the greatest teams
GOLDEN ICE

Stan Fischler

Research Editor: Jeff Resnick

WYNWOOD™ Press
New York, New York

Copyright © 1990 Stan Fischler

All rights reserved. No part of this publication may be reproduced, stored in a retrieval system or data base, or transmitted, in any form or by any means, electronic, mechanical, photocopying, recording, or otherwise, without the prior written permission of the publisher.

ISBN 0-922066-52-3
1 2 3 4 5 6 7 8 9 AP 9 8 7 6 5 4 3 2 1 0

First published in 1990 by
McGraw-Hill Ryerson Limited
330 Progress Avenue
Scarborough, Ontario   M1P 2Z5

Care has been taken to trace the ownership of any copyright material contained in this text. The publishers welcome any information that will enable them to rectify, in subsequent editions, any incorrect or omitted reference or credit.

Canadian Cataloguing in Publication Data

Fischler, Stan, 1932-
  Golden ice : the greatest teams in hockey history

ISBN 0-07-549963-0

1. Hockey - Clubs - History.   2. Hockey - History.
I. Title.

GV846.5.F57 1989   796.96′26   C89-095211-6

Printed and bound in Canada

To Shirley, Ben, and Simon, my favorite team.

CONTENTS

Preface v
Acknowledgments vii

    THE MONTREAL CANADIENS, 1956–60 1
    THE NEW YORK ISLANDERS, 1980–83 29
    THE MONTREAL CANADIENS, 1976–79 41
    THE TORONTO MAPLE LEAFS, 1946–51 55
    THE EDMONTON OILERS, 1984–88 67
    THE TORONTO MAPLE LEAFS, 1962–67 81
    THE DETROIT RED WINGS, 1950–55 95
    THE BOSTON BRUINS, 1970–72 113
    THE MONTREAL CANADIENS, 1944–46 123
    THE DETROIT RED WINGS, 1936–37 133
    THE BOSTON BRUINS, 1939–41 143
    THE NEW YORK RANGERS, 1928–33 151
    THE MONTREAL CANADIENS, 1930–31 161
    THE BOSTON BRUINS, 1929 179
    THE NEW YORK RANGERS, 1940 191
    THE TORONTO MAPLE LEAFS, 1932 199
    THE MONTREAL CANADIENS, 1916 207
    THE CHICAGO BLACK HAWKS, 1961 221
    THE PHILADELPHIA FLYERS, 1974–75 231
    THE CHICAGO BLACK HAWKS, 1934 249

HONORABLE MENTION

THE OTTAWA SILVER SEVEN, 1905 — 257
THE UNITED STATES OLYMPIC TEAM, 1980 — 265
THE NEW YORK AMERICANS, 1925–42 — 279
THE SOVIET NATIONAL TEAM, 1972 — 287

Preface

The challenge in selecting the best 20 hockey teams of all time, *in order of greatness*, was not unlike the difficult chore in picking the best 100 players anywhere, any era, as I did in the companion book, *Hockey's 100*.

While the picks are subjective and based on personal opinion and first-hand viewing, a number of criteria were established to justify the position of the various teams.

This, of course, will not satisfy everyone, particularly when it comes to a comparison of teams from different eras. The Montreal Canadiens of 1916 played a game that in no way resembled contemporary hockey other than the fact that players used a stick and a puck while skating on ice.

In the early days of hockey, most players skated for a full 60 minutes, helmets and face masks were unknown. Ice conditions were primitive, to say the least, and the strategy employed was vastly different from the techniques we see today. (Nobody in the 1920s, 1930s, 1940s, or 1950s could ever have imagined a goaltender actually scoring a goal, as Ron Hextall of the Philadelphia Flyers did during the 1988–89 season.)

Comparing teams from different eras just added to the difficulty but also made the writing of this work all the more intriguing. In the case of teams that preceded my time, I based my findings on interviews and conversations over the years with various people connected with pro hockey in its earlier years. Hall of Famer Frank Boucher was a major source of information. He was general manager of the New York Rangers in 1954–55 (my boss) during the season when I was an assistant publicist for the team. Boucher, coach Murray (Muzz) Patrick, the son of the immortal Lester Patrick, would regale me with stories about hockey in the younger days of The Game.

I witnessed my first hockey game in 1937 and have seen thousands of games since then, first as a fan and then as a reporter and columnist. Each of the top-rated teams, starting with the Montreal Canadiens, 1956–60, was observed first-hand even to the point of being in the cramped, steamy Boston Garden dressing room of the Habs immediately after they won The Stanley Cup on April 20, 1958.

From the start of the 1940s when the New York Rangers won their last Stanley Cup, I have examined each NHL champion intensively enough to provide a proper evaluation. For the preceding teams, I relied on research, interviews with participants, and forms of oral history.

To obtain a precise determination of where each team should be placed, a number of criteria were used. These included championships (Stanley Cups as well as first-place finishes during the regular season), All-Star players, trophy-winners, and unusual accomplishments.

The Toronto Maple Leafs of 1947–51 were higly rated because they became the first team to win three consecutive Stanley Cups. By contrast, the Chicago Black Hawks of 1961 *should have* won three straight, considering their talent, but wound up with only one. While that was sufficient to drop them down near the bottom of the list, no team with Hall of Famers like Bobby Hull, Stan Mikita, and Glenn Hall could be omitted altogether.

In order to settle some very close races, such as the one between the Islanders and Oilers, several yardsticks were used including the number of consecutive playoff series won, and that decided it in the Islanders' favor.

Another yardstick was the quality of competition. Some might argue that the Bruins team that featured Bobby Orr, Phil Esposito, and Gerry Cheevers rated higher than eighth place. But that Boston squad, which won the Stanley Cup in 1970 and 1972, played in the era immediately following the NHL's expansion from six to twelve teams. Never in league history was the quality of opposition (the six new teams, comprised predominantly of minor leaguers) been so weak. The Bruins 1970 Cup win over the St. Louis Blues was more farcical than any championship in memory.

Leadership, team character (a good example being Toe Blake's Canadiens and Al Arbour's Islanders) also was considered as well as the solidity of the organization as a whole. In addition, the team's impact on The Game was a major consideration. Both the Bruins' and Rangers' first Stanley Cup-winners had considerable influence on the growth of hockey in the United States as well as in their respective cities.

The significance of individual stars on their teams, cities, and the NHL itself also was a factor. In that regard, the 1947–48 Maple Leafs received a major boost because collectively the Leafs presented the finest three centers — Max Bentley, Syl Apps, Ted Kennedy — any team offered at any time.

In the end, though, you the reader will decide whether the rankings are acceptable. If not, drop me a line and we'll resume the discussion.

Stan Fischler
New York City

April 1990

Acknowledgments

This is a book about teams — great teams. They became great because of a special melding of talents and the ability to cooperate and press forward toward a common goal. The result, in many cases, was a Stanley Cup.

Another kind of teamwork is just as important in the production of a book. In this case, the author received a significant amount of help from experts in hockey history as well as former National Hockey League players willing and able to provide time, insights, and anecdotes.

A team is made of several components; the first line, second line, defense, goaltender, and specialists such as penalty-killers and power play operatives. So, it was on this book others were of immense help in the areas of research, typing, and consultation on just who should be placed where, and why.

One of the key members of the team is the captain; in my case, editor Glen Ellis, who had the idea that this book could work and provided the encouragement any linemate needs when the chips are down.

Other teammates who provided invaluable assistance included David Starman, an expert on the United States 1980 Olympic team whose contacts with various team members helped make the chapter possible.

No less helpful were Kay Ohara, Kelli O'Reilly, Dave Katz, Linda Lundgren, Andy Schneider, Arthur Staple, Eli Polatoff, Joe Glus, Keisha and Kell Ciabattari, Dennis Nolan, Victor Lavella, Neil Dorosin, Joe Dionisio, and Rich Joline.

Montreal Canadiens, 1956–60

The Greatest Ever — Montreal Canadiens 1956–60

What the Murderer's Row New York Yankees of the 1920s meant to baseball, the 1956–60 Montreal Canadiens were to the National Hockey League. Quite simply, the greatest team of all time.

In Jacques Plante, they had one of the best, most creative goaltenders ever; in Doug Harvey, the best defenseman to grace the ice — even better than Bobby Orr; in Maurice (Rocket) Richard, Henri (Pocket Rocket) Richard, Jean (Le Gros Bill) Beliveau, and Bernie (Boom Boom) Geoffrion, the most awesome array of shooters any goaltender ever faced.

And that was just the beginning. Left wing Dickie Moore and defenseman Tom Johnson from that squad also are in the Hockey Hall of Fame along with coach Hector (Toe) Blake, who was perfectly suited to lead the Habitants.

The Canadiens didn't have a weakness. Period.

"Their third line," said former Ranger Aldo Guidolin, "was better than most first lines on other teams."

He was referring to players like Claude Provost, a remarkably efficient defensive forward, and slick centers Ralph Backstrom, Phil Goyette, and Don Marshall.

"I don't think there was as good a team anywhere," said Blake, and there could be little argument.

Spearheading the club was its captain, Rocket Richard, the Babe Ruth of hockey. The Rocket dominated by force of personality as well as his scoring talents. No less influential was the majestic Beliveau, the flawless Harvey, and the explosive Geoffrion, the latter of whom introduced the slapshot to big-league hockey.

The Canadiens' power play was so overwhelming that the NHL actually changed their rules to curb its effectiveness. Previously, the league compelled a player to remain in the penalty box for a full two minutes. So strong was the Habs' power play that they frequently scored two or three goals during one 2-minute sequence, rendering the game hopeless for the opposition. "They simply wanted to limit our power," said Maurice Richard, "but that still didn't stop us."

From 1955–56 through 1961–62, the Canadiens finished first six times and won five consecutive Stanley Cups — 1956, 1957, 1958, 1959, and 1960. It was the era of the six-team league at a time when the Red Wings also was a powerhouse; a factor that magnifies the Canadiens' accomplishments.

Contemporary hockey analysts have argued that the game was slower during the 1956–60 era and lacked such armament as the slapshot. Perhaps, but the Beliveaus and Moores were better stickhandlers and bodycheckers. "We had to face the five best goalies in the world," said Harvey, "not counting our own. Now there are dozens of goalies and they all make a lot of mistakes."

Only a nitpicker could quarrel that the Richardian Canadiens weren't the ultimate team. They could well have won six straight Cups by winning in 1955 (which they almost did, and would have, but for the unfortunate all-playoff suspension of Rocket Richard) and again in 1961. In the latter series against Chicago, they were without Maurice Richard who had retired following the fifth Cup win. His absence, spiritually, hurt more than anything.

No team has ever won five straight except for the Montreal Canadiens, and for that reason among many, they are at the top of the list.

The pity of it all is that the world's greatest hockey team — any time, anywhere, any era — performed in an era when the NHL on television was still not widespread and when the league, itself, still was a six-team cocoon, hardly known in vast portions of the United States and Europe.

The Montreal Canadiens, who owned The Stanley Cup from 1956 through 1960, were so overflowing with stars and innovators, that truly creative and accomplished players such as Bernie (Boom Boom) Geoffrion, inventor of the modern slapshot, were often overshadowed by the total team effort or such individual heroes as Montreal's most famous athletic personality, Maurice (The Rocket) Richard.

Credit for extracting the most out of Richard's potential as well as Jean Beliveau, Dickie Moore, and Doug Harvey, must go to the team's unassuming general manager, Frank Selke, who had learned the business while working as Conn Smythe's aide in Toronto when Smythe founded and developed the Maple Leafs.

Selke moved to Montreal at a time when the Canadiens were on a decline, following the heroics of Richard, Lach, and Blake in the early 1940s. By the late 1940s, Blake and Lach had reached the end of their playing careers and major changes were necessary. Selke decided to build a new club around The Rocket. To do so, he created an octopus of a farm system that stretched all across Canada. A typical example was the city of Regina, Saskatchewan where the Canadiens sponsored the Regina Patricias junior team. There were 400 teams in Regina's park league that funneled skaters up to the Patricias.

But the majority of the future aces would come from the province of Quebec, where nearly every kid dreamed of playing for the Canadiens. "Drive through the streets of Montreal or Three Rivers or Valleyfield or St. Jean on any clear, cold winter evening," wrote Jack Newcombe, "and you will see them, wearing toques (wool caps) and white woolen shirts with the royal blue and red letters *CH* on the chests, their skates and hockey sticks slung over their shoulders, heading for the bright glow of the floodlighted outdoor rinks. There, for an hour or two, they will play the part of Rocket Richard."

Among the legion of kids were Bernard "Boom Boom" Geoffrion, Dickie Moore, Jacques Plante, Doug Harvey, Dollard St. Laurent, Jean-Guy Talbot, Claude Provost, Phil Goyette, Henri Richard, and perhaps the most important young hockey star of all — Jean Marc Beliveau.

A product of small-town Quebec provincial hockey, Beliveau grew to 6'2" and 192 lbs., but he had uncanny speed and maneuverability for a man his size. Most important of all, he could score goals.

One would have imagined that the Canadiens could have obtained Beliveau merely by snapping their fingers, but it was not so easy. Jean Marc was something very special, and the citizens of Quebec City were quick to recognize it. By 1951 Beliveau virtually owned the town. If he went into a clothing store to buy a couple of suits, the proprietor would forget the bill. Having *le gros* drop in was honor enough.

Beliveau's team, the Quebec (junior) Citadelles, were technically considered amateur, but Beliveau grossed more than $20,000 in the 1950–1951 season, including a new car presented to him by admiring fans. However, Jean Marc was as impressed by a ring given him the same night by his teammates. "Beautiful ring they gave me," he remarked proudly. Had he chosen politics, Big Bill could have become the mayor of Quebec City.

"Jean Beliveau in Quebec," remarked author Leonard Shecter, "is like Mickey Mantle and Joe DiMaggio in the United States. When Jean Beliveau walks down the street in Quebec, the women smile, the men shake his hand, and the little boys follow him."

It was understandable that Jean Marc was reluctant to leave Quebec City, no matter what the Canadiens had to offer. There was another factor at work in his decision: the less urbane citizens of Quebec resented the Montreal sophisticates, and they were determined to keep Beliveau, who had put Quebec City back on the map.

When Beliveau became too old to play junior hockey for the Citadelles, he could easily have moved into the Quebec Senior League. But the ramifications of Big Bill's remaining in Quebec ran as deep as the well of politics. Several Quebec City businessmen had backed construction of the handsome Colisée, which was equal in size to many NHL rinks. Without Beliveau to fill the seats either as a junior or as a member of the Quebec Aces, the Colisée and its backers would lose money.

It was freely noted that these same Quebec businessmen-politicos were pressuring the Canadiens to lay off Beliveau and threatening to cut off the Montreal Forum's beer license if they did not do so. All these factors were brought to bear in August, 1951, because Jean Marc was about to turn 20 and would soon be too old for the Juniors.

While Beliveau was still 19, les Canadiens invited him for a couple of trial NHL games. After watching Big Bill in one turn on the ice, coach Irvin waxed ecstatic and told the world that Beliveau would be a big-league star the moment he signed an NHL contract. "He's the closest thing to Lester Patrick that I've ever seen," said Irvin. "He didn't make one mistake in the two games with us."

The Aces made no mistakes either. Prior to the 1951–52 season they managed to sign Beliveau to another "amateur" contract, this time in the fast Quebec Senior League. Beliveau became the dominant force in the circuit from his very first game with the Aces. Crowds that had previously filled the Colisée to watch the Citadelles were now coming to see the Aces. Beliveau might still be enjoying life in Quebec were it not for the irresistible pressures on him from Montreal and Quebec City itself. The two seemingly opposing forces united to form an interesting *entente cordiale*, which eventually squeezed Beliveau out of his Quebec cocoon and into a Canadiens uniform.

The most obvious lobbying was done by Selke and his Montreal colleagues. More subtle efforts were launched by backers of Quebec's other junior team, the Frontenacs, who were losing money now that Beliveau was drawing all the crowds to the senior games. They allied with the Canadiens to get Beliveau out of their hair.

By exerting pressure in the proper places les Canadiens hoped to persuade most members of the Quebec Senior League to abandon the "amateur" label and become true professionals. Were this to happen, the Canadiens would have the right to sign Beliveau, and there would be no way he could avoid coming to Montreal. At the time, Punch Imlach was coaching the Aces, and he employed all the know-how at his command to thwart the move. He succeeded for two years, until the summer of 1953, when the representatives of the Quebec Senior League teams (with the exception of Imlach) voted to turn the league professional. It was then that the Canadiens finally annexed Beliveau. Meanwhile they had to do without him, but that was not really hard to manage because of the continued excellence of the Rocket and the coming age of Bernard Geoffrion.

Nicknamed "Boom Boom" because of the reverberation of his stick hitting the puck and the puck hitting the end boards, Geoffrion had many of the incendiary qualities of Richard. "Remember, the Rocket always was my idol when I was a kid in Montreal," the Boomer would say. "When Maurice doesn't score, he's not happy, and he doesn't want to speak to anyone. I'm the same way."

The Geoffrion character had one ingredient that was missing in the Richard psyche: a flamboyant sense of humor. For the most part the Rocket was quiet and introverted even when life was agreeable, but when Geoffrion was scoring easily, he became an opera-singing clown and led Montreal's laugh parade. He began delighting teammates late in the 1950–51 season after scoring 103 goals in 57 Montreal Junior League games. Like Beliveau, Geoffrion was under great pressure to turn pro with the Canadiens, and he resisted until there were only 18 games remaining in the 1950–51 schedule. Geoffrion realized that the Calder Trophy for Rookie of the Year was given to players who had skated in 20 or more games. By waiting until there were fewer than 20 games in the 1950–51 schedule he became eligible to win it the following season.

When he was approached by Selke, Geoffrion laid the facts on the line, "I'll lose my chance for the Calder. It's too late in the season to catch up with the other guys."

The Boomer was no fool. He opened the 1951–52 season with two goals, including the winner, against Chicago in a 4–2 Montreal victory and immediately established himself as the newest Canadiens hero. For Geoffrion it was relatively easy. Not only was he an excellent young prospect, but he had recently married Marlene Morenz, the daughter of the late Howie Morenz.

"I was a figure skater at the time," Marlene remembered, "and I was practicing at the Forum for an ice carnival. While I was doing a spin, I missed a piece of cardboard on the ice and took a bad spill. As I looked up, deeply embarrassed, I noticed this big fellow laughing his head off. I was furious and was still furious after the show when a knock sounded on the dressing room door. It was my brother (Howie Morenz, Jr.), who wanted me to meet a friend of his from junior hockey. It turned out to be the same fellow who had been laughing at me. And that's how I met Boomer. Soon we were all laughing."

Not long after Geoffrion's opening scoring burst, les Canadiens visited New York, and Geoffrion was interviewed by *New York Daily News* sports columnist Jimmy Powers. The writer observed that the NHL had a prize crop of rookies and wondered just who the Boomer thought would win the prize.

"Me," said Geoffrion, in as candid a reply as Powers could hope for.

Then the Boomer set about the business of proving himself correct, while the

Montreal brass attempted to thwart a revolt between Irvin and his veteran defenseman Butch Bouchard. The 31-year-old Bouchard had just opened a lavish new restaurant in Montreal and was apparently eating too many of the tasty dishes. Irvin claimed that Butch was overweight, and Bouchard said that if Dick didn't apologize, he'd quit.

Irvin and Bouchard quickly came to terms, and everything seemed about normal in the Canadiens camp. On October 31 the Habitants visited Toronto, lost the game 1–0, and the Rocket clashed with a few Leaf fans as well as the team physician, Dr. Jim Murray. The Rocket had been frustrated in his attempt to score his 300th NHL goal and took exception to a remark tossed by the doctor.

The episode lit the fuse for the explosion that would take place the following night at the Forum. It began sputtering in earnest when the Rocket and Fern Flaman of the Leafs exchanged blows in the second period. Referee Bill Chadwick sent Flaman to the dressing room and Richard to the penalty box. As the Rocket was about to take his seat, defenseman Bill Juzda of the Leafs delivered a few indiscreet remarks to Richard. The Rocket left the box and skated straight for Juzda.

"Richard lashed a jolting right from behind one of the officials," said Gord Walker of the *Globe and Mail*, "and it found a target on Juzda's left eye. Juzda dropped heavily and lay on the ice for almost a minute." The Rocket had scored another TKO.

A few miles away at a local Montreal rink, another Richard was also exploding. This one was 15-year-old Henri Richard, the Rocket's kid brother, who had betrayed signs of becoming as big a star as brother Maurice. Some critics cautioned that it was premature to foresee the NHL for Henri; unlike the Rocket, Henri was small and showed no signs of filling out. Besides, another of the Richard brothers, Jacques, had failed after showing some sign of the Rocket's ability. Said Baz O'Meara of the *Montreal Star*, "Jacques didn't have the same drive as his famous brother, nor the tenacity to make the big time. On the other hand, Henri has hockey players' legs, a very good shift, and if he listens to his older brother, he might become a star."

In time Henri would join the Rocket on the same line. In the meantime, Irvin sought a left wing to round out the abridged Punch Line. Both Maurice and Elmer Lach had sprung ahead in the scoring race, first with Bert Olmstead on left wing and later with Dickie Moore, a Montreal-bred youngster with all the zip of Rocket Richard. But in 1952 there was something in the Rocket's system that perplexed doctors. Several examinations produced nothing but an announcement that Richard was suffering from a "stomach ailment" and would be sidelined indefinitely. Meanwhile the Canadiens struggled for a playoff birth.

"Richard owns the most famous bellyache in sports since Babe Ruth's burps," said a Toronto writer. In New York, Ranger manager Frank Boucher charged that the Canadiens, especially coach Irvin, were a bunch of "cry babies." Irvin took the charge seriously and replied that if Ranger coach Bill Cook would play for the Rangers in their game against the Canadiens on January 13, Irvin would take the Rocket's place on right wing for the Canadiens. Boucher immediately accepted the challenge on behalf of Cook.

"I'll guarantee that if Irvin takes the ice, Cook will skate out and make him look sick — just as he always made Irvin look sick when they played against each other," said Boucher.

Needless to say, neither Irvin nor Cook dressed for the game because Richard had returned the night before. He swung into action by scoring a three-goal hat trick as Montreal routed Chicago 8–3 at the Forum. "Irvin hit a new low in childishness, and he should be taken to task for it," said Jim Vipond, sports editor of the *Globe and Mail*. Irvin couldn't have cared less about the bleats from Toronto as long as his club stayed in playoff contention. Now that the kids were producing, he dismissed his critics with a wave of the hand.

As he had so candidly predicted, Geoffrion had become the Rookie-of-the-Year candidate. Although he may not have realized it at the time, Geoffrion had become a hockey revolutionary. Instead of using the traditional forehand wrist shot or the backhand shot for his tries at the goal, Geoffrion would draw his stick back like a golfer and slap the puck. The result was the "slapshot" that would eventually be adopted by most of the leading scorers in the NHL and would dramatically change the face of the game.

The essential characteristic of the slapshot was the extraordinary speed Geoffrion generated, harder than anything the league had seen, including the bullet-shooting Charlie Conacher of the early thirties. Toronto coach Hap Day, who had played with Conacher on the Maple Leafs, had no qualms about putting the Geoffrion shot in proper perspective.

"It's definitely harder than anything Conacher shot. I watched Geoffrion closely on one play. I saw him draw the stick back, but I didn't see the puck until it bounced off the goalpost."

Geoffrion and Dickie Moore weren't galvanizing the Canadiens alone. A speedy youngster named Paul Meger was shining on the forward line along with Dick Gamble. Young Tom Johnson and Doug Harvey offered goalie McNeil formidable protection on defense. "We Like Moore," said Jim Vipond in his *Globe and Mail* column. "He's a chippy operator who mixes with the toughest and still knows how to stick-handle and skate his way to the opposition net. He's not unmindful of Milt Schmidt, as he leans far forward in gaining top speed. These Montreal kids are making the customers forget Maurice Richard."

But the Rocket wouldn't let anyone forget him. Recovered from his stomach ailment after a Florida vacation, he returned to Maple Leaf Gardens on March 19, 1952, to aid the Canadiens in their second-place battle with Toronto.

Montreal won the game 3–0 and beat out Toronto for second place. That night, the Rocket was the catalyst, and he put on one of his displays of pure fury on ice. "The Rocket's goal was typical," wrote Gord Walker in the *Globe and Mail*. "On a two-man break in the second period, Lach was covered by Jimmy Thomson. He still got over a perfect pass to Richard, who appeared to be blanketed by Jimmy Morrison. Yet the Rocket somehow got his stick around and zipped the puck into the net."

Richard's histrionics had already become too numerous for most fans to remember. Some rooters preferred to recall only the goals he scored. Others remembered the fights, and still others pointed to the bizarre episodes that made Maurice unique.

"The impact Richard had on the Canadiens," said Peter Gzowski, "and through them on the rest of the league, seems to me, beautifully summed up in one incident that occurred in Toronto. It was the time that, soaring head over heels as the result of an artful Maple Leaf check, Richard shattered the 'unbreakable' Herculite glass that had just been installed in Maple Leaf Gardens around the top of the boards. No one had nicked it before, and only Eddie Shack has broken it since, and Shack hit a faulty piece. Richard put the *heel of his skate* through it. There was something perfect about its being the Rocket, the epitome of recklessness, of untrammeled fire and fury and abandon on the ice, who did it."

Few players upstaged Richard. One of those who did was Gordie Howe, and the Red Wing immortal managed to pull the surprise on "Rocket Richard Night" at the Forum. As the presentation was coming to an end, Richard headed for the sideboards when Howe called out, "Hey, Rocket!" As Richard turned, Howe pulled off his leather gauntlet and extended his hand. For a brief second the Forum crowd was hushed as the arch-foes shook hands at center ice. "It was a sort of unrehearsed spontaneous gesture, and it caught the big crowd completely by surprise," said Elmer Ferguson.

The crowd remained silent for another moment; then they burst into an ovation that gave veteran press-box viewers a case of goose pimples. When play resumed, Howe went out and scored a big goal for the Red Wings.

The Canadiens finished in second place during the 1951–52 season and went up against the fourth-place Boston Bruins in the opening Stanley Cup round. Those who had doubts about Richard's health were put at ease in the very first game, when he scored twice. Montreal romped to a 5–1 win. The Rocket was held scoreless in the second match, but Geoffrion, who was to win the Rookie-of-the-Year award, helped Montreal to a 4–0 victory with a three-goal hat trick.

The Canadiens received a stunning surprise as the Boston sextet swept the next three games and put Montreal squarely on the ropes. In the sixth game, Boston virtually completed the upset, scoring twice in the first period and blanketing Montreal with severe checking.

When the Canadiens skated out on the ice for the second period, they pecked away at the staunch Bruin blue-line corps and finally found an opening at 4:53. Eddie "Spider" Mazur shot the puck past goalie Jim Henry, and Montreal was alive again. Still, Boston held the lead, and the Bruins continued to nurse the one-goal margin well into the third period.

At the 11-minute mark, captain Milt Schmidt of the Bruins allowed the puck to slip off the blade of his stick. The Rocket, hovering nearby, seized the opportunity and dashed straight down the middle of the ice. His 30-foot shot fooled Henry, and the teams went into sudden-death overtime, tied 2–2.

Neither team scored in the first extra period, but early in the second session Doug Harvey organized a rush at the Bruins net. His shot was blocked by Henry, but rookie Paul Masnick, who had been recalled from the American League, snared the rebound and beat Henry at 7:49 of the second overtime.

The seventh and final game of the semifinal was played at the Forum on April 8, 1952, and there are those who consider it the most exciting hockey match ever played. There was no disputing the assertion that it was Maurice Richard's most courageous display of hockey skill.

Each team managed a goal in the first period. Then they settled down to vigorous exchanges of end-to-end rushes, and the ice looked like an endless stream of downhill ski racers. With one major exception the game was, as one reporter noted, "clean, hard-fought, and played a vital role in the game's ultimate evolution.

With the score tied 1–1 in the second period, Leo Labine, a Bruin forward with scant acquaintance with the rulebook, took a dead aim at Richard as the Rocket knifed through the Boston defense. Richard had tripped and already fallen to his knees when Labine ruthlessly charged him. Labine's stick thudded against Richard's head, and his knees rammed into Richard's stomach with the impact of a battering ram.

Already down, the Rocket keeled over on his back. He seemed to be dead. His legs spread out in an inverted V formation as trainer, Hector Dubois, physiotherapist, Bill Head, and teammate, Bert Olmstead hovered over Richard's limp body, searching for some signs of life. In time he responded to smelling salts, and with his face smeared with blood, Richard clambered to his feet and groggily skated to the Forum first-aid room. There, the deep cut over his eye was stitched and repaired. He returned to the bench and took in the action with the special kind of reflex that only the very unusual athlete possesses.

"My legs felt fine," Richard recalled after the game, "but my head . . . was I dizzy! I didn't remember anything after I got hit. They told me it was Labine. I don't know. I didn't even know the score when I went back to the bench."

Toe Blake, the retired member of the Punch Line, was standing in the press box, high in the Forum rafters, when Richard returned to the ice. Blake spotted his old buddy and turned to one of the reporters. "You watch," Blake said, "the Rocket will get one in the last five minutes of the game."

It became apparent as the third period moved along without a score that the next goal would decide the series. It also was obvious to most observers that Richard would *not* score that goal.

"After receiving his stitches," commented one Montreal newspaperman, "he was in a partial coma for a while, his head fuzzed up from pain, his eyesight impaired, with dull noises ringing in his ears."

More than 16 minutes had elapsed in the third period when Bruin veteran Woody Dumart carried the puck toward the Canadiens zone. Butch Bouchard thrust out his stick with rapier-like speed, jabbing the puck away from Dumart. The Montreal defenseman looked up for a moment and spotted Richard near the blue line. The Rocket captured the pass as Dumart tried, without success, to bat down the puck. Richard wheeled around Dumart like a speeding car, skirting a disabled auto on the highway. First he reeled to center; then he cut sharply to the right, jabbing the puck ahead of him with short pokes from his blade.

Bill Quackenbush, one of the most experienced and intelligent defensemen in the NHL, skated backward on the Bruin defense, prepared to meet the ominous challenge, for Richard was now in full flight, his eyes blazing madly and his destination known to all. Quackenbush was traveling at about ten miles per hour in reverse as Richard bore down on him at more than twice that speed. Quackenbush hurled his black-shirted body at the Canadien ace, but he might as well have been checking a phantom.

Nevertheless, Quackenbush had done his job, for he had forced Richard to take so circuitous a route along the right side that the Rocket appeared to have taken himself right out of the play. "He looked to be too deep for a shot," said Baz O'Meara of the *Montreal Star*, "but then he suddenly did a deft cut to the left."

A right-handed shot playing right wing would have been cradling the puck too far to his right to release a threatening drive, but Richard was a left-handed shot. The puck was on his left side, closer to the net, as he barreled past the flailing Quackenbush. "Sugar" Jim Henry, both eyes blackened from previous injuries and barely recovered from a broken nose, guarded the right corner of the net, . . . allowing Richard nothing but the "impossible" angle shot to the far left corner.

When he was almost on top of Henry's bulky goal pads, Richard finally released his drive. It was low and hard, and Henry didn't even see, let alone touch, the puck. "One minute I was facing him, waiting for a shot. The next he had whizzed by, and the puck was in the net."

The ovations that have traditionally greeted Rocket Richard goals have had the impact of a thunderclap, but this time the din shook the very foundation of the Forum. According to Baz O'Meara, "Richard has received ovations in his day the likes of which have never been seen in the Forum, but the ensuing roar, which lasted fully four minutes followed by a paper shower, left all others in the also-ran class."

Reactions to the goal were as surprising as the score itself. Elmer Lach, who was sitting on the bench watching the Rocket in orbit, leaned forward onto the sideboards and fainted. Art Chapman, manager of the Buffalo hockey club, simply stood, mouth agape, after the red light flashed. "Only Richard could score like that," he said later.

"He is like Babe Ruth was," said Irvin. "He adds that little extra flourish to everything."

That little flourish provided the Canadiens with the winning goal, although Billy Reay added another score with less than a minute remaining. Montreal won the game 3–1. When the final siren wailed, reporters searched their minds for the proper adjectives to describe Richard's feat. Baz O'Meara, who had seen more hockey games than any other member of the press corps, summed it up this way. "In all his storied, starry career, Richard has scored some of the most spectacular goals of hockey history. No player has ever matched him as a thrill-producer. No one has come close to him for versatility of execution. Of all the goals credited to him, none ever excelled that game-winner against Boston. . . . None ever drew a greater ovation, more gasps of admiration, because it was scored under the pressure of pain."

The pain had not entirely dissipated when the Rocket fell onto the bench in Montreal's joy-filled dressing room. His father, Onesime Richard, walked in and put his arm around the Rocket's shoulder and hugged his son. No longer able to control the emotion that welled within his battered frame, the Rocket broke down and cried.

Decimated by injuries, the Canadiens were no match for the Red Wings, who were well rested after their four-game sweep of the Maple Leafs. The Detroit sextet swept the Canadiens in four consecutive games to win the Stanley Cup, although some observers argued that Detroit benefited from the officiating throughout the playoffs.

"The Wings can put the best seven men on the ice of any team in the league," said Toronto's managing director, Conn Smythe.

To which Irvin added, "And the referee must be one of them!" Bitter to the end, Irvin refused to congratulate the winners. He slammed the dressing room door in the faces of Detroit reporters.

Irvin's grumpiness and the general depression in the Montreal dressing room was not reflected by the even-tempered Selke. He realized that his plans were jelling and that only a few more years were required before his rebuilding job would be complete. In the meantime, he bathed in the fading sunlight generated by such veterans as Bouchard and Lach. Although Elmer had vowed to retire a few seasons earlier, he appeared at the 1952–53 training camp with the same vigor he had displayed as a rookie, and he continued to excel as the campaign got under way.

On Saturday night, November 8, 1952, the Black Hawks were playing the Canadiens at the Forum when Lach scored his 200th NHL goal. Not surprisingly it was the Rocket who fed him the lead pass, and Richard was the first to congratulate his old buddy. "Keep piling up the points," kidded Maurice, "but keep away from those fractures."

The partisan crowd lustily cheered the pair, but they were more anxious to see the Rocket score. His next goal would be number 325 and would break the NHL record, held by Nels Stewart. Only 30 seconds after Lach's historic score, the Rocket throttled past the Black Hawk defense and reached his newest plateau. This time it was Lach who did the congratulating and the needling. "Nice going, Rocket," he laughed, "and no more broken bones, please!"

Paced by Lach, Richard, and the energetic youngsters, Montreal finished second behind Detroit and went into the fourth playoff semifinal, a heavy favorite to defeat the fourth-place Black Hawks. But Chicago was not the traditional doormat of yester-year. They presented a creative coach in Sid Abel and a superb, but underrated, goaltender named Al Rollins. They still would not have presented a problem for les Canadiens except for an unexpected development: goalie Gerry McNeil had become overwrought with nervousness and suffered an awesome letdown in the series.

Before Irvin could get command of the situation, Chicago had advanced to the lip of victory in the semifinal round with a 3–2 advantage in the best-of-seven series. With an ironic twist of strategy, Irvin suddenly benched McNeil and inserted Jacques Plante, an unusual goaltender if ever there was one.

In his spare time, Plante had a hobby of knitting *toques*, the French-Canadian wool caps worn by his ancestors. He was confident to the point of being cocky, and he displayed a bizarre goaltending style, which would soon be copied by other netminders around the league. It was Plante's idea to aid his defensemen by roaming out of his cage and behind the net when the pucks were caromed off the boards. By so doing, Plante controlled the puck and passed it off to a teammate; then he would scramble back to his goal crease before any shots were taken.

Plante's theory was new and fascinating, but experimenting with the Canadiens in the playoffs was something else. Irvin had made a commitment, however, and

Plante was his goalie. Jacques the Roamer immediately went into the cage and stopped the Black Hawks cold. He foiled a breakaway early in the fifth game, and with that impetus les Canadiens won two straight games and captured the first round.

Meanwhile, the Bruins had stunned the league-leading Red Wings with a 4–2 upset in the other semifinal round, and they qualified to meet Montreal for the Stanley Cup. After building up a 3–1 lead in games, les Canadiens clinched the Cup when the Rocket passed the puck to Lach in a sudden-death overtime, with the score tied 0–0. Elmer converted the pass for a goal.

The success of the Canadiens was soon to boomerang on them. In the early fifties it had become apparent that the Bruins, Rangers, and Black Hawks were suffering attendance setbacks, which were also complemented by great deficiencies in player personnel.

Pressure from the three losing cities was finally felt in the NHL hierarchy, which responded by creating a draft system. Selke contended — and rightly so — that the new draft was aimed at diluting his dynasty. He fought the draft on the grounds that Montreal should reap the rewards of its hard-earned success. In a significant display of altruism, Selke sold highly regarded young Ed Litzenberger to the Black Hawks for only $15,000, although the crack forward was worth more than four times that amount. It was that same Litzenberger who spearheaded Chicago's march to the Stanley Cup in 1961.

One of the prime reasons for the "Curb-the-Canadiens" movement was Selke's own triumph in signing Jean Beliveau for the 1953–54 season. The Beliveau negotiations were conducted in the atmosphere of excitement that might have greeted the signing of the North Atlantic Treaty. Le gros Bill, accompanied by an accountant and an attorney, came away with one of the largest salaries in hockey history.

Beliveau's premiere was widely trumpeted throughout the league. His decision to stay in Quebec had merely served to whet the interest of hockey fans throughout the NHL, and they came out in extraordinary numbers to see what he was all about. At first he suggested that he would be the most overrated flop since the aluminum hockey stick!

Beliveau was the antithesis of Richard, Geoffrion, and Moore. His long strides indicated that he was not really trying very hard and his phlegmatic disposition contrasted to the volcanic teammates who surrounded him. Even worse, Beliveau displayed no thirst for fighting, a trait that would prove to be his downfall in his rookie year.

Every low-salaried skater from New York to Chicago was determined to get a piece of le gros Bill, and many of them succeeded. He suffered a cracked fibula after being heavily checked in Chicago shortly after the start of the season, and he was sidelined a total of 26 games for assorted injuries during the season. But Beliveau had a good sense of perspective, and he realized that his teammate Rocket Richard had endured a similar spate of injuries when he broke into the NHL. "If my career turns out like the Rocket's, all of this will really be worthwhile," he said.

Occasionally Beliveau offered cause for favorable comment. His stickhandling ability suggested that he had an invisible string linking the puck to his stick blade, and his shot was hard and accurate. "The playing of Beliveau is poetry in action," commented Canadian novelist Hugh MacLennan.

But Beliveau's production left him overshadowed by his teammates' histrionics, which were abundant in 1953–54. Clearly established as a star, Geoffrion found himself assailed and assaulted, just like the Rocket. The Boomer's boiling point was equally low, and in November, 1953, he was fined $250 for charging referee Frank Udvari. A month later Boom Boom immersed himself even deeper in hot water during a game against the Rangers at Madison Square Garden. The rivalry between New York and Montreal had remained keen ever since a classic 1947 brawl and was no less sharp on this night, when several players, among them Geoffrion and Ron Murphy, piled up along the sideboards in a high-sticking joust.

At the time of the collision Geoffrion had lost his stick. Murphy, who had been standing at the perimeter of the general melee, still had his, and he used it on Geoffrion. Press-box observers took it for granted that the trouble would soon be calmed; nobody expected Geoffrion to retaliate with anything more than a counter-shove. But the stickless Boomer felt the blood on his head, and he bolted from the bout, frantically searching for his lost stick.

From the grandstands it appeared that he had gone temporarily berserk as he regained his stick and moved menacingly toward Murphy. The young Ranger conducted a disorderly retreat toward center ice, where he finally stopped, alone, with 15,000 spectators looking on with expectant horror. Geoffrion advanced on his foe, stick over his shoulder in a swinging position. Up until then it appeared that the Boomer was merely taunting Murphy, goading him to drop his stick and engage him in a bare-fisted fight. But Murphy stood transfixed at the center-ice circle with his stick in hand.

When Geoffrion had skated to within arm's length of Murphy, the Boomer pulled his stick even farther back and took a cut at the Ranger's head. Somehow he missed, but he quickly drew back his stick to try again. This time he felled Murphy with a direct clout on the side of his head. The Ranger fell to the ice in a pool of blood while Geoffrion stood over him, his eyes on the other Rangers, who advanced to the scene. Except for an exchange of words and some idle pushing, no further blows were struck, and Geoffrion was led away from the scene by teammates. Murphy, disabled by a fractured jaw, was taken to the hospital. The incident was thoroughly reviewed by President Campbell, who suspended Geoffrion for eight games and Murphy for five.

"L'Affaire Geoffrion" did nothing to cool New York's enthusiasm for the Flying Frenchmen. Some observers marveled at such veterans as the Rocket and Lach. Others raved over the kids, and still others admired the raw intensity with which the Habitants approached the game.

"Before every game," said television commentator Bud Palmer, "they must put in 30 minutes of silence. They just sit there, backs to the wall, and their heads are down, as if in prayer."

Nevertheless, the Red Wings remained the class of the league and proved their skill in a stirring Stanley Cup final with les Canadiens. The teams' seventh and final game was decided on a rather innocent long, soft shot by Tony Leswick of Detroit. Goalie McNeil, who had made a brief comeback with the Canadiens, appeared to have it in hand, when defenseman Doug Harvey attempted to deflect it out of danger. Harvey managed to get only a piece of the puck, and it caromed off his left gauntlet and into the net behind the startled McNeil.

That was enough for McNeil. He permanently retired after four full seasons in the NHL and never fulfilled the promise Selke had held for him when he hired McNeil to replace Durnan. The great Lach also retired, but neither of the older players would be terribly missed. Plante would be an excellent replacement in goal, and the front line was fortified with the likes of Richard, Beliveau, Moore, Olmstead, and Floyd Curry.

"One of the most remarkable facts about the team — and a tribute to Frank Selke's talent-seeking abilities — has been the way it has been able to refresh its strength from new, young players whenever a group of older ones begins to disintegrate," wrote Peter Gzowski.

Yet the balance wheel of the dynamo that was les Canadiens remained the galvanic Richard. Consequently, he continued to be the target of incessant abuse from the rank-and-file among his opponents. One of his archrivals was Bob Bailey. During the 1954–55 season, the Maple Leafs owned Bailey, a third-rate player who had a habit of wielding his stick as a weapon.

Bailey and Richard battled several times, and one of their most severe clashes caused referee Red Storey to dispatch the Rocket to the dressing room. According to Frank Selke, Irvin leaned over the boards as Richard was heading for the showers and said something to his star. The Rocket wheeled in his tracks and accosted Storey with an assortment of epithets before retiring to the dressing room once and for all.

The dispute would have ended there were it not for Conn Smythe, who happened to have had movies taken of the game. Armed with the films, Smythe showed them to Campbell and NHL governors from Boston, Chicago, and New York. "All of the gentlemen demanded that something be done to curb Maurice Richard, whose greatest fault was defeating their teams and filling their arenas to capacity," said Selke.

Campbell summoned Richard and Selke to his office and presented the filmed evidence. Selke properly countered that it was unjust for Campbell to have held a kangaroo court with the three governors without permitting the Rocket to defend his action. Selke later asserted that Campbell was "ashamed" of the governors' meeting, "but an ugly black mark was placed alongside Richard's name."

Richard was more concerned with the scoring race than anything else. For the first time in his long career it appeared that Maurice was going to lead the league in points, with teammates Geoffrion and Beliveau close behind. As the Canadiens faced the Boston Bruins at Boston Garden with only one week remaining in the schedule, nobody doubted that the Rocket was home free.

The Bruins were not a very good team in those days, but they knew how to hit. They tormented the Canadiens with an assortment of body blows in the first and second periods. This action rankled Irvin, who had become more and more irritable as the season progressed. Part of the problem was the fact that Irvin was uneasy about his future.

Sometime late in December, 1954, he had conferred with Conn Smythe, his former boss, and mentioned to Smythe that he wouldn't mind coaching the lowly Black Hawks *if the price was right.*

Surprised by Irvin's remark, Smythe later called Selke and mentioned the conversation to him. Since Selke had no idea of Irvin's thinking, he was surprised and vexed. Later, when Selke confronted Irvin with the information, the coach replied that he wasn't really interested in Chicago, and the two left it at that. It has been Selke's conviction that Irvin's vitriolic temperament was having an unfortunate effect on Richard. The Bailey incident was one example, and the late-season game in Boston was to be even more significant — and damaging — to all concerned.

By the end of the second period in Boston Garden, Irvin had become dismayed by the abuse his team was absorbing from the Bruins. He urged them to come out fighting in the last period, and some of them, notably the Rocket, emerged from the dressing room lusting for combat. The Bruins, supported by a frantic crowd, provided plenty of cause for trouble, but the chief culprit turned out to be an ex-teammate, Hal Laycoe. The bespectacled defenseman crashed into Richard and opened a bloody cut in the Rocket's scalp. Maurice responded by challenging Laycoe to fight, and the Bruin executed an orderly retreat. The Rocket continued in pursuit but was intercepted by both teammates and linesman Cliff Thompson, a former defenseman who had played for the Bruins. Instead of calmly buffeting Richard from Laycoe, the linesman used an assortment of antagonizing holds that merely exacerbated a worsening situation. Richard and Thompson fell to the ice. The Rocket was suitably penalized for his outburst, and the episode would have ended there, had not a subjective and thoroughly biased Boston press demanded that sterner action be taken against Richard. Campbell responded by ordering Richard, Irvin, and Ken Reardon to his office for a hearing along with a contingent from the Bruins.

After studying the testimony, Campbell shocked the hockey world with an extraordinary announcement. Richard was suspended for the remainder of the regular session *and* the playoffs! Based on the ill-handling of the situation by Thompson and the provocation delivered by Laycoe, the Rocket's penalty was unfair in the extreme and a classic example of Campbell's negative treatment of Richard. But there was no appealing his decision. It was upheld by the other teams, who envisioned a Richard-less Montreal team as a sitting duck in the playoffs. Les Canadiens had to make do without him.

Montreal had three remaining games on its schedule: Thursday night at the Forum against the Red Wings, Saturday night at the Forum against the Rangers, and Sunday night at Detroit against the Red Wings. Up until the suspension, the Canadiens were expected to nose out Detroit and win the league championship. "Without Richard," said Selke in *Behind the Cheering*, "the team had lost its soul. Our boys were certain that, in one fell stroke, they had lost both the league championship and the Stanley Cup."

The same feeling permeated the devoted Montreal fans, who were enraged over Campbell's decision. By game time on St. Patrick's Day, 1955, the city was in an uproar. Several fans had phoned threats against Campbell's life and warned him to stay away from the Forum when the Red Wings played the Canadiens. Undaunted by the challenge, Campbell had made up *his* mind to attend, although there was mounting evidence that potentially violent protests would be staged on Ste. Catherine Street West, outside the arena. The evidence proved correct.

Placard-carrying fans marched along the sidewalk calling for Campbell's dismissal, if not execution, in several variations of French and English. But none of the demonstrations had an effect on the start of the game.

Without the Rocket, the Canadiens were a shadow of their former selves, and the Red Wings knew it. They seized the opportunity and quickly took the lead. Campbell had not yet arrived. He reached the Forum well after the opening face-off. Since his presidential box was well known to most Montreal fans, it was not difficult to discern his arrival, and a resentful murmur spread across the building as Campbell climbed the steps to his seat.

Officials of the Canadian Arena Company contend that the audience was unusual in one respect. There was a group of leather-jacketed toughs lining the standing-room arena not far from Campbell's seat. Not long after the president had arrived, one of the anti-Campbell men stalked over to his seat and attempted to attack the league boss. Soon a hail of debris, rotten fruit, and vegetables descended on Campbell, while other patrons attempted to get in a good shot at him. One assailant managed to crush a rather large tomato on Campbell's head.

Police moved in to protect the president, but the crowd was so surly that it appeared that the police would have difficulty preventing an attempt on his life. Precisely at this moment, Campbell was saved by a mysterious and completely unexpected incident. Someone in the audience of 14,000 exploded a tear-gas bomb directly in front of Selke's box. The rising fumes and acrid odor completely distracted the fans from the destruction of Campbell, and chaos reigned as spectators made their way to the exits. The public-address announcer attempted to restore calm. Soon, the fire chief ordered the building cleared, and the game was called off, forfeited to the Red Wings. As the teams repaired to their dressing rooms and the fans groped their way out to the street, it seemed that the worst was over. But it was only the beginning.

Campbell managed to escape through the rear of the Forum after first finding a sanctuary in the first-aid room. But when the spectators emerged from the rink and onto Ste. Catherine Street West, they were confronted by the huge crowd that had gathered in the park directly across the street from the Forum lobby.

Bands of vandals tossed everything from bricks to vegetables at the Forum, passing trolley cars, and automobiles. Newspaper kiosks were set afire and burned down, and roving bands proceeded east along Ste. Catherine Street, smashing store windows and looting at every turn. The rioting continued on into the night, until it finally dissipated of its own accord. When the final tally was in, damage was estimated at more than $100,000.

By the next morning, the "Richard Riot" was headline news around the world. *The New York Times*, in an unprecedented move for a "hockey story," played it on page one, as did other distinguished dailies. Everyone deplored the affair, and everybody appeared to blame everybody else for letting it develop. First, Campbell came under attack for showing up. His retort was legitimate enough: he was doing his duty as league president, and he wasn't about to be intimidated by fans or hoodlums. The police chief was accused of not having enough protection. Finally, there were those who charged that the Forum could have done a better job of preserving order.

In an editorial, the *Montreal Star* indicted the citizens of the city. "Montreal," said the *Star*, "stands convicted of emotional instability and lack of discipline. . . ."

Strangely enough, one of the most calming agents was the Rocket, who went on radio and television pleading with the community to accept Campbell's decision and to look forward to his return next season.

The Rocket's plea became a balm to all, and fans turned once again to the business of the pennant race. The Canadiens regained enough equilibrium to defeat the Rangers on Saturday night, but they were beaten by Detroit in the final game and had to settle for second place. That loss, however, was the lesser of the two tragedies in the eyes of Montreal fans.

The major catastrophe developed when Boom Boom Geoffrion made a determined bid to score goals and assists in the final two games. The Boomer was in the most difficult position of his career. On one hand, he wanted his idol, Richard, to win the scoring championship, but on the other, he wanted to help the Canadiens to annex first place. The best way to do that was to score goals or at least set up goals for his teammates. By the time the third period of the final game had ended at Detroit, Geoffrion had passed the Rocket and won the scoring championship. Richard was runner-up, and Beliveau finished third.

The Canadiens pulled themselves together and routed Boston in five games of the Stanley Cup semifinal, while Detroit took the measure of Toronto in four games. Montreal then extended the Red Wings to seven games before bowing out in the final match, 3–1. The defeat was harder than ever for Selke and Irvin to swallow. The coach placed the blame directly on Campbell for not curbing Richard's assailants and for suspending the Rocket. The manager considered Irvin at least partially at fault for the tragedy. He reasoned that Irvin had goaded Richard above and beyond the call of duty, and this goading had led to his squabbles and ultimate suspension.

Unknown to Selke at the time, Irvin was suffering through the first stages of bone cancer, which would cost him his life two years later. Soon after the final game, Selke summoned his old friend Irvin into his office and informed him he could remain with the Canadiens in "another job," but not as coach. He also made it clear that he would have no objections to Irvin's moving to the coaching job in Chicago.

Irvin, whom many regard as the greatest coach hockey has known, considered Selke's proposal and said he would move to the Windy City. Selke had inherited Irvin when he made the switch from Toronto to Montreal in 1946, and he had never before had to face the problem of selecting a new coach for the Canadiens. Selke had a difficult decision to make.

There were plenty of qualified coaches to choose from, but the task of controlling the Canadiens was something special. No team in the NHL had the distillation of French-and English-Canadians that the Montreal sextet possessed. Selke would have to find a man who, like Irvin, would be able to maintain harmony in the club. On top of that, he required a personality who could command the respect of aces such as Richard, Beliveau, and Geoffrion and who could follow in Irvin's difficult footsteps as a winner.

One rumor had it that Selke would be obliged to select a French-Canadian. One suggestion was Butch Bouchard; another was Roger Leger. Both were former players, well respected in the French-speaking community. Others speculated that Billy Reay, though not a French-Canadian, would wind up with the job. Several of the Forum directors were partial to Reay, and he and the favorite, Hector "Toe" Blake, were the only ones seriously in the running for the job.

Blake, "the Old Lamplighter," had studied coaching well in the Quebec Senior League. He was partially French-Canadian, and he was admired by all the players, particularly Richard. Kenny Reardon, who had moved up to a key front-office position with the Canadiens, was a strong advocate of Blake, and ultimately the opinions of Selke and Reardon prevailed. On June 8 the signing of Blake was officially announced before a standing-room crowd at the Forum, and the Canadiens were ready to become the greatest team in hockey history.

Toe Blake eventually wielded a dictator's baton over the Canadiens, but at first he ruled them like a benevolent despot. This was easy because all the players respected Blake, and vice versa. The pivotal personality on the team was the Rocket, and he went out of his way to assure the Canadiens' hierarchy that he backed Blake to the hilt.

Now it was up to the Old Lamplighter to produce. All the ingredients were there: a competent goaltender; a strong, intelligent defense; and the most explosive collection of scorers in history. It was simply a matter of stirring them and heating without creating the fire hazard of previous years. Richard Riots were to be avoided at all costs.

"Blake and Selke were trying to give the Rocket all they had by way of a tranquilizing program," says Josh Greenfeld. "They started giving him de-pep talks long before the season began. They pointed out to him that he was 35 years old, that he did not have to carry the emotional burden of victory alone, that he still would be treated with sufficient respect by the other players around the league even if he went a little easier on the roughhouse, and that the important thing was not one game, not one fight, but to lead the team to a Stanley Cup victory."

The Canadiens' organization was still smarting from the black eye it had received from the St. Patrick's Day disaster. A unique community spirit seemed to engulf the team right from the start of training camp, in nearby Verdun, Quebec. "I could see immediately," said Blake, "that we would have good harmony in the club. The boys were greatly disappointed with the way they'd finished the last two years. One year a bad goal beat them, the next year a bad fuss. They were determined they were not going to let anything beat them this time, least of all themselves."

The major roadblock would be provided by the Red Wings. Fortified by the Production Line of Sid Abel, Alex Delvecchio, and Gordie Howe, an excellent bench, and good goaltending, Detroit seemed as powerful as ever. To dethrone them would be a major accomplishment and would require adroit manipulation of lines — right down to the third unit. When the Beliveau line or the Richard line was exhausted, Blake had the good fortune to call upon Floyd "Busher" Curry, one of the essential unsung heroes, Claude Provost, and a very capable rookie, Don Marshall.

His scrubs, such as defenseman Jean-Guy Talbot and Bob Turner, were good enough to be first-liners on almost any other team, which was a credit to Selke's superb farm system. The galaxy dazzled nobody more than it did Blake. "I couldn't help being amazed once we started holding our first workouts," said Toe. "I was glad I was as young as I was. Otherwise, I would have been killed. All those great shots. The puck was flying around with such speed I thought I was in a shooting gallery."

It is impossible to project just how the 1955–56 Canadiens would have reacted to Dick Irvin, but one can surmise that the results would not have been as positive as they were with Blake. Irvin was confounded with a ramshackle Black Hawks team in October, 1955, and although they failed to make the playoffs, he managed to give them an aura of respectability. The condition of Irvin's health was worsening, and by the start of the 1956–57 season he had to be given a sabbatical. Irvin died in May, 1957.

When Blake took over as Montreal coach, the memory of Irvin lingered on. His success at Valleyfield in the Quebec Senior League was well known to management, but it hardly made an impression on the rank-and-file fan, who had as many doubts about Blake as did Toe himself. "I was nervous," the rookie coach allowed. "I felt I had to produce with a club like that. So much potential. And it was a big test for me. But the Rocket went out of his way to help me. So did Kenny Mosdell and Floyd Curry and Butch Bouchard.

"Sometimes it's tough to coach players you once had as teammates. But these fellas went out of their way to make it easy for me. Even from the beginning we were like one big happy family."

This camaraderie was virtually a miracle because Blake's Canadiens boasted a number of extroverts who bordered on egomaniacs. One of them was Jacques Plante, who eventually collided with Blake one time too many. Geoffrion was very much a team player but also a clown, given to renditions of Pagliacci in the dressing room, television singing appearances, and occasional dashes of braggadocio. The Rocket remained basically a loner, and Beliveau exuded a princely humility that endeared him to practically everyone. "Jean is so modest," said Selke, "he blushes when anybody says anything nice about him."

To that, Beliveau would reply, "If people are saying I am good, it is nice to hear. But to play good hockey you must be lucky to be born with ability. Then you work hard at it the rest of the time. I work hard for my job, and I think this team is a good one. We are one big happy family here."

The "happy family" theme would be a recurring one. Normally a hockey team splinters into small groups of players after each game. With the exception of Richard and Plante, the Canadiens would travel *en masse* to a movie, a tavern, or a restaurant.

One might have suspected that the Rocket would be jealous of the Young Turks grabbing the spotlight from him, but the opposite was true. The Rocket went out of his way to make life comfortable for le gros Bill and was quick to praise the big youngster. "He gets along with everyone, and he's the best center I've seen since I've been in the league," said Richard.

Still another young center captured the Rocket's attention. Henri Richard, the Rocket's 19-year-old brother, was invited to training camp for an audition, a rudimentary procedure with the Canadiens. After a week or so of scanning the youngsters, the high command would distribute them to any one of several farm teams. Certainly a kid straight out of Junior hockey and as small as Henri was not going to crack the varsity.

At first Henri was named "Flash," but this was soon changed to the "Pocket Rocket" as he displayed less and less inclination to be dropped from the varsity. This fact disturbed management because everyone agreed that at least a year in the minors would be most beneficial to young Richard.

For experimental purposes, Blake inserted Henri at center, with his brother at right wing and Dickie Moore at left wing. Whenever he stepped on the ice, Henri controlled the play, dashing around the rink with his lilting hop-steps. The appearance of his kid brother seemed to galvanize 35-year-old Maurice, while Moore complemented the line perfectly with his tough checking and superb shooting. It was no contest. Henri Richard made the team in his first try.

"He's a little small yet, but with his speed we keep telling him not to try to go through the big opposition defensemen, just go around them," said Toe Blake.

Henri's arrival enabled Blake to compose a second line of Beliveau, Geoffrion, and Olmstead, while mixing Mosdell, Curry, Marshall, Provost, and Jackie Leclair in varying combinations for his third unit. "I'm lucky I was a member of that team," recalled Beliveau. "We had everything. We had great scoring, we had checking, we had great goaltending. And we had great blending, the ideal combination of experienced veterans and good young rookies. And also great team spirit."

Experts varied in their opinions of the final standings for 1955–56, but Dick Irvin had no qualms about rating his former team: "They should win the championship by ten games!"

Blake agreed, "If we finish anywhere but first, I'll feel I've done a very bad job. If things go right, yes, we should win by ten games. But any hockey man will tell you that in hockey things don't always go right."

The gears didn't mesh perfectly for Blake. His club was baffled by an uncommon number of injuries. Yet, whenever one ace was side-lined, another filled the breach to play just as well. As the Canadiens approached the midpoint in the season, they were already six games in front of the pack. The Rocket was having another splendid season, and everyone hoped that *this* time he would win his long-coveted scoring championship. But it was not to be. He would be deprived of this honor by a changing Beliveau who was beginning to adopt some of Richard's old belligerence.

Up until 1955–56, Beliveau had become known as "Gentleman Jean" because of his abhorrence of rough and dirty play. As a result, the league bullies punished him severely. Just before Irvin left Montreal, he persuaded Beliveau that he had better fight back if he wanted to survive in the NHL jungle. Beliveau began retaliating in 1955–56. His penalty minutes mounted alarmingly, but his scoring totals jumped just as fast.

"Like the other great players, Jean smartened up when he saw the opposition getting the better of him," said Irvin. "He'll never be the type to go around looking for trouble, but now he can be as tough as anybody."

Blake had one more worry. By placing the two Richards on the same line he was inviting trouble. "We figured that if they were together they'd always be looking for each other or if the Pocket got into a scrape, the Rocket would be over in a second and explode," he explained. Blake kept his fingers crossed and played *les frères Richard* with Moore. Sure enough, there was trouble.

When the Canadiens played the Rangers at Madison Square Garden, the Pocket Rocket rammed the much bigger Lou Fontinato into the boards, and the Ranger defenseman retaliated by pushing both gauntlets into Richard's face. In a trice, the Rocket arrived on the scene and did battle with Fontinato. The scene was repeated in other arenas, but soon it became clear to Maurice that Henri could handle his dukes better than most players in the NHL. The Pocket Rocket was afraid of absolutely nobody.

Selke was a very happy man at the start of 1956. There was no longer any doubt that Blake had been a wise choice. The Rocket was temperamental, to be sure, but he managed to maintain decorum at the right time; and his prize catch, Beliveau, had become the talk of hockey.

"Big Jean is Great," said Black Hawks manager Tommy Ivan, "because he takes the direct route. No long way around for him. He has the size and the weight to hold his own. He's tremendously strong, a beautiful skater, a superb stickhandler, strictly a team man, with a perfect sense of playmaking. He'd be a star on any hockey club."

Beliveau was different from Maurice Richard in one area. "Jean doesn't have the desire to score that Maurice has," said Blake.

This comment was meant more as an analysis than as criticism. "With Maurice," said Selke, taking the issue a step further, "his moves are powered by instinctive reflexes. Maurice can't learn from lectures. He does everything by instinct and with sheer power. Beliveau, on the other hand, is probably the classiest player I've ever seen. He has a flair for giving you his hockey as a master showman. He is a perfect coach's hockey player because he studies and learns. He's moving and planning all the time, thinking out the play required for each situation. The difference between the two best players in the game today is simply this: Beliveau is a perfectionist; Richard is an opportunist."

The Rocket and le gros Bill formed two-fifths of the most devastating power play, the five-man charge when the enemy is shorthanded, in hockey history. Doug Harvey and Boom Boom Geoffrion were stationed at the left and right "points" near the blue line. Beliveau, Richard, and Bert Olmstead played up front, and Olmstead did the major digging in the corners for the puck. "Of all the players," Blake once observed, "I don't think Olmstead received all the credit he deserved."

More often than not, Olmstead would head for the boards to fetch the puck. If he fed it to Harvey, the relaxed defenseman would calmly look around and thread-needle a pass to someone near the net. If everyone was covered, he'd skim it across the ice to Geoffrion, whose potent shot was the fright of every goalie. For purposes of variety or deception, the Boomer might feed the puck to Beliveau or Richard, who were stationed closer to the net.

Statistics underlined the potency of Montreal's power play. Les Canadiens scored 25 *percent* of their goals on it, a fact that terribly distressed their five opponents. At a meeting after the season, the NHL voted against Montreal's opposition to change a rule terminating a minor penalty at the scoring of a goal. The rule was specifically aimed at curbing the Canadiens' awesome power. "When they're playing that power play right, it is a beautiful picture to watch," said Blake.

Finding a flaw in this armament was virtually impossible. The best the critics could do was charge that Selke's dreadnaught was too old a club to last very long. "They can say what they want," the manager replied. "When our old men stop producing, we'll bring up younger fellows who will start producing." He would then unveil charts indicating that the Canadiens had strings on some 10,000 players on 750 teams across the continent. Launched in 1946, Selke's farm system was bigger than the farm systems of all other NHL clubs combined.

There was no need for replacements in 1955–56. By the end of January, Montreal's lead was substantial, but three games with the hated Red Wings loomed on January 29, February 2, and February 4. The loss of all three, or even two of the three games, could have induced a panic, a slump, and loss of first place.

The teams played a 1–1 tie in the first game at Detroit. The Rocket and Beliveau scored in the second match, giving Montreal a 2–0 win. Le gros Bill scored twice in the rubber game, and les Canadiens came from behind to win 2–1. They now sported a 15-point lead, and the battle for first place was over.

Blake, nevertheless, continued to run a tight ship while allowing for healthy injections of humor here and there. Once Blake reminded his players that he had imposed an eleven o'clock curfew. "Gee, coach," said Harvey with a straight face, "does that mean we have to wait until eleven to go to bed?"

Even the Rocket got in on the banter. Andy O'Brien, sports editor of *Weekend* magazine, was accompanying the team on a trip to New York when he noticed most of the players posing for a photographer, kissing their wives goodbye at the railroad station. The Rocket stood by, biting on a long stogie. O'Brien sauntered over and wondered why Maurice did not kiss his wife goodbye. "Not on short trips," quipped the Rocket.

By this time the Pocket and the Rocket had jelled perfectly with Moore. Despite the Rocket's age, he managed to keep pace with his younger cronies, although one afternoon he nearly regretted it. The Canadiens were in the midst of a workout when Henri rounded the net at full speed from one side and Maurice approached on the same track from the other direction. They collided, and both fell unconscious to the ice. When they were finally revived, both were escorted to the first-aid room. Maurice needed 12 stitches to close his wound, and his kid brother required 6.

In a masterful understatement, Maurice intoned, "You'd better watch yourself, Henri. You might get hurt."

Only once did the Rocket nearly approach the fury that engulfed him in previous seasons. The Canadiens were playing the Rangers at Madison Square Garden in a game that was so wild and turbulent that columnist Red Smith likened it to a Roman circus. Late in the second period, the Rocket and New York's Lou Fontinato clashed. Fontinato connected with a hard right that opened a wound over Richard's left eye. The bloodthirsty New York crowd went into transports of joy at the sight. Richard seethed with contempt for Fontinato and continued stewing in his quiet rage as the Canadiens trooped into the dressing room for the break between the second and third periods.

Ken Reardon, by that time a major executive with the team, dashed down to the dressing room from the press box. Reardon had more than a passing knowledge of temper tantrums and had played with the Rocket long enough to know how to deal with him. As soon as he opened the locker room door, Reardon went straight to Richard's bench and talked hard but calmly to him. He stressed the obvious. Fontinato had hit him a lucky punch and it would be better for all concerned — Maurice and the Canadiens — if he cooled it this time.

The Rocket listened impassively like a boxer more intent on getting back into the ring than listening to the ministrations of his trainer. For a few seconds it appeared that all hell would break loose again and the Rocket would be in the middle of it. Without notice, Doug Harvey came up with a droll remark, and the sullen dressing room erupted with laughter. An almost embarrassed smile crossed the Rocket's face. Soon he was laughing with the rest of them, and he was never in real trouble again.

"Sometimes," said Blake, "I had to cool the Rocket on the bench. He'd glare at me, but he took it."

A year after his suspension, the Rocket was virtually canonized in Montreal. A French-Canadian record company pressed a disk in his honor, as well as one for Geoffrion, and an English outfit came up with a hillbilly version of the St. Patrick's Day riot called "The Saga of Rocket Richard." His goals received as thunderous a response as ever, and from time to time, when Gordie Howe visited the Forum, the crowd would boo whenever Howe carried the puck.

Conversely, the Forum faithful took a dim view of Geoffrion. They resented the fact that he had wrested the scoring championship away from Maurice while the Rocket was under suspension, and they generally made life miserable for the normally ebullient Boomer. Geoffrion was so despondant about the negative reaction that he seriously considered retiring before the 1955–56 campaign.

"It was not my fault the Rocket was suspended," Geoffrion would say in defense of his position. "I couldn't deliberately *not* score. So I was sick of the whole thing. Even thinking about hockey made me throw up. I wanted to get away from hockey. But then before practices began, Beliveau and Richard visited me. They urged me to stay in the game."

Plante was another eccentric, not only because he knitted *toques* in his spare time or traveled far and wide from his goal crease. Some people contend that he was a hypochondriac. Others noted that he did, in fact, suffer from asthma, and in cities such as Toronto he would divorce himself from the team and stay at a select "nonasthmatic" hotel. Blake didn't mind. "Starting that season, for five years he was the greatest goalie the league has ever seen," said the coach.

Interestingly, the Montreal defense was not all that tough, but it didn't have to be. With the forwards outskating the opposition at every turn, the defensemen were mobile enough to outwit the enemy with brain power and speed, without resorting to violence — unless suitably provoked.

Once, during a game with the Rangers in New York, Harvey planted the pointed blade of his stick in Red Sullivan's gut and sent the Ranger center to the hospital with a ruptured spleen. Sullivan's condition was so grave that he was given last rites of the Catholic Church. Fortunately, he recovered completely and returned to play out his career in the NHL. Honest to a fault, Harvey never denied the attack, but he pointed out that Sullivan had developed an obnoxious, not to mention dangerous, habit of "kicking skates," so that when the two went into the corner of the rink, Sullivan would kick Harvey's skates out from under him, making it very easy for the Montrealer to fall on his head. According to Doug, he warned Sullivan about his unfortunate proclivity, and when the warning went unheeded, the stick was plunged into Sullivan's stomach.

Harvey had one "flaw" as a defenseman. He was so laconic in style, so calmly sure of himself, that he executed plays of extreme complication with consummate ease. Lacking the flamboyance of Eddie Shore or other Hall of Fame defensemen, Harvey was slow to receive the acclaim he deserved. But by 1955–56 it was apparent that he was superior to Shore in many ways. "Doug Harvey was the greatest defenseman who ever played hockey — bar none," said Blake. "Usually a defenseman specializes in one thing and builds a reputation on that, but Doug could do everything well."

Inevitably, Harvey has been compared with Hall of Famer defenseman, Bobby Orr of the Bruins. In all fairness to both athletes, Orr was not in the league long enough to merit a fair comparison to Harvey. On specific performance, Orr never matched Harvey *defensively*.

"Often Harvey's cool was mistaken for disinterest," said Josh Greenfield. "Actually it was the result of an always calculating concentration." By contrast, Orr often appeared to make outrageously obtuse plays in his own defensive zone and occasionally betrayed moves that suggested panic.

Harvey was a superb rusher, but he lacked the blazing shot that characterizes Orr's arsenal. There is little doubt that Orr has the advantage offensively but not as much as current statistics would suggest. "Harvey," wrote Greenfield, "could inaugurate a play from farther back and carry it farther than any other defenseman."

Not far behind Harvey in all-round ability was Tom Johnson, a well-coordinated puck carrier and a solid man behind the blue line. "It took everybody a long time to know that Johnson was as good as we knew he was," said Blake. In 1970, Johnson was inducted into the Hockey Hall of Fame.

With this abundance of stars, Blake was careful not to introduce any stratagem that would disrupt the team. Under Irvin, the Canadiens had become renowned for what was known as "Firewagon Hockey," which accented the rush, rush, rush until the enemy was run through the ice with exhaustion. Peter Gzowski said he preferred to describe the Canadiens' trademark as *élan*. "On the ice," he wrote, "the Canadiens swoop and gambol, skating like fury and burning with zeal: they are somehow romantic, like Scaramouch or Cyrano or Jean Gascon."

Blake was acutely aware of this quality. All he did was improve on Irvin's failing psychology. Everything else fell perfectly into place. "Your style of coaching has to depend upon the players you have," said Blake, "because if you try to change the styles of your players, you're in trouble.

"If you're connected with so many superstars as I was, then you've got to let them go all out and let the defense look after itself. But I told my team that four or five stars don't make a team. Everyone in uniform is important."

With Blake orchestrating his club to perfection, the Canadiens romped home first with ease — 24 points, or 12 games, ahead of Detroit. Four of the top seven scorers were Canadiens. Beliveau led the league with 88 points while the Rocket was third with 72. Beliveau, Richard, Harvey, and Plante were named to the First All-Star Team. Plante's 1.86 goals against average gave him the Vézina Trophy. Harvey captured the James Norris Trophy as the league's best defenseman, and Beliveau was awarded the Hart Trophy as the most valuable player in the NHL. The club set a record by winning 45 games, losing only 15, and tying 10, for 100 points.

These prizes, however, were quickly forgotten once the playoffs began. To hockey fans, the Stanley Cup round is a completely new season: the triumphs and achievements of the season gone by are ancient history. For a change, the Rangers had won a playoff berth, and having finished third, they were slated to meet Montreal in the opening round. New York was coached by the one-time Canadien Phil Watson, and from time to time the New Yorkers generated enough power to be considered a threat to any team.

The Rocket's hat trick defused the Rangers in the opening game at the Forum, and the Canadiens romped to an easy 7–1 victory. Everyone in Montreal expected the second game to be just as easy. Gump Worsley, the Rangers' regular goalkeeper, was injured, and Watson was compelled to use 31-year-old Gordie Bell, a weather-beaten minor-league goaltender with virtually no NHL experience. Somehow the Rangers rallied around Bell and defeated Montreal, 4–2. Heartened by the upset, the Rangers returned to New York, hoping to win the next two matches on Madison Square Garden ice.

The Rangers fought gamely, but the Canadiens didn't fool around either. Montreal won both games in Manhattan and eliminated New York with a 7–0 victory in the fifth game at the Forum. Once more, the Rocket starred, setting up five of the seven goals. "Now I've become a playmaker," he kidded in the dressing room after the game.

Only the Red Wings stood between the Canadiens and the Stanley Cup. Detroit had moved into the finals on the strength of a 4–1 sweep of the Maple Leafs and impressed Toronto's King Clancy enough to persuade him to predict that Montreal would lose to the Detroiters. For a couple of periods in the first game at Montreal it appeared that Clancy might have something there. The Canadiens fell behind 4–2 and appeared to be in a state of inertia.

"Sometimes," said Blake, "your aces get heavily checked in the playoffs. When that happens, you have to hope that your lesser lights can come up with a couple of goals and bail you out."

Jackie Leclair did the spade work on Montreal's third goal, and Jean-Guy Talbot spearheaded the fourth and tying goal. Then big Jean Beliveau came through with the tie-breaker, followed by an insurance score from the stick of Claude Provost. Before the Red Wings could turn around, they had been swept off the ice, 6–4.

The Red Wings were no match in the second game, and they bowed 5–1. Only once, in the third game, was the Detroit club to perform respectably. The Wings prevailed, 3–1, but they lost their next home game 3–0. They returned to the Forum for what 14,151 fans expected would be "the kill." They were disappointed throughout the scoreless first period and waited expectantly as the second period moved along without a goal. But late in the session, Harvey spotted Floyd Curry breaking toward the Detroit goal. His pass was radar-perfect, and Curry moved swiftly, with Beliveau flanking him on the other side. Curry's pass was true, and Beliveau's shot beat Glenn Hall in the Red Wing goal.

The second period had still not ended when the Rocket detonated another explosive roar as *he* beat Hall. Boomer Geoffrion made it three for Montreal in the third period, and Alex Delvecchio scored for Detroit. Meanwhile, the clock ticked closer and closer to the 20-minute mark, and when the siren wailed, signaling the end of the game, the crowd launched into a roar that reached new heights in decibel counts. The Canadiens had regained the Stanley Cup. Butch Bouchard, the captain who was on the verge of retirement, accepted the trophy at center ice, and the champagne flowed. A day later, the citizens who were the shame of the NHL a year ago proudly toasted their heroes with a 30-mile parade through the city of Montreal.

"Perhaps to some Montrealers it was as if Bonnie Prince Charlie had become king," said Josh Greenfeld, "perhaps to others it was like the restoration of the Bourbon dynasty. But all of hockey-mad Montreal was happy — in any language."

It was more than that. The deafening cheers were an expression of retribution for the previous year's "crime" against the Rocket as well as a feeling of jubilation about the rosy future, what Canadiens' publicist Camil Desroches called "those wonderful five years."

Armed with basically the same lineup as they had iced in 1955–56, the Canadiens won an unparalleled five Stanley Cups in succession and finished in first place in six out of seven years. "I saw the old Canadiens with Morenz and Joliat," said Muzz Patrick, the Rangers manager. "There's no comparing that team with this one. This Montreal outfit is many, many times better."

"Nobody seems able to skate with them, to shoot with them," said New York columnist Jimmy Powers, "and if, as happens, they have a bad night and get licked, it is an event." Such was the case until 1960, although the Canadiens were experiencing an inner upheaval of major proportions.

There was only one thing different about the Canadiens when they launched the 1960–1961 campaign, but that one thing made all the difference in the world. Rocket Richard was no longer skating for Montreal. On September 15, 1960, after a career that spanned the eras from 1942 through April, 1960, the Rocket announced that he was finished as a player.

During his career, this extremely high-strung, dedicated man scored 626 goals and left an indelible impression on the Canadiens and big-league hockey throughout the NHL. Without the Rocket around to explode, life just wasn't the same for the Montrealers or the rest of the league.

The Canadiens, led by The Rocket, were the greatest team ever in that glorious span in the 1950s and it could never be the same without Maurice Richard.

But Henri Richard remained with the team and, along with Beliveau, led the Canadiens dynasty to more Cup wins. Beliveau's last championship was in 1971.

Then, Henri became captain, and in May, 1973, he underlined the glorious tradition by spearheading another Montreal Cup victory.

But some purists insist that the Canadiens lost their ferocious flair when Maurice Richard retired. "It is quite unlikely that similar excitement would attend any future idol," concluded Canadiens-watcher Herbert Warren Wind.

He was right.

The New York Islanders, 1980–83

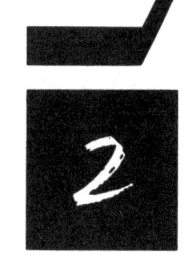

The Best of the 1980s — New York Islanders

The Islanders must be considered the second greatest team of all time because they succeeded in winning 19 consecutive playoff series, beginning in 1980 and concluding in 1984. No other team can make that statement.

In that period, the team coached by Al Arbour and managed by Bill Torrey had to regularly meet their fierce cross-county rivals, the Rangers, in most of the playoffs and always disposed of them, although the toll was great. (The 1984 five-game New York–New York series, particularly Game Five, is regarded as a playoff classic.) In addition to the 19 consecutive playoff series wins, the Islanders won four straight Stanley Cups and did so with the best-balanced club of the post-expansion era.

They featured one of the all-time snipers in Mike Bossy, the best two-way hitting center ever in Bryan Trottier, the best clutch goaltender in Bill Smith, and more significant role players than any team in an era. Bob Bourne was the NHL's fastest forward; Clark Gillies the most productive fighting left wing (when provoked); and Butch Goring, a fleet second center who doubled as penalty-killer checker-of-stars.

Whether Al Arbour was the best, second-best, or third-best coach of all time is a moot question. Suffice to say that Arbour was ideal for his team. He had played on Punch Imlach's multi-championship Toronto Maple Leafs as well as the Chicago Black Hawks Cup-winners in 1961. He studied under the masters and learned well.

"I remember something Arbour said to us the season after we'd won our first Cup," recalled former Islanders defenseman Jean Potvin. "We'd played badly in a couple of games and lost them both, and Al was really upset with us. 'You should have won those games,' he told us at practice one morning, and one of the guys said, 'Geez, Al, you can't expect us to win every game.' And Al just got this hard look on his face and said, 'WHY NOT?' "

In many ways the Islanders of the early 1980s resembled the super-Canadiens who won five straight Stanley Cups. There were no weak links in the lineup. "They could play you any way you wanted to play them," recalled Herb Brooks, who coached the rival Rangers at the time. "They had skilled players like Bossy, Trottier, and Potvin and tough guys like Garry Howatt and Bob Nystrom. They could finesse with anyone or grind with the best of them."

They were a better team than the Oilers of the late 1980s because of the equitable balance between offense, defense, and goaltending. Edmonton boasted good netminding and a scary offense, but defense was not in the Oilers vocabulary; not for defensemen and not for checking forwards. It was a deficiency that was only partially remedied after high-scoring defenseman Paul Coffey was traded to Pittsburgh.

By contrast, the Islanders defense was stout to the core. Denis Potvin was the best two-way defenseman of the post-Doug Harvey era and his sidekick, Stefan Persson, emerged as the most underrated solid backliner in the league. Dave (Bammer) Langevin supplied the lusty bodychecks, while Gord Lane, Tomas Jonsson, and Ken Morrow all filled in nobly.

Management, headed by president-general manager Bill Torrey and Arbour, was insightful, steady, and consistently superior, beginning in the late 1970s when the Islanders dynasty was developed.

The Islanders had become a power in 1978 and even stronger in 1979, but in both years were unable to reach the Stanley Cup finals. Torrey realized there was a missing link. He required an experienced, digging center to supplement the vigorous Trottier. Another requirement was a stay-at-home defenseman who could complement the oft-rushing Potvin.

Both pieces fit neatly into the puzzle before the trade deadline in March 1980. Torrey dealt right wing Billy Harris and defenseman Dave Lewis to Los Angeles for fleet center Butch Goring. It was the perfect fit. With Goring's arrival, the Islanders went on a winning tear that carried into the 1980 playoffs.

Previously, they had been accused of being too tight in crunch situations but they responded in series wins over Los Angeles, Boston, and Buffalo before reaching the finals against the Philadelphia Flyers. For the first time the Cup was within their grasp and the Islanders came through with a four games to two win over Philadelphia. Bob Nystrom, who scored the sudden-death winner, would prove to be as effective a clutch performer as Maurice Richard had been with the Canadiens.

In 1981, the Islanders marched past the Maple Leafs, Oilers, and Rangers before disposing of Minnesota in a five-game final. They got a major scare in 1982 when Pittsburgh led by two goals in the decisive fifth game of the semifinals, but the Islanders displayed their patented comeback qualities and took the series in overtime on John Tonelli's goal.

They then edged the Rangers in six games and wiped out Quebec in four as they did Vancouver in the finals. But their most impressive run took place a year later. They topped Washington (four games), the Rangers (six games), and the Bruins (six games) before taking on the powerful Oilers, led by Wayne Gretzky. The combination of Smith's superlative goaltending and timely scoring was too much for Edmonton. The Islanders swept the series in four straight.

In many ways the Islanders "Drive For Five" in 1984 was even more heroic. Fighting their way through three brutally difficult preliminary rounds, Arbour's sextet was riddled with injury by the time it took on the Oilers in the finals.

The teams split the first two games at Nassau Coliseum and then moved on to Edmonton for a resumption of the series. At this juncture, a quirk in playoff scheduling turned the series in the Oilers favor. Instead of playing the next two games in Edmonton and then returning east, the teams were required to play three games at Northlands Coliseum. The move clearly favored the Oilers in many ways and they exploited this advantage as well as the Islanders injuries to wrest the Cup away from the New Yorkers in five games.

Not only was the Islanders' run of 19 consecutive playoff series victories remarkable, it demonstrated a staying power, combined with high-quality performance, that has been unmatched at any time in history.

Additionally, the Islanders oozed the kind of class that few other teams could boast except for the Canadiens of the Blake-Richard era. There was none of the wise-guy braggadocio that was part of the Oilers persona and no running from reporters in defeat, a trait that characterized so many other teams.

The Islanders were a class act; perhaps the classiest group of skaters who ever graced an NHL rink. And, as their four Cups and 19 series triumphs in a row indicate, they deservedly are the second greatest team in history.

In September 1983, when the New Jersey Devils' financial problems were made public, NHL Players' Association boss Al Eagleson suggested that there was one team that could offer hope to the Devils. That team was the New York Islanders.

"The Islanders," said Eagleson, "are living proof that you can bleed and bleed for four or five years, then make a lot of money — if you win."

The Islanders did win — and they won big — to the tune of four consecutive Stanley Cups. But the wins did not come easily, although they did arrive a lot swifter than many people believed.

The roots of the Islanders can be traced to 1966 when the NHL launched its first major expansion from six to twelve teams. It proved so successful that still further expansion took place. Buffalo and Vancouver were added and they, too, were instant hits at the box office. When Nassau Coliseum was constructed in Uniondale, New York, at the start of the 1970s it was inevitable that Long Island would be represented in the majors with a hockey club.

The price of an NHL franchise had leaped from $2,000,000 in 1966 to $6,000,000. The club that invaded the New York Rangers' territory would also have to pay an indemnification fee — estimated at $4,000,000 — to Madison Square Garden, owner of the Rangers. This apparently failed to faze Roy Boe who, with 19 partners, purchased the NHL franchise for Long Island on December 30, 1971. Now, he was a hockey man with challenges he never dreamed possible just five years earlier when he sat behind a desk on Seventh Avenue, running Boe Jests.

Having received the green light from the NHL, Boe embarked on his first recruitment drive. The immediate goal was to find a general manager with the qualities of intelligence, patience, fortitude, and humor.

On February 15, 1972, Boe announced his choice of William Arthur "Bill" Torrey, a 37-year-old native of Montreal who was born across the street from the Forum. Torrey, a graduate of St. Lawrence University, where he played for the varsity hockey team, had been business manager and public relations director of the Pittsburgh Hornets in the American Hockey League. He also spent two years with the California (Oakland) Seals, of which six months were under the baton of Charles O. Finley. Torrey had helped lift the Seals from last place in the Western Division in 1967–68 to playoff berths the following two seasons.

With the job of organizing a team confronting him, Torrey's prospects for finding first-rate players were exceptionally dim.

"I don't expect my NHL brothers will be overly generous with me in the draft," said Torrey. "I don't think anyone will throw a 25 or 30-goal scorer at us. We will beg and borrow any talent we can."

Torrey knew what he wanted, however, and his "three-to-five-year plan" to build a winner was clear. "I committed myself to youth," he said. "We decided to draft people who will be around for years rather than those who will not be with us after a year or two."

The neighboring New York Rangers, one of the most powerful organizations in the NHL, oozed with players who had been well known in the metropolitan area for years; veterans such as Rod Gilbert, Jean Ratelle, and Vic Hadfield. Even so, Boe relished the idea of playing in the same division with the Rangers.

"This," said Boe, "makes for a great natural rivalry."

Much would depend on Bill Torrey's choice of aides as well as his selections in the decisive June 1972 draft. He immediately signed two scouts, former Toronto Maple Leaf goaltender Ed Chadwick and erstwhile New York Ranger center Earl Ingarfield. Torrey and his aides-de-camp criss-crossed the continent, from Swift Current, Saskatchewan, to St. Catharines, Ontario, in search of prospective talent. Unlike his predecessors in the NHL who were confronted only with competition from within the league itself, Torrey also had to contend with the just-organized World Hockey Association which had already begun raiding the NHL clubs in preparation for its 1972–73 campaign.

"I was convinced," said Torrey, "that the WHA was a fact of life. I knew we had to take them seriously because we were going to have to battle them for players. We did have an edge in one respect; the NHL was — and is — THE league. All things being equal, hockey players want to be in the NHL, rather than any new league."

A decisive milestone in the Islanders' young life was reached in June, 1972 when the expansion draft would enable them, along with the Atlanta Flames, to stock their rosters with experienced players. It would not be as much a qualitative as a quantitative step for Torrey and his high command. "I told Roy Boe to expect nothing from the draft. I even told him we'd have to get rid of most of the players we drafted just as fast as we could."

Torrey stayed up all night prior to the draft meeting on June 6. At the player selection ritual, a flip of the coin with Atlanta manager Cliff Fletcher gave Torrey the right to select first in the amateur draft. He picked Bill Harris of the junior Toronto Marlboros. In the selection of professionals, the Islanders and Flames each wound up with 21 players, including two goaltenders.

By far, the best-known Islander pick was Eddie Westfall, a superb defensive forward who had played for the Boston Bruin's Stanley Cup championship club in 1970, and again in 1972. Westfall was one of three Islanders still with the team through the 1976–77 season. The others were goalie Billy Smith and defenseman Gerry Hart.

Also drafted by the Islanders were Gerry Desjardins, the Chicago Black Hawk goalie who had a permanently bent arm following an injury, and Terry Crisp, who had been an effective utility player with the St. Louis Blues.

As anticipated, complications set in immediately following the draft. The WHA bird dogs started to zero in on the NHL teams. When the dust had cleared they came away with seven of the players the Islanders had selected. The Islanders then got some good news when the Montreal Canadiens made goalie Denis DeJordy available to them.

On July 27, 1972, the Islanders made another meaningful move when they signed their second and third amateur draft choices, center Lorne Henning and right wing Bob Nystrom.

Finding an adequate coach was another story. Following a spate of rumors, Torrey finally selected 38-year-old veteran center Phil Goyette to lead the new team from behind the bench. To say that he had a difficult task would be an understatement. Even Torrey admitted that.

In the first hockey game ever played at Nassau Coliseum, on September 27, 1972, the Rangers defeated the Islanders, 6–4. It was an exhibition game. Despite the defeat, the Islanders came away with some critical praise.

On the official opening night, October 7, 1972, a crowd of 12,221 turned out to see the Flames edge their young rivals, 3–2.

Although coach Goyette remained optimistic, the on-ice results were less than encouraging. In mid-November, for example, the Islanders had played well until 16 minutes were left in the game. Then they collapsed and lost, 7–2, to Montreal. Eventually Goyette was fired.

"Hapless was the word," Torrey recalls in his reflection over the various jibes hurled at his first-year club. "The Rangers play the hapless Islanders tonight. The Bruins get a breather against the hapless Islanders. Les Canadiens rout hapless Islanders. Cripes, I thought hapless was the only word in the English language."

When the won-lost record was compiled at season's end, it showed that the Islanders had captured only 12 games — a record low — and lost 60, a record high. They had finished 72 points behind the Rangers. Yet, somehow, it wasn't all that calamitous. For one thing, the team rallied around new coach Earl Ingarfield and played a more competitive brand of hockey in the homestretch. For another, their last-place finish guaranteed the first pick in the amateur draft. That meant that Torrey had a better than fair chance of signing 19-year-old Denis Potvin, a defenseman with the Ottawa 67s who had broken all of Bobby Orr's junior hockey scoring records.

To ensure the acquisition of Denis Potvin, Torrey swung a late season deal with the Philadelphia Flyers and obtained Denis' older brother, Jean, in exchange for Terry Crisp. The Islanders knew that Denis wanted to play alongside his brother. And they were right.

At first it appeared that the pursuit of Denis Potvin would be as difficult as the signing of the Islanders drafts picks in 1972. Denis had been well scouted by the World Hockey Association and clearly would be the prize plum in the 1973 junior crop. Earl Ingarfield, who was soon to return to his scouting chores, had offered a terse but definitive report on the husky Denis. "He scores extremely well, carries the puck well, and is a tremendous hitter at mid-ice."

The WHA made their pitch for Potvin but, fortunately for the Islanders, Denis rejected it. ("I always wanted to play in the NHL and only the NHL.") He jetted to New York with his mother, Lucille, and father, Armand, for a contract-signing ceremony at the Islander headquarters. He puffed on a meerschaum pipe and told newsmen he'd rather be known as the first Denis Potvin rather than another Bobby Orr.

The 6 foot 205-pound Potvin arrived with a reputation that almost transcended the one preceding Orr's entry into the NHL. Denis was tough and, unlike Orr, liked to hit the enemy as much as he liked to score goals. Articulate in both English and French, Potvin wasted no time telling newsmen about his career objectives.

"Now that I'm here," he said, "I ask myself what am I going to do next? Well, I want to be the best. I set my goals high. It keeps you working; it keeps you alive."

If anything, Potvin needed a coach who would stress the defensive fundamentals which might have eluded him in the junior ranks. When Ingarfield asked to be relieved of the coaching job, Bill Torrey offered the assignment to Al Arbour. Al had long been considered the "defenseman's defenseman" when he skated for the Chicago Black Hawks, Toronto Maple Leafs, and the St. Louis Blues.

Arbour, who had coached the Blues on and off from 1970 to 1973, hesitated at first because of his sour opinion of the Big Apple. But, when he and his wife discovered the more bucolic atmosphere to be found on Long Island, he accepted the position.

Having an insightful coach to assist him through his rookie season and a sensitive brother to provide tips on the opposition — Jean Potvin had been around the NHL since 1970 — made life easier for Denis, who reached his 20th birthday on October 29, 1973. This showed up in his performance during that first 1973–74 season. He handled the attack as if he had been around the NHL for more than a decade. Rinksiders were astonished at his effortless skating and his ability to pace himself at all times. "He's like Gordie Howe in that respect," said Coach Arbour.

Potvin was the major headline-grabber among the Islander defenders, but there were others who unobtrusively helped solidify the backline in the club's second season. One of the least heralded defensemen was Bert Marshall, a 29-year-old drafted in June 1973 from the New York Rangers. Marshall was a handsome, husky veteran who had previously played for the Detroit Red Wings and the California Seals.

General manager Torrey's acquisition of Marshall was typical of his adroit moves that rapidly bolstered the team, but puzzled sports commentators. They wondered why he hadn't selected centermen Bobby Rousseau or Lou Angotti or left winger Glen Sather, all of whom were available at the time.

Time would prove Torrey correct. "Marshall," he said, "is the guy who could do the most good for our club. He has experience, he has size, and he can play right or left defense. He can knock down a few people, too. We need to get our goaltenders out of the shooting gallery. The area we needed to plug most was defense; which is why I went for Marshall."

Without fuss or fanfare, Marshall stabilized the defense while providing useful advice to another young defender, Dave Lewis, who, like his mentor, played a conservative game on the blue line.

Lewis epitomized the youth movement which Torrey had advocated from the Islanders' inception. There were others. The 5'9", 170 lb Garry Howatt (who suffered from epilepsy) was regarded by some railbirds as too small for the big time, but he took on the goliaths of the NHL. By the time the 1973–74 season had ended he was revered as one of the most ferocious forwards in the NHL. Blond, energetic Bob Nystrom overcame early skating problems — he took lessons from power-skating specialist Laura Stamm — and provided a positive robustness up front to complement his steady improvement as a goal scorer.

The Isles were league leaders by 1974–75 and had definitely established themselves as a playoff threat for the first time in their brief NHL existence. By the midpoint of the 1974–75 season, Arbour's skaters had displayed a marked improvement over their play of the previous year. After the same number of games (44) they had 34 points in 1974–75 compared with 12 the previous season. Their goals-against total dropped a significant 14% while the goals-for total skyrocketed 37%.

Torrey still was not content with the results; he wanted more oomph up front and went to the NHL marketplace in search of scorers. To his amazement he learned that Minnesota North Stars' GM Jack Gordon was prepared to unload two crafty forwards with superb scoring credentials; J.P. Parise and Jude Drouin. In return, Gordon was willing to accept Ernie Hicke, Doug Rombough, and Craig Cameron, a trio of forwards who had made only a minimal contribution to the Islander cause.

Al Arbour's patience and the Islanders' vigor produced a playoff berth two years before most observers thought it possible. They had played 80 games and had won 33 (compared with 19 the previous season and 12 in the first miserable year). They lost 25 games (compared with 41 the previous season and 60 in the rookie campaign). They tied 22 times and finished in third place with 88 points, 32 more than they had in 1973–74.

Now it was time for the Stanley Cup playoffs. In the first round, a best-of-three event, the Islanders would face the New York Rangers, still one of the more powerful clubs in the NHL. The Islanders were as confident as a young team that had made the playoffs could be; but were still somewhat awed by their "cousins" in the big city.

"We know we can beat the Rangers," said Denis Potvin. "We're younger, stronger, better. For some reason, though, we have too much respect for them. We treat them like gods. I guess we really have a bit of an inferiority complex, probably because we believe too much of what we hear and read about them."

This attitude would be reversed — within one week, or three games — two at Madison Square Garden and the other at Nassau Coliseum. The Isles upset the Rangers in three games and then went on to other miracles.

Prior to the 1975 Stanley Cup playoffs, the only National Hockey League team ever to lose three consecutive games in a best-of-seven round and then counter-attack to win the next four in a row, was the 1942 edition of the Toronto Maple Leafs.

However, the Maple Leafs club which ultimately defeated the Detroit Red Wings in that series was a formidable outfit, well-sprinkled with All-Stars. They were expected to win. This was not the case with the three-year-old Islanders who rose from a last-place finish in 1973 to come within one game of reaching the 1975 Stanley Cup finals.

The saga began with the upset win over the Rangers. The Islanders then came back to sweep the Pittsburgh Penguins in four straight — after falling behind three games to none. For finishers, they scared the daylights out of the Philadelphia Flyers, rebounding from another 3–0 deficit, before finally bowing to the Stanley Cup champions in the seventh game.

The following are the highlights of that remarkable playoff run, beginning in April, and ending in mid-May 1975.

April 11 — The Islanders beat the Rangers in overtime in the third game of their opening round and take the series two games to one. J.P. Parise accomplishes the feat with a goal at 11 seconds of the sudden-death period.

April 17 — The Islanders are two down to the Pittsburgh Penguins and they lose game three, 6–4. The Islander goaltending has been weak, while Pittsburgh goalie

Gary Inness frustrates them time and again with exceptional saves. All-Star defenseman Denis Potvin is playing with a bruised left thigh and right wing Bobby Nystrom is in a slump. He has yet to score in the playoffs after scoring 27 goals during the regular season. It seems impossible for the Islanders to successfully counterattack.

April 20 — To inspire the club, Arbour makes a change in goal, inserting Glenn Resch who has not seen action since the second game of the Ranger series. With the capacity crowd at Nassau Coliseum chanting "Chico, Chico!" and with signs urging the Islanders to *Souvenez-vous les Maple Leafs* (Remember the Maple Leafs), the Islanders win, 3–1. The New York defense keeps Pittsburgh out of the slot and Resch turns back 27 of 28 Penguin shots. Although still alive in the series, the Islanders face impossible odds.

April 26 — Getting superb goaltending from "Chico" Resch, the Islanders take the next two games to draw even, facing a seventh game in Pittsburgh. Although the Penguins insist they are loose — and although the odds are on their side — the game is tight, remaining scoreless well into the third period.

At 14:42 of the finale, Ed Westfall takes a pass from defenseman Bert Marshall and fires the puck behind Pittsburgh goalie Inness. It is enough. Resch holds fast and the Islanders sweep the Penguins out of the Stanley Cup contention. The Islanders are now in the semifinals, against the defending Stanley Cup champs, the Philadelphia Flyers.

Astonishingly, the Islanders lose the first three games to the Flyers, then win the following three before dropping the seventh and deciding game.

In 1972, Manager Bill Torrey had talked about a five-year plan for producing a playoff contender. He had done much better. In three years the Islanders had not only annexed a postseason berth but had come within a game of reaching the Stanley Cup finals. They were well ahead of schedule, but now the Isles had to contend with the traditional postscript to a standing ovation — what to do for an encore!

The encore, if there was to be one, would have to take place in the 1975–76 season. That such an event was possible, was due in large part to a 19-year-old center named Bryan Trottier; the cohesive action of goalies Glenn Resch and Billy Smith; and the continuing ascendency of Denis Potvin's defensive play and such foot soldiers as Gerry Hart, Lorne Henning, and Garry Howatt.

By mid-December, 1975 it was possible to put the Islanders in perspective and compare them with the previous year's team. Critics such as Robin Herman of the *New York Times* did just that and came away persuaded that the Islanders actually had improved. "The Islanders," said Herman, "are better than last season and each week another group of Arbour's players seem to improve."

"We achieved balance and movement," said Captain Westfall. "You need good balance among the guys involved."

In the aftermath of the 1976 Stanley Cup playoffs, the Islanders emerged with nearly as much praise as the ultimate winners, the Montreal Canadiens. The champions routed the Chicago Black Hawks in four straight and similarly shellacked the defending champion Philadelphia Flyers.

Montreal outscored Chicago, 13–3, and Philadelphia, 14–9. Only the Islanders gave the Canadiens a run for their money. Al Arbour's skaters came out of the playoffs with their heads held high. They were the only stickhandlers to defeat Montreal (5–2 in the fourth game), and came distressingly close to winning both the first and second matches at the Forum. At that, the Canadiens outscored the Islanders by a mere 17–14.

Ken Dryden, the Canadiens' analytical goaltender, lavished praise on the four-year-old team from Long Island. "Believe me," said Dryden, "they're going to be just as good — or better — in years to come. They've got pride and they're not going to be psyched out in any situation. They've developed a certain amount of mental toughness. It's obvious that this is one team that doesn't discourage easily and it proves that they've developed considerable maturity."

They also developed superstars. In June, 1976 Denis Potvin was voted the Norris Trophy as the NHL's top defenseman and Bryan Trottier came away with the Calder Trophy as the league's best rookie. Several independent surveys named Al Arbour as the premier NHL coach.

"We've got a young team," said Arbour. "If we keep giving more than we've got to give, the way we did in the 1976 playoffs, we're going to get that Cup yet."

The Islanders knew they had marched close to hockey's holy grail but that there was still more marching ahead. "We needed some big goals in those first three games against Montreal," said Denis Potvin, "and we didn't get them. But we have the kind of guys who will get 'em next time because they're on our team right now and gaining the experience we need. We won't have to change much in the coming years."

The Islanders began their ascent for real in the late 1970s, capping their climb with an unexpected Stanley Cup triumph in 1980. With stars such as Mike Bossy, Bryan Trottier, Denis Potvin, and Billy Smith, the Islanders dominated the NHL from 1980 through 1983, when they won four consecutive Stanley Cups.

Comparing the Islanders four-year dynasty with NHL empires past is like discussing the relative merits of Michael Jackson, Frank Sinatra, and Bing Crosby. It makes for good arguments and there's something to be said for each but, really, we're discussing apples and pomegranates. (Which is also fun.)

Dynasty, by NHL definition, is a label that can only be affixed to teams that have won three or more Cups in succession. Thus, in addition to the Isles, only two other teams qualify; the Toronto Maple Leafs who twice won three straight Cups (1947–8–9 and 1962–3–4) and the Montreal Canadiens, mug-winners five straight times (1956–7–8–9–1960), and four-in-a-row (1976–7–8–9).

The most ancient of these power-houses, the Leafs of the '40s, resembled the Isles in several ways, particularly the goaltending. Turk Broda, Toronto's net-minder for the Cup run (as well as the 1942 and 1951 championship teams), was the *original* money goalie; at his best in the playoffs. However, Billy Smith has far surpassed Broda in major playoff wins. Toronto's coach, Hap Day, was, like Al Arbour, a retired former defenseman who so matched Arbour in personality and deportment it's scary. For one of the Cup years (1948), *the Leafs boasted the three best centers any hockey club ever iced at one time* — Syl Apps, Max Bentley, and Ted Kennedy. The Leafs defense, anchored by Jim Thomson and Gus Mortson, was solid, but unspectacular and singularly lacking a rusher in the mold of Denis

Potvin. Also missing was a gunner like Mike Bossy. Checking was a Leafian forte as it was for the Islanders.

The second Toronto dynasty, orchestrated by GM coach Punch Imlach (which included Al Arbour as a player) could also be likened to the Islanders. Goalie John Bower, like Smith, played his best in his 30s and was solid in the clutch, although not in Smitty's class. Imlach's clubs majored in defense and more defense (Carl Brewer and Bob Baun led the pack, followed by Tim Horton and Al Stanley) along with superior checking forwards. Missing was a Bryan Trottier. The Bossy of Imlach's Leafs was Frank Mahovlich. It was a good club but not in a class with its predecessors from Toronto, and not nearly in a class with the Isles. Imlach's autocratic rule created a continuous aura of tension that eventually led to the breakdown (physically and psychologically) of Mahovlich and, to a lesser extent, Brewer. As a leader, Imlach lacked Arbour's class.

Scotty Bowman, who steered the Canadiens to four straight Cups in the late 1970s was not unlike Imlach when it came to antagonizing his troops, but Bowman did it with a more tolerable panache, that even bordered on appealing. Guy Lafleur, Larry Robinson, Serge Savard, and Ken Dryden formed the nucleus of that impressive crew molded by GM Sam Pollock. Ask Pollock and he'll tell you that Dryden was better than Billy Smith.

"I put Dryden in the same category as Terry Sawchuk and Jacques Plante, which is the highest," said Pollock. "Smith is a real money player but I'm not ready to put him in that league yet." However, Smith passed Dryden in Cup wins and I rate him over Dryden. Also, Trottier rates over any of the Montreal centers, headed by Jacques Lemaire. The Habs lacked beef up front, a Clark Gillies-type, although Bob Gainey occasionally came through with a heavy hit. As for Bossy and Lafleur, respected Montreal Daily News columnist Tim Burke observed; "Bossy may not be as spectacular as Lafleur but he's just as effective. I give the edge to the Isles on overall talent and productivity."

Most significant is the analogy between the Isles and the *only* team to win five straight Cups, Toe Blake's Canadiens. "I don't think the Isles are as good a team," said Blake. And, here again, I disagree. The arithmetic is on my side as you will see.

In five Cup-winning springs, the Canadiens won a total of 10 *series*, good for 40 *wins*. Over the four Cup-winning springs, the Isles totalled 19 *series wins* and 72 *victories*. Therefore, they beat the Habs, 19–10 in series and 72–40 in wins.

But the margin doesn't stop there. The Isles demonstrated that they are far and away *the better pressure team*. Never in all five of the Cup years were the Canadiens forced to come from behind to win a series. As front-runners they were terrific. But, one wonders, what would have transpired had they been in the situation such as the one confronting the Isles in 1982 when they trailed the Pittsburgh Penguins by two goals with five minutes left in the decisive fifth game of the series, yet managed to tie and win in overtime. They were behind in the other series and faced the hated Rangers in three of those Cup-winning years, beating them each time.

Furthermore, Blake's Canadiens enjoyed the luxury of playing during an era when a team required only two series — a semifinal and the finals — to win the

Cup. Under that system, the Isles, with 19 series wins, would have annexed nine consecutive mugs.

Sentimentality favors the 1956–60 Canadiens. They had a number of virtuosos — Rocket and Pocket Richard, Dickie Moore, Jean Beliveau, Bernie Geoffrion, Plante — and a marvelous unit. But the players skate faster today, shoot harder, and the game is infinitely more sophisticated. If it were possible, I would love to see a series between the dynamic Isles and their Montreal counterparts.

It is abundantly clear that there is much in the way of evidence supporting the claim that the Islanders could be rated the number one team of all-time. In the end, however, the Canadiens get the nod because they remain the only team that has won five consecutive Stanley Cups.

The Montreal Canadiens, 1976–79

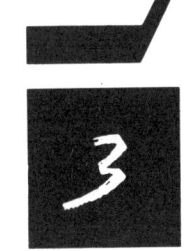

Scotty's Canadiens — Montreal, 1976–79

Toe Blake's five-straight Cup-winners of the 1956–60 period was a tough act to follow, and nobody did, because no other hockey team ever possessed as many headliners as Rocket Richard, Boom Boom Geoffrion, Jean Beliveau, Doug Harvey, Dickey Moore, and Jacques Plante, to name a few luminaries. And no other club ever won five straight Stanley Cups again.

But one Montreal team came close. The Habitants of the 1976–79 epoch had many of the ingredients that Blake boasted, but in a less ostentatious form. For example, goalie Ken Dryden, who worked for Scotty Bowman, was excellent at his craft, but not quite in the Plante class. Guy Lafleur was a dazzling performer on the attack, but lacked the explosiveness of a Maurice Richard. Larry Robinson was a tower of strength on the blueline, but could not match Doug Harvey for pure defensive skills.

This is not to be construed as a knock against Bowman's Canadiens, but merely as a measuring stick to demonstrate why they cannot be rated at the very top. After all, a club that wins four straight Stanley Cups must be blessed with talent. In the case of the 1970s unit, the talent started behind the bench where Bowman emerged as one of the most commanding leaders the game has known. "You did it Scotty's way," said one Canadien, "or you took the highway!"

Bowman frequently lauded Dryden for the club's high attainment and other fine hockey minds backed him up. "Anytime you were fortunate enough to catch Montreal playing badly, Dryden stopped you anyway," said Bruins general manager Harry Sinden. "In order to have a dynasty you have to have strong goaltending."

Dryden backstopped a mobile defense that featured (in addition to Robinson) Serge Savard, Guy Lapointe and, in the last Cup year, Rod Langway.

Lafleur, Steve Shutt, and Jacques Lemaire were among the more gifted scorers, but the Habs also featured a number of grinding checkers, not the least of whom was Bob Gainey whose bodycheck on Rangers defenseman Dave Maloney in 1979 helped win the fourth Stanley Cup.

"We had lots of good players on that team," said Savard, "but Lafleur was the most important because he had the ability to dominate a game."

The Canadiens launched their Cup run with a four straight sweep of Philadelphia in the 1976 finals. Among other things, the victory showed that the Habs could play a tough game as well as a skilled one. Robinson's muffling of Dave (Hammer) Schultz amply demonstrated the point.

In 1977 and 1978, the Canadiens disposed of the Bruins in four straight and then six games, respectively. A hot Rangers team gave them a brief scare in 1979, winning the opener in Montreal and then taking a 2–0 lead in Game Two at The Forum. But the Habs regrouped and won Game Two, 6–2 and romped through the next three games for the fourth Cup.

One wonders whether the fifth Cup win might have been possible had Bowman remained with the squad. His replacement, Claude Ruel, was hardly in Bowman's class as a motivator or tactician. The Canadiens were stunned in the quarter-finals by the Minnesota North Stars four games to three and the era was over.

All things considered, the four-year streak was a remarkable feat of endurance, let alone skill. Bowman's conducting of the team was firm and enlightened. "It didn't hurt that he had Lafleur," said Don Cherry, who coached the Bruins against the Canadiens in several series. "And Dryden wasn't bad either."

Bowman's Canadiens merit high ranking but because there was a touch less talent than a couple of other clubs, not the very highest.

Bowman's Canadiens are rated behind the Islanders for several reasons. Most important is that the Montrealers won their four Stanley Cups during a period when the quality of play in the NHL was at a relatively low point.

Raids by the World Hockey Association had diluted the NHL talent base, as did the addition of two new NHL teams in Washington and Kansas City in 1974. By 1977, when the Canadiens were on their roll, the WHA had reached a level of high quality because of defections from the NHL. Therefore, the Canadiens were competing at a time when the level of play was of less intensity than the years that immediately followed.

When the NHL absorbed four WHA teams and the young league folded in 1979, the NHL regained its vitality and in the ensuing years became a high-quality league again. The regeneration of the NHL began with the 1979–80 season, *after* the Canadiens had won their fourth straight Cup under Scotty Bowman. Significantly, it was the Islanders who dominated in the new period of high-quality play and that is an important reason why the Isles were given the edge over the Canadiens. That and the fact that the Habs were unable to match the Islanders record of 19 consecutive series wins in the playoffs.

While the Canadiens' dynasty of the late 1950s stands supreme in the pantheon of puckdom, other Montreal clubs have distinguished themselves enough to merit comparison. And if one is called upon to name the second-best-ever edition of The Flying Frenchmen, the unit that spanned the decade of the 1970s would have to be the choice.

It was led through a good part of the way by a seemingly fragile young French-Canadian with the most unusual (for hockey) nickname, "The Flower." Guy Lafleur epitomized everything that was wonderful about Montreal hockey; grace, speed, artistry and *élan*. He was, in truth, a latter-day Howie Morenz if there ever was one.

The defense was as well-balanced as Toe Blake's backline, if not better. A mighty triumverate on the blue line comprised Serge Savard, Guy Lapointe, and Larry Robinson and they were supplemented by competent teammates such as Bill Nyrup, J.C. Tremblay, and Pierre Bouchard from time to time.

Like so many dynasties, the Cup-winning crew was developed years before it actually won the championship. In the case of the 1976–79 Canadiens, the seeds were planted at the turn of the decade and began sprouting with the advent of Ken Dryden in goal during the spring of 1971 and the arrival of Scotty Bowman as coach for the 1971–72 season. This followed the Canadiens totally unexpected Cup win in 1971 under Al MacNeil, who was summarily moved out following protests from team captain Henri Richard.

It took Bowman only two seasons to find the championship groove. In 1971–72, the Canadiens were bumped out of the playoffs in the opening round, losing to the Rangers in six games. The re-tooling was minor. Dryden had matured between the pipes and produced a 2.26 goals against average in 1972–73, while Jacques Lemaire, one of the most underrated solid forwards in Canadiens annals, pumped in 44 goals, and led the team with 95 points.

The road to the Stanley Cup was bumpy, but featured few detours. The Habs defeated Buffalo four games to two in the opening round. Their second round foe, the suddenly fearsome Philadelphia Flyers, stunned the Habs with a 5–4 overtime win in the opening game of the semifinals, but the Canadiens swept the next four and moved into the finals against the Black Hawks. Chicago had an impressive club, but the defection of superstar Bobby Hull to the WHA had robbed the Hawks of their biggest star, and Chicago fell in six games.

What loomed as the first of a succession of Stanley Cups turned into a nightmare the following season. First, the Habs lost Dryden, who sat out the season to study law, win a bigger contract, and do some T.V. work on the side. Neither Wayne Thomas nor Bunny Larocque were in Dryden's class. Without clutch goaltending, the Canadiens were ousted in the first round by the Rangers, four games to two.

The Flyers won the Cup on the strength of Bernie Parent's superior netminding. This proved to Bowman that Dryden had to be lured back to the fold for 1974–75, and he was. But Scotty also realized that more had to be done.

Bowman had made up his mind during the summer of 1974 that the forthcoming 1974–75 season would be different for his hockey club.

Sitting under an old apple tree on his cattle ranch in the eastern township of Quebec and meditating about the problems to be faced, Bowman concluded that his troops needed more physical conditioning.

"Some people say that off ice training is no good. That's just hogwash." To members of the press who asked about it, Bowman stated "I'm not qualified to say how much good it'll do, but one thing's sure — it can't hurt."

Apparently, it didn't hurt. In training camp, the Canadiens looked especially crisp. Several rookies, among them forward Doug Risebrough and defenseman Rick Chartraw looked specially sharp. Goalie Ken Dryden, following his year's sabbatical was back in the nets sporting a new multi-colored mask.

Dryden took his place in the crease on opening night at the Forum against the New York Islanders and the indications were that he still was somewhat stale after being out of NHL action for that one year. The Islanders put five shots past Ken in the 60 minutes of play but, fortunately for the Habitants, with two minutes remaining, they turned a 5–3 deficit into a 5–5 tie. Big Peter Mahovlich, who had scored an earlier goal, tied the match for Montreal with goals at 18:06 and 19:03 of the final period.

The first match having been completed, everybody, it seemed, felt better for it. "It's good to have that one out of the way," said rookie Chartraw. "The first one is like facing a mountain."

Unfortunately, the mountain loomed larger and larger for the Canadiens in the opening weeks of the schedule. There were incidents that created friction, such as when captain Henri Richard feuded with coach Bowman after being omitted from the lineup one night. Bowman later apologized, but Richard said he didn't think the coach was sincere.

"It has to start with the players," said managing director Sam Pollock. "If Dryden plays well and Savard and Lapointe play well and a few others . . . and they win."

Slowly, but surely, the Canadiens began putting it all together in December, 1974. They routed the St. Louis Blues, 7–1, at the Forum and coach Bowman breathed easier. "I wish," said Scotty, "they were all like that."

Soon, many would be. Later that month the Canadiens were turned on by their kids — center Risebrough and right wing Mario Tremblay. Risebrough, only 20 years old at the time, provided some pizzaz in the Montreal checking department, while Tremblay, who had just passed his 18th birthday, dazzled the enemy with his footwork.

In a perverse sort of way, the Canadiens also got a lift when captain Richard suffered a broken ankle. With Henri out of the lineup, the Montrealers seemed to blend better, a fact that was apparent to others such as Vancouver coach Phil Maloney.

"I think the best thing that happened to Montreal was Richard's injury," Maloney asserted. "I'm not saying that Henri isn't a great player — he is, but he kept saying the Canadiens didn't have any pride. Now that he's out, the guys are trying to prove he was wrong."

If Maloney was right, the Canadiens did an effective job of doing just that — proving Richard was wrong. They moved to the top of the James Norris Division and engaged in a neck and neck battle with Los Angeles for first place. With Richard absent, a lighthearted feeling pervaded the dressing room. Skaters such as Pierre Bouchard, Steve Shutt, and Peter Mahovlich kidded around with each other as if they were a Montreal version of "Laugh-In."

"Hey, Pierre," Shutt shouted over to Bouchard one day after a workout, "do you know what my bonus is?"

"No, what's your bonus?"

"I get off Pete's line!"

Later Bouchard came back with his squelch, asking Shutt why he, Guy Lafleur, and Pete Mahovlich are known as the Doughnut Line.

"Why are we called the Doughnut Line, Pierre?"

Bouchard smiled, "Simple, no center!"

As always, center or no center, the Canadiens forte was skating. The Flying Frenchmen were really flying now and nobody knew it better than their opponents. "They are so good skaters," said Chicago Black Hawks coach Billy Reay, "they don't need Henri Richard or Guy Lafleur. This is the best skating Canadiens team ever."

Equally important were the positive psychological factors produced by winning. Coach Bowman appeared more relaxed by mid-season and better able to communicate with his players, and he and the men could also kid with each other. One day, for example, Bowman recalled that he and referre Wally Harris had played junior hockey together.

"Harris," said Bowman, "hasn't liked me ever since I beat him out of a spot with the Junior Canadiens."

Peter Mahovlich overheard the remark and chimed in, "If that's the case, Scotty must have beaten a lot of people out of spots with the Junior Canadiens."

Bowman kept smiling through February and March, 1975. His Canadiens, who never used to lose at home, now kept winning on the road. By early March, 1975 they had extended their unbeaten road record to 21 games.

"For some reason," said goalie Dryden, "we seem to be at our best on the road. I guess we feel more confident in Montreal and, as a result, we concentrate less and play more of a wide open game. That's really not what suits our style of play. In other words, we are tight on the road and play more by the book."

The problem, for Montreal, was that the Los Angeles Kings were also playing by the book, and winning, too. A decisive game at the Los Angeles Forum late in the season would, to a great extent, determine which of the two contenders would finish on top. As expected, the Canadiens came out charging. The four days prior to the game, Bowman kept the players in seclusion at Squaw Valley, California. The Frenchmen were really ready to fly.

The Montreal team roared ahead, 2–0, but stalled when Dan Maloney and Bob Berry scored for the Kings. Then, big Larry Robinson, who more and more was becoming a leader of the Montreal backline, put the Canadiens back in front, 3–2. Berry tied the score once again but that was the Kings' last gasp. In the traditional manner of les Canadiens, Jacques Lemaire broke the tie on a Montreal power play and Serge Savard followed moments later with a shorthanded goal. The Canadiens won, 5–3, and went on to annex first place in the Norris Division.

There were several reasons for this renaissance. Bowman's more relaxed attitude was important. The ability of the foot soldiers to compensate for Henri Richard's absence helped. But it was the new faces that really sparked the Habitants with vitality. Lambert, Tremblay, and Risebrough, in particular, were the catalysts, and emerged looking like a cross between the Three Musketeers and the Dead End Kids.

"You look at their production," said Bowman, "and their aggressiveness and you have to conclude that they gave us everything, more than we hoped. When we put them together, they just clicked. It's chemistry or whatever, and when it works it's really something. It doesn't happen too often, but it worked with those guys."

Risebrough, the most truculent of the trio, expanded on the theme. "What makes it so good is knowing that the other guys aren't trailing. If you're on a rush, they're with you. If something happens — like a fight developing — you know you've got friends."

Risebrough and friends completed the regular season with 47 victories, 14 defeats, and 19 ties for 113 points in 80 games. They tied for most points with Buffalo of the Adams Division and Philadelphia of the Patrick Division. Now, it was time to learn whether the chemistry would bring success in the "other" season — the Stanley Cup playoffs.

The Canadiens opponents in the opening round of the 1975 Stanley Cup playoffs were the surprisingly successful Vancouver Canucks. They were an expansion club whose first year of play had been the 1970–71 season, and who after finishing out of the playoffs for four straight years, finished first in the Conn Smythe Division. The best-of-three series was to open at the Forum in Montreal.

"If you want to get anywhere in the playoffs," said Vancouver coach Phil Maloney, "you have to meet the best, sooner or later. In the games in which we played them (Montreal) this season, I thought they didn't beat us as much as we beat ourselves. And we usually played well in their building."

With high hopes, the Vancouver team traveled across Canada to meet their foe. However, paced by Guy Lafleur's two goals, the Canadiens walloped Vancouver, 6–2. "That Lafleur," moaned Vancouver defenseman Mike Robitaille, "is just dynamite. He cracked the game wide open."

Then, although not expected, the Canucks rebounded smartly to win the series' second game.

In the third and deciding match, Montreal wrapped up the series with a 4–1 win.

The Canadiens' second round opponents were the Buffalo Sabres, coached by Floyd Smith and managed by George "Punch" Imlach. Only five years old, the Sabres had matured into one of the new NHL powerhouses. During the regular season, Buffalo had consistently over-powered Montreal, taking four from the Canadiens, tying one, and losing none.

Bowman was hoping that the Flying Frenchmen would be able to edge the Sabres with superior goaltending. Ken Dryden appeared to have recaptured his previous skills in the playoffs, while the Sabres were saddled with an ailing veteran Roger Crozier, rookie Gary Bromley, and a refugee from the WHA, Gerry Desjardins.

If the Canadiens could match Buffalo's firepower — believed possible because of Lafleur's emergence as a major shooter — Montreal would have an edge in defense and, hopefully, be able to win the series.

But theories on paper aren't always developed on the ice.

The series' first two games were to be played at Buffalo's Auditorium. In each of them, the Sabres came out on top. Then the tournament shifted to Montreal for games three and four.

Now, it appeared that the Canadiens had finally found themselves and all was once again well with Les Habitants.

They clobbered Buffalo in both matches by the startling scores of 7–0 and 8–2. Very effectively, the Montrealers stifled the Sabres' high scoring French Connection line of Rene Robert, Gil Perreault, and Richard Martin. Bowman constructed a checking line of Jacques Lemaire, Bob Gainey, and Jim Roberts to harass the Connection. Lemaire guarded Perreault, Gainey followed Robert, and Roberts shadowed Martin.

If the Canadiens could maintain this blanket into the fifth game at Buffalo, they would enjoy an excellent chance of winning the series. But, this time, Richard Martin carried the attack — physically and verbally — to his Canadiens tormentors.

"I'm going to take this stick and put it right through your guts," Martin told Roberts during one exchange before a faceoff.

The newly inspired Sabres built a 3–1 lead in the first period but the Canadiens promptly counterattacked and tied the score, 3–3. Early in the third period, Montreal moved ahead when Henri Richard returned to the Canadiens' lineup after having been out most of the regular season. He broke away with the puck on a three-on-two and set up Roberts for the Canadiens' fourth goal.

With Dryden now playing at the top of his form, it appeared that the Canadiens could contain Buffalo's attacking forces. And contain them they did, up to a point. Because the score was still so close, Montreal's checkers were bodying and poke-checking the Sabres off the puck as often as possible.

At one point, rookie Risebrough attempted to poke the puck away from Buffalo defenseman Jerry Korab. Risebrough missed the check and tripped Korab. Referee Lloyd Gilmour whistled Risebrough into the penalty box for two minutes. Before Doug was able to return, Buffalo tied the score, 4–4, which was where it stayed until the final light. The game was then forced into sudden death overtime.

For six minutes, it was a toss-up as to which team would flash the winning red goal light. Finally, Buffalo forced a faceoff deep in Montreal territory. Sabres' coach Smith sent the French Connection line onto the ice. Bowman quickly countered with the Lemaire, Gainey, and Roberts checking line. It appeared relatively secure for the Canadiens.

Perreault moved in for the face-off against Lemaire. The puck was dropped and went directly to the Buffalo center. Swiftly, he shoveled it back to teammate Robert and, in a trice, the Sabre swiped it past startled goalie Dryden. The Sabres had won, 5–4.

But Montreal still had high hopes. It was a packed Forum at Ste. Catherine Street West as the series returned to the Canadiens' home base for game six. Everybody seemed "up" for it, except the Canadiens. Buffalo's Craig Ramsey, trying to kill a penalty, scored an early shorthanded goal for the Sabres. Then Martin blasted a slap shot between Dryden's legs, putting Buffalo on top, 2–0.

Peter Mahovlich got one back for the Frenchmen, but Buffalo continued to dominate the match and with two more scores, moved into a 4–1 lead without any noticeable sweat. In the third period, the Canadiens scored a pair of fluke goals, narrowing the margin to 4–3, but those two were all there were. It wasn't enough.

Buffalo held fast and won the game and the series, and nobody argued about the result.

"The best team won," said Canadiens' defenseman Don Awrey.

On July 14, 1975, after wearing the red, white, and blue of the Montreal Canadiens for 20 years, Henri Richard hung up his skates for good. At his retirement Henri was 39, the same age as his brother Maurice "The Rocket" was when he retired.

Henri's retirement was no surprise since he had been toying with the idea since the previous year. After breaking his ankle in November, 1974, the "Pocket Rocket" said, "It's only a simple fracture. I'll be in the cast for six weeks and I'll need a little extra time to get back in condition. It shouldn't take too long."

It did take long though. Instead of six weeks, Henri was out until the semifinal round of the Stanley Cup playoffs against the Buffalo Sabres, almost six months later.

With Henri gone, the Canadiens last remaining link with their great Stanley Cup dynasty, the teams that had won the Cup for five consecutive years, 1956 through 1960, was severed.

In some ways, the retirement of Richard would benefit the Canadiens for what would be their run of four consecutive Stanley Cups. Henri's departure made room on the roster for younger legs. And if the Canadiens had anything as they opened the 1975–76 season, it was speed and more speed.

Lafleur, who was fast reaching his prime, led the team with 56 goals, 69 assists, and 125 points. There was no speedier, skilled player in the league.

Likewise, the defense was equally mobile. Guy Lapointe totaled 21 goals, 47 assists, and 68 points on defense, while the future Hall-of-Famer Larry Robinson went 10–30–40. Another who was reaching his prime was Dryden, who won 42, lost 10, and tied 8 for a goals-against average of 2.03.

Standings-wise, the Habs were supreme. They finished first in the Norris Division with 58 wins, only 11 losses, and 11 ties and danced through the playoffs with ease. They routed Chicago in four straight games — Dryden permitted only three goals, total! — and then eased past the Islanders in five games.

This set the stage for the climactic final against the Broad Street Bullies from Philadelphia. It was a Stanley Cup round that aroused more passion and interest than most because, in the view of many hockey students, this was really a case of good vs. evil.

The Flyers, in the eyes of many, represented everything bad about hockey, from their penchant for fighting to the sinister reputation carried by players such as Dave (Hammer) Schultz and Bob (Hound) Kelly. It was feared by several critics that the Flyers would use every intimidation tactic available to bet the Canadiens, and if they succeeded, not only the Montrealers but the NHL would suffer a black eye.

No fool he, Bowman was prepared for the bludgeoning. Although his club was totally bereft of goons, Bowman did have strong, character players like Big Bird defenseman Larry Robinson. Very quickly, Robinson deflated Schultz and a message was delivered loud and clear to the Flyers; the Canadiens would not be intimidated.

That didn't mean it would be an easy series. In fact, Philadelphia led 3–2 midway through the third period of the opening game of the finals at The Forum, but Lemaire tied the score at 10:02 and Lapointe scored the winner at 18:38. In the second game the Habs again won by one; this time, 2–1.

If The Spectrum was to frighten the Habs, it wasn't apparent. Dryden held fast in Game Three, which the Canadiens won 3–2. The Flyers had one last gasp — a 3–2 lead until the final minute of the second period in Game Four — but Cournoyer tied the count at 19:49 and Lafleur won the game at 14:18 of the third. The final score was 5–3 and the Canadiens had swept the series to win The Stanley Cup.

The 1976 Stanley Cup win not only was hailed by Montrealers, but by the NHL as well. Just ridding itself of the Bullies from Broad Street was like curing a two-year hockey headache. The Canadiens represented all that was good about The Game and continued to improve, which made the future look even brighter. Meanwhile, the Canadiens were being deified in their native province. As Allan Turowetz, co-author of *The Lions of Winter*, noted:

"Style took on a new importance as Quebec looked at itself in the collective mirror with new eyes, and liked what it saw. Guy Lafleur was part of Quebec's emerging elan. He had moved to centre stage when he chucked his helmet and began scoring goals with panache, his blond hair trailing behind him like the trail of Halley's Comet.

"Others were filling the net in the NHL: Phil Esposito, Rick Martin, Reggie Leach, Jean Pronovost, Danny Grant, Marcel Dionne, and Pierre Larouche. Only Larouche could match Lafleur for style and he labored in near anonymity in Pittsburgh. As far as Montreal was concerned, the others were plodders, possessors of big shots, cannons which simply blasted the rubber into the net. Lafleur was *un artiste*, a magician who could lift 18,000 people from their seats with his end-to-end rushes. At home, Lafleur's linemate Steve Shutt increased his scoring in increments of 15, with consecutive years of 15, 30, 45, and 60 goals, but was never considered a threat to Lafleur's deity. A very smart man who often hid his intellect behind a ready smile and constant kidding, Shutt took the pressure off the fans by describing himself as a 'garbageman' — someone who 'just hangs around and picks up the leftovers of Lafleur, Lemaire, or Mahovlich.'"

The best way to explain the Canadiens' domination of the 1976–77 season is to look at the record — 60 wins, 8 losses, and 12 ties for 132 points. The runner-up Flyers were a full 20 points behind! If that doesn't say enough, the playoffs provide the clincher. They won 12 games enroute to The Cup and lost only two; both to the Islanders in the semifinals. The Blues were demolished in four, scoring a grand total of four goals and the Bruins went out in four as well. At least Boston managed six goals. Dryden had four shutouts.

Because his nucleus was young, Bowman had to make few changes in the lineup and the Canadiens' prime concerns were not as much the foe from without, but the enemy within. Injuries, obviously, were always a problem. Then, there was the threat of fat-catedness.

"Success can do strange things to championship teams," said Bowman. "There was always the possibility that some of the boys might get lazy."

Bowman did his best to ensure against that problem and succeeded. The Canadiens' 59–10–11 record in 1977–78 indicated that he kept them as strong as they had been the previous year. Their playoff opposition was slightly tougher. They needed five games to beat Detroit in their opening round, then they beat Toronto in four straight before meeting Boston in the finals. With Don (Grapes) Cherry behind the bench, the Bruins had the series deadlocked at two games apiece before the Habs broke the dam with a pair of back-to-back 4–1 wins to annex their third straight Cup.

Lafleur led playoff scorers with 10 goals and 21 points, and was at the very apex of his career. What friends wondered was how long his body could withstand the checking on the ice and what had become well-known as his zest for the good times off the ice. In an interview with *Weekend* magazine, Lafleur described his home life in these words:

"She knew what the situation was before she married me, and understood. It's tough for me and tough for her to accept. Lise is not really a hockey fan, but she is, I think, my biggest supporter. I want her to be happy. We both pursue separate activities by mutual agreement. If I'm home one night a week and that's the night she usually goes out, that's fine. At heart I am a family man, but when I'm home I can't sit still. So after I wash the car and play with Martin, I drive Lise crazy sometimes.

"Sometimes, I think she is glad to be rid of me. We are discussing more children, but I don't want them right now. I don't want to father them and then hit the road; that's not right."

Lafleur's glitzy lifestyle in no way detracted from his performance. With Shutt and Lemaire meshing like clockwork, Lafleur's only concern was being the victim of enemy goons and for the most part he was spared. Opponents realized that if they trifled with the Flower they'd quickly hear from Larry Robinson and some of the other bigger Canadiens.

Mostly though, Guy succeeded because of the old hockey bromide, "You can't hit what you can't catch."

The balance of power began shifting somewhat during the 1978–79 campaign. A young Islanders team moved to the top of the Patrick Division and led all teams — Canadiens included — over the regular schedule with 116 points. Montreal had 115.

Bowman still had his big three on defense and now the farm system had added a young blocker in Brian Engblom, with Rod Langway on the way. With Dryden in goal, there was little to fear but injuries and overconfidence.

No problem. The Habs swept Toronto four straight in the first challenge. It seemed like smooth sailing until the third game of the semifinals against Boston. With a two-games-to-one lead, the Canadiens looked like a shoo-in.

Not this time. Boston rallied to tie the series at three and came awfully close to winning the round in Game Seven which has become a much-discussed classic, particularly in Boston where they still talk about *the* blunder that led to the dissipation of the Bruins' 4–3 lead late in the third period.

At the time the Bruins appeared in total command, having done a splendid job of shadowing Lafleur and keeping the rest of the Canadiens snipers at bay. Then, it happened. The Bruins were caught having too many men on the ice. All of a sudden Montreal had a power play and Lafleur was once again on the ice.

Don Cherry, who was behind the Bruins' bench, was employing every defensive device at his disposal while keeping his fingers crossed that Lafleur could be curbed. Here in Cherry's own words is a description of what followed:

"The time out was over. There was a face-off and the puck was in motion. I couldn't believe what a terrific job we were doing of killing the penalty. A minute had gone by and we still had the lead. Now it was 70 seconds elapsed and we were still ahead.

"But the Canadiens mounted a counterattack. Jacques Lemaire, one of the most underrated players on that Montreal team, took a pass near our blue line. Lafleur was moving down the right side like the Japanese Bullet Train. Lemaire dropped the pass over to Lafleur. I figure he was going to try to move in on Gilbert, try a few dekes and get into a really good scoring position.

"He was way over to the right, far, far out, sort of where I wanted him. A shot from there would be desperate, but he drew his stick back. He was desperate. For a split second I almost felt reassured. Then, his stick swung around the big arc and the blade made contact with the puck.

"I can't tell you precisely how fast that puck traveled but anything faster than that shot had to break the sound barrier. Almost in the same moment Lafleur slapped the rubber, it bulged the twine in the left side of the net behind Gillie. There went the lead. *Boom*! Just like that.

"We left the ice tied, 4–4, at the end of regulation time. The way my players plodded into the dressing room you would have thought that they had just finished a trek across the Sahara Desert — in uniform. I have seen teams in my 11-year coaching career that were down, but none as thoroughly subterranean as this one.

"I knew that even getting them to a reasonable state of battle readiness for the overtime would be the chore of my life.

"Before going into the room I had to get my frustrations out. It does no good for the players to see their coach frustrated. So I left them alone for a while. Then I took a deep breath and walked into the room.

"It was like a morgue. No jokes this time. I said to them, 'Look, when we were down two games to none in this series going back to Boston, if I could have said to you, "Would you be happy to go into overtime of the seventh game?" what would you have said?' And they all yelled, 'YES!'

"I didn't know if I believed it, but they did and that's most important. They were banging at the doors to get going. There never was, nor ever will be, a better bunch of guys. I love them.

"And, before you knew it, the buzzer was sounding for the start of sudden-death overtime.

"To my surprise, we came out with more drive than I thought we had in us. Marcotte took a pass from O'Reilly when Dryden had one knee down on the ice. Marcotte shot it for the upper corner and started to raise his stick in celebration, as if the puck was going in. But Dryden, who was so damn big, got his shoulder in front of the puck — more by accident than by skill — and my heart was still in my mouth. The rebound came out to O'Reilly and, with an open net waiting to greet his shot, the puck bounced over his stick.

"Back and forth the play whirred at a dizzying pace. The clock ticked past the nine minute mark and there was still no tie-breaker. My guys — particularly the older ones — were struggling. Park, Schmautz, and Cashman had blood running into their underwear but they keep on going.

"At last, Lafleur was off the ice and it seemed as if we might have a respite, but Bowman had some excellent infantrymen. One of them was a kid named Mario Tremblay who had gone into orbit along the right boards. Another was Yvon Lambert, who always looked as if he had two left feet until he put the puck behind your goalie.

"Al Sims was alone on defense, with Park coming back, and I could see the fear in Al's eyes as Lambert sped to the goal crease while Tremblay, tantalizingly, waited for the precise moment to deliver the pass. Lambert eluded Park, accepted the puck at the lip of the net and pushed it past Gilbert before the goalie could slide across the crease.

"The pain I felt when the red light flashed behind our goal cannot be measured in traditional human terms. To say that a piledriver applied to my stomach would not have created a deeper hurt would simply be minimizing the ache."

Having disposed of the Bruins, the Habs then confronted an upstart Rangers team in the finals. Most fans had expected the Islanders to be the Canadiens' opponents but the Rangers upset the Isles in six games, marched into The Forum, and whipped the Habs 4–1 in Game One of the finals.

The Broadway Blueshirts then jumped into a quick two goal lead in Game Two before the Canadiens rallied for a 6–2 triumph. New York put up a good fight in Game Four before losing, 4–3. Surrounding that match was a pair of 4–1 Montreal wins and for the fourth straight year there was dancing on Ste. Catherine Streets, East and West.

For the first time, however, there was an air of hostility mixed in with the jubilation, not to mention concern. Dryden had decided to call it a career and would next surface as a "color" commentator during the 1980 Winter Olympic Games.

The Cup win notwithstanding, nobody was unhappier than Bowman. He had coveted the general managership of the Canadiens, and when it became clear that he was not going to get it, he decided to leave the Montreal organization and hook up with the Sabres, who were delighted to sign him on as GM.

The twin losses of Dryden and Bowman would be difficult to overcome. Neither Bunny Larocque, Denis Herron, nor Richard Sevigny were able replacements and new coach Bernie (Boom Boom) Geoffrion was plain out of his league behind the bench. He was replaced 30 games into the season by Claude Ruel who did well enough getting the Canadiens into first place in the Norris Division.

Naturally, Montreal fans were clamoring for a fifth straight Stanley Cup and Ruel got off on the right foot with a three games to none preliminary round sweep of the Whalers. The next opponent was the Minnesota North Stars, a team that normally would be a pushover for the Frenchmen.

Some pushover! The North Stars invaded The Forum and swept the first two games. Montreal then rebounded to take the next pair, but the series was destined to go the limit. Game Seven was played at The Forum on April 27, 1980. The North Stars won 3–2 and another era of Montreal hockey dominance had come to a close.

"Would it have been different had I been there?" said Bowman in response to the obvious question. "Who knows?"

Certainly, it would have been, especially if Scotty had been able to persuade Dryden not to retire. But there was no reversing the tide. The Canadiens were a club on the decline and would remain so until 1986, when they defeated the Calgary Flames to add to their Cup collection.

The Toronto Maple Leafs, 1946–51

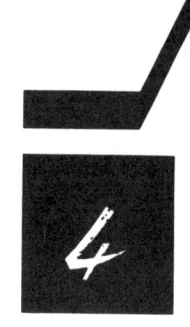

The Little Major's Leafs — 1946–51

Not only were the Toronto Maple Leafs, circa 1946–51, one of the most arresting teams of all time, but they were a notable bunch for yet another reason. The club, managed by the irrepressible Conn Smythe and coached by scholarly Clarence (Hap) Day — later, for the 1951 Cup win, by Joe Primeau — became the NHL's first legitimate dynasty and, concomitantly, hockey's first post-World War II power.

Curiously, the Leafs had no business being a major force in the league if their previous season was a barometer. They had missed the playoffs with a fifth-place club and opened training camp in September 1946 with an amalgam of unknown rookies and veterans, some of whom had just recently packed away their Canadian army uniforms.

In some cases, the returning veterans had been beneficial to their teams. The most obvious case was the Boston Bruins, who welcomed back "The Kraut Line" of Milt Schmidt, Woody Dumart, and Bobby Bauer, a trio who had served in the Royal Canadian Air Force. The Krauts hardly missed a step in their reappearance on NHL rinks and proved a force in the immediate post-war years.

On the other hand, the New York Rangers suffered terribly. Just after Pearl Harbor, the Broadway Blueshirts had dominated the NHL, finishing first in the 1941–42 campaign, thanks to stars such as Mac Colville, Muzz Patrick, and Sugar Jim Henry. But they disappointed in various ways on their return and, as a result, the Rangers struggled in the post-war years. (New York failed to make the playoffs from 1943 through 1947). The Leafs were more fortunate.

With few exceptions, their veterans were in mint condition and formed a formidable nucleus around which Day would arrange his gifted rookies. Some of the rookies ripened faster than anyone had believed possible, particularly the defensive tandem of Gus Mortson and Jimmy Thomson, otherwise dubbed "The Gold Dust Twins."

Still, other youngsters displayed unusually mature leadership characteristics for their age. Prime among them was Ted (Teeder) Kennedy, a center whose labored skating style belied his creativity with the puck. While Kennedy was not the team captain — that honor belonged to the distinguished center Syl Apps — Teeder often played the part in a most natural way, giving Day not one, but two, extraordinary centers who could rally the team in crisis.

Likewise, the defense was anchored by a crowd-pleasing puck-rushing defenseman named Wally Stanowski, who was more than willing to help "The Gold Dust Twins," not to mention other untested backliners such as Garth Boesch and Bashin' Bill Barilko. The coalescence of the young defense in time for the 1947 playoffs proved to be one of the more remarkable achievements of the Day regime; a tribute to the coach, patient veterans and, most of all, manager Smythe, who was willing to gamble on the youth movement although it could very well have backfired on the club.

Smythe's ace-in-the-hole was superior goaltending. Walter (Turk) Broda had been a pre-war ace and delivered a Stanley Cup in 1942, when the Leafs had rallied from a three-game deficit in the finals to top the Detroit Red Wings, four games to three. Broda was one of the veterans whose style was hardly affected by his armed forces stint. He was superior during the regular season and even better during the playoffs.

This was particularly evident during the 1947 playoffs when Broda outgoaled the Montreal Canadiens formidable Bill Durnan, enabling the Leafs to pull off one of the more amazing upsets in Cup history. Man for man, Toronto was no match for Montreal in that series, but the blend of youth, veterans playing up to their potential, Day's astute coaching, and Broda's goalkeeping combined to produce the unlikely victory.

A year later, the Leafs, after engineering *the* most sensational deal ever until that time, had all the pieces in place. By acquiring super-center Max Bentley, Toronto had the best-balanced attack in the game, and organized the first significant power play in NHL annals, with Bentley patrolling the right point.

Certainly, a case could be made for the 1948 Leafs as the greatest team to that point in time and, perhaps, the best ever because of the galaxy of stars and overall accomplishment in a highly-competitive six-team league. Their 32–15–13 (77 points) record hardly tells the story. To reach the top, the Leafs had to outdistance a mighty Detroit team that featured The Production Line (Gordie Howe–Ted Lindsay–Sid Abel), a robust defense, and nifty goaltending from future Hall of Famer Harry Lumley.

Toronto finished five points ahead of Detroit and then confirmed their superiority by humbling the Red Wings in four straight games of the finals. The last two games were symbolic; 2–0 and 7–2 victories.

What separates the Leafs from those above them among the all-time teams — and, in the end, drops them down a few pegs — was the abrupt retirement of

Apps following the 1948 Cup win and the trade convulsions that followed. During this time, Smythe attempted to compensate for the egregious loss and fill the gap.

To say the Leafs were never the same without their peerless captain would be an understatement. They did, however, fill the opening better than could be expected and went on to win a third straight Cup with Cal Gardner replacing Apps. They won a fourth in 1951 with Gardner again playing a major role. But none of the post-1948 teams were good enough to finish first through 1951 and that fact in itself is enough to keep this Leaf club from the top of the all-time list.

Of all the NHL's super teams, the Maple Leafs of the late 1940s have received the least credit for their accomplishments. This is hard to figure when one takes into account that the NHL already was 30 years old before any team managed to win three Stanley Cups in a row.

The feat was executed by Conn Smythe's Toronto team in most extraordinary fashion, in the era immediately following World War II. Smythe, otherwise known as "The Little Major," for his stature and legendary wartime exploits both in World War I and World War II, had long experience in creating hockey teams.

He had begun at the University of Toronto in the early 1920s and had been hired by Madison Square Garden to fashion the original New York Rangers. He did just that, but was fired before his team ever took the ice, following a dispute with the Garden high command.

After developing the Maple Leafs, Smythe sipped Stanley Cup champagne in 1932, 1942, and 1945. Each was an extraordinary championship team. The 1932 winners were special because they were the first. The 1942 team still is the only one in history to have dropped the first three games of the finals and then rebound to win four straight, and The Cup. The 1945 team was a patchwork collection forced upon the franchise by the loss of aces to the armed forces. Its goalie Frank McCool had chronic ulcers and its crack center Ted Kennedy was too young to vote. Still, they managed to win, but everyone knew it was a fragile team and this was proven the next year when the Leafs missed the playoffs completely.

The Toronto Maple Leafs were Conn Smythe's team, and the players did what their general manager told them to do. And Smythe told them loud and clear: "If you can't beat'em in the alley, you can't beat'em on the ice."

Sometimes the Little Major showed his players what he meant, like the night a Detroit fan hurled a chair at one of Smythe's defenseman, Gus Mortson. The Little Major leaped up, hobbled down the aisle, and tossed a left, a right, and another left at the fan. That was that.

Following the Little Major's lead, the Toronto Maple Leafs fought and won, as few hockey teams ever have. They won the Stanley Cup in 1947, 1948, and 1949 — a feat never before accomplished — and took it home again in 1951. The 1948 champions, considered the greatest of the four, are the players we're most concerned about here, but the nature of the clubs was such that you have to talk about them collectively.

All the Leafs bore the hallmark of their combative Little Major, who spent 14 months in a German prison camp in World War I and organized an anti-aircraft battery in World War II.

The Little Major knew what it was to be defeated occasionally, but he never knew how to accept it. He fanned the same flame of competition in his players. He was considerably angry at the Maple Leafs' state of affairs when he returned to Canada after his World War II tour of duty. After winning the Stanley Cup in 1945, the Leafs plummeted to fifth place the following season, finishing out of the playoffs.

It was then that Smythe fashioned what was to be his extraordinary dynasty. His plan was to take the best of the returning veterans and blend them with an outstanding crop of youngsters; then he would hope for the best. The rebuilding job began in April, 1946, immediately after the Leafs were unceremoniously deposited in fifth place, and it ended at the start of the 1946–47 campaign.

With Clarence "Hap" Day back as coach, Smythe decided that the fabulous fat man, Walter "Turk" Broda, would do fine as full-time goalie. Acknowledged as the best playoff goaltender in NHL history, Broda was back from the wars. He had lost none of his edge.

The problem would be the young men guarding Broda on defense. Wally Stanowski, a magnificent skater whose end-to-end rushes were the delight of Maple Leaf Gardens, was the only experienced regular taking a full turn on defense. The other regulars, Jimmy Thomson, Gus Mortson, and Garth Boesch, were talented, but inexperienced.

This tactic was the essence of Smythe's gamble. He figured that a large dose of enthusiasm would erase most of the consequences of inexperience. He was right. Thomson and Mortson became known as the "Gold Dust Twins," and the mustachioed Boesch emerged as a surprisingly poised defender.

The philosophy of all Smythe-run teams maintained that you won with "strength down the center." Led by captain Syl Apps, and backed by young Ted "Teeder" Kennedy, the Leafs had two of the best pivots in the NHL. Apps centered for rugged, but calm left wing Harry Watson and the equally tough, but tempestuous "Wild" Bill Ezinicki. They comprised a remarkably diverse line. Apps had everything — a hard, accurate shot, enormously strong skating strides, and the ability to play defensive as well as offensive hockey. The phlegmatic Watson owned a potent shot, and he was able to barrel up and down his wing without flinching; he usually absorbed most bodychecks as if nothing had happened. By contrast, Ezinicki's unexpected and usually crunching blasts were the scourge of the league. As a result, enemy radar usually zeroed in on Ezinicki, and Apps and Watson were able to roam free.

Smythe's second line was so effective that they were dubbed the "Second Kid Line," a compliment alluding to the Kid Line of Busher Jackson, Joe Primeau, and Charlie Conacher, who terrorized enemy goalies in the early thirties. Kennedy centered for the brush-cut whirlwind Howie Meeker on right wing, while bulky Vic Lynn, a converted defenseman, anchored the left side.

Meeker symbolized the Maple Leafs' spirit. A grenade blast that nearly shattered his leg threatened to end his hockey career, but he returned home, recuperated, and eventually skated in the NHL. Kennedy had been obtained in a deal with the Canadiens, while Lynn came to Toronto in a deal with Detroit. Smythe and Day arranged the line during training camp in September, 1946, and they immediately clicked.

"Kennedy was the puck-carrier and playmaker," said Toronto broadcaster Foster Hewitt. "Meeker and Lynn were both fast skaters and good shots. They were as full of rollicking dash as pups, and each was a born fighter. They weren't the best line in the league that year, but they were improving all the time."

The third line was a problem, if only because Smythe could not find a center to equal Apps and Kennedy. With such players as Gaye Stewart, Gus Bodnar, and Bud Poile, the Leafs could ice a competitive, if not overwhelming, third line.

Almost immediately, the Leafs demonstrated that they would be a contender in

1946–47. Broda had found his old-time form, Apps was as good as ever, the Kid Line clicked, and the Gold Dust Twins played as capably as any defense team in the league. By midseason, the Leafs were challenging the Canadiens for first place and making trouble wherever they went.

"They are the worst team in the league for holding, tripping, and interfering," said Rangers manager Frank Boucher.

Even such mild-mannered Leafs as Harry Watson managed to get into the brawling act, usually in an amusing way. One night the Leafs were playing their arch-foes, the Red Wings, and a typical full-scale brawl erupted on the ice. Suddenly, Watson found himself face-to-face with the equally mild Bill Quackenbush of Detroit.

In a trice, Quackenbush grabbed Watson by the shoulders and stunned his opponent with a question. "Shall we waltz?" said Quackenbush with a big smile.

"No," chuckled Watson. "Let's get in the middle and start shoving a bit. I think they're going to take pictures!"

On other occasions Watson was less cordial. Antagonized by Boston defenseman Murray Henderson, Watson broke the Bruin's nose with one punch. Another time he floored Red Wing defenseman Lee Fogolin with a mighty bodycheck. When Fogolin got to his feet, he skated over to Watson and snapped: "Watch what you're doing or I'll cut your head off, you big clown."

A few days later, Watson easily captured a loose puck at center ice and had only Fogolin to beat en route to the goaltender. He went around the husky defenseman with ease and shot the puck into the net. This time Fogolin approached Watson and sounded a bit more penitent. "That is the last time I'll ever call you names," he said.

The Leafs made a gallant run for first place, but they couldn't catch the speedy Canadiens. Toronto finished the regular 1946–47 season a solid second, and went up against the Red Wings in the semifinal round of the Stanley Cup playoffs.

Although the Leafs squeezed out a 3–2 overtime win in the opening game, in the second contest it appeared that their inexperience had finally caught up with them. Detroit piled up nine goals to Toronto's one, and all appeared lost as the teams entrained for Olympia Stadium in Detroit.

But Conn Smythe had a theme, and his players took it to heart. "Defeat does not rest lightly on our shoulders," said the Little Major, and he was right. Toronto beat Detroit 4–1, 4–1, and 6–1 to sweep the series in five games, sending the Maple Leafs into the Stanley Cup finals against Montreal.

The Canadiens, with veterans Maurice Richard, Toe Blake, and Elmer Lach, were favored to sweep the young Toronto skaters off the ice and retain the Stanley Cup they had captured a year earlier. Sure enough, the Canadiens smothered their opponents 6–0 in the first match, and a shudder went up and down the spines of all Toronto fans.

By contrast, the Leafs themselves appeared unconcerned. By now they had become welded into a mighty machine, and they proved it by winning the next three games from Montreal. The Canadiens did manage one more triumph, but Smythe's sextet wrapped up the series with a 2–1 win at Maple Leaf Gardens and took the Cup.

It was a monumental upset and a tribute more to Toronto's tenacity and drive than to the Maple Leafs' ability. Even the Little Major was willing to concede that. He knew he had a good team, and he realized that Kennedy, Mortson, Thomson, and Meeker would get better. But he also knew that he had a way to go to create a superteam. He knew he needed one more super player, a center, to fit the last piece into the complicated puzzle.

The player was in Chicago, and his name was Maxwell Herbert Lloyd "Max" Bentley. At the time Max was centering for the Black Hawks famed "Pony Line" with brother Doug Bentley and Bill Mosienko. They were a marvelous unit, all speed and pinpoint passes, with Max providing the hardest shot, despite his seemingly fragile frame. One observer said, "Max would lead the way with his huge nose, threading a path up center, past clutching arms and outthrust sticks.

Normally, a team would not dare to break up such an ideal unit, but the circumstances in Chicago were desperate. Aside from the Bentleys and Mosienko, the Black Hawks were a terrible team, acutely short in personnel. By November, 1947, it became obvious that one of the three Chicago aces had to be traded, and nobody knew it better than Smythe. He entered serious negotiations with Black Hawks manager Bill Tobin and made it clear that Max had to come to Toronto.

They haggled for days, and finally the two hockey bosses hammered out an agreement that left the hockey world gasping for breath. Smythe traded five of his Stanley Cup champions — nearly an entire on-ice team — for what amounted to one player.

Gus Bodnar, Gaye Stewart, Bud Poile — the complete "Flyin' Forts" line — and defensemen Bob Goldham and Ernie Dickens were dispatched to Chicago for Max Bentley and an inconsequential rookie named Cy Thomas. It was the biggest deal in the NHL and apparently a beneficial one for both clubs. The Black Hawks obtained the experienced manpower they so desperately needed, and the Leafs got their superstar. The only people who seemed sad about it were the Bentleys, their family, and their friends.

"I couldn't sleep a wink all night on the train taking me from Chicago to Toronto," said Max. "I just lay there thinking about the trade. I'd been with the Black Hawks for eight years, and it wasn't easy to leave Chicago. Doug felt the same way. But we figured that it was the only way out for the Black Hawks in the long run. There was nothing else they could do."

With Apps, Kennedy, and Max Bentley in the lineup, Smythe had the best collection of centermen ever seen on one team at one time. It was an insult to Max's reputation to say that he was centering the "third line," but that's where he was, alternately working with Joe Klukay and an assortment of wingers.

Max was not an instant sensation. He missed Doug and Mosienko, and he found coach Hap Day's disciplined style cramping to his free-wheeling philosophy. But, genius will out, and Max Bentley was a hockey genius.

A month after the extraordinary deal had been completed, Max began clicking on all cylinders, and the Leafs launched a serious challenge for first place and the Prince of Wales Trophy that goes with it. At times, Smythe thought he had a basket case on his hands because Max, among all his talents, also happened to be a hypochondriac.

"There's always something ailing him," said Black Hawks publicist Joe Farrell. "Hardly a day goes by that he doesn't think he's got cancer or kidney trouble or ulcers or something. He's never healthy."

Of course, Farrell wasn't telling the Leafs anything they didn't know. "It's true," confirmed Cy Thomas. "And the nights Max says he's dying are the nights he'll go out and play his greatest hockey."

Max did play some of his greatest hockey for the Maple Leafs, but he wasn't on the ice alone. Captain Apps was at the top of his game, and goalie Broda never made more clutch saves. Wild Bill Ezinicki was belting everyone in sight, and the Kid Line developed into one of the most exciting units since the days of Primeau, Jackson, and Conacher.

More than anyone, though, another youngster came along to give the Maple Leafs a zip that had all the pulsating qualities of the 1946–1947 outfit. His name was Bill Barilko. A bushy-haired youngster from Northern Ontario, Barilko was given an emergency try-out with the Leafs in February, 1947, when the Toronto defense corps was riddled with injuries.

Only 19 years old at the time, Barilko had been playing for the Hollywood Wolves of the old Pacific Coast Hockey League. Smythe phoned coach, Tommy Anderson for a report on Barilko. "He's pretty green," said Anderson, "but he's a big boy, not afraid of anyone, and he learns fast."

Anderson's prediction was accurate. Barilko learned fast, and by the 1947–1948 season he had developed a "snake-hips" bodycheck that put the fear of God into every opponent who skated down Bill's side of the rink. Elmer Lach of the Canadiens said: "Barilko is the hardest hitter in the league. When he hits you, he hurts you."

Of course, the Leafs' quest for complete dominance would have been futile if Max Bentley hadn't come through as expected. Oddly enough the turning point of the season was marked by the arrival in Toronto of Max's wife, Betty, and his two youngsters, Lynn and Gary. In the next game Max scored a three-goal hat trick against his former Chicago teammates, as Toronto romped to a 12–5 victory. "I guess all I needed was Betty's home cooking," said Max. "Just watch me go from now on."

And go he did. A night later at the Chicago Stadium, Max broke the hearts of Black Hawks fans by scoring the winning goal with only four minutes remaining. Toronto had a 3–2 victory. "Scoring that winning goal," said Leaf publicist Ed Fitkin, "was worth ten goals to Max. It gave him the confidence he needed. Even when injuries necessitated shakeups in his line, Max kept going at a remarkable clip."

More than that, Max gave Toronto the most fearsome power play in the league. He played the right point at the blue line when the face-off was in the enemy zone. The Maple Leafs plan was to win the face-off and somehow get the puck back to Max at the blue line. Then, employing an uncanny zig-zag skating style and a blinding ability to move the puck back and forth on the blade of his stick, Max would wend his way toward the enemy net. Since the opposition usually was falling over backward in a desperate attempt to wrest the puck from him, Max usually had the option of passing off to a free teammate or firing his speedy wrist shot on goal. In either case, the results were so successful that Max climbed to second in the scoring race, right behind captain Apps, and the Leafs became the terrors of the NHL.

"I don't know where we'd be if we hadn't gotten Max," said Smythe. "He's really been the 'Old Equalizer' and the greatest thing we've had at Maple Leaf Gardens since Howie Morenz and Aurel Joliat."

Max not only was colorful on the ice; he was good copy off the ice as well. On a trip to New York Bentley told Herb Goren of the old *New York Sun* that the secret of his quick wrist shots was attributable to milking cows back on the farm in Saskatchewan. "My dad has had eight cows on the farm back in Delisle ever since I can remember, and I milked those cows every day — two hours in the morning and two hours at night. That's a lot of milking, but it gives a guy strong wrists."

Just as Smythe had hoped, Max became the toast of Toronto. Wherever he went, the public chased him for autographs. Once he thought he had escaped the crowds when 50 youngsters descended on him on Carlton Street, just outside Maple Leaf Gardens. "Okay, okay," Bentley agreed, "but you've got to line up." They did so, and Max made sure that every one of them obtained his signature.

With all their talent, the Leafs simply couldn't run away with the NHL race. An injury to Apps on January 30, 1948, slowed them down, and when he returned, the Detroit Red Wings were bearing down on Toronto.

As NHL races go, the home stretch drive in 1948 was the all-time thriller. Toronto and Detroit battled neck and neck down to the final weekend of the season, when the arch-rivals were to play in a home-and-home series. The rival goalies, Turk Broda and Harry Lumley, were tied in the Vézina Trophy race, and Apps, with 198 goals in his record, needed two more red lights to reach the coveted 200-goal plateau.

Most important of all was the fact that Toronto held a bare one-point lead over Detroit, which meant that the Maple Leafs could clinch the Prince of Wales Trophy with a win on either night. The first of the two matches was played at Maple Leaf Gardens. When the game was over, Teeder Kennedy emerged as the star, scoring two goals en route to Toronto's 5–3 triumph. Broda was less than brilliant, but Lumley was a study in the jitters and fell two goals down as the teams met at Olympia Stadium in the final match of the regular season.

This time Broda starred, and the Leafs mauled Detroit, 5–2, guaranteeing Turk the second Vézina Trophy of his career. However, the hero of the night was none other than captain Apps, who scored a three-goal hat trick and tallied up a lifetime mark of 201.

The train carrying the Maple Leafs triumphantly home to Toronto exploded with revelry. The affable Broda was the center of attraction. He kidded his pals and kidded himself over the heartwarming win. "If I stay in this league a few more years," he said, "they'll be calling it the Broda Trophy. Yes, sir, the Broda Trophy."

Defenseman Jimmy Thomson piped up that it was the backline corps who really won the trophy for Turk. "Won it for me!" shouted Broda. "I must have stopped a million shots tonight. How many shots did I stop?"

A reporter checked the statistics, which revealed that Lumley had stopped 25 and Broda 30. "You see what I mean?" said Broda. "Thirty shots. I've been holding you guys up all year."

"You couldn't even hold yourself up on Saturday night," snapped Teeder Kennedy. "I thought you weren't even going to stop *one* shot."

Not to be outdone, Wally Stanowski added, "Vézina would have turned over in his grave if he'd seen the way you and Lumley played that one."

Captain Apps received his share of the twitting. The players realized that Syl was seriously considering retirement, although he was in the prime of his hockey career. "You've started on 300 goals now, Cap," one of the Leafs kidded. "You can't quit now."

True enough. Apps was the picture of perfection in what was to be his last regular season game, and so were his linemates, Bill Ezinicki and Harry Watson. Appropriately, Apps's 200th goal was the result of an unselfish decision by Watson. Ezinicki started the attack inside the Detroit blue line. Wild Bill outmaneuvered the Detroit defense until Watson cut in from the left; then Ezinicki skimmed a perfect pass to Watson. The big left wing could have easily scored, but he heard Apps in the background, noticed that Syl also was in perfect scoring position, and delivered the puck to him.

"I just blasted it with everything I had," said Apps. The puck hit the twine at a lucky 7:11 of the second period. It was a dandy goal, but everybody realized that it was Watson who made it possible.

"I've always thought highly of Harry," said coach Day, "but he went up even higher in my estimation because of that play."

Toronto's might made the Maple Leafs favorites to win the Stanley Cup, but to do so they had to dispose of the Boston Bruins. That they did, after demonstrating the amazing depth from Apps, Kennedy, and Bentley right down to the last man on the bench, Nick Metz, a versatile utility player and the oldest man on the team.

With the score tied 4–4 and 17 minutes gone in sudden-death overtime, Metz came through with the winner to set Boston down 1–0. In the second game, Kennedy blasted four goals into the Boston net and the Leafs won 5–3. "Those goals," wrote Jim Coleman in the *Toronto Globe and Mail*, "were a belated tribute to the persistence he has shown all season."

It was Kennedy again in the third game, this time figuring in three goals by scoring one and setting up Meeker and Boesch. Boston won the fourth game but bowed out in the fifth, as Kennedy scored the winner. Thus, the Leafs once again were pitted against Jack Adams's Red Wings for the Stanley Cup.

From the beginning, Toronto outclassed the Detroit sextet, and the Leafs never let up. They won 5–3 and 4–2 at home; then they moved on to Motor City, where the Red Wings were trounced 2–0 and 7–2. The Stanley Cup remained in Toronto, and when the triumphant Leafs returned home the next day, they were hailed by one of the greatest civic receptions ever accorded a group of athletes.

Thousands of people lined the parade route from Union Station in downtown Toronto to City Hall, where another 10,000 toasted the champions. "This is the greatest team our organization has ever had!" said Conn Smythe.

It was. Although Apps retired, the Maple Leafs went on to win an unheard-of third consecutive Stanley Cup in 1949. They might have made it four in 1950, but the Red Wings beat them in sudden-death overtime in the seventh and final game of the semifinal round.

Nevertheless, the Maple Leaf power reasserted itself in 1951, when the Toronto club defeated Montreal 4–1. The decisive goal in the fifth game was scored by Bill Barilko in sudden death. Taking a passout from Howie Meeker, Barilko executed a magnificent lunging ballet shot at 2:37 of the first overtime period. The puck sailed over Canadiens goalie Gerry McNeil, and delirious teammates hoisted Barilko to their shoulders.

The 24-year-old defenseman was the toast of hockeydom, the pillar around which Smythe was building his continuing hockey empire. It appeared that the sky would be the limit for the Leafs. They had Kennedy, Bentley, Thomson, Mortson, Meeker, and Watson. But most of all, they had exuberant Bashing Bill Barilko, and it appeared that Stanley Cups would keep coming his way.

Then tragedy struck.

On Sunday, August 26, 1951, Barilko and his friend Dr. Henry Hudson, a Timmins, Ontario, dentist, took off from the James Bay town of Rupert House in Hudson's plane. They were on the last leg of a fishing trip from Seal River to Timmins, but they never made it. Their plane crashed in the vast, lake-studded bush country of Northern Ontario, killing Dr. Hudson, Barilko, and, for all intents and purposes, the Maple Leafs dynasty.

Without Bashing Bill to provide the zing, the Toronto club flattened out in the 1951–52 season, and the Leafs were eliminated in the first round of the playoffs by Detroit in four straight games.

"One thing is certain," wrote Ed Fitkin, who knew Barilko well, "Toronto fans will never forget him. The 1951 Stanley Cup victory will always be remembered as Bill Barilko's Cup win."

It was 11 years before the Maple Leafs won another championship.

The Edmonton Oilers, 1984–88

Gretzky's Greats, The Edmonton Oilers

No two teams were more alike in their failure to achieve all-time greatness than the Detroit Red Wings of the 1950s and the Edmonton Oilers of the 1980s. The Detroiters owned Gordie Howe, the best player of the pre-expansion era, and the Edmontonians were headlined by Wayne Gretzky, the finest performer of the post-1967 epoch. Each had a world class goalie — Terry Sawchuk in Detroit and Grant Fuhr in Edmonton — and the right blend of forwards and defense to dominate the league.

Neither the Oilers nor the Red Wings ever won more than two straight Stanley Cups, although each team was capable — on paper, at least — of doing better. The Edmonton general staff certainly expected more than it obtained. After the Oilers had won championships in 1984 and 1985, assistant coach John Muckler opined, "If we keep working and keep our heads and don't get fat, there is no reason why we can't win four, five, or even six in a row."

The difference between the Oilers and Islanders is that the former believed it could win by accenting the run-and-gun philosophy at the expense of goalie Grant Fuhr. The thinking was that somehow or other, Fuhr would come up with the big save when rushing defensemen like Paul Coffey were trapped up ice. It was a pleasant thought; the only trouble was, it didn't always work.

During the 1986 playoffs against Calgary, the Oilers were unquestionably the superior team — on paper. But the Flames' Mike Vernon outgoaled Fuhr, Calgary's checkers drove the Oilers' forwards to distraction and, unlike the Islanders, the Oilers collapsed in the clutch.

No one was more disappointed than Oilers' president general manager coach, Glen Sather. He helped create the team from Day One of its formation in the late 1970s. (Remember, the Oilers originally were in the World Hockey Association.) Sather was tempted to break up the combination that lost to Calgary, but, instead, he did some minor tinkering and went back for more.

Sather acted wisely. The Oilers were built around the incomparable Wayne Gretzky, Mark Messier, Jari Kurri, and Glenn Anderson up front and Kevin Lowe and Paul Coffey on defense. Grant Fuhr and Andy Moog were the original goaltenders, with Fuhr eventually taking over the number one job.

To insure that Gretzky was not mauled by enemy goons, Sather employed such heavyweights as Dave Semenko, Kevin McClelland, and Marty McSorley, each of whom was effective at keeping the peace. Although many teams tried, few were able to intimidate the Oilers at any time during their reign.

It began in 1984 with a four games to one finals victory over the Islanders and, at the time, it seemed destined to go on through the end of the decade. "We do not want to go down in history as one of the great teams who ended up winning only two Stanley Cups in a row," said Coffey.

The second Stanley Cup win over the Philadelphia Flyers in 1985 was as convincing as the first. The young aces, such as Gretzky and Messier were just reaching their prime, and Sather was continually adding new blood including Mike Krushelnyski, Craig MacTavish, Steve Smith, and Esa Tikkanen. None, however, could fortify the Oilers' weak underbelly, a disturbing frivolousness that betrayed a lack of character. It would ultimately do the club in during the 1986 loss to the Flames.

If nothing else, the loss to Calgary had a maturing effect on the team and the Oilers rebounded smartly to win the prize in 1987, beating the Flyers in a terribly exciting seven game final. Ironically, the win betrayed many more Edmonton flaws. "We should have beaten them in four games, not seven," said Lowe. "We left them for dead after the third game and they just got off the floor and nearly knocked us out."

The win also revealed strains of discontent among the hard-core Oilers, particularly Coffey who had become more and more rancorous over Sather's constant badgering of him. When the defenseman balked over his contract and walked out on the team before the 1987–88 season began, Coffey was put on the block and traded to the Penguins. This marked the beginning of the end of the Oilers' golden era.

Coffey's departure caused discontent, especially among his close friends — Gretzky, Lowe, and Messier. Sather, who had been palmed off by the media as the "players' manager," was fast turning into an ogre in the eyes of his skaters. But even without Coffey, the team survived. Craig Muni and Jeff Beukeboom stepped in and proved adequate. Gretzky was still Gretzky, and when the dust had cleared in the spring of 1988, the Oilers were on top once more. Then, IT happened. Gretzky was dealt to the Los Angeles Kings and the Oilers, despite Messier, Lowe, Kurri, and Fuhr, became just another good hockey team; but not good enough to get out of the first playoff round.

Because of superlative performers such as Gretzky, Messier, Kurri, and Fuhr, the '80s Oilers have to be regarded among the better clubs of an era. But they were far from being the best.

After the New York Islanders won four consecutive Stanley Cups, several hockey experts predicted that the parlay of four straight championships would never be accomplished again, simply because the odds would be too high and the competition too keen. So far this call has been borne out, and it is conceivable that we will never see a four straight run again.

However, the Edmonton Oilers of the late 1980s almost changed all that. They were not the greatest hockey team of all-time or even the runner-up, but they certainly arrested the imagination and produced a number of headliners worthy of their six figure salaries — Wayne Gretzky, Paul Coffey, Mark Messier, and Grant Fuhr to name a few.

The story of the champion Oilers of the 1980s is the saga of two leagues and two personalities. The leagues are the now-defunct vagabond World Hockey Association and the staid, perennial National Hockey League. The individuals are Canadian entrepreneur Peter Pocklington and Mister Hockey himself, Wayne Gretzky.

To understand the evolution of the Oilers, one must also understand the birth, growth, and eventually the expiration of the WHA; its merger with the NHL and the ripening of the Oilers — and most importantly, Gretzky — within the established league's structure.

For the Oilers, the starting point was an unlikely development at the start of the 1970s, but one which would shake the very foundations of hockey's superstructure. Defying all hockey shibboleths, a group of California entrepreneurs launched, what they labeled a second major league of the ice sport, in 1972. Organized by Santa Ana attorney, Gary Davidson, and promoter, Dennis Murphy, the World Hockey Association took on the National Hockey League as a decided underdog. Neither Davidson nor Murphy had any previous hockey experience, and because of that fact alone, the imminent demise of the WHA was freely predicted by NHL rivals right from the beginning. Furthermore, the WHA chose to collide head-on with the established cities — New York, Boston, Toronto, among others — where there already was a team with a strong following.

On February 12, 1972 the WHA held its first player draft at the Royal Coach Inn in Anaheim, California. Until then, the WHA had no profound impact on the NHL. Elders of the established circuit refused to recognize the new threat, and moved along with plans for further expansion of their own league.

Two weeks later, the NHL received its first tangible shock, when Bernie Parent, one of the most gifted young NHL goaltenders, made public his intent to sign with a WHA team. At the time, it was believed that he would align with the Miami Screaming Eagles, although he later officially joined the Philadelphia Blazers. Parent's decision was the catalyst for other NHL players to jump to the new circuit and, one-by-one, signings were announced.

WHA teams spirited the likes of Bobby Hull, Derek Sanderson, Ted Green, and J.C. Tremblay from the NHL. The league opened with 12 teams spread over two divisions. New England (Boston), Cleveland, Philadelphia, Ottawa, Quebec, and New York were in the Eastern Division. Winnipeg, Houston, Los Angeles, Alberta (Edmonton), Minnesota (St. Paul), and Chicago represented the West.

The WHA opened its first season on October 11, 1972, with Quebec at Cleveland and Edmonton at Ottawa. Edmonton's Ron Anderson scored the first

WHA regular-season goal. In the playoff finals, New England defeated Winnipeg, four games to one, to win the WHA's first championship trophy.

Not only did the WHA survive its first year of operations, it also held its first All-Star game on January 6, 1973 at Quebec City and even had one of its games shown on the CBS television network. Danny Lawson became the first WHA player to reach the 50-goal plateau on February 22, 1973 in Ottawa.

Some NHL officials took the WHA challenge seriously. As a result, secret meetings were held in April, 1973 between Gary Davidson and a NHL group, led by William Jennings, president of the New York Rangers. An effort was made to hammer out an agreement, but no pact was forthcoming. Davidson announced that the WHA would continue to operate independently. "We believe the NHL's reserve clause to be wrong," said Davidson. "It would be impossible for us to consider any formal association with the NHL so long as it has it." More importantly, the old guard among the NHL governors was adamantly opposed to an agreement with the WHA, and proclaimed a full-scale war in hopes of eliminating the maverick league.

In its second year, the WHA added to its trophy collection by making a deal with the AVCO Financial Services organization. The company, which provides financial counseling and loans through more than 1,500 offices in the United States, Canada, Australia, and Great Britain, lent its name to the WHA's version of the Stanley Cup. Hereafter, the winner of the WHA playoff would become the holder of the AVCO World Trophy. It wasn't very classy, but at this point in time, the WHA wasn't about to quibble; it would accept help whenever and wherever posssible. In May, 1974 the Houston Aeros captured the AVCO World Trophy in 14 games, losing only to Minnesota, while sweeping four straight from Winnipeg and Chicago.

Like the NHL, the WHA was struggling through tumultuous times and reorganization seemed to be the order of the day. In June, 1974 the league divided into three divisions (Canadian, West, East) and a wild-card team playoff format was adopted. Pheonix and Indianapolis were the new expansion teams. Another blow was dealt the NHL when the WHA's Toronto Toros persuaded superstar Frank Mahovlich to leave the established league.

In contrast to the NHL, the WHA owners realized there was a motherlode of talent to be mined in Europe. The Winnipeg Jets, in particular, thought nothing of stocking their rosters with Swedes rather than Canadians. Soon Ulf Nilsson and Anders Hedberg of Sweden teamed with Bobby Hull to become one of the most formidable attacking units of the 1970s. The WHA made another meaningful inroad on the international level when it persuaded Soviet hockey officials to sanction an eight-game series between WHA All-Stars and a similar team from Russia. The tourney took place in the fall of 1974, with the Soviets easy winners.

Setbacks notwithstanding, the WHA continued to grow because of one pivotal element: the spectacular growth of new arenas throughout the country and the demand, in each city, for a suitable tenant. Whereas the NHL was infinitely more demanding in setting forth conditions for entry, the WHA would gladly accept any franchise bidder as long as an attractive arena was located in the city in question. Thus, Cincinnati, which was not likely to become an NHL entry, was welcomed into the WHA in 1975, upon completion of the handsome river-front arena.

Cleveland — actually the building was located in distant Richfield, Ohio — also had a new arena, as did Indianapolis and Edmonton.

From the very beginning, one of the most frequently debated questions was the quality of WHA play in relation to the NHL. Clearly, the new league lacked the depth of stars still in the established circuit, but it did offer some interesting talents in the Swedes, as well as two Finnish players and two Czechoslovakians, along with Bobby Hull, Gordie Howe, and his two youngsters, Mark and Marty. Scoring came easier in the WHA. When Bobby Hull equalled Maurice Richard's venerable NHL record of 50 goals in 50 games on February 14, 1975, the achievement was greeted with less than overwhelming enthusiasm.

Some players who made the leap from the NHL to the WHA reconsidered and returned, among them were Bernie Parent and Derek Sanderson; but others, such as Bobby Hull, remained true to the new league. More than anyone, Hull proved to be the foremost gate attraction in the WHA and further helped the league's cause by his graciousness with fans and the media. On December 14, 1975, Hull received still more attention when he became the first WHA player to score 200 goals in league play.

More franchise rumblings were heard after the league realigned into two new divisions — Eastern and Western. The Toronto Toros could not compete with the NHL's Toronto Maple Leafs and emigrated to Birmingham, Alabama, and were renamed the Bulls. Likewise, the Crusaders became a losing proposition in Cleveland and moved to St. Paul. Birmingham proved to be a pleasant addition to the league but St. Paul could not make it past 42 games before folding. It was a portent of things to come. By the end of the 1977–78 season, the league had dwindled to eight teams — a year earlier it had opened with 12 — having lost St. Paul, Calgary, Phoenix, and San Diego. But Edmonton remained strong.

There was, however, new hope on the diplomatic front. Howard Baldwin, new WHA president, enjoyed a very positive relationship with key NHL leaders: Ed Snider, owner of the Philadelphia Flyers, and John Ziegler, new president of the NHL. The endless WHA-NHL war was bleeding both leagues, and a spirit of reconciliation once again brought the leaders together. This time there was more understanding on both sides of the bargaining table and a realization that a peace pact of some kind was in order. The result was that four WHA teams — the Edmonton Oilers, the Hartford Whalers, the Quebec Nordiques, and the Winnipeg Jets — were admitted to the NHL following the 1978–79 season. The WHA, after seven seasons of tumultuous operation, went out of business.

In many ways the WHA had a profound impact on the North American professional hockey scene. The competition for talent sent players salaries skyrocketing to all-time highs. The WHA spread pro hockey to new areas, but all too often these gains were offset by shabby management practices that angered the fans and, ultimately, turned them away from the game. As a result, cities that had been acclaimed for their hockey support — among them San Diego and Cleveland — became hockey wastelands.

The progressive nature of the WHA leadership resulted in a heavy accent on European talent — a trend later followed by the NHL — and an increase in many of the skills of the game. Further, the WHA recognized cities heretofore ignored as big-league centers that had been dismissed as potential moneymakers by the

NHL. Quebec, Edmonton, Winnipeg, and Hartford later demonstrated that they could attract as many fans, comparatively, as established centers such as Detroit and Chicago. On the legal front, the WHA fought many battles with the NHL and won a significant number of them. It was the WHA that signed the electrifying Wayne Gretzky, at a time when the NHL leaders were disparaging the lad as too thin, too unskilled, and not likely to become a factor in the major league game.

The WHA spawned interest, created a group of gifted hockey executives, and offered an interesting form of sports entertainment throughout the 1970s. But, in the end, the league demonstrated, more than anything else, that there is no room in hockey for more than one major professional league. And that is why the World Hockey Association is now a footnote in the lore of the game.

The WHA did open the door for the Edmonton Oilers and that franchise, in turn, provided the format for the inimitable Gretzky. Curiously Gretzky's debut was not with Edmonton but with the Indianapolis Racers. But, millionaire Peter Pocklington, who owned the Oilers, had his eye on Gretzky. Pocklington realized that Racer owner, Nelson Skalbania, needed cash in a hurry and picked up on the SOS. Skalbania and Pocklington huddled and a deal was struck. Gretzky, as well as left wing Peter Driscoll and goaltender Eddie Mio, was sold to the Edmonton Oilers for $850,000.

The deal, at least momentarily, enabled the Racers to stay in the hunt and released Skalbania from a commitment to pay Wayne $1,750,000 over the next seven years. Peter Pocklington wasted no time renegotiating Gretzky's contract so that he was coupled with the executive they call Peter Puck for nine years, including two six-year options, for a total of 21 years. Wayne would be guaranteed approximately $300,000 a year.

On paper, the figures looked good, but on the ice Gretzky did not look that good. "Would he be another Pat Price?" Jim Taylor wondered. "For Wayne Gretzky, it is not going to be easy. He is, after all, only 17. With all those dollar signs, his age is too easily forgotten."

Gretzky's puck was now in the Edmonton Oilers' end of the rink. How he would skate it out would determine the fate of his career.

The distance from Indianapolis to Edmonton is approximately 1,500 miles. But the cities are worlds apart, particularly when it comes to the care and feeding of hockey players. Less than a hockey hotbed, Indianapolis had never been a place where young stickhandlers cavorted on outdoor rinks under the lights. Edmonton was literally smothered with hockey players, a number of whom either had made it or were in the process of graduating to the professional ranks. It was a place where a young talent such as Wayne could feel right at home — and he did. Edmonton was a great hockey town and Gretzky would prove to be the best player in the burgh. He was the Oilers' leading scorer his first year with 46 goals and 64 assists for 110 points, 39 more than his nearest teammate, Blair MacDonald.

His new coach, Glen Sather, was a testy, former third-line National Hockey League journeyman who had once teamed with Bobby Orr on the Boston Bruins, and later skated for the Pittsburgh Penguins and the Montreal Canadiens, among other clubs. Sather developed the patience, insight, and understanding of the average athlete that made him a superior leader and coach.

Gretzky, of course, was a special case and one who would demand unusual treatment. If anything, Sather would have to be especially vigilant in dealing with Gretzky's defensive flaws, the only obviously weak part of his game. During a match with the Cincinnati Stingers, a Gretzky defensive blunder provided Cincinnati with the puck and the Stingers promptly scored. The Kid returned to the bench and awaited his next turn on the ice.

The turn never came. Sather deliberately bypassed Gretzky and kept him on the bench until he felt that the lesson had been learned. A period later The Kid got the high sign and returned to action.

"He could have pouted and sulked," said Sather. No way; not the Brantford Bullet. He scored a three-goal hat trick enabling the Oilers to overcome a 2–1 deficit and triumph 5–2. "That," Sather added, "was the turning point in his career. Not just anyone could keep the motivation with a contract like his. But he wants to be the best."

Gretzky's arrival in the NHL in 1979 was viewed with as much concern by those who believe he would be brutalized, as it was with delight by others who were persuaded that he was, in fact, the second coming of Howie Morenz, or Eddie Shore, or Gordie Howe, or Bobby Hull. Certainly, those who purchased tickets at Edmonton's Coliseum were tickled by the prospect to the tune of 14,600 season tickets. That the Oilers might be overmatched in the NHL seemed to disturb no one, least of all Larry Gordon, the Oilers general manager.

"We've got the guy to build a team around," said Gordon. "Now we're just going to try to give him some help."

Supporting Gretzky at center ice for the Oilers was Ron Chipperfield, once nearly as highly regarded as Wayne, and Stan Weir, a former Toronto Maple Leaf with a bit more than journeyman potential. Among the other competent forwards were Blair MacDonald on right wing and Brett Callighen on the left. Dave Semenko and Peter Driscoll were the heavy hitters up front.

While not terribly awesome, the Oilers defense showed some promise, particularly with the acquisition of Lee Fogolin, a 24-year-old backliner whose father, Lee Sr., had been a bone-crusher for the Chicago Black Hawks in another era. Fogolin would be complemented by Pat Price (the fellow who had not been able to handle instant fame as well as Gretzky), Colin Campbell, Kevin Lowe, Al Hamilton, and Doug Hicks. Dave Dryden, who had performed so nobly the previous season, would take another crack at puckstopping. All in all, it was a team with infinite promise and awesome potential, but with just as many doubts, particularly about Number 99. Would The Kid, who had nearly won the WHA scoring championship, be able to execute as expertly in the NHL?

Superficially, at least, there seemed no way he could be prepared for the likes of such behemoths as Barry Beck, Larry Robinson, and Jerry Korab. After all Gretzky, on a heavy day, weighed in at only 165 pounds, still hadn't started shaving, and often behaved like a kid tuned to a distant tape deck in the sky.

"He looked like a high school kid in a locker room full of big league pros," said veteran author Bill Libby.

Gretzky averaged a point a game after the Oilers first seven tests. With two goals and eight assists, he seemed less than overwhelming, but he was far from out of place in his new surroundings.

"The pace seems a little faster in this league," he admitted, "but the WHA was a good league. I feel I did well for my first year. I will do my best and hope it's good enough."

Did he have a particular style in mind?

"I try to stay out of trouble. I'm hard to hit. A lot of players took shots at me when I first got into the WHA and a lot are taking shots at me now in the NHL, but I can take it. I'm not a fighter, but I practice self-defense."

The beginning was rocky for both Gretzky and his Oilers. They made the playoffs, and skating against the rugged Philadelphia Flyers in the opening round of the 1980 playoffs, played competently and courageously. In the opener, the Oilers fought back from a 2–0 deficit (Gretzky tied the count at 2–2) to take a 3–2 lead in the third period. They held the lead until Rick MacLeish scored with less than a minute left in the third period. Bobby Clarke won it for Philadelphia in sudden-death overtime.

Although the Flyers romped 5–1 in the second game, the Oilers regrouped in Game Three and took a 2–0 lead (with Gretzky opening the scoring) into the second period. But the Flyers rallied to tie the count and sent the game into sudden death. Neither team scored in the first overtime period, but Ken Linseman beat Ron Low at 3:56 of the second sudden-death period to end the game and the series.

The season was over for Gretzky and the Oilers and now it was time to take stock of what The Kid had accomplished as an NHL freshman. Not only did he tie Marcel Dionne in the point parade, but he also won the Lady Byng Trophy as the NHL's most gentlemanly player. Wayne was also voted the league's most valuable player, for which he received the Hart Trophy. As an added fillip, Oilers' owner, Peter Pocklington presented the Kid with a Ferrari.

By the 1981–82 season, the Oilers had become the biggest draw in the NHL. "We had scalpers outside the building for a game late in the (1981–82) season, something we'd never seen before," said Terry Schiffauer, public relations director for the Pittsburgh Penguins. "A couple of them told me they needed a map of the city to find their way to the rink. They'd never worked a hockey game before. Thanks to Gretzky we were sold out more than three weeks ahead of time and were able to put the match on live television locally, which was something really extraordinary. We'd do about 13,000 people on a Saturday night but this was a capacity crowd, 16,033. Gretzky gets credit for those extra 3,000 people, or roughly $30,000 in gate receipts. But that's not an accurate measurement of what he did for the franchise in the brief time he was in Pittsburgh. You couldn't put a price on it."

Gerry Helper, Buffalo Sabre's public relations director, had a similar story to tell about the night Gretzky broke Esposito's record. "We sold out, which we expected, but we had 200 media people, compared with the usual 70. Burt Reynolds and Goldie Hawn were there. And what sticks in my mind was that Gretzky didn't let anybody down."

Certainly, he wasn't letting the Oilers down as he steered them to the top of the Smythe Division and a second-place overall in the regular schedule. The Gretzky Effect was such that, despite coach Glen Sather's attempts to limit his availability, he was constantly being stared down by a newsman or a cameraman. Once, when he was in a fast food emporium, waiting for a milk shake, his teammate Dave Semenko noticed the lens of a security camera ten feet from Wayne.

"Hey Gretz," chided Semenko, "there's another camera. You should get in front of that one, too."

Even after the season had concluded, Gretzky continued to inspire raves. Before splitting up for the summer, the Oilers were required to visit the University of Alberta, where the players were put through a two-hour testing session. Among other things, the examination was designed to indicate the strength of the respective players' hearts and lungs, the power in their legs, the percentage of body fat, and the strength of their upper bodies.

Among the conclusions reached by Howie Wenger of the University staff was that Gretzky had a remarkable recovery rate after strenuous exercise. His heart beat registered 183 halfway through the vigorous bicycle test, but minutes later dipped to a relaxed 60. Wenger described the result as fantastic.

Sather used the same adjective to describe just about anything his prodigy would do. "He's the premier attraction in the National Hockey League," said Sather. "He's the most exciting young player in the league."

The Hockey News confirmed Sather's endorsement by voting Gretzky Player of the Year.

The next question was, where do he and the Oilers go from here?

As it happened, the sky was the limit for both Gretzky and the Oilers. Wayne was not the only one to emerge a star. There were aces like Mark Messier, defenseman Paul Coffey, Finnish winger Jari Kurri, and goaltender Grant Fuhr. Everyone seemed to be coming into his own at the right time.

With this lineup, the Oilers were getting closer. However, after the stunning first-round playoff exit at the hands of the Los Angeles Kings in 1982, and the embarrassing sweep by the Islanders in the 1983 finals in which the high scoring Oilers managed only six goals, people began to wonder whether this collection of superstars could put it all together and bring the Holy Grail to Edmonton.

The Oilers finally won their first Stanley Cup in 1984, gaining revenge against a determined Islander team in quest of its fifth consecutive championship.

In a truly memorable opening game, the Oilers shut out the mighty Islanders 1–0 on a goal by Kevin McClelland and the flawless goaltending of Grant Fuhr. In Game Two, also at Nassau Coliseum, the Islanders knotted the series at one game apiece by making up for their lack of scoring the night before with a 6–1 decision. If the Islanders did not savor this victory, they were not to get another chance. The series shifted to Edmonton, and the Oilers delighted the home crowd by promptly disposing of the Islanders with three straight decisive victories. The Stanley Cup's four-year tenure in Long Island was over. Its new home would be Edmonton, and the Oilers were more than hospitable hosts.

With their personnel, whispers were being heard regarding a possible "dynasty" in the making. A second Stanley Cup would certainly offer some proof. The Oilers would not disappoint.

After finishing in their usual first-place spot in a much improved Smythe Division in 1984–85, the Oilers were just warming up. There wasn't much the Kings could do in the opening round that spring, losing three straight, and from there it was on to the pesky Winnipeg Jets. One of the most improved teams in the

National Hockey League last season, the Jets played their hearts out only to come up short to the steamrolling Oilers.

The semifinals pitted the Oilers against the hard-hitting Black Hawks. At this point, nothing was going to stop the Oilers' drive for a second straight Cup. Getting past the Hawks was no easy task, but the Oilers were only looking ahead. Taking on a rejuvenated and inspired Philadelphia Flyer team, headed by rookie coach Mike Keenan, the Oilers received only mild interference when they lost the opening game. They then went on to take the next four in a row for their second straight championship, silencing the critics and adding a little more validity to the "dynasty" tag.

Kevin Lowe: "When we won the Stanley Cup in 1984, there were plenty of critics who claimed our win was a fluke, same as they did when the Islanders won their first Cup in 1980. So, there was only one thing to do: win it again and quiet the critics.

"The Oilers are going to get even better. Our best players haven't even reached their peak. Our general manager, Glen Sather, somehow provided two or three new players each season. And we have the other key ingredient we may have lacked the first time around — experience.

"We've proved now that we can play it any way the opposition wants, from high-scoring to tight-checking to a goaltenders game, and still win. I can't see any team winning the Stanley Cup this year but the Edmonton Oilers!"

He was almost right. On paper, the Oilers *should* have won a third straight Cup and established themselves alongside the Maple Leafs of the 1940s and 1960s, who did just that, but two vital factors were working against Sather's skaters; luck and internal character flaws.

Unlike the Islanders who had preceded them as champions, the Oilers were not a class act. They were too full of themselves — partly because of The Gretzky Effect and partly due to team-wide immaturity — and lacked the attention span of a more mature team like the Islanders or Canadiens of the 1950s. When the coaches pointed out flaws, the Oilers more often than not, laughed them off and went their own undisciplined way.

Not surprisingly, the result was disaster, although it wasn't immediately apparent. The Oilers completed the regular season with an awesome 56–17–7 record and appeared capable of overrunning all opposition enroute to The Cup.

They did just that in the opening round against Vancouver, which set up the Smythe Division finals against the traditional enemy, Calgary. As always, the intra-province battle was intense, and while many observers expected the Flames to put up a good show, few anticipated the eventual result.

Calgary won the opener, 4–1 at Northlands Coliseum and, from that point on, the champions were off-balance. Edmonton tied the count in Game Two, although overtime was required. Now the Oilers realized they had a genuine challenge on their hands, particularly after the Flames took a two games to one lead in the series after it moved to The Saddledome. Back and forth, the playoff rocked until Edmonton pulled even, after falling behind three games to two.

The finale was at Northlands Coliseum and once again the Flames showed they meant business, pulling ahead 2–0. Edmonton roared back and tied the score. Early in the third period, with the count 2–2, Oilers defenseman Steve Smith attempted a long clearing pass from a position to the left of and behind his net. The pass was set on an angle from left toward the right boards at the blue line, but the puck never reached its destination. Smith's pass ricocheted off goalie Grant Fuhr's leg and fell into the Edmonton net. *Shazam!* Without lifting a finger, Calgary had a 3–2 lead.

The Oilers had three-quarters of a period to tie the score; normally child's play for them, but now they faced a determined Flames defense and unusually adroit goaltending from young Mike Vernon. Time and again the Oilers penetrated the Calgary zone but they were repulsed either by the backliners or Vernon. Time finally ran out on Edmonton and the Oilers quest for a third straight Stanley Cup.

"We gave them a game plan and they didn't follow it," explained Sather in his post-game rationale for the defeat.

Others on the Edmonton general staff concurred, as did some players. "In the games we lost, we didn't have any sustained forechecking," said Kevin Lowe. "We had a forechecking system but the guys refused to do it."

Strange as it was, the loss to Calgary would have profound implications for the Oilers. For one thing, it reduced their chances of becoming known as the greatest team of all time; something that Sather, Gretzky, Lowe, Messier, & Co. truly believed possible. For another, it pointed up egregious flaws in the hockey club which required work. Many were addressed, and when the Oilers returned to the starting gate for the 1986–87 season, they were determined to get back on track.

They did with a vengeance, finishing first again (50–24–6) and, this time, looking formidable enough to conquer the Flames. But, alas, Calgary was eliminated from the playoffs by Winnipeg, while the Oilers were knocking off the Kings. Edmonton then disposed of the Jets and Red Wings to reach the finals against the Philadelphia Flyers.

The Broad Street Bullies were a trifle less vicious than they had been during their 1974–75 Stanley Cup reign, but no less pugnacious. Their rookie goalie Ron Hextall had played better than anyone would have imagined, leading the Flyers not only to the finals but to a seventh game finale with the Oilers at Northlands Coliseum.

For a few scary moments, it appeared that the Flyers would do to Edmonton what the Flames had done a year earlier. They jumped into a quick 1–0 lead, but for a change the Oilers got hold of themselves and rebounded. They tied the count and then went ahead 2–1 in the second period.

Try as they might, the Flyers couldn't beat Fuhr again. With less than three minutes remaining, Glenn Anderson beat Hextall and the game — and Cup! — was clinched.

Ironically, the reaction in the Oilers' dressing room was a curious counterpoint between joy and bitterness. While most of the Edmonton skaters sipped champagne and toasted their victory, super defenseman Paul Coffey, a key player both on attack and defense, went public on television declaring his unhappiness with the Peter Pocklington regime. He was also dismayed over Sather's criticism of his play over the past few years. "A lot of things were said that hurt me personally," Coffey opined. Quietly, Gretzky agreed.

As the Oilers returned for the 1987–88 season, more storm clouds gathered. Two of the European stars of the Oilers 1987 Cup win, Kent Nilsson and Reijo

Ruotsalainen, chose not to return to Edmonton and Coffey began a holdout that would eventually lead to his being moved to the Pittsburgh Penguins without ever playing another game for Edmonton.

True, the Oilers still had Gretzky, Messier, Anderson, Lowe, and Fuhr, but they weren't the same team without Coffey. They finished second in the Smythe — Calgary was on top — with 99 points, the fewest for the club since 1980–81 when they managed only 74. But they still had one thing in their favor — playoff savvy.

It helped them to a relatively simple first round win over the Jets and set up the Smythe Division finals against, of all people, the Flames. And, what do you know, Calgary was favored for a change.

Perhaps, but the Flames wilted faster than Italian ices in the Mohave Desert. One-two-three-four games, a sweep, and Calgary was eliminated from the playoffs. If the Oilers missed Coffey, you couldn't tell by their performance. "Without Paul," said Lowe, "we knew we needed a team defense — and we got it."

They also got another stellar series out of Gretzky, superior goaltending from Fuhr, and strategically smart coaching from Sather, who outguessed his Calgary counterpart, Terry Crisp, at every turn. "From that series on," added Lowe, "we were confident we could go all the way to The Cup."

And they did just that. True, they lost a couple of games to Detroit in the Campbell Conference finals. No sweat. Next came the doughty Bruins in the finals. Boston simply was no match. The series went five games — one contest, incredibly, was postponed after a power failure at Boston Garden interrupted play — and Edmonton so thoroughly dominated the series it was almost embarrassing.

In five seasons, the Oilers had won four Stanley Cups. "If we win another," said Lowe, "we'd have to be considered one of the greatest teams of all time — if not the greatest of them all."

It was not to be. In the most startling trade hockey has known, Gretzky was dealt to the Los Angeles Kings during the summer of 1988, along with Marty McSorley and Mike Krushelnyski. Edmonton received Jimmy Carson and four first-round draft choices, as well as $15 million.

Gretzky's friends, particularly Lowe and Messier, were furious with Pocklington and Sather. They even talked of going on strike, but they eventually settled back into a playing mode. Without Gretzky, the Oilers dropped to third place.

Carson, clearly, could not fill The Great One's skates — could anyone, for that matter? — and the Oilers almost appeared ordinary, although Jari Kurri did his best to carry the club through the difficult winter.

The Oilers had one last chance to redeem themselves. They faced Gretzky's Kings in the opening round and actually led the series at one point, three games to one. But Los Angeles rallied to take the next three games and the series.

Postscript: The Edmonton Oilers, 1989–90

The value of Edmonton's 1980s nucleus would be enhanced, most experts believed, if somehow the Oilers could win one more Stanley Cup without Wayne Gretzky in the lineup. "Certainly," said coach John Muckler, "we didn't expect it (the Cup win) to happen in 1989–90. At least we didn't think we had the goods when training camp opened in September '89. We were only in the rebuilding stage then."

Sather enhanced and accelerated the rebuilding by constantly turning adversity to sweet use. There was no better example than *L'Affaire Jimmy Carson*. A Detroit native, Carson came to Edmonton with considerable fuss and fanfare in the Gretzky deal. Nobody would have faulted him had Jimmy simply went about his job of scoring goals; but, pretty soon he made it clear he loathed Edmonton. Even worse, Carson skipped the team early in 1989–90, causing Sather no end of embarrassment and forcing a trade.

Normally, a general manager backed into such a deep corner is forced to make a deal not to his liking or advantage. In this case, Sather dealt Carson and over-the-hill enforcer Kevin McClelland to Detroit for Petr Klima, Joe Murphy and Adam Graves. "Carson didn't want to play for us," said Sather, "so I had no choice. We were lucky that the kids worked out."

Edmonton finished second in the Smythe Division and not first due, in part, to the club's lack of a mobile defenseman to play the point on the power play. At the eleventh-hour of the trade deadline, Sather obtained fleet veteran point man Reijo (Rexy) Ruotsalainen from the New Jersey Devils in exchange for defenseman Jeff Sharples, who also had been procured from Detroit. "Rexy had been with us before," noted Sather, "and he just fit right in, ready for the playoffs."

When the first puck was dropped to launch the 1990 Stanley Cup round, the Oilers were far from being considered favorites to regain the championship. Calgary was the choice of most experts because of the Flames' overall balance and the addition of Soviet ace Sergei Makarov. "We didn't mind being in the underdog role at all," said Kevin Lowe. "It took a lot of pressure off our younger guys."

The Oilers did little to enhance their Cup designs in the first four games of the opening round against Winnipeg. With Grant Fuhr sidelined, rookie coach Muckler was forced to employ Bill Ranford—and the backup was pointedly awful in the Game One defeat. With comparative ease, the Jets ran up a three-games-to-one series lead and appeared quite capable of ousting the Oilers in one of the three remaining games.

"We never panicked," Muckler insisted, "and never diverted from our game plan. The important thing was that we got help at the right time from the right people, starting with our kids."

Sure enough, the Oilers reeled off three straight wins to edge Winnipeg and move into the Smythe Division finals against the Kings, who had disposed of them in seven games a year earlier. This time the Oilers took no prisoners. Injured Wayne Gretzky was shown no mercy when he did play—*poof!* just like that—the Kings were overthrown in seven games.

By now the Flames had been unceremoniously wiped out of playoff contention, and the trail to the Cup suddenly loomed as a superhighway for Muckler's men. "We certainly didn't want to get over-confident," said captain Messier, "but we knew that with Calgary out, we had an awfully good shot at the mug."

Chicago was the next challenge just as the Black Hawks had been two years earlier. Having come off a pair of seven-game series against Minnesota and St. Louis respectively, the Hawks appeared ready to be caged. This, however, was not to be as easy as it appeared on paper. Coached by resourceful Mike Keenan, the Black Hawks were not awed by Edmonton. They split the first two games at Northlands Coliseum and then spanked the Oilers, 5–1, at Chicago Stadium to grab a two-one series lead.

Edmonton fans panicked. The Edmonton media panicked. And the Oilers calmly went about the business of retooling the machine. Muckler took a leaf out of the Sather Book of Coaching Surprises and inserted Soviet import Semenov into the lineup for the critical fourth game, although the Russian had never played an NHL game—let alone a critical playoff contest—in his life. "Maybe," theorized Muckler, "it'll shake the boys up a bit."

Did it ever! Messier took command and appeared capable of defeating the Black Hawks singlehandedly. Edmonton not only won Game Four but also wrapped up the series in six matches. Enter the Boston Bruins, a team that had led the entire 21-team league in points and had just come off a persuasive four-game sweep of the Washington Capitals. What's more, the series opened on the cramped Boston Garden ice.

The Bruins dominated the first three periods of Game One, yet they had to rally in order to force overtime. Neither team scored in the first or second sudden-death period nor in 15 minutes of the third. That's when Muckler went for his trump card—ex-Red Wing Klima. The Czech had been benched most of the game and, hence, was well-rested. Within seconds of taking the ice, Klima accepted a Craig MacTavish pass and deposited the puck past goalie Andy Moog.

After Game One, The Kid Line of Graves, Murphy and Martin Gelinas took over and, despite a Bruins' win in Game Three, the finals were dominated by the speedy Oilers. When The Kid Line tired, Messier took over, and when the Captain exhaled, Glenn Anderson stepped forward with a spectacular pass or goal. Goalie Ranford, who had been reviled when the playoffs had begun, was so superior, he was named Conn Smythe (playoffs' most valuable player) Trophy-winner immediately after Edmonton had annexed the Stanley Cup in Game Five at Boston Garden.

In just eleven seasons the Oilers have won five Stanley Cups. This gives them a distinctive mark of excellence, but it also most be noted that there was a character flaw—or flaws, as the case may be—that prevented them from doing what the Islanders, Maple Leafs and two Canadiens teams have done: string three straight Cup years together. *That* is the mark of a true dynasty and until the Edmontonians do that, they must be placed behind the other great ones on our all-time list.

The Toronto Maple Leafs, 1962–67

Punch Imlach's Maple Leafs — 1962–67

For almost three decades, one, and only one, man dominated the Toronto Maple Leafs hockey club. That was its founder, voice, manager, and inspirational leader, Conn Smythe. "The Little Major" was there in the Roarin' Twenties when the Toronto St. Patricks became the Maple Leafs. He was there when The Gashouse Gang of Joe Primeau, Busher Jackson, and Charlie Conacher steered the Leafs to a Stanley Cup win in the midst of The Great Depression, and he was at the helm during the amazing 1942 comeback playoff triumph, as well as the dynasty years when his faithful coach, Hap Day, orchestrated three consecutive Cup wins, the first time such a feat was ever authored in the NHL.

It would be hard to imagine anyone — no matter how strong the personality — casting as distinct an imprint on an organization as Smythe did with his Maple Leafs, but someone did and his name was George (Punch) Imlach.

Until he was hired by the Leafs, Imlach had been a career minor leaguer, first as a player with the Quebec Aces in the then powerful Quebec Senior Hockey League, and later as coach in Quebec and eventually Springfield in the American League. Caustic and commanding, Imlach had a Pattonesque personality that drew attention to him even when he roamed the minors. For a time it appeared that he would be hired to run the Boston Bruins but, instead, it was the Maple Leafs who hired him to resurrect a crumbling franchise.

Imlach was an abrasive genius who originally was signed as assistant general manager, but in no time at all was promoted to general manager, while also assuming the coaching duties. His process of converting a dismal loser into a playoff club would involve a number of clever signings as well as the development of youngsters in the farm system.

Two of Punch's first moves would be so thoroughly insightful he wouldn't have to make another deal to be hailed as a superior talent appraiser. First he signed Johnny Bower, an aging goaltender who seemed to have played his best hockey years ago and who looked too old for the NHL grind. He then made a deal for Allan Stanley, a stay-at-home defenseman who had been booed (literally) out of Madison Square Garden when he was a New York Ranger and then played unspectacularly for both the Chicago Black Hawks and Boston Bruins.

Under Imlach's baton, Bower played a goaltender's symphony. He seemed younger than ever, sharper than when he starred for the Rangers in 1953–54 and so good for so long under Imlach, that he eventually was inducted into the Hockey Hall of Fame.

The Stanley metamorphosis was even more remarkable. While well-schooled in basics, "Big Allan" often seemed lethargic and considerably less than authoritative on the blue line. Imlach was to Stanley, what the genie was to Aladdin. Wearing the royal blue and white of the Maple Leafs, Stanley seemed to glow in Toronto's defensive zone. He became a bodychecking threat, a leader in the locker room and, without question, one of the NHL's best defensemen; so good over the long haul that he, too, was named to the Hockey Hall of Fame.

Stanley would team with rugged Tim Horton and form one of the finest defensive duets in the NHL. "Allan," said Imlach, "went on to play more than six hundred games for Toronto in the next ten years, as honest and dependable a hockey player as a coach could hope for."

Imlach, who stressed defense above all aspects of the game, was blessed with two young blueliners who graduated from the Leafs' Junior club, the Toronto Marlboros. They had almost instant impact. Carl Brewer and Bob Baun were to Imlach's Leafs, what Gus Mortson and Jim Thomson had been to coach Hap Days's 1947, 1948, and 1949 Stanley Cup-winners; a pair of young, robust exuberant skaters who boasted innumerable skills.

Never was the genius of Imlach more evident than in his handling of Leonard (Red) Kelly, a defenseman who had carved out a brilliant career with the Detroit Red Wings but who had fallen into the doghouse of Jack Adams, the Motor City hockey boss. Like Bower and Stanley, Kelly seemed stuck in an irreversible tailspin when Punch obtained him from Detroit. That, in and of itself, was not at all remarkable, but it was Imlach's following decision that startled the hockey world: he converted the defenseman Kelly into a center and Red became an instant star up front.

More than anything, Punch infused a spirit into the previously lifeless Leafs. Before he had been able to assemble all the necessary parts, he nonetheless got the message across that the word surrender was not in his vocabulary. This was demonstrated late in the 1958–59 season when the Leafs pulled off the single greatest comeback in the homestretch of any NHL campaign. With two weeks left in the schedule, Toronto trailed the Rangers by *nine points*. On the final night, Imlach steered his club past New York!

Punch discovered that it was one thing to make the playoffs and yet another to win the Stanley Cup. In 1961, the Black Hawks took the mug with aces such as Bobby (The Golden Jet) Hull, Stan Mikita, and Glenn Hall. Imlach might not have been able to match Chicago, luminary for luminary, but he did boast a couple of glittering personalities of his own, the most noticeable being Frank (Big M) Mahovlich, a huge left wing with enormous strides and a shot that occasionally sent enemy goaltenders reeling backwards into their nets.

The Big M flowered into a superstar just as the Maple Leafs were making their first serious bid for the Stanley Cup. Kelly was his center, and an efficient, hard-checking forward named Bob Nevin (surely, one of the most underrated players of the 1960s) patrolled the right side.

No less effective was smallish center Dave Keon whose speed reminded some oldtimers of the legendary Howie Morenz. Keon centered for diligent Dick Duff, with captain George Armstrong on the right side. Another line featured Bob Pulford, who came along with Baun and Brewer, flanking Bert Olmstead and Eddie Shack.

If ever there was a superb blend of scorers, checkers, tenacious skaters, and sore losers this was it. From top to bottom and bottom to top there was not a weak link in the chain. For example, the defense was so formidable that a respected blue liner such as Al Arbour never could break into the lineup on a regular basis. Other excellent reserves included playmaking Billy Harris; versatile Ron Stewart, who could double on defense but essentially was a hard-checking forward; and big Ed Litzenberger who had starred for the Black Hawks' Stanley Cup-winners in 1961.

Once veterans such as Bower, Stanley, and Olmstead had established that they still were in mint condition, Imlach was ready to roll; and roll he did. Pacing behind the bench, his bald pate topped by the ubiquitous fedora, Imlach stopped the Black Hawks in their bid for a second-straight Stanley Cup in the spring of 1962.

The Cup-winning game was a classic and revealed the comeback qualities that would be a hallmark of Punch's teams. Bobby Hull had broken a scoreless tie with a dynamic goal that had the Chicago Stadium rafters shaking from the crowd thunder. It was in the third period and the home club seemed destined to roll over the Leafs. But a delay caused by debris-throwers enabled Toronto to regroup. In no time at all, the Leafs tied the score and then put the winner past Glenn Hall for Imlach's first Stanley Cup triumph. It was the start of something big; very big!

Employing the same core, Imlach produced another Cup champion a year later, and in most convincing fashion. First, Toronto routed Montreal four games to one and then repeated the feat against Detroit. In the spring of 1964 the scenario was almost the same; only the length of time needed for the *coup de grace* was different. A full seven games was required to dispose of Montreal in the semifinals and then seven to defeat Detroit for The Cup.

Three Stanley Cups in succession are credentials enough for a ticket to the all-time great team list. But how high should the Imlach Leafs be rated? To put them in better perspective, one must also consider their performance during the regular season. In 1961–62, Toronto finished a distant second to

Montreal. In 1962–63, the Leafs were first, but only one point ahead of the runner-up Black Hawks. Prior to the third Cup, Imlach could manage only a third-place spot, seven points behind league-leading Montreal.

Like Hap Day before him, Imlach hoped to arrange a skein of four consecutive Cups. The difficulty was with Punch, himself. He had carried his disciplinary measures too far and so antagonized some stars that they ceased to be effective. In the 1965 semifinal round, Montreal defeated Toronto four games to two and the streak was over.

Nevertheless, Imlach the manager wheeled and dealed enough in the next two years to produce one more winning combination — and a Stanley Cup in 1967, the final playoff year before expansion. The total was four Stanley Cups between 1962 and 1967, a commendable performance for Punch.

The club cannot be placed in the top echelon because of its regular season failures; its inability to produce a true superstar other than Mahovlich, and, ironically, Imlach's destructive behavior when the team still was riding high. This is hardly meant as criticism, but rather an assessment of what was one of the more interesting collection of athletes seen in the NHL, and certainly one of the better clubs.

Contemporary Toronto Maple Leafs fans know the feeling of rooting depression better than most hockey followers. More than two decades have passed since a Stanley Cup has graced the arena at Carlton and Church Streets, and in that time the club's fortunes have slipped from bad to worse to hopeless.

At times like these, supporters of the Royal Blue and White need only hark back to the 1950s for a lesson in rebuilding a decrepit franchise into a champion. Following the Stanley Cup win in 1951, and subsequent plane crash death of playoff hero Bill Barilko, the Leafs fell into an abject state of disrepair in the years that followed.

They were rescued by one, and only one, man. George (Punch) Imlach, rebuilt the club slowly and painstakingly, and in the process made some of the most dramatic — and in the case of Red Kelly — revolutionary moves imaginable.

A persnickety type, who had spent his entire playing career in the minors, Imlach blended some good, old-fashioned luck with adroit player moves and the result was the revitalization of a team that could prove to be a beacon for the present Toronto ownership. Unfortunately, there is no Imlach around today.

He was in the right place at the right time. Although the Leafs were starting the 1958–59 season with most of the skaters who had finished last the year before, Imlach inherited a spate of promising youngsters, some of whom would climb the ladder to All-Star status. On defense there were Carl Brewer, a swift skater and nasty defender, and Bobby Baun, a chunk of concrete who loved to hit. On the attack, Frank "the Big M" Mahovlich showed enough stickhandling and shooting talents — not to mention enormous size — to compel raves from friends and foes alike. Other effective forwards were Bob Pulford, Dick Duff, Bill Harris, and Bert Olmstead, an irascible veteran who had played for Montreal's championship teams.

Goaltending was the weak underbelly of the Maple Leafs hockey club before Imlach arrived. When the club finished last in 1957–58, Ed Chadwick was goaltender in all 70 games and finished the season with a 3.23 goals against average, worst of all the league regulars. Billy Reay, Imlach's predecessor behind the Leaf bench, scouted the minors for a replacement.

Reay's first choice was Al Rollins, who had starred for the last Leaf Cup-winner. Rollins was playing for Calgary in the Western League, but he played poorly on the night Reay was scouting him and lost his return ticket to the NHL. The second choice was Johnny Bower, a veteran who had bounced around the minors for years and had a brief stint (1953–54) with the New York Rangers before returning to the bushes.

Cynical about past treatment and uncertain about his NHL future, Bower rejected Reay's first offer. "I was happy in Cleveland," he said. "I'd had my fling at the NHL, and besides, I didn't think I could help Toronto."

Another consideration was that he was almost 34 years old, ancient for a goaltender in those days. Then something changed Bower's mind, and he decided to sign with the Leafs. It was the best break Imlach ever received. Unfortunately for Reay, he soon was fired, and he never received full credit for landing Bower in the first place.

Bower played 39 games during the 1958–59 season, and Chadwick was in the nets for 31 contests. Bower outgoaled his teammate 2.74 to 3.00. There no longer was a question as to who would be the first-string Toronto goalie.

Bower was a glutton for punishment, especially during practice sessions, during which he performed as diligently as the rawest of rookies. "I've always had to work hard," Bower explained. "I don't know any other way to play the game."

Hard work also was Imlach's story, and the two blended together ideally, which was more than could be said for the rest of the Toronto team. They struggled through more than three-quarters of the 1958–59 season in what appeared to be a fruitless pursuit of the fourth-place Rangers.

With only two weeks remaining on the schedule, New York and Toronto played a home-and-home series, starting on a Saturday night at Maple Leaf Gardens. A Rangers victory in either game would virtually clinch a playoff berth for the New Yorkers, but Imlach would have none of that. While the press and radio and television commentators had all but conceded the fourth spot to New York, Imlach kept telling his players they *could* catch the Rangers. He told the media that they *would* catch the Rangers and went to work proving that he was right.

In the first of the home-and-home series of games, Toronto blasted New York 5–0. The next day, at Madison Square Garden, goalies Bower for the Leafs and Gump Worsley for the Rangers were shaky, as the lead bounced back and forth until the Rangers tied the match at 5–5 with less than five minutes remaining. A draw would have been as welcome as a win for the staggering New York sextet, but the Leafs pressed on.

At last the persistent Pulford took a pass from Olmstead and fired a long, seemingly impossible, shot at Worsley. It flew directly over the goaltender's arm, glove, and leg pad. Toronto won the game 6–5. And they never stopped winning after that. With Imlach exhorting them, the Leafs kept on winning until they reached the final night of the season only one point behind the Rangers.

If coach Phil Watson's Rangers won their game at Madison Square Garden against the Montreal Canadiens, it was all over. But if the Rangers lost, the Leafs could climb into fourth by beating the Red Wings at Olympia Stadium in Detroit.

The staggering Rangers just didn't have it. They scored the first goal of the game early in the opening period and got another late in the last period. The Canadiens scored four against Worsley and won the game 4–2. It was up to Imlach and his troops.

The Leafs wobbled, straightened themselves out, staggered again, and finally put everything together in the third period, on goals by Dick Duff and Billy Harris to beat Detroit, 6–4. Imlach and his skaters had performed a miracle, and the first root in the new Maple Leaf dynasty was planted.

Winning the Stanley Cup was another story. Twice, in 1959 and 1960, the Leafs reached the finals, and twice they were eliminated. In 1961 they were knocked off in the semifinals. But Imlach knew he was working on the right combination, and the key was Red Kelly.

Long an All-Star defenseman with the Red Wings, Kelly fell into the bad graces of Detroit manager Jack Adams during the 1959–60 season. At first, Adams tried to peddle Kelly and Billy McNeill to the Rangers for Bill Gadsby and Eddie Shack, but Kelly refused to report to New York and was suspended. Imlach quietly sought out Kelly and learned that Red would be willing to play for Toronto. But Punch didn't want him to play defense — he had bigger plans.

"I knew Kelly could help us," said Imlach in *Hockey Is a Battle*. "My big aim at the time was to build a team for one function: to beat the Canadiens. To do that we had to be more powerful at center. Red had played a little left wing for Detroit from time to time. I knew how well he skated, checked, made plays, and so on. I figured he could play center and that he was one guy I could put out against Jean Beliveau and make Beliveau work for any goals he got."

Although the league raised some objections about the deal, Imlach prevailed. Kelly did everything Imlach had asked of him, including bringing the Stanley Cup back to Toronto.

According to Imlach, the Leafs actually should have won the Cup in 1961. Kelly had become a splendid center, the defense was near-perfect, and Bower was en route to the Vézina Trophy as the league's best goalie. In fact, Toronto held a six-point first place lead over Montreal on February 12, 1961.

That night the Leafs were playing the Red Wings in Detroit. It was a rough game and a close one. Toronto was ahead 3–2 in the third period, when Detroit defenseman Howie Young watched Bower skate to the side of his net to clear the puck. Normally goaltenders are not considered fair game for bodychecks, but the rule is unofficial and, in any case, Howie Young was not much for the rulebook in those days. He charged Bower, crashing him backward to the ice. Johnny finished the game, but he was badly hurt and missed the next five critical weeks of the season. Montreal came on strong and edged the Leafs out for first place by a single point.

"I've always thought if Bower hadn't been hurt by Young we would have been so far ahead by the last week of the season that nobody could have caught us. And nobody would have stopped us in the playoffs," said Imlach.

The Detroit Red Wings torpedoed the Leafs in the 1961 Stanley Cup semifinals, but Toronto's injury list included Bower, Shack, and Olmstead. "To my mind," Imlach insisted, "we had the best team in hockey that year."

Maybe he did, maybe he didn't. But that year, Imlach did have the best left wing in Frank Mahovlich. With his long, sweeping strides, the Big M was virtually unstoppable. After 1961, Mahovlich never was the same again. According to Imlach, the trouble was that Mahovlich lost his aggressiveness. In the 1960–61 season, Mahovlich did things he never repeated — he'd skate right over a defenseman if he couldn't skate around him. Mahovlich, in that season, was precisely what the beauty of hockey is all about. The same could be said for Johnny Bower in goal.

"The big guys puts 'em in, and the old guy kicks 'em out," said an admiring Jack Adams.

Bower wasn't the only old guy on the team. A cornerstone of the Imlach philosophy had it that a good veteran will often do the job better than a good young player. As a result, Imlach entrusted his fortunes to such "pappy guys" as Allan Stanley, George Armstrong, Ed Litzenberger, Olmstead, and Kelly. Injuries stalled the Leafs' first-place drive (they finished second behind Montreal by 13 points), but Imlach had everything in order for the big playoff drive.

Toronto's first-round opponent, the Rangers, gave the Leafs a run for their money. The series was tied two games apiece when Toronto got the decisive edge on a bizarre overtime goal against, of all people, Gump Worsley.

The teams had been deadlocked 2–2 after regulation time, and neither club scored in the first sudden-death overtime. Just past the four-minute mark of the second overtime, the Leafs swarmed to the attack. A shot was hurled at Worsley, who fell to the ice and made the save. It was a peculiar kind of save: Gump was flat on his back, and he *knew* that the puck was somewhere beneath him. But he wasn't sure where.

Expecting that the referee would whistle a time-out, Worsley leaned forward, exposing the puck directly under his neck. At that very moment, Red Kelly of the Leafs skated by and simply pushed the uncovered rubber into the net. The referee had not blown his whistle, and Toronto had the goal — and the game! The broken-hearted Rangers were no match in the next game. They bowed out, 7–1 losers.

While this was going on, the Chicago Black Hawks, a strong third-place club, stung the first-place Canadiens in a bruising six-game semifinal round. Thus Chicago came head-on with Imlach's Maple Leafs.

Paced by Bobby Hull and Stan Mikita, Chicago displayed as withering an attack as any club in the NHL, but Johnny Bower was equal to the occasion. The Leafs won the first two games by 4–1 and 3–2 scores at home. The Black Hawks breathed fire on their noisy Chicago Stadium ice and outscored the Leafs 3–0 in the third game.

Chicago was hot. In the fourth game, one of Bobby Hull's big shots sent Bower sprawling. Johnny was hurt, and he had to be replaced by goalie Don Simmons, who gave up three goals in a 4–1 losing cause. A lot of critics thought the Leafs were dead at this point. They noticed how Chicago's heavy hitters seemed to bash some of the smaller Toronto skaters with impunity, and they also took into account the momentum generated by Hull and Mikita.

But Imlach's pros were not impressed with momentum, and they showed it by routing Chicago 8–4 in the fifth game. Simmons played it tough in goal, and Bert Olmstead returned to the lineup after being sidelined for six weeks. Both were outstanding, convincing Imlach that there's nothing like a "pappy guy" when it comes to winning big hockey games.

Few better hockey games have been played than the sixth match of the 1962 Chicago-Toronto final in the Windy City. Goalies Glenn Hall for Chicago and Don Simmons for the Leafs extended themselves beyond all required limits, and two periods elapsed without a goal.

Into the third period they raced until Bobby Hull finally broke the ice past the mid-point in the period. The 20,000 fans jamming the old building on West Madison Street nearly tore it apart. Confetti, playing cards, beer cans, and even ink bottles poured down on the blotched ice in a seemingly endless flow of debris.

When the storm finally ended, more than ten minutes were required for workmen to clear the ice. Unfortunately for the Black Hawks, the zany demonstration by their fans did more damage to them than the Maple Leafs' attack. The debris-throwing disrupted the Black Hawks' surge, and the hiatus cooled down what had been a very hot hockey team.

By the time play had resumed, the Black Hawks were flat. In no time at all Bob Nevin, the Toronto right wing, broke through the Chicago defenses and beat Hall to tie the game once more. The din turned to a funeral quiet, as if the 20,000 spectators knew what soon was to come.

And it came.

Defenseman Tim Horton wound up on his own end and began trading passes with Toronto forwards as the attack gained speed at his blue line, the center red line, and, ultimately, the Chicago blue line. Regaining the rubber, Horton caught smallish wingman Dick Duff busting in on Hall. Duff eluded the panicking Chicago defense, nabbed the pass, and beat Hall.

The Black Hawks were stunned to the core and helpless, as their death knell was counted off on the clock above. Punch Imlach's troops had won the Stanley Cup for Toronto for the first time since 1951.

Everyone on the Toronto bench went berserk, including the injured players in civvies. They pounded each other on the back and raced toward the end of the building and down the stairway leading to the visitors' dressing room. One by one, champagne bottles popped as the young Leafs hooted with joy. One of them, defenseman Brewer, crawled around on the floor screaming with delight.

The pappy guys were exhausted and collapsed on their benches. When Imlach stopped to pump veteran winger Olmstead's hand, he was too tired to get up. "It's been a long haul, Punch," he said.

That it was, but it was well worth the effort. Punch at first declined the offer of a City Hall reception. But when the team returned home, he realized that it was more than worth the effort when an enormous throng jammed downtown Toronto to hail the champions a few days later.

"It hit me very hard. And it hit the team as well. I was glad we'd done it, when it seemed to mean so much to the people," said Imlach.

Imlach and his shock troops were on the top of the hockey world, and they would remain there for several glorious seasons. No season would stand out more than 1962–63, when they took it all. It wasn't easy for Punch. As gratified as he was with the work of old-timers such as Olmstead, he still had an NHL draft to contend with. Finally, he decided to leave his redoubtable left wing unprotected. To Punch's chagrin, Olmstead was immediately selected by the Rangers, and just as quickly he retired from the NHL.

Meanwhile, Punch pulled off one major trade, sending four young minor leaguers to Eddie Shore's Springfield club for defenseman Kent Douglas, one of the most gifted backliners in the minors. The wisdom of that move was underscored months later when Douglas was voted the NHL's Rookie of the Year.

The 1962–63 season opened and closed with a bang for the Maple Leafs. Explosion number one occurred in October when Chicago Black Hawks owner Jim Norris offered the Maple Leafs $1 million in a straight cash bid for Frank Mahovlich.

Several cynical reporters have charged that the "deal" was a ploy to push baseball off the sports pages. Others have insisted that Norris was not quite sober at the time of the discussions. However, Imlach has maintained that the deal was on the level, and Black Hawks manager Tommy Ivan insisted that Norris knew exactly what he was doing.

Whatever the case, Norris's offer was refused. For one thing, the Leafs, who sold out their building for every game, did not need the money. For another, Mahovlich was considered too valuable a property to exchange for Jim Norris's bankroll, no matter how big. Imlach's theory had it that a million-dollar check could not score goals for him, and he was right.

Mahovlich proved Imlach's point by scoring 36 goals and 73 points. One of those goals was considered, at least by Imlach, as the turning point of the big season for Toronto. When the Black Hawks visited Maple Leaf Gardens, Toronto was in third place, nine points behind first-place Chicago with four weeks remaining in the season.

The Big M scored in the first period and sent the Leafs winging on to a 6–3 triumph. Against the Rangers at Madison Square Garden, he broke up a tie game with only 62 seconds remaining to give the Leafs another two points. Meanwhile, the Black Hawks were staggering, and within two weeks the teams were tied for first place. By then it was generally agreed that nobody would stop Imlach's big blue machine, least of all the Black Hawks. Toronto clobbered the Hawks 3–0 and went eight games without a loss, winning six and tying two. Toronto clinched first place and the Prince of Wales Trophy when little Dave Keon slipped home a shot with eight seconds to go in a game against the Canadiens. It gave the Leafs a tie against Montreal and the point required for the top.

Imlach's grand plan to stop the Canadiens was devised. He always maintained that he wanted to beat them in the *finals* for the Stanley Cup, but in 1963 he was confronted by Montreal in the semifinal round.

Just about everything worked out according to the blueprints. Punch had Red Kelly handy to take care of Canadien captain Jean Beliveau, and Beliveau scored only two goals in the five games. His favorite athlete, Johnny Bower, played remarkably agile goal, and the leafs disposed of Montreal in five games, highlighted by Bower's 5–0 shutout in the final contest.

The final round was Toronto vs. Detroit. Although the Red Wings boasted such aces as Gordie Howe, Norm Ullman, and Alex Delvecchio, and Terry Sawchuk in goal, they fell apart in front of Imlach's skaters.

Detroit managed only one victory — 3–2 at home in the third test — and headed for the exit on April 18 when the Leafs clinched the Stanley Cup with a 3–1 triumph before the home crowd. Once again, Imlach led a ticker-tape parade through downtown Toronto, but it was the first time he did so with the Prince of Wales Trophy and the Stanley Cup.

Nobody would have dreamed it, but Punch had reached the crest. Ever so slightly — so slightly that it was almost not discernable at first — he was beginning a long road that would lead him out of Toronto.

Several factors contributed to the decline and fall of Imlach's dynasty. For one, a few of his stalwarts had become jaded. Red Kelly had run for the Canadian Parliament and won, and he was carrying the burdensome load of playing a full NHL schedule and tending to his political duties. Many observers believe that the dual assignments impaired his hockey-playing ability.

For another, Frank Mahovlich's productivity and enthusiasm waned, and his relationship with Imlach began a long, but steady deterioration. Aces of other years — Kent Douglas, Dick Duff, Bob Nevin, and Ed Litzenberger — all had difficulties of one kind and another. Imlach saw the handwriting on the wall and decided to make a major deal.

On February 21, 1964, Imlach finally concluded a stunning trade with the New York Rangers. He sent Dick Duff and Bob Nevin, both regulars, minor leaguers Bill Collins and Arnie Brown, and junior ace Rod Seiling to the Rangers in exchange for Andy Bathgate, the Rangers high scorer, and Don McKenney, a forward in the twilight of his career.

In terms of the short-range goals, Imlach did well. Bathgate gave new oomph to the Maple Leafs attack, and McKenney was an asset in the home stretch. Toronto finished third.

Once again Punch had genius written all over him. Bathgate fit neatly on the line with Red Kelly and Frank Mahovlich, and McKenney seemed like the ideal skater to complement Dave Keon and George Armstrong. They excelled in the seven-game opening round victory over Montreal, and they reached new limits of exertion during the finals against an aroused Detroit sextet, which at one point led the series 3–2.

One of hockey's most dramatic moments occurred in the sixth game. Defenseman Bobby Baun broke a bone in his leg, but somehow he managed to have the doctor fix him with pain-killer so that he could play in the sudden-death overtime. Baun completed the amazing script by scoring the winner at 1:43 of the first overtime session!

Bathgate confirmed Imlach's faith in him by scoring the lead goal in the seventh match. Detroit desperately counterattacked, but Bower was, as his nickname suggested, like a China wall. The Leafs went on to score three more times and win the Stanley Cup for the third straight year.

One might imagine that such an uplifting *dénouement* would stir the spirits of the Maple Leafs and inspire another march on first place in the 1964–65 season. But quite the opposite developed. Resentment against Imlach's rigorous practices began brewing early in the season, and soon after the Leafs were eliminated from the semifinal round of the playoffs, the friction burst into print.

Surprisingly, the anti-Imlach brigade was led by none other than Bathgate, the hero of April, 1964. "There's a limit to an athlete's endurance," Bathgate said. "Imlach pushed a few of the players past that limit physically and mentally."

Imlach's answer was right to the point. "The older you get, the harder you work," he said.

Punch also made certain that Bathgate wasn't around his dressing room anymore. The gifted right wing was traded to Detroit in May, 1965, as part of a large package of skaters. Bathgate's Red Wings finished fourth, and Imlach's Leafs were third. Neither team won the Cup. A year later the Leafs were third again, and Detroit finished fifth.

However, third place was a rather deceptive finish in terms of the upheavals that cracked the foundations of the Leaf team. Imlach seemed to be losing rapport with more and more players. Even young stalwarts such as Brian Conacher were displeased with Punch.

"While the team was winning under its own steam," said Conacher in *Hockey in Canada*, "they were prepared to put up with Punch's idiosyncrasies and excessive training methods, as long as it didn't threaten the structure that they had as a team. However, by the time I joined the team, the Leafs were becoming more vocal as to the way they were being treated, or not treated.

"What the Leafs needed was a coach who could lead the team rather than threaten it. It seemed as far as Punch was concerned, there was no room for reasoning; everything was black or white. You were either with him or against him. And if you were against him, as far as he could see, you weren't good for the team. I think Punch had fear and respect confused."

Conacher was not far off the mark. At one point during the season, Toronto lost ten consecutive games, and Imlach was admitted to the hospital with ulcer problems. His replacement, King Clancy, used a looser approach to training and practice, and soon the Leafs were winning again. They clinched a playoff berth in March, 1967.

Imlach returned and enjoyed his last moments of genuine glory. Chicago provided the opposition in the first round, and it was a dandy. After four games, the evenly matched clubs were tied at two apiece with the fifth game in Chicago Stadium. Punch started Bower in goal and had the veteran Terry Sawchuk available for emergency duty.

The emergency occurred early. Bower was hurt, and Sawchuk skated out between the pipes. Within minutes, Bobby Hull of the Black Hawks tested him with a rising slapshot that smashed against the goalie's shoulder. Sawchuk was down for the count and, at best, appeared incapable of finishing the game. But since Toronto had no other goalies, Sawchuk had to go on — and he did.

"From that moment on," said Brian Conacher, who skated in front of Sawchuk that night, "I saw the greatest goaltending exhibition that I had ever seen take place. Sawchuk was invincible. Time and again he robbed the Hawks on shots that looked like sure goals."

The Leafs won the game 4–2 and moved up to the finals with a 3–1 decision at Maple Leaf Gardens.

Imlach, who always felt gratified at the prospect of challenging the Canadiens in the finals, got his wish in April, 1967. Ironically, it was Conacher whom Imlach had been grooming to replace Red Kelly, who teamed up *with* Kelly to produce a key goal in the fifth game of the series, which was tied at 2–2.

Centering for Ron Ellis and Conacher, Kelly crossed the Montreal blue line flanked by his mates. Ellis and Conacher zeroed in on the net, while Kelly stickhandled around the Canadiens near the blue line. At last, Red released the shot, which was blocked by goalie Vachon, but fell out and on to Conacher's stick. In a split second the puck was behind Vachon.

"It was such a perfect scoring play because of the way Kelly had played it," said Conacher. Brian's goal was the winner in a 4–1 victory. In the sixth game, at Maple leaf Gardens, Imlach's shock troops held fast and emerged with a 3–1 win and another Stanley Cup.

Perhaps clouded by the heady nectar of victory, Imlach overlooked the internal problems on his hockey club. It wasn't until the 1967–68 season that dissension really ripped the Maple Leafs apart. They finished fifth, out of the playoffs for the first time since the Imlach stewardship. A year later, during a brief renaissance, they climbed to fourth, but they were eliminated in the Stanley Cup quarterfinals.

The Imlach era in Toronto ended minutes after the final game, when Maple Leafs President Stafford Smythe walked into the dressing room and told Punch Imlach that he had been fired.

The Detroit Red Wings, 1950–55

The Production Line in High Gear, Red Wings 1950–55

It was clear as soon as the soldiers returned home from Europe and the Far East in 1945, that the most successful teams in the post-war era would be those with the most extensive farm systems. With that in mind, Detroit Red Wings' general manager Jack Adams — with the complete cooperation of the club's multi-millionaire owner Jim Norris — laid out an elaborate network of teams on the minor league, senior amateur, and junior levels.

"We wanted to cover all bases," said Adams, "and that way bring in the best possible prospects. Within a couple of years after the war, the results were coming in and they were very good."

The first tangible evidence of success developed in 1948–49, when the Detroiters ran away with the regular season schedule, finishing a comfortable nine points ahead of the Boston Bruins. The euphoria was short-lived, however. Toronto wiped out the Red Wings in a four-straight final series, forcing Adams to regroup.

He tinkered here and there and in 1949–50, had assembled one of the most powerful teams on record. The Production Line of Gordie Howe, Ted Lindsay, and Sid Abel, in the view of some critics, was the single greatest offensive unit in NHL history. The defense featured powerful Black Jack Stewart, Leo Reise, Jr., and one of the world's best puck-rushing defensemen, Leonard (Red) Kelly. The goaltender in 1949–50 was young veteran, Harry (Applecheeks) Lumley.

It wasn't easy, but the Red Wings went on to win The Stanley Cup in April 1950, although the Rangers forced the final series to seven games and into double overtime before a third-stringer named Pete Babando scored the winner.

At this point, the Red Wings were on the threshhold of a dynasty, and by all rights should have won about three or four Stanley Cups in a row. The club ripened in 1950–51 with the addition of Terry Sawchuk in goal. Nevertheless, the Wings were beaten in a six-game opening round playoff with the Canadiens, and this defeat proved to be a major embarrassment to the team.

The Wings recovered and flexed their muscles the following year, winning the playoffs in eight straight games. Sawchuk produced four shutouts, and in only one game did he give up more than a single goal. "As great as they were, the Red Wings seemed to have a flaw," said defenseman Larry Zeidel, who played for them in the early 1950s and later against them. "Some teams were able to find a weakness and knock them off, even in the best of times."

So it was in the 1953 playoffs. An inferior Bruins club was able to get outstanding defensive checking from ancient Woody Dumart and clutch scoring from Jack McIntyre, to beat Detroit four games to two in the opening round. The inimitable Gordie Howe was reduced to mediocrity and Sawchuk was eminently vulnerable; at least then.

Still, the Red Wings were too good to be kept down for very long. They won the Cup again in 1954 and 1955 and almost made it three in a row in 1956 but, by now, the Canadiens were coming on strong and erased Detroit's hopes with a four-games-to-one win in the finals.

Had Detroit been able to win a Stanley Cup in either 1951 or 1953, they could very well have made the very top of the list. Still, four Cups (1950, 1952, 1954, 1955) in six years is as good as the Edmonton Oilers could do in the 1980s. The Red Wings dominated the regular season, finishing first 6 consecutive years. That, coupled with the four Cups, is enough to associate that club with *la creme de la creme* of any era.

The Detroit Red Wings probably would not have become what some critics have labeled hockey's greatest team if it were not for the persistence of a 12-year-old lad in the city of Saskatoon, Saskatchewan.

Tall, raw-boned Gordon Howe had been designated by his teacher, R.H. Tricky, at the King George public school to play goal for the King George varsity. Young Howe was an awkward skater, seemingly too clumsy to be an effective forward, but he was a rather steady and cool customer between the pipes.

"We won the city championship that year," said Howe, "but I didn't like playing goal. It was too cold standing there doing nothing on an open-air rink with the temperature below zero. And besides, I wanted to *score* goals, not stop them. Mr. Tricky told me I should stick to being a goalie, that if I ever left the nets I'd never get out of Saskatoon as a hockey player."

Howe, the fourth oldest of nine children, considered his teacher's advice and rejected it. Finally he was reassigned to a defense position, and a year later he skated with enough polish to lead his school once again to a city championship. In 1942 he won an audition with the Saskatoon Lions amateur team, *at right wing*. Howe excelled again and paced his team to the provincial midget championship.

Unlike defense work and goaltending, playing on the right side gave Howe a feeling of comfort. His skating had improved to the extent that he no longer could be outdistanced or knocked off his feet by opponents. In 1943, Gordie Howe was a diamond in the rough, and the first to realize his potential was a scout for the New York Rangers, who invited the youngster to the Ranger hockey school at Winnipeg at the close of the season.

Unfortunately for the Rangers, their camp director was less perceptive than the Saskatoon scout. Virtually ignored, Gordie finally approached the head counselor and asked for an appraisal of his talent. The reply has gone down in Rangers history as the classic blunder in the club's rich and long history.

"You're not doing too good," he said. "In fact, you'd better pack for home. You'll never be a major leaguer."

The words stung, and the prediction remained stuck in Howe's mind throughout the summer. If he was to do nothing else in his life, he would prove that the Rangers had made a mistake. In 1944, Gordie won an invitation to the Red Wings training base at Windsor, Ontario. Jack Adams, the vitriolic manager of the Red Wings, immediately noticed the big fellow and summoned his aide, Tommy Ivan. Adams was particularly impressed with the tall kid's ability to shoot the puck from both his right and left side with consummate ease. Even the major leaguers couldn't do that.

"Who's the big kid?" Adams asked Ivan. "The kid who can shoot 'em either way?"

Surprised by the question, Ivan paused momentarily. "I don't know," he replied. "There are so many kids here I've forgotten just who he is." Ivan walked over to the sideboards and waved to Howe, who was skating at another end of the rink. Howe immediately skated over to Ivan.

"What's your name son?" Ivan asked.

Gordie was embarrassed because he realized that left winger Syd Howe, one of the best Detroit Red Wings players in the team's history, was on the ice at the time.

Gordie blurted, "Howe. But I'm not related to that guy over there." At this point Adams moved in on the conversation. He knew he had a winner, but he realized that the player was still young. "You're doin' all right, sonny," said the crusty boss. "I like your style. Just keep on working like that, and you'll be up with the Red Wings one of these days."

Gordie Howe played his first National Hockey League game at Detroit's Olympia Stadium on October 16, 1946. The Red Wings had not won the Stanley Cup since 1943 and had not known a dynasty since 1937, when they won the second of two Stanley Cup championships. They were, in fact, rebuilding when Howe was promoted to the team. Although the insightful Adams probably knew it at the time, he said nothing about Howe's being the cornerstone of what was to be Detroit's mightiest dynasty.

When Howe joined the Red Wings for the 1946–47 season, having been promoted from Omaha, the big teams in the National Hockey League were the Montreal Canadiens and the Toronto Maple Leafs. The dominant player was Montreal's Rocket Richard. On Detroit's first road trip during his rookie season, Howe collided with Richard during a game at the Montreal Forum. Richard swung, and Howe ducked. Then Gordie swung at Richard and caught him flush on the jaw. The Rocket toppled to the ice, but he got to his feet within a few seconds, more embarrassed than hurt. But as he got up, Richard heard Abel shout at him, "That'll teach you not to fool with our rookies, you phony Frenchman." Richard promptly skated over to Abel, threw a punch, and broke Abel's nose in three places.

It would be nice to say that Howe achieved instant stardom, but he did not. True, Howe scored a goal in his first NHL game, beating Turk Broda of the Maple Leafs. "The puck was lying loose ten feet from the net," Howe says of his first goal. "I just slapped it in." He retrieved the puck and took it home to his family. But he notched only 6 more goals that season and added 15 assists, for a total of 22 points.

Even as a rookie of 18, however, Howe betrayed flashes of brilliance that marked him for future greatness. There was, for example, the game against Boston in which Howe outfoxed the veteran defenseman Dit Clapper, whose NHL longevity record was later broken by Howe. As Clapper went to check him, Howe changed hands on his stick and, with his body between Clapper and the puck, got off a clean shot on the net. "I think," Ted Lindsay has remarked, "that that's when Dit decided he'd quit hockey."

"What helps you on stickhandling," Howe says, "is that when you're a kid, you play with a tennis ball. There was a family in Saskatoon that had a rink with sideboards between the house and the barn. We'd go all day there with a tennis ball, 15 guys to a side, and when the ball got frozen, we'd go over and knock on the window of the house. The lady would open the window, we'd throw in the frozen ball, and she'd throw out the other one. That way you learn to stickhandle and pass without looking at the puck or where you're going to pass it. If you kept your eyes on the puck, you'd end up in the rafters. You take glances at it, but you know it's there by the feel."

Detroit finished fourth during Howe's rookie season and lost in five games to Toronto in the first round of the Stanley Cup playoffs. Against the Maple Leafs,

Howe failed to pick up a goal or an assist, but he did accumulate 18 minutes in penalties, battling continually with Toronto rookie Howie Meeker and assorted other Leafs.

Gordie showed a marked improvement during his second season with the Wings. He netted 16 goals and added 28 assists, for a total of 44 points in 60 games. The Red Wings wound up in second place, but bowed to the Maple Leafs in the finals of the Stanley Cup competition.

The following year, Howe missed 20 games because of torn cartilage in his right knee. The fact that the torn cartilage was one of the few injuries he has sustained is also part of the amazing Gordie Howe story.

Hockey, like football, is basically a contact sport. Of the two, hockey is probably the more dangerous, simply because NHL players skate at speeds up to 25 miles an hour. When two players collide on ice, chances are that one — and sometimes both — will suffer an injury, ranging anywhere from a minor cut to a fractured skull.

The hard rubber puck also poses a danger, particularly when it comes off a stick at 100 miles an hour, and skates can cause injuries, especially during pileups in front of the net. And sticks can become lethal weapons, sometimes intentionally and sometimes not. Several years ago, for example, Detroit's defenseman Doug Barkley was the victim of a near-fatal accident. He lost an eye after being hit by the sharp edge of a stick blade.

There were reasons for Howe's seeming immunity to really serious injury: his brute strength, his magnificent reflexes, and his great instinct for avoiding dangerous situations. Another, and perhaps more important, reason was Howe's habit of keeping himself in top condition during the off-season as well as in season. For instance, he does not smoke and never has.

"Early in my career," Howe explains, "my coach told me it wouldn't do me any good to smoke cigarettes, so I never tried them. All I know is that when I see a boy smoking, I know he's either a little shot trying to be a big shot, or he's gone over to the social side and doesn't want to be a hockey player."

The most bizarre of Howe's injuries occurred at the Montreal Forum in 1961. There was a face-off in the Detroit end, and Howe was the Red Wing involved in it. Just before the puck was dropped, defenseman Marcel Pronovost skated over to Howe and asked him to step aside when the puck went down the ice. Pronovost wanted a clear shot at a Montreal player who had dealt him a stiff check a few minutes earlier. Howe did as he was asked, but the play got fouled up and Gordie shifted himself right into the line of fire. Pronovost missed his target and slammed full tilt into Howe. Gordie ended up with a broken shoulder, and he missed six games.

"Naturally, I felt pretty bad about it," Pronovost said in relating the incident. "But all Gordie said in the first-aid room was, 'Marcel, you're a rotten bodychecker. You better get your eyes tested.'"

The damaged cartilage in his right knee was repaired, and Howe appeared in 40 games during the 1948–49 campaign. He netted 12 goals, added 25 assists, and was selected for the second team of All-Stars. It was a creditable performance for a third-year man, especially when the man in question was only 21 and coming back after knee surgery.

Yet there was a nagging suspicion among some Detroit fans — and some players around the league, for that matter — that Howe had been overrated, that perhaps he had matured too early and had reached his peak as a teenager. After all, 35 goals in three seasons was hardly anything to write home about. Certainly he continued to display flashes of brilliance on the ice, but he had failed to correct two faults that had marked his formative years in the National Hockey League.

One was his irritating tendency to misuse his talents for the sake of showmanship. Sid Abel recalls, "Gordie would come in and stickhandle around a defenseman . . . then he'd swing back and stickhandle around the same defenseman again, beating him a different way. I guess he just wanted to show that the first time was no fluke."

Gordie's second great shortcoming was a tendency to draw too many needless penalties. It is one thing not to be intimidated by opponents; it is another to go looking for fights, which is exactly what Howe did during his first three seasons in the league. Finally, Jack Adams took Howe aside and snapped at him: "What do you think you have to do, Howe, beat up the whole league player by player? Now settle down and play some hockey."

Howe got the message in time for the Stanley Cup playoffs. Detroit had finished atop the league and had little trouble beating the Canadiens in the opening round. But in the finals against Toronto, the Wings came out second best. The Detroit setback was no fault of Howe's. In fact, Gordie emerged as the star of the Stanley Cup competition by scoring 8 goals and adding 3 assists in 11 games, which was tops in goals and points. Recalling that performance, Howe says with a grin:

"I still wasn't so sure I was a star, because one day, back home in Saskatoon, a kid came up and asked for my autograph. While I signed it he said, 'Mr. Howe, what do you do in the winter?' "

But, of course, he *was* a star. His overall performance against Montreal and Toronto in the playoffs had pushed Howe over the thin line that divides the good players from the greats.

The following season (1949–50) Howe scored 35 goals — matching his total for the three previous years — and added 33 assists, for a point total of 68. For the second consecutive season he was voted to the second team of All-Stars, again finishing behind Rocket Richard in the voting for the right-wing position. More important, Howe was the league's third highest scorer. Only his linemates, Lindsay and Abel, compiled higher point totals.

The Howe-Lindsay-Abel "Production Line" had become one of the best in the history of professional hockey, and Howe, more mature and confident, blended in perfectly. For hockey fans of that era, there were few greater thrills than watching Howe, Lindsay, and Abel on a rush into enemy ice. The Production Line helped Detroit to a first-place finish that year, and the Wings were favored to win the Stanley Cup.

It was at that point, at the start of the semifinal round, that Gordie Howe was struck down, nearly for life.

There was an air of optimism around Detroit's Olympia Arena on March 28, 1950, as the Red Wings prepared for the opening round against the Toronto Maple Leafs. Detroit had finished the regular season schedule 14 points ahead of third-place Toronto. Jack Adams, general manager of the Red Wings, frankly told reporters: "There'll be no alibis if we don't take the Cup. Barring injuries, we have the team we think can take it."

But the Red Wings were confronted with two very significant obstacles, both mental. They realized that the Maple Leafs had won the Stanley Cup for three consecutive seasons, the last time with a fourth-place club. Furthermore, the Leafs had won 11 straight playoff games from Detroit and had knocked the Wings out of the running for three straight seasons.

When someone remarked to Leaf coach Hap Day that the Wings appeared more worried over the outcome of the series than did the high-spirited Leafs, Day said with a wry smile: "That's the trouble."

On the eve of the opening game headlines in the *Toronto Globe and Mail* pretty well summed up the feeling in the respective camps: "Leaf Boss Prescribes Hard, Honest Toil for Cup Retention . . . Wings Feel Leaf Jinx Has Run Its Course."

The bitterness that flamed among the players on the opposing teams was reflected best by Ted Lindsay. "This is our profession. It's a game you get paid for — but when it comes to the Leafs, we'd play them for nothing."

Referee George Gravel knew he had an unusually difficult game on his hands when he skated out to center ice. Gravel possessed a rare sense of humor, and the first thing he did upon reaching the face-off circle was to bow from the waist in the direction of the press box.

But Gravel's humor failed to infect the antagonists. In the first period, Marty Pavelich and Fleming Mackell slugged it out. Red Wing Pavelich bloodied Mackell's nose, and both received major penalties. Later, Bill Juzda, the tanklike Leaf defenseman, and Howe swung freely at each other, and both were sent off the ice with major penalties.

Neither team scored in the first period, but after ten seconds of the second, Max Bentley of the Leafs outdrew Max McNab and got the puck to Bill Barilko. The huge defenseman saw Joe Klukay scooting to the right side. Klukay called for a pass, got it, and flipped a backhander past Detroit goalie Harry Lumley.

Additional goals by Barilko, Johnny McCormack, and Cal Gardner had fortified Toronto with a 4–0 lead as the clock ticked away toward the middle of the third period. The cause of the Red Wings appeared hopeless, as Toronto captain Teeder Kennedy methodically lugged the puck out of his territory toward the Detroit goal.

Kennedy was six feet from the left boards as he reached center ice. Behind him in pursuit was defenseman Jack Stewart of the Wings. Sweeping in from the right side was Howe, who attempted to crash Kennedy amidships. Howe was a trifle too slow to hit Kennedy with full force, and it appeared that the best he could do would be to graze the Leaf player and throw him off balance.

But Howe appeared to miss even that opportunity, and as Kennedy stopped short and then pressed forward, Howe tumbled, face first, into the thick wooden side boards.

"I don't know how he got it," said a worried looking Kennedy in the noisy Leaf dressing room after the game. "I avoided his check along the boards and didn't feel anything hit me, although he may have struck my stick. It could have happened when he crashed into the boards."

Seconds after Howe rammed the boards, his face was a bloody pulp, and he lay unconscious on the ice. He had suffered a stiff concussion of the head, a bruised cheekbone, and a broken nose. As 13,659 fans sat awestruck by the scene, he was carried off the ice on a stretcher and removed to Harper Hospital. Doctors there described his condition as "serious."

His head injuries were indeed so serious that the doctors ordered him into the operating room, where neurosurgeons probed for additional injuries. They decided to operate to relieve pressure on his brain. For several hours there was doubt that Howe would survive the ordeal. He did survive the first-night crisis, but he remained in critical condition.

Still, some doubted that he would live. A call was put through to Saskatoon, and Gordie's mother was urged to take the first plane to Detroit so that she could be at her son's bedside. Mrs. Howe, accompanied by her daughter, Gladys Lyell, arrived in Detroit on Thursday, two days after the accident.

Gordie wasn't told that his mother was coming to Detroit. When she walked into his room, he exclaimed, "Why, Mom, what are you doing here?"

"You seem just like my old Gordie," she replied, and they embraced.

Dr. C.L. Tomsu, the Red Wings' physician, said that the visit from Gordie's mother was better medicine for the injured star than anything a doctor could prescribe. "He still has a headache," said Mrs. Howe, "but he's feeling fine. I certainly feel much better at finding him so well."

But the episode was hardly finished. What started out as a typical brushfire feud between the two rival teams, soon would erupt into one of the biggest conflagrations in the league's history. It was fed by verbal gasoline poured on by antagonists from both sides. The Red Wings camp charged that Kennedy had purposely injured Howe.

"If he (Kennedy) didn't hit Howe with his stick, why did he skate over and apologize?" charged Detroit coach Tommy Ivan. "I'm not saying it was deliberate, but it was a check made with the butt end of Kennedy's stick."

Visibly shaken by the chain of events, Kennedy offered to take an oath that he did not cause the injury. "I saw Howe lying on the ice with his face covered with blood," said the Leaf captain, "and I couldn't help thinking what a great player he was and how I hoped he wasn't badly hurt. Then Detroit players started saying I did it with my stick. I knew I hadn't and, as I've always regarded Ivan as a sensible, level-headed man, I went over to the Detroit bench and told him I was sorry Howe was hurt, but that I wasn't responsible.

The Toronto camp countercharged that Detroit captain Sid Abel tried to chop down Kennedy with his stick after Howe was injured. The chain reaction of events so disturbed Jim Vipond, sports editor of the *Globe and Mail*, that he sharply criticized Abel in an editorial: "Sid Abel, a fine performer and a veteran of the game, who should have known better, disregarded the puck when play finally was resumed. Instead, he slashed at Kennedy's ankle, and Ted has a nasty welt to show for it."

Leaf defenseman Garth Boesch suggested that Howe was hurt by his own teammate Jack Stewart's stick, an opinion that was shared by other members of the team. Al Nickleson, who covered the game for the *Globe and Mail*, observed:

"From the raised press box, directly across the rink from where the incident occurred, it appeared to this observer that Kennedy, in stopping short, had raised his elbow as a protective gesture and that Howe had struck it, before smashing into the boards with his face as he fell. However, Kennedy repeated that, as far as he knew, no part of his person had touched Howe."

Red Burnett, writing in the *Toronto Daily Star*, added: "Referee George Gravel saw the mishap to Howe and didn't call a penalty. That proves, as far as we are concerned, that Kennedy did not hit Howe."

Soon the war spilled over into the journalistic realm, and Detroit writers began to attack Toronto writers over their handling of "l'Affaire Howe."

Paul Chandler, who covered the Red Wings for the *Detroit News*, needled his Toronto colleagues with a story headlined: 'Toronto Town Hot, Bothered'.

Chandler wrote: "The Toronto Telegram has made Kennedy a martyr, an innocent man put to torture by a cruel conspiracy between the Detroit sports writers and the Detroit Red Wings. 'Kennedy Cleared' screamed the *Telegram* on page one of its news section the day after Howe was injured.

"Cleared of what? The paper said Kennedy has been accused of chopping down Howe with the butt-end of a stick and that Detroit papers were assassinating Kennedy. The *Telegram* even posed a picture to show how the accident took place. They posed three individuals, labeled 'Kennedy,' 'Howe,' and 'Stewart,' on skates in Maple Leaf Gardens. In two views that showed 'Howe' speeding behind 'Kennedy' and smashing into the boards."

It didn't take long for the antagonists to find a common enemy. NHL President Clarence Campbell was singled out for his failure to prevent the brutality and violence that preceded and followed Howe's injury. Bob Murphy in the *Detroit News* said: "Campbell might do anything at any time, but nothing ever showing any real leadership or courage."

Despite the wave of criticism, Campbell quickly took a stand on the Howe case and promptly exonerated Kennedy. He made it clear that game officials had absolved Kennedy of any blame in connection with Howe's injury, and he branded "very vicious" Tommy Ivan's charge that Kennedy had butt-ended Howe on the play. Campbell pointed out that Kennedy could not have fouled Howe by way of a butt-end.

"Kennedy," said Campbell, "as a right-handed player, had the butt part of his stick tight to the fence as he was going up the ice. He was being checked from his right. The injuries to Howe were on the right side of the head. Kennedy had stopped to avoid the check, and Howe went in front of him."

Interpreters of the president's analysis concluded that Howe's right side was away from Kennedy. The Toronto player was further exonerated when referee George Gravel submitted his report, which coincided with the report of linesman Sammy Babcock. It read:

"Jack Stewart carried the puck into the Toronto end and was checked by Kennedy, who carried the puck into the center zone right close to the fence on the players' bench side. I turned to follow the play and Stewart was trying to check Kennedy and was right close to him. Just as Kennedy crossed the Toronto blue line, I saw Howe cut across toward Kennedy, skating very fast. Just before Howe got to Kennedy, Kennedy passed backhanded and stopped suddenly. Howe just brushed him slightly and crashed headlong into the fence and fell to the ice. Stewart fell on top of him. Play carried on for a few seconds as Toronto had possession."

Campbell said the only official statement he had received from the Detroit club on the Howe injury was that it was "a very unfortunate incident." The president added: "There is no doubt Gravel saw it all from beginning to end. One linesman, Babcock, also had a very good view. Both their reports are substantially the same."

This contrasted sharply with the report in one Detroit paper, which quoted Gravel as saying he didn't see the Howe incident. The report accused officials and the league governors of incompetence. One of those governors was the vitriolic Conn Smythe, manager of the Maple Leafs.

"It seems," Smythe shot back, "every time the Leafs go out to defend the championship, they have to defend their right to play. Loose accusations against players have no place in the game. Neither has rough hockey. Kennedy always has been a great and clean player . . . this is the roughest, toughest, hardest, and fastest-thinking game in the world today."

Not to be outdone, Mayor Hiram McCullum of Toronto squeezed himself into the controversy and dispatched a message to Kennedy: "The people of Toronto know absolutely no blame in any way can be attached to you for the accident to Gordie Howe. They are 100 percent behind you all the way and know you will go on and continue to play wonderful hockey . . . leading the team to the Cup. We regret very much the injury to Howe as he is a great player but at the same time know that he was the aggressor in attempting to crash you on the boards."

By the time the opening face-off approached for the second game of the semifinals, on Thursday, March 30, a pitch of bitterness of infinite intensity had been reached. In the Red Wing dressing room players were chanting, "Win this one for Gordie." In the Maple Leaf dressing room there was a grim feeling that the Detroiters were going to try to "get" Kennedy.

They were right, but it is doubtful that the Toronto players had any idea of the extent of the brutality they would encounter.

The game began calmly enough. Only two penalties were called in the first period, as Detroit ran up a two-goal lead on scores by Red Kelly and Sid Abel. Joe Carveth got another goal for the Wings midway in the second period, and for a few more moments it appeared that rationality would prevail. Then it happened.

"Somebody pulled an invisible trigger," said Jim Vipond, sports editor of the *Globe and Mail*, "and mayhem broke loose."

It started when Lee Fogolin sent Kennedy rolling to the ice with a stick trip. As play halted and referee Butch Keeling thumbed Fogolin to the penalty box, Ted Lindsay rushed up and cross-checked Kennedy to the ice. Gus Mortson flew at Lindsay, and fights broke out all over the ice. About 20 feet out from the Detroit goal, Jim Thomson fell to the ice, and Leo Reise struck him across the head and shoulders with his stick. Thomson was defenseless and dazed as Reise, apparently not satisfied, slashed away. Blood flowed. By this time, Kennedy was on the other side of the rink, and Reise moved over to put in some more stickwork, this time across Kennedy's shoulders.

Lindsay returned and rushed at Kennedy, his stick held high; then Abel rushed, flailing with his fists. A fan grabbed Kennedy and manacled him as other Wings struck the Leaf captain. Toronto goalie Turk Broda, handicapped by 35 pounds of leg pads, trundled to the scene to assist his teammate, but Abel and Lindsay persisted in their attempt to get at Kennedy.

Veteran onlookers were stunned by the panoply of terror. "This writer," said Vipond, "has often avowed that no player would intentionally injure another player, but not after tonight. There could be nothing more brutal and deliberate than the Detroit players' attempt to even a trumped-up injustice to one of their mates."

The fighting finally subsided, but it erupted again in the final minutes of the third period, when several other battles kept the referee on a belt line to the penalty box. When the ice had cleared, the Wings had won the game. They trooped happily into their dressing room with Lindsay at the head of the march yelling, "We won it for Gordie."

Meanwhile, Howe was still in critical condition in Harper Hospital. Doctors had refused to permit him to hear the game or to be told the result until the following day.

Kennedy emerged from the fracas with more dignity than most. He had not backed away from any of his assailants, and he left the ice with a discolored eye and a cut above his lip. "He was supposed to be slowed up because of a charley horse," said his boss, Conn Smythe. "He played a terrific game. His line scored our only goal and had no goals scored against it. He's still the greatest hockey player in the world."

Across the hall, Detroit's manager Jack Adams was saying: "The Red Wings are champions of the world . . . and don't forget we played without the greatest player in the world — Gordie Howe."

"All Kennedy would say was, "The game's over. They won it."

Now the Howe episode was threatening to move to the courts. The Wings charged that Conn Smythe commented after the injury: "Two years ago Detroit broke my Gus Mortson's leg, and last year they broke the jaw of Elmer Lach of the Canadiens in the playoffs."

Adams countered: "We are now suing a Montreal newspaperman for $75,000 for saying we broke Lach's jaw. Smythe is taking a lot on himself, making the ruling that is to be decided by the Canadian courts."

Antagonists were in agreement on one point: NHL president Campbell was the man who could calm the tempers. "Too much blood and thunder can ruin the game," wrote Tommy Devine in the *Detroit Free Press*. "Campbell would do well to make his warnings against violence sharp and then make them stick."

This time Campbell responded. He sharpened the teeth of the NHL rules and warned that "very substantial fines and suspensions" would be applied, if necessary, to stop bitter feuding between the Maple Leafs and Red Wings. He ordered the stand-by referee to act as a linesman in future games and ordered the managers and coaches of both teams to a meeting to settle "any possible misunderstandings . . . of what is being done."

"Hockey is a tough and rugged game at the best of times," said Campbell, "but the stick-swinging which took place has no place in the game at any time."

Campbell's statement obliquely indicted the Red Wings, and many critics insisted that he was speaking directly about Leo Reise's clubbing Jim Thomson over the head. Still, the Red Wings insisted they were innocent.

"Never at any time did I tell any of my players to go out and do anything to that boy (Kennedy)," said Detroit coach Tommy Ivan. "I can only repeat that I did not have any thoughts of my players' seeking revenge. You can confirm that statement by talking to my players. Responsible lads like Red Kelly will back me up. We're not interested in trying to get anybody. We've got to win hockey games, and I really want to win this series. But we certainly won't win by doing anything so foolish as to injure players."

Armed with Campbell's edict, referee Bill Chadwick ruled the third game, played at Maple Leaf Gardens, with an iron hand. He whistled off Howie Meeker in the opening minute of the game and penalized only two other players. He didn't have to do any more. The mental equilibrium of the players had been restored, and they were playing hockey according to the book. The Leafs scored twice in the second period on goals by Joe Klukay and Max Bentley and won the game, 2–0, to take a 2–1 lead in the series.

Detroit tied the series with a 2–1 victory in the fourth game; then the Leafs went ahead again, blanking the Wings 2–0, to skate to within a game of winning the bloody series. But Detroit still had some energy left, even though it now was apparent that their star, Gordie Howe, would be lost to them for the playoffs. They defeated Toronto 4–0 in the sixth game, carrying the semifinal to a seventh and deciding game at Detroit.

The final game of the 1950 series is regarded as one of hockey's classics. The teams battled through three periods of regulation time without a goal. Checking remained close through the opening eight minutes of the sudden-death overtime. That night Olympia Stadium was not for the weak-hearted.

Coach Tommy Ivan sent out a line of George Gee, Steve Black, and Joe Carveth against Toronto's Max Bentley, Fleming Mackell, and Vic Lynn. The Leafs had Bill Juzda and Bill Barilko on defense, while Detroit's defenders were Jack Stewart and Leo Reise.

Gee, Black, and Carveth launched a dangerous rush for the Wings, backed by Stewart and Reise. Several times the puck bounced dangerously close to the goal line, only to be cleared; but the Leafs couldn't quite get the disk out of their own zone. Finally Gee captured the puck and slid it across the ice to Reise, who was standing near the blue line 60 feet from the goal.

His shot went straight to the net, where goalie Turk Broda appeared to have the short side blocked with his skate, pad, and stick. But the puck bounced over Broda's stick and hit the back of the net. Detroit won 1–0.

The final round against the New York Rangers might have been anti-climactic except that it, too, was decided in sudden-death overtime in the seventh game. In fact, the Wings and Rangers went into the second overtime before Detroit's Pete Babando took a pass from George Gee and backhanded a 15-foot shot past goalie Chuck Rayner to give the Wings a 4–3 victory and the Stanley Cup.

Gordie Howe was in the arena that night, and when the ancient silver mug was pushed out to center ice, the 13,095 fans spontaneously chanted: "We want Howe!

We want Howe!" As Gordie gingerly stepped on the ice, Lindsay grabbed his hat and sent it flying into the stands. Then he tapped the head of his star linemate and joked, "You big lucky stiff. You sit in the seats and watch us go out and make a couple of thousand dollars for you."

When the ceremony at mid-ice had ended, Howe was given the Cup, and he carried it through the milling, cheering crowd to the Detroit dressing room. He was well on his road to recovery, ready for even greater accomplishments than before.

Less than three months after his near-fatal injury, Howe was well enough to start playing baseball in the Northern Saskatchewan League. By the time he reported to the Red Wings training camp, he was in near-perfect condition; as the 1950–51 season opened, Howe pronounced himself ready to go.

Still, Howe's teammates and opponents wondered if Gordie would play as aggressively as he had before the accident. Had he left a little bit of heart back in the hospital room? Would he be gun-shy? Would he occasionally take his eye off the puck and glance about for a defender when he was near the boards? Would he slow himself down just a bit at the blue line and lose that valuable half-step? Would he pass up the opportunity to throw a hard check at an enemy forward?

Howe answered these doubts — and perhaps his own fears as well — in the best of all possible ways. He scored 43 goals and added 43 assists, good enough to lead the league in both goals and total points.

The Wings again finished first, only to be upset by Montreal in the first round of the Stanley Cup playoffs. But the loss of the Cup was no fault of Howe's. He had four goals and three assists in the six-game series.

During the 1950–51 campaign, Howe also reached the first of many a personal milestone: he scored his one-hundredth NHL goal on the night of February 17, 1951. The goalie was Montreal's Gerry McNeil, and the game was played at the Montreal Forum. Most significant — and perhaps embarrassing — of all, it happened on "Rocket Richard Night."

Perhaps that hundredth goal was an omen of things to come, for at the end of the season Howe displaced Richard at right wing on the first team of All-Stars. Howe was fast displacing Richard as the most celebrated player in professional hockey. The 1940s were Richard's era, but the 1950s belonged to Howe. The question of who was the all-around better player is still being debated by hockey fans and experts today.

Richard's style of play, explosive, aggressive, and at all times colorful, reminds one of Babe Ruth. Howe, on the other hand, can probably best be likened to Joe DiMaggio, although he has displayed Ruthian qualities on many occasions. Richard was first and foremost a scorer. Probably no player in the history of professional hockey was as fearsome as Richard inside the enemy's blue line.

In Montreal, for example, they still talk about what is referred to simply as the "Boston goal." Richard scored it late in the third period of a Stanley Cup playoff game against Boston in 1952. The Bruins had just completed a rush on the Canadien goal. Richard retrieved the disk in front of the Montreal net and started up ice. He swerved around a Boston wingman who was trying to check him, cut to the right boards at the red line, and he headed toward Bruin ice.

At the Boston line Richard fended off a Bruin defenseman with his left arm, but still he was steered into the corner to the right of the Boston net. It appeared that the puck would be frozen there, but somehow Richard managed to break free from the defenseman. With a swoop of his stick he recovered the puck and skated laterally toward the Boston goal. With a quick feint, Richard brought the goaltender to his knees; then he fired into the upper right-hand corner of the net. Richard's score broke a 1–1 tie and gave Montreal the game.

Richard was a furious and feverish hockey player, completely obsessed with scoring. "When he came flying in toward you with his stick," says Chicago goalie Glenn Hall, "Richard's eyes were all lit up, flashing and gleaming like a pinball machine."

Richard had relatively little use for the other aspects of the game. His defensive play was often loose, sometimes downright sloppy. He never was much of a checker, nor was he overly concerned with the *assist* column of the scoring sheet. Given the option of shooting or passing to a teammate with better position, Richard would shoot. This may seem like nitpicking, since Richard still ranks as the most explosive scorer in the annals of the NHL, but it does help to point out the major difference between the Rocket and Gordie Howe.

Several years ago, six coaches then in the National Hockey League were asked to define the best qualities of both Howe and Richard. They replied that Richard had the most accurate shot in the league and was the game's best man on the breakaway. Howe, they said, was the best puck-carrier, best playmaker, top passer, and the league's smartest player.

More recently, "Boom Boom" Geoffrion was asked whether Howe or Richard was the greater hockey player. Geoffrion responded by saying: "From the waist down, I'll take the Rocket. From the waist up, give me Howe. Howe could kill penalties, pass, and do almost everything. The Rocket concentrated on scoring. But from the blue line to the other team's post, give me the Rocket. If my team needed a goal, I would want the Rocket with the puck near the boards."

The embarrassing demise of the Red Wings from the Stanley Cup playoffs in April, 1951, stung the Detroiters to the core. They vowed to avenge the calamity, and in the following season they did so with a vengeance. Gordie led the league in scoring for the second straight year, and his colleagues finished atop the NHL, winning 44 games, precisely the amount they had captured the previous year.

Haunting the Red Wings, however, was their hasty exit in 1951. More troubling was the fact that the Red Wings would go up against the Maple Leafs in the opening round. The Toronto sextet had enjoyed more success against the Wings than any other club, winning four and tying four in 14 games. "The breaks," said Jack Adams, "will be decisive in the series."

As events later indicated, Adams had uttered the understatement of the half-century. If breaks were needed, the mighty Red Wings would somehow manufacture them. Whatever Adams's club did, it did right.

The first game was a 3–0 romp for Detroit, with 102 penalty minutes called. "It started like a tea party," said Toronto's *Globe and Mail*, "and blew itself into a roaring tempest of penalties."

In a move to infuse more spirit into his club, Leafs manager Conn Smythe benched young goalie Al Rollins and replaced him with the veteran Turk Broda, a remarkably efficient playoff goalie who was beloved by his mates. For a while it appeared that Smythe had come up with the winning formula.

The elderly Broda summoned all the tricks at his command and foiled every Detroit play but one. During a first-period power play, Broda stopped a shot by Metro Prystai, but Johnny Wilson sped for the rebound and pushed it into the open net. After that Broda was impregnable, but it was too late. The Leafs lost the game 1–0, sending the Red Wings on to Toronto with a 2–0 lead in the series.

Playing before the hometown fans at Maple Leaf Gardens, Toronto appeared ready for a comeback. Broda once again was in the nets, and the crowd roared for Leaf goals. But it wasn't to be. Detroit pumped six goals past Broda, and the next day the *Globe and Mail* flashed a headline that said it all: "Let's Face Facts! Too Much Class!"

Smythe went with Rollins in the fourth game, but it was a futile gesture. Despite a mighty Maple Leafs effort, the Red Wings easily marched past them with a 3–1 victory and annexed the series in four games. Gordie Howe was indestructible, and the Detroit defense, anchored by Red Kelly and Leo Reise, never was more powerful.

There were other stars, and captain Sid Abel was one of them. "He makes us go," said Adams. "He's the needler out there." Left wing Ted Lindsay was another. "We need Ted out there," said Abel. "He's the guy who holds us together. He keeps us at a high pitch. He won't allow anyone to let down when he's on the ice."

Neither Lindsay nor Abel would allow a letdown against the second-place Montreal Canadiens, who faced them in the 1952 Stanley Cup finals. But if any Red Wing needed reassurance, it was 22-year-old goalie Terry Sawchuk, who was already being hailed as "Hockey's New Mister Zero."

Acclaimed as the best young goaltender in all of hockey, Sawchuk nevertheless was in goal the previous year when Rocket Richard and the Canadiens knocked Detroit out of the playoffs. Coach Tommy Ivan was doing everything possible to perfect Sawchuk's near-flawless style for the Canadiens series.

Sawchuk said: "Tommy has practiced straight-on shots with me. Meanwhile, I'm perfecting my style. I try to concentrate on the puck. I'm not a holler guy. I have a very low crouching style; my reflexes are that way, I guess. I can see better through the legs than over some tall guy's shoulder."

The Canadiens knew that Sawchuk feared the Rocket, and they knew he had one soft spot in his goaltending repertoire. "His weakness," said Montreal coach Dick Irvin, "is a shoulder-high shot on the right side. Personally, I think we'll have the Stanley Cup by April 19th. Remember that."

Sawchuk was hardly the picture of overconfidence, especially when he discussed Richard. "No matter where the Rocket shoots from," said Sawchuk, "it's always on the net. His backhand is even tougher than his forehand, and he shoots a heavy puck. When you stop it, it feels like it's going through you."

But once the series started, the Rocket's best shots were blunted by Sawchuk, and Detroit won the opening game 3–1. There were just too many stars in the Red Wings galaxy for even the mighty Canadiens to handle. One of them was Red

Kelly, who could score goals as handily as he could defend against them. Even Montreal's high command recognized that.

Montreal's managing director Frank Selke said: "Kelly is as good a player as I've seen in my long connection with hockey, which dates back to 1906. More than that, he exemplifies everything that is desirable in a young man, and the Detroit club is fortunate to have a man of his integrity and character in its lineup."

By contrast, Lindsay was the hard-nosed type, and he thought nothing of shoving his stick across an enemy's face or ramming him from behind. As a result, Lindsay was a marked man throughout the league, especially in Montreal. "I take the boos right along with the cheers, if any," Lindsay said. "With the price a fan pays for his ticket, he gets the right to howl at me. I expect it."

It was Lindsay who bounced the puck off defenseman Butch Bouchard's chest in the second game of the finals, to give the Red Wings a 2–1 victory and a 2–0 series lead. When the teams moved on to Montreal, Howe took over and scored twice, leading Detroit to a 3–0 triumph. "The Red Wings," said the *Canadian Press*, "stand on the threshold of the greatest Stanley Cup sweep in the modern-day, big-league game."

An eight-game sweep was unthinkable in the Stanley Cup playoffs. Surely, a team, no matter how powerful, would suffer a letdown along the route, or the enemy would obtain a surplus of breaks, or the hometown crowd would provide a lift to the contenders and encourage them to win at least one game. At least this had always happened in the past.

But there never had been a player like Gordie Howe before. "They should use two pucks every time Detroit plays," said Hap Day, who had coached Toronto to three straight Stanley Cup wins from 1947 through 1949. "Give one to the other team and the second one to Howe. He's always got the puck anyway."

Curiously enough, Howe did not score a single goal in the fourth and final cup match. Metro Prystai scored twice, and Glen Skov scored once, to spearhead the Wings to another 3–0 triumph and the Stanley Cup in an astonishing eight-game sweep.

Clearly this team was one of the strongest collections of hockey players ever to skate in the NHL. At first Jack Adams was cautious. After the first round he had been asked whether the 1951–52 edition was the greatest Detroit hockey team of all time. Adams said that critics would have to wait until the Wings had finished the final round against the Canadiens. When that was over, he was emphatic about his club's niche in hockey history: "This is the best-balanced club I've had in 25 years in the NHL. I'll let the figures speak for themselves and let any other club try to match them."

The Detroit dynasty had been built, and as Adams pointed out, the figures spoke for themselves. Between 1949 and 1955 the Red Wings finished first seven consecutive times and won the Stanley Cup in 1950, 1952, 1954, and 1955.

Adams realized that he had to pump new blood continually into the Detroit lineup. "We won the title in 1935–36 and 1936–37," Adams said. "The next year we stood pat and finished last in our division. That taught me you can't be sentimental in hockey and still be a winner."

The proof of Adams's philosophy was there for all to see. He had unloaded such stars as Jack Stewart, Harry Lumley, Bill Quackenbush, Sid Abel, Leo Reise, and

Metro Prystai. After winning the Stanley Cup in 1955, he traded Tony Leswick, Glen Skov, Johnny Wilson, and Benny Woit to Chicago for Dave Creighton, Johnny McCormack, Bucky Hollingworth, and Jerry Toppazzini. Two weeks later he stunned the hockey world by trading Terry Sawchuk, Vic Stasiuk, Marcel Bonin, and Lorne Davis to Boston for Bruin captain Ed Sandford, Real Chevrefils, Warren Godfrey, Gilles Boisvert, and Norm Corcoran.

Of course, Adams had to defend his wholesale housecleaning. "When a boy on one of our farms has reached maturity, we believe in giving him a thorough trial with the Red Wings. We don't bury our players. We felt Sawchuk was ready to play big-league hockey in 1950, so we brought him up to replace Harry Lumley. Now we think Glenn Hall is ready to replace Sawchuk."

Adams also elevated rookies Johnny Bucyk and Norm Ullman from his Edmonton farm club and looked forward to the 1955–56 season with his usual great expectations. But in spite of his enthusiasm, the dynasty was crumbling.

Hall proved to be a very capable goaltender, but Adams soured on him after only two seasons. In fact, nearly all of the players obtained in the off-season trades turned out to be duds in one form or another. "Nobody in hockey really believed the breakup of the Red Wings would result in a breakdown," wrote the late Jack Zanger, who chronicled the Red Wings saga for *Sport* magazine, "but that's what happened, slowly but surely, over the following years."

With Gordie Howe playing brilliantly, as usual, the Wings finished second in 1956, but Detroit was eliminated by first-place Montreal in the finals. The great machine developed by Jack Adams and carried by Gordie Howe had lost its horsepower. Detroit would never again win the Stanley Cup.

The Boston Bruins, 1970–72

Orr's Bruins, 1970–72

In terms of flamboyant personalities who blended art with bombast, few teams could match the Boston Bruins, who launched the decade of the 1970s with a Stanley Cup. "Bobby Orr and the Big, Bad Bruins," as they were known to fans across the continent, were as equally feared for their toughness as they were for their talent.

Until the Bruins came along, marauding through the NHL in the late 1960s (before they actually won The Cup), no Stanley Cup-winner ever had been labelled "intimidating" in the ferocious sense. Toronto's dynastic Maple Leafs of the 1947–51 era had a healthy sprinkling of rugged performers (Wild Bill Ezinicki, Bashin' Bill Barilko, Gus Mortson), but they came short of using violence as an art form.

Coached by Harry Sinden, the Bruins were different. They were a product of the expansion era which began in 1967 and ushered in "goon" hockey. Sinden's inner core of stars included Phil Esposito, Bobby Orr, Ken Hodge, and Johnny Bucyk. Each a gifted offensive force, they were to concentrate on their scoring while the enemy was distracted by Boston's corps of enforcers.

As tough teams go, the Bruins boasted a collection of belligerents matched only by the Philadelphia Flyers (a.k.a. Broad Street Bullies) a few years later. In Terrible Ted Green, Boston had a defenseman who could mesmerize a foe just by glaring at him. Wayne Cashman could score, but he would just as soon send an enemy through the boards with a bodycheck; and he could fight. When Cashman wasn't worrying the foe, there was Derek (Turk) Sanderson, another talented offensive force who loved to cause trouble, and Johnny (Pie) McKenzie, who wouldn't have second thoughts about impaling an opponent if he thought it would mean a win.

The Sandersons, McKenzies, and Cashmans created so many distractions, that the incomparable Orr and Esposito were able to execute their talents without significant interference. And considering the prodigious talents of each, that meant many, many wins for Boston.

Prodigious scoring alone does not make a championship team. This was apparent to Sinden, who built a solid defense around Green and Dallas Smith. His goaltenders were Eddie Johnston and Gerry Cheevers, both better than average. Cheevers was more noticeable because he was as truculent as anyone who went between the pipes, he enjoyed venturing far from his crease, and — like Ron Hextall of the current epoch — relished fencing with oncoming forwards. By contrast, Johnston was a stay-at-home type who rarely lost his cool and played his angles to perfection.

The seeds of this extraordinary team were planted at the time of the NHL's first major expansion in 1967 when the prodigy Orr arrived in Boston. When Esposito, Hodge, and Fred Stanfield became Bruins soon after, the club became a threat, if not a power, in the league.

Maturity was a problem at first, especially with such controversial characters as Sanderson on the squad. The understanding Sinden was willing to allow some leeway to his troops, while administering discipline when necessary. By 1970, the perfect chemistry had been attained. Esposito had peaked as a goal-scorer; Orr had blossomed into the most productive offensive-defenseman, while second liners such as Ed Westfall (a remarkably efficient penalty-killer) and McKenzie were doing all that had been asked of them.

When Boston won The Stanley Cup in 1970, all signs pointed to a long reign of at least three more championships; maybe four. It would depend on several factors, the most important of which were health, discipline, motivation, and stability. In each case there were failings, which helps explain why the Bruins cannot be rated among the top five of all time.

Orr, the balance wheel of the club, was hampered by gimpy knees, which ultimately forced a premature retirement. Discipline became a problem soon after the first Cup win. Adulation caused fat heads and a diminution of discipline. This was partly responsible for the Bruins' early playoff exit — one of the most startling upsets in NHL annals — in 1971. Motivation was not a concern at first, but after the 1972 championship, some of the desire that had been so important to the unit began to disappear.

The most telling blow of all was the lack of stability and this was directly attributable to the birth of the World Hockey Association and the WHA's constant raiding of NHL rosters. For example, the Bruins lost Cheevers, Green, and Sanderson to the WHA in 1972 and never fully recovered from the blow. Surely, that trio could have made the difference in 1974 when Boston lost to Philadelphia (the first expansion club to win a Stanley Cup) in the finals.

As long as Orr and Esposito were operable, the Bruins would be an impressive challenger, and they were. But the loss to an expansion team proved to have as much a psychological effect on the Bruins as it did in any other way. From 1974 on, the team slowly, deliberately, disintegrated. The Bruins remained big, and often bad, but the championship ingredients were gone and, soon, Orr would be gone, too.

In retrospect, it is almost unbelievable that such a consummately gifted team could not have accomplished more than the 1970–72 Bruins. Obviously, they were partly detoured by circumstances beyond their control, especially in the case of the WHA. But maintaining discipline was within control, especially in the classic 1971 series with the Montreal Canadiens when an inexperienced rookie goalie named Ken Dryden moved to center stage and baffled the Bruins.

Because the Bruins failed to attain their potential and because they won two Cups when four would have been within their means, they must be relegated to a lower plane among the super teams and this, despite Orr, Esposito, and Cheevers.

If Boston is the Athens of North America, as many residents along the Charles River like to boast, it also is the hockey capital of the United States in terms of history, enthusiasm, and the number of people who play and watch the sport in New England.

Thus, it was virtually a statewide tragedy when the Bruins suffered through eight consecutive seasons, from 1960 through 1967, without gaining even a playoff berth. Despite the abysmal performances regularly offered by the Bruins, the fans continued to fill Boston Garden and to display a rare faith in the future of their beloved hockey team.

That faith would eventually be repaid. Down in the amateur Ontario Hockey Association skated a young man who, one day, would grace the National Hockey League and lead the Bruins up to the heights they had known in the Eddie Shore era and, later, during the dynasty of Milt Schmidt and the Kraut Line.

The lad's name was Robert Gordon "Bobby" Orr, and he played for the Oshawa, Ontario, Generals. At the age of 16, his skills were so superior to those of his colleagues, that nobody felt any hesitation about predicting instant NHL stardom for Orr and relief for the beleagured Bruins. For Boston hockey fans, the turnabout came in 1966–67, when Orr joined the Bruins and promptly established his credentials by winning the Rookie of the Year award.

In virtually no time at all, every manager, coach, and player who watched the blond marvel speed from one end of the rink to another, declared that he would be the most accomplished skater of the seventies, if not the all-time savior of the Bruins.

Orr's magic had little effect on the Bruins' standing in 1966–67. The club finished in sixth place (it was the last year before expansion), but it showed signs of jelling around Orr's orchestration. But no matter how talented one individual might be, he can't do the job alone. It was obvious to manager Milt Schmidt that the Bruins needed more help on the offensive and more size to go with Orr's speed.

It was Schmidt's luck to encounter Chicago Black Hawks manager Tommy Ivan in May, 1967, when Ivan was disturbed about Chicago's early exit from the playoffs, despite a first-place finish. A shake-up was deemed imperative in the Windy City, and Ivan made it clear to Schmidt that he was prepared to swing a major deal with the Bruins. The deal that eventually evolved became the key to Boston's future success and one of the most unbalanced trades in NHL history.

Schmidt dealt minor-league goalie Jack Norris, defenseman Gilles Marotte, and center Pit Martin to Chicago for Phil Esposito, Fred Stanfield — a pair of centers — and right wing Ken Hodge.

Almost overnight, the Bruins had been converted from patsies to menaces. Suddenly the Bruins not only were big, they were *bad* — they literally skated over the smaller opponents.

Somehow disparaged in Chicago, Esposito became the league's leading playmaker in his rookie year with Boston. Hodge started to score goals like never before, and Stanfield turned into a smaller version of Esposito. As a result, the Bruins climbed to third place in the East Division, and everyone who knew anything about hockey muttered that the Hub sextet couldn't help but go higher.

Orr was at the helm. In his sophomore season he was voted the NHL's best defenseman, although he was sidelined for nearly half the schedule because of injuries. He won that same award every season he played since then.

Meanwhile, Schmidt was increasing his beef trust. Wherever possible, a big, husky player would replace a smaller stickhandler. Even such smaller types as Johnny McKenzie were so dynamic that they intimidated larger players on other teams. By 1968–69, tall, testy Wayne Cashman had been elevated from the minors, and the Bruins had the toughest collection of hockey players any contemporary observer could recall. Boston Garden fans loved them and encouraged them to battle; and battle they did, with a ferocity that frequently infuriated the opposition.

Toronto's assistant general manager, King Clancy, referred to them as "butchers." New York's manager, Emile Francis, said that playing in Boston Garden was like "going into a bullring."

One of the many superb analyses of the Bruin phenomenon was authored by Paul Dulmage, hockey writer for the *Toronto Telegram*. "Unless you have been to Boston this season," Dulmage wrote in the spring of 1969, "you cannot be aware of the intense, almost suffocating aura of the physical nature of the Bruins. They were the most penalized team in the NHL and richly deserved to be such.

"Had their aggression been penalized at a rate equal to that applied to other clubs, the Bruins might have had to play the entire season without ever getting a sixth man on the ice. One referee cannot possibly see everything, nor can he call it. The Bruins give you the stick, the trip, the elbow, and the shove away from the play. They hunt heads. They traded away most of their little men for big strong forwards, and, egged on by the world's unruliest and most obscene fans, they hit everything that moves."

Milt Dunnell, then sports editor of the *Toronto Daily Star*, described Boston Garden as a "nuthouse." Charles MacGregor, sports editor of the *Telegram*, labeled the Bruins' home rink a "zoo." *Telegram* assistant sports editor George Gross preferred comparing Boston Garden with a "lunatic bin." He added, "The only thing missing was the straight jackets."

"We know they will play rough," said Montreal Canadiens coach Claude Ruel. "We expect it. They always do. . . . They hate Canadiens. The Bruins are the only team that tried to intimidate you."

Such vivid descriptions of the Bruins style were not limited to Toronto, Montreal, or New York. They were heard throughout the 12-team NHL and, sometimes, in Boston. After the April 2, 1969, match between Toronto and Boston, Bill Liston of the *Boston Herald-Traveler* opened his story this way:

"In one of the wildest encounters ever seen on Boston Garden ice, Boston police had to save Toronto defenseman Pat Quinn from a crowd of raging fans after Quinn flattened Bruin superstar Bobby Orr. . . . At least two policemen and possibly several fans suffered cuts when the glass partition separating the Toronto penalty box from the promenade seats was smashed as Bruin backers attacked Quinn."

Bruin officials spent their energy trying to moderate the killer image that their team had generated through the 1968–69 season. Schmidt tried to make light of it one afternoon in the press room of the NHL at a New York hotel in February, 1969, but the media apparently thought otherwise. One national magazine alluded to Schmidt's collection of players as "Bobby Orr and the Animals." Bruin coach Harry Sinden also tried to diminish the ugly image his troops had obtained, insisting that they play rough — but not dirty — hockey. He also pointed out, with justification, that his team was loaded with virtuosos. The fact is that the Bruins had more individual stars than any other club in the game.

Bobby Orr was regarded as the best defenseman, Phil Esposito the best center, Ted Green the toughest defenseman, and Derek Sanderson the finest young center, among other talents.

Yet with the effusion of talent and the surplus of stock, the Bruins failed to hold first place in the homestretch of the 1968–69 season. They ultimately lost it to Montreal in a decisive game on the final weekend of the campaign. "We overreacted," explained Sinden. "I never saw a Boston team so tight. We stood around for 15 minutes waiting to see what they'd do, and when we found out they were going to score, we were in trouble."

Given the chance to handle the Canadiens in a best-of-seven series, the Bruins failed again. This time they went out in six games, losing three out of three sudden-death overtime games. Montreal went on to win the Stanley Cup and emerged from the 1968–69 season as the true champion. The Bruins came out of it all as the kings of brawling.

To put this collection of bashers in proper perspective, one should compare them with the old St. Louis Cardinal Gashouse Gang. The Cards, man for man, were as tough and rollicking a group of messer-uppers as you'll find anywhere. The same held for the 1969–70 Bruins.

There is, however, one key exception. In baseball, the most damage the Gashouse troupe could inflict on the enemy was a cleat in the face on the basepaths or a rock of a baseball in the batter's ear. That's not peaches and cream, but it's a lot more pleasant than the arsenal the Bruins had at their command: heavy pointed sticks, hard padded elbow guards, rocklike gauntlets, and the semiprotection of a rulebook that is very vague about the fine line between legality and mayhem.

Physical contact between the Bruins and their enemies was constant, reckless, and brutal. The Bruins had been a hell-bent outfit for years. This, plus the addition of quality performers, provided the distillation that nearly put them on top of the East in 1969–70. But it should be recalled that Schmidt was preaching hard hockey back in 1958 when he coached the club. "Sure, penalties are good," he admitted. "Teams won't skate against you with their heads down following the puck when you play rugged hockey. They have to keep looking around to see where you are." The same lines could apply today. The question remained of whether such a penalty-ridden club could make it all the way to first place and the Stanley Cup.

To teach the summit, the Bruins first had to dispose of the club that had reigned supreme for most of the past decade, the Montreal Canadiens. Unlike the Bruins, the Canadiens were a classic team in the tradition of artistic hockey. Their three centers, Jean Beliveau, Ralph Backstrom, and Henri Richard, were lyrical skaters and stickhandlers. Most of their other forwards followed the pattern and, true to the Montreal tradition, were on the lighter, nonbelligerent side.

"You can intimidate those guys," said one Bruin mauler. "I talk to them all the time. I tell them they better not turn their backs on me. Things like that."

This was said in the Bruin dressing room after a typically rough game. In another corner of the room, center Derek Sanderson, one of the most explosive sticks of TNT in sports, put it another way: "You sit on the bench, and it dawns on you that you're gonna lose if you don't start hitting."

What Boston did to the Canadiens, they did with even more vengeance to the Rangers. The two clubs can be reduced to a simple comparison: the beach bully and the 97-pound weakling.

On one of Toronto's visits to Boston, the Leafs started the game with five defensemen on the ice — a bruiser at every position — instead of using only two defensemen. The theory was that by putting out five heavyweights, they'd defuse the Bruins.

Their strategy served only to inspire the Bruins. They hit, hit, hit until the Leafs wilted and Boston walked off with the game. By the end of January, 1969, the Beantowners had gone unbeaten in 14 games.

Many hockey analysts were anxious to isolate 21-year-old All-Star defenseman Bobby Orr as the cause of the Bruin renaissance. This was easy. Fortified with a $400,000 contract, a mop of blond hair, blue eyes, and a large helping of talent, Orr was a natural for the cover of many national magazines in the United States and Canada. But as often happens, the subtle factors were overlooked, although when you discuss Ted Green, you're hardly dealing in subtlety.

Green, the toughest of the tough, had been buried in obscurity as the writing world lavished praise on Orr. But it was Green who helped mold the personality of the Bruins and who went unheralded far beyond the call of reality. At 206 pounds, Green was one of the most feared players in the NHL. There were other hard guys — Gordie Howe, Ted Harris, John Ferguson, to name a few — but none of them combined the total destructiveness of Green, who was named to the Second All-Star Team in 1969. "In addition to his muscle," the *Toronto Daily Star* observed, "Green is a capable defender, an able puck-carrier, a fine pointman, and a take-charge type."

Schmidt, who developed the Bruins team, believed that his 1968–69 club improved 25 percent over the previous year. "All three lines have been scoring," said Schmidt. "Another reason we're better is that our guys got into the playoffs in 1967–68 for the first time in eight years. They got a whiff of that hay, the extra money, and they liked it. Now they want more of it."

Surprisingly, the Bruins were eliminated on April, 1969, in six games, by the Canadiens. Many observers contend that coach Sinden erred. Al Dickie, who covered hockey in Kingston, Ontario, when Sinden was a player-coach there, pointed out that Sinden never was a roughhouse hockey stylist himself.

"Harry was more the Doug Harvey type," Dickie told me. "He used his head more than his body and played the game much in the manner of the Montreal Canadiens. If he had used that style a little more and the aggressiveness a little less, chances are he would have done a lot better against the Canadiens."

In a review of the Bruins, the *Toronto Daily Star* noted: "The Bruins are at their best when a lenient referee is on deck. If the official calls things tightly, the Bruins are inclined to run into trouble. At such times you question their self-discipline."

Sinden, a former minor-league defenseman who never made it in the NHL, directed the Bruin plan of aggression articulated by Schmidt. He realized that the Bruins were ripe for retaliation, and he expressed mild concern.

"Every team is starting to give us its best shot," said Sinden. "It's getting to be like the old Yankees. Remember when they always used to see the best pitchers. Every team we see is starting to come right at us. They're lying in wait, trying to knock us off."

Sinden's concern was exaggerated. The Bruins were becoming invincible. They had the best balance, the best defense, the best scorers, and a pair of adequate goaltenders.

On top of that, they had *fighters*. Green led the way, but Don Awrey and Orr could hit. Up front there was McKenzie, a persistent intimidator, and Sanderson, Hodge, and Ed Westfall. When they were smitten with injuries, they hauled up a kid named Jim Harrison, who fought every opponent in sight — and with good results.

"Lack of size had been one of our troubles in the past," said Schmidt. "I got to thinking of guys who played for the Bruins in the days when we were winning. I thought of Dit Clapper, Eddie Shore, Johnny Crawford, Ray Getliffe. At the time they used to say that if you could get through the door, you couldn't play for the Bruins. Actually, there were some small Bruins, too — great ones. It was true, though, that Boston liked big players."

The first sign of dividends paying off on Boston's beef trust came in the spring of 1970 during a neck-and-neck race with Chicago for first place in the East Division. Actually, first place would not be decided until the final night of the season, since both Boston and Chicago were deadlocked with 97 points apiece going into the last match of the campaign.

Chicago was playing at home against the Canadiens, and the Bruins went up against the Maple Leafs at Boston Garden. If the Black Hawks won their game, they would clinch first place because of a league technicality that provided that the team with the most wins gains first if the clubs are tied in points.

The Bruins went out and trimmed Toronto 3–1, despite some astonishing goaltending by Marv Edwards of the Maple Leafs. But Chicago took the measure of Montreal. Thus, the Hawks compiled 45 wins, 22 losses, and 9 ties, for 99 points, while the Bruins had 40 wins, 17 losses, and 19 ties, for 99 points. Unfortunately for Boston, the wins had it!

"We lost fewer games and scored more goals than Chicago," said coach Sinden. "I give them credit for a big weekend, but that doesn't ease the pain."

Just about everybody in hockey, with the possible exception of the Black Hawks, believed that the Bruins were superior. But Sinden's team had developed a habit of letting up against seemingly easy teams and losing points they should easily have won. "We have only ourselves to blame," said Bobby Orr. "I can recall half a dozen spots where we either settled for a tie or blew a game we should have won. We're the best team. I know it, and the guys know it."

To prove it, the Bruins would have to march through the Stanley Cup playoffs in convincing fashion. And that is precisely what they did. First of the victims were the New York Rangers, who were dropped in six hectic games, during which Derek Sanderson emerged as the Bruin "heavy." He battled nearly every Ranger in sight and topped them all. "The win over the Rangers really psyched us up," said Sanderson.

The Bruins needed all the psyching they could get because their second-round opponents were none other than the Chicago Black Hawks. But here, Sinden's club came into its own. They came together as a team, and nobody helped make this possible more than Phil Esposito, who shared the leadership role with Orr. "If we lose," said Esposito on the eve of the Chicago series, "it will be because someone stops working and lets us down. Believe me, I'm going to be the first one on the guy who stops working."

Esposito need not have worried. Boston bombed Chicago 6–3 in the opening game of the series on Black Hawks' ice and kept on winning. The Bruins stunned Chicago Stadium spectators with an easy 4–1 victory in the second match and wrapped up the series with a pair of wins at Boston Garden. Then they beat St. Louis in four straight to win the Stanley Cup.

Propelled by Esposito's scoring and Orr's multi-talents, the Bruins were heavy favorites to retain the Cup. But they went up against the regal Montreal Canadiens, who surprised Boston by starting rookie goalie Ken Dryden. A graduate of Cornell University, where he had been an All-America choice, Dryden frustrated the Bruins, and the Canadiens disposed of Boston in seven games for one of hockey's most dramatic upsets.

However, the Bruins rebounded in 1971–72, finished first again, and this time routed Toronto, St. Louis, and New York to regain the trophy they had so embarrassingly lost to Montreal a year earlier.

Johnny Bucyk, who had been a Bruin since 1957, underlined the fact that the 1972 champions represented the high point of the Schmidt-built dynasty. "This is the best of the Bruins teams," said Bucyk.

Ed Westfall, who first became a Bruin in 1961, was inclined to agree. "We matured more," said Westfall. "We were not as chippy as we used to be."

Under normal circumstances, the Bruins as they were constituted in May, 1972, suggested a club that could remain champions for at least another three seasons. Orr and Esposito were in their prime. Goalie Gerry Cheevers had honed his style to a new sharpness, and the second- and third-liners such as Sanderson, Dallas Smith, Don Awrey, Fred Stanfield, and Don Marcotte seemed to be improving.

But May, 1972, was not a normal time. The World Hockey Association had burst onto the scene, and overtures were made to several Bruin stalwarts. In addition, the NHL added two new teams, Atlanta and the New York Islanders, which meant that the Bruins would be stripped in the league draft.

By September, 1972, it was apparent that severe damage had been done. Goalie Cheevers and forwards Sanderson and Johnny McKenzie had switched to the WHA along with defenseman Ron Plumb, a highly promising youngster.

Even more damaging to the Bruins, Westfall had been drafted by the Islanders, and gifted young goalie Dan Bouchard — who normally would have replaced Cheevers — was drafted by Atlanta.

Further aggravating the deteriorating situation was the condition of Bobby Orr's left knee. Surgery had been performed on it for the third time during the off-season, and the *Wunderkind* apparently had not fully recovered. He was unable to play his normal game through the 1972–73 season.

True, the Bruins still had Esposito, Hodge, Cashman, and Bucyk, but the loss of such peppy players as McKenzie, Cheevers, and Sanderson removed the heart of the hockey club. The Bruins dynasty, which offered so much promise a few months earlier, was dead.

The Montreal Canadiens, 1944–46

Montreal Canadiens — The Punch Line Era

They were called "The Punch Line," and if there ever was an appropriate title for an attacking threesome, this is it. Elmer Lach was the center. He was a tough hombre from Saskatchewan who ladled soft passes to tenacious Hector (Toe) Blake on the left, and Maurice (Rocket) Richard on the right.

They were wedded as a unit during World War II and remained united through the post-war era when injuries cancelled the careers of Blake and Lach.

Unlike other Canadien super-teams, this one cannot possibly be placed in the upper echelon because of its limited reign at the top of the league. With the Punch Line providing the pizazz, Montreal won two Stanley Cups, but one of them was accomplished during wartime when the quality of most rosters was diluted because of armed forces enlistments. The Habs surely would have been given higher marks here had they come through — as everyone had expected — in 1947 when they met the underdog Toronto Maple Leafs in the Cup finals. The Flying Frenchmen were knocked out in six games (Lach was also KO'd with a devastating check by Don Metz) and never took another cup during the Punch Line's era.

As every opponent knew, there was more to Montreal's club than Richard, Lach, and Blake. Goaltender Bill Durnan (the best ambidextrous netminder of all time) was well schooled in the minors and immediately became a hit in his rookie season, 1943–44. His defense of Leo Lamoreaux, Mike McMahon, Glen Harmon, and Emile (Butch) Bouchard would have been formidable in any era. Up front, the Habs supplemented the power of the Punch Line with the likes of Buddy O'Connor, Gerry Heffernan, and Murph Chamberlain.

They finished so far ahead of everyone in 1943–44 that to call it a runaway (83 points to Detroit's 58) would be understating the case. A year later, they finished first with 80 points to Detroit's 67.

It was in the 1944 Stanley Cup round that the Punch Line came to the fore. Montreal routed Toronto four games to one in the semifinals and then ousted the Chicago Black Hawks in four games, to win the Stanley Cup.

Most experts expected another romp in 1944–45, since the Montreal team was intact from wise coach Dick Irvin on down. But the Habs ran into a hot Toronto goaltender in the opening round and were wiped out in six games.

They atoned for that sin a year later, again finishing first — this time the lead was only five points over the Bruins — and then steam-rolling through the playoffs. In the opening round against Chicago, they not only beat the Black Hawks in four straight, but outscored them by an overwhelming 26–7. Boston gave them a good run in the finals, keeping both the scores and the games close, but in the end, Montreal prevailed, taking the series four games to one.

The Canadiens remained the dominant team over the regular schedule in 1946–47, but faded quickly thereafter. Their fifth place finish in 1947–48 was a humiliation for the entire city of Montreal, not to mention Richard, Blake, and Lach. It would be the last campaign the Punch Line would endure. Blake retired after the 1947–48 season, while Lach hung on through the early fifties.

Though not in the class with their successors, the Jean Beliveau-Rocket Richard-Henri Richard-Bernie Geoffrion Canadiens, the Punchliners were very special in other ways, and fully deserve top rating.

When one considers that the Montreal Canadiens have won 23 Stanley Cups, and clubs like the New York Rangers and Chicago Black Hawks have each won only three silver mugs, it is difficult to imagine the Habs in a depressed period.

Anyone who followed the Canadiens in the early 1940s would be quick to remind you that, yes, the Montrealers were down and out at the start of the 1940s. They finished seventh and last in the 1939–40 season, and only by the grace of the horrible New York Americans, did the Canadiens manage to climb to sixth during the following two seasons.

The turnabout in the Canadiens fortunes could be compared to the renaissance of the New York Yankees in the early 1920s, when George Herman (Babe) Ruth was traded to the Bronx Bombers from the Boston Red Sox.

In Montreal's case, the hero was a youngster who had been born and reared in a French-speaking section of Montreal and who was determined to make a career out of professional hockey. Joseph Henri Maurice Richard was the man.

The season of his debut, 1942–43, is one that goaltenders will never forget, although there had been scant indications in early scouting reports that the Habs had a superstar on their roster.

The slick-haired kid had little trouble making the NHL team in his first try, but he was overshadowed by such new Montreal additions as Gordie Drillon, who had been obtained from Toronto, and Dutch Hiller from Boston. Richard's significance to the Canadiens at the time was summed up in the official NHL history with only one line: "Another new face was a fast-skating right wing named Richard."

Irvin inserted Richard on a line with the veteran Tony Demers and young center Elmer Lach. The line clicked immediately and Demers scored two goals, as the Canadiens won their opening game from Boston, 3–2. The result was especially appealing to one of the game's linesman, Aurel Joliat.

On November 8, 1942, Richard played his third NHL game. Montreal's opponents in the Forum that night were the Rangers who had beaten them on the previous night in New York. This time Les Canadiens were the winners by a score of 10–4. The highlight of the game was a pulsating end-to-end rush by Richard, who made his way through the Ranger defense like a pinball bouncing its way past the obstacles to the goal. Richard's shot beat Ranger goalie, Steve Buzinski, and even so critical an analyst as Newsy Lalonde raved about the rookie.

After fifteen games, Richard had played commendably, if not always spectacularly. His record was five goals and six assists for eleven points, and the Canadiens, as a team, appeared refreshed by his vitality. Then, in the sixteenth game, it happened again. The Canadiens were skating against the Bruins when Jack Crawford, a big but clean defenseman, collided with Richard and sent Maurice sprawling to the ice in pain. He had suffered a clean break just above his right ankle and was finished once again for the season.

"It looked as though the Flying Frenchmen had picked an easily-bruised-and-busted lemon," said Bill Roche. "Richard seemed destined only to be number one on the Canadiens' injury list."

Only a young man with exceptional perseverance and grim determination could surmount such a collection of injuries. Richard was troubled by his misfortune and seriously considered quitting hockey, but neither Irvin nor Gorman was persuaded that he was through. They bided their time through the summer of 1943 and eagerly awaited the start of training camp when Irvin announced that he was forming a new forward line with Richard as the balance wheel.

More than anyone, it was the short-tempered, vitriolic Irvin who convinced Richard he would become a star. "Not only will he be a star," Irvin predicted at the start of the 1943–44 season, "but he'll be the biggest star in hockey!"

Irvin had theorized that Lach was the ideal center for Richard, but he wasn't so sure about left wing. He finally decided that Toe Blake would be worthy of an experiment on the unit, and in no time, the line was made for keeps. The trio, soon to be named "the Punch Line," finished one-two-three (Lach, Blake, Richard) in scoring on the team, with Richard collecting thirty-two goals and twenty-two assists for fifty-four points in forty-six games.

He was, however, buried in fifteenth place on the scoring list and certainly wasn't regarded with the same awe as his two linemates. That is, not until the first round of the Stanley Cup playoffs against Toronto. In the opening game, Richard was held scoreless by the Maple Leafs' expert checking forward, Bob Davidson. But in the second game, on March 23, 1944, Davidson's most determined efforts proved feeble against Richard's towering performance.

Maurice scored three goals in the second period, breaking a scoreless tie, and added two more in the third period. The final score was *Richard* 5, Toronto 1! The first time a player had scored five or more goals in a Stanley Cup match was in 1917 when Bernie Morris scored six against Les Canadiens for Seattle.

After disposing of Toronto, the Canadiens challenged Chicago and, once again, Richard dominated an entire game. The Montrealers defeated Chicago, 3–1, on April 6 in the second game of the final round and Richard scored *all three goals*! Just to prove it was no fluke, Maurice practically single-handedly saved Montreal in the fourth and last game of the series, after Chicago had mounted a 4–1 lead after two periods.

Richard's second goal of the game tied the match 4–4, sending it into sudden-death overtime. Then his pass to Blake set up the winning goal, and minutes later, Richard, Blake, and Lach were sipping champagne from the Stanley Cup.

As for the kid from Rivière des Prairies, in his first full season in the NHL he had set two big records. One for scoring five goals in a single game (a modern record), and another for amassing twelve goals in the complete playoff series.

Oddly enough, the reaction to Richard's accomplishments was not totally enthusiastic. Some viewers suggested that the "injury jinx" would soon catch up with him again. Others predicted that he would burn himself out. "He won't last" was a familiar cry whenever Richard was discussed. "Let's see what he'll do next year" was another.

When "next year" arrived, Les Canadiens iced virtually the same team they had when they won the Stanley Cup in April, with only a few exceptions. Phil Watson was reluctantly returned to the Rangers and the Canadiens received Fern Gauthier and Dutch Hiller. Another key addition was Ken Mosdell, a tall rangy forward who had just been released from the armed forces. The Punch Line remained intact and launched the season with the same syncopated attack that had stirred the fans in 1943–44. Richard seemed particularly bolstered by a full season under his belt without serious injury, and he broke from the post like an overzealous thoroughbred. His scoring was becoming so prolific that opposing coaches began mapping specific strategies to stop Maurice alone, on the theory that if you could blockade Richard, you could beat Les Canadiens. These strategems took on many variations over the years. One of the favorites was simply to goad Maurice into a fight. This was not exactly difficult, since the brooding French-Canadian still couldn't speak English and was rather sensitive and self-conscious about his language barrier.

One of the most effective methods for inciting Richard to riot was for an opposing coach to select one of his less-effective hatchet men to pester Maurice with an assortment of words, elbows, high sticks, and butt ends, until Richard retaliated. Both players would then likely be penalized, but at least Richard would be off the ice. The Rangers tried this ploy in Madison Square Garden on December 17, 1944.

Midway in the second period, Bob "Killer" Dill, a young Ranger defenseman, challenged Richard a few seconds after Chuck Scherza of the Rangers and Leo Lamoureux of the Canadiens had started their own private war. Up until then, Dill's chief claim to fame was the fact that he was a nephew of Mike and Tom Gibbons of fistic fame. From that night on, however, Dill became renowned as the man who lost two knockouts to Maurice in one period!

In the first bout, Richard disposed of Dill with a hefty right to the jaw. When the Ranger recovered, referee King Clancy sent him to the penalty box with a major penalty for fighting and doled out the same sentence to Richard. In those days, the penalty benches were constructed without a barrier separating players of opposing teams, so it was no unusual for the combatants to exchange insults while they awaited their release.

Still smarting from his knockout, Dill challenged Richard to a return bout. Maurice didn't quite understand Bob's English but there was no mistaking his sign language. Dill tossed the first punch and the two were off and swinging on the dry wood of the penalty box.

"Here Maurice the Mauler again measured his man," wrote Dan Daniel. "Roberto suffered a cut left eye and other bruises and contusions."

Richard's performance against Dill intrigued the imagination of New York sportswriters. One suggested that boxing promoter Mike Jacobs arranged a return flight between the pair in the ring rather than on the ice. Another described it as "the most interesting wartime set-to on local ice." Opinion was unanimous that Maurice was one of the best one-two punchers to come along since Joe Louis. "Richard scored two widely separated but emphatic knockdowns," said a boxing writer, "and he won on points!"

There was no longer any question that Richard had orbited into a very special position among the galaxy of hockey stars. Hy Turkin, of the New York *Daily News*, dubbed him "the Brunette Bullet," and added that his sidekick, Lach, was a "sandy-haired stick-handling Svengali." On Richard's first return to New York following his decision over Dill, more than fifteen thousand fans jammed Madison Square Garden to see him. One newspaper carried a two-column photo of

Richard's eyes alone and added, "He is the main event wherever he goes." For the first time in Richard's career he was being favorably compared with such Hall of Famers as Howie Morenz and Aurel Joliat.

"He may prove to be one of the great players of history," suggested sportswriter Joe King. "Those who saw Morenz will remember him for his flashing straight-away speed and his boundless daring. He was an arrow whizzing through the defense. He did not know caution. No momentary gap in the defense was too small for him to attempt.

"Richard is extremely speedy, but he is not the breathtaking adventurer that Morenz was. He is on a different pattern, with more guile in his makeup. . . . Maurice makes much more use of the change-of-pace, the trickery of speed and stick-handling than did Morenz. Richard swoops around the defense, while Morenz dared the guards to stop him dead on."

Ranger manager Lester Patrick, who was in a position to know, said Richard was more a copy of Jack Laviolette than of Morenz. Phil Watson echoed Patrick's sentiments. "There's no doubt," Watson asserted, "that Richard is the best wingman in hockey today." *Daily News* columnist Jim McCulley referred to Les Canadiens as "Richard & Co." And, needless to say, Maurice reinforced his reputation on each visit to New York.

With four games remaining in the season, Les Canadiens, snug in first place, invaded Madison Square Garden and routed the Rangers, 11–5. Banging two shots past goalie Ken McAuley, Richard lifted his goal-scoring mark to an astonishing forty-eight in only forty-seven games. "McAuley," observed Hy Turkin, "acted shell-shocked."

Overlooked by most readers consumed with the uproar over Richard was a small item out of Montreal carried by the Canadian Press. It said: "Howie Morenz, Jr., who a few weeks ago was warned that he would have to cut down on his hockey because of 'athlete's heart,' has sliced his playing time in half with encouraging results, his doctor said today. Young Morenz had been playing with Catholic High School and with the Junior Canadiens. He has dropped the Canadiens."

Acclaim for Les Canadiens was not as warm in Detroit and Toronto as it was in New York. The Red Wings peppery manager, Jack Adams, sniped at both Irvin and Richard, calling Montreal's coach, Dick Irvin, "a poor sport" and suggesting that Richard was becoming too self-important and far too touchy when checked by opposing players. Toronto's manager, Conn Smythe, criticized Richard for his weak back-checking.

Such commentary was regarded as so many sour grapes by Tommy Gorman, who launched a verbal counterattack. Gorman accused Richard's foes of deliberately fouling Maurice and singled out Smythe's Maple Leafs as the worst offenders.

Maurice seemed to rise above the smog of blather and cruised speedily along at a goal-a-game pace. He had surpassed Joe Malone's goal-scoring record, for which he received a standing ovation at the Forum, and the pressing question remaining was whether or not Richard would reach the hitherto unattainable plateau of fifty goals.

He scored number forty-nine on March 15, with only two games remaining on the schedule. In the next-to-last game, against the Black Hawks on Forum ice, Les Canadiens triumphed, but somehow Maurice was thoroughly blanked. That left only one more match, the final game of the season at Boston Garden. This time Richard came through in a 4–2 win over the Bruins and he finished the season with fifty goals in fifty games.

Having defended their first-place championship with ease, the Canadiens now turned to the business of defending their hold on the Stanley Cup. Toronto's Maple Leafs, the robust third-place finishers, would be the opening-round opposition and it didn't take very long for Conn Smythe's outfit to prove it had come to play.

Leaf coach, Hap Day, once more assigned Bob Davidson the thankless job of manacling Richard and this time he succeeded. Toronto upset Montreal, 1–0 and 3–2, in the first pair of games on Forum ice and Richard was completely neutralized. Although Montreal won the third game, in Toronto, by a score of 4–1, Richard was held scoreless. The Leafs captured the fourth game of the series with a 4–3 win and Richard finally scored. Maurice then exploded for four goals in the fifth game in which Toronto was routed, 10–3. Richard's inflationary output created the mirage that Montreal was about to dispose of the upstart Leafs, but when the teams met on March 31 in the sixth game, Richard was nullified and Toronto came away with a 3–2 win, stunning Les Canadiens with elimination.

The fact that Toronto went on to win the Stanley Cup hardly consoled the Canadiens' front office. But Irvin was quick to guard against a panic shake-up and decided to launch the 1945–46 season with virtually the same lineup that he had employed the previous season. There was one very significant addition, Ken Reardon. A boisterous prospect who had quit hockey to join the armed forces, he had returned to Montreal, and Irvin immediately invited him to training camp.

Reardon was a rare bird. Taken at face value, his hockey skills were minimal. In fact, he never so much as betrayed the likes of a star as far back as anyone could remember. As a youngster in Winnipeg, Manitoba, he played second fiddle to his older brother, Terry, and appeared content to watch his sibling develop into a big-league defenseman. "Ken had courage," said a friend of the family, "but little else as far as hockey was concerned."

Yet, somehow, his brother's success inspired Ken to pursue a hockey career. He would slog his way through sub-zero temperatures to find a practice rink where he could hone his game to sharpness. Despite a seemingly innate clumsiness, he pursued his goal and obtained a tryout with the Edmonton Athletic Club, after writing a letter to the team executive requesting a chance to play. He made the team, and at one point was closely scouted by the New York Rangers, but the Garden bird dogs finally rejected him because of his abject skating failures. Not long after the Ranger experts had departed, a Montreal scout took up the trail. He found Reardon's truculence to his liking. Working on the assumption that Kenny would never lose his guts and would improve his skating, the scout recommended that Reardon be signed. Reardon's first two seasons in Montreal were inconsequential, and before he could make a hockey name for himself, he joined the 86th Bridge Company of the Canadian Army and was next heard from in dispatches from the front.

One of them told how Reardon stood in a drizzling rain to receive a Certificate of

Gallantry from Field Marshall Bernard Montgomery. Another indicated that he was rarin' to rejoin the Canadiens at war's end to display his hockey skills. Reardon was discharged from the army in 1945 and immediately returned to the NHL to open up his own war on ice. "He has built a fearsome reputation," said one observer. "His feuds are becoming of national interest."

Forum fans immediately took him to their hearts, while spectators in out-of-town rinks were quick to despise him. In one of his earlier games in New York, Reardon was severely heckled by a fan sitting in a seat along the boards. During a stoppage in play, Ken gathered together a hunk of ice shavings, pressed them into a ball, and tossed it in the fan's face.

That, more or less, was what the Canadiens did to their opponents in the 1945–46 campaign, despite dire predictions that they would be routed by the rejuvenated opposition. World War II had ended and many of the stars of Boston, Detroit, New York, Chicago, and Toronto had returned. It was assumed that the opponents *had* to get better, while the Canadiens would inevitably slip.

It would prove to be more wishful thinking than reality.

Aubrey "Dit" Clapper, the professional player-coach of the Boston Bruins, was one of the more outspoken detractors of Les Canadiens. It was Clapper's boast that his Kraut Line, composed of Milt Schmidt, Bobby Bauer, and Woody Dumart, would obliterate the Punch Line in the eyes of postwar hockey fans. Clapper could be forgiven for his optimistic outburst. After all, the Krauts were one of the best offensive units before the war, and Boston fans nurtured the hope that they would regain their touch after being mustered out of the armed forces.

When Irvin declared, "Only an atomic bomb can stop the Punch Line," Clapper countered, "And we have that atomic bomb in our Kraut Line."

Dick realized he was being suckered into the brand of argument that would do his club no good. He was convinced that he had the best club in the NHL, but Irvin kept telling himself he would be better off keeping his mouth shut when it came to discussing the league's balance- or imbalance-of power. "If the other clubs make up their minds that we have the best team," he reasoned, "they'll all gang up on us."

But it was the Canadiens who did the ganging up. They routed Chicago, 8–4, in the opening game of the 1945–46 season; then swept past Toronto, 4–2, and Detroit, 3–1. However, they had yet to be tested by Clapper's Krauts, and on November 4, 1945, Les Canadiens invaded Boston Garden ice for what was to be the first chapter in a new Boston-Montreal grudge series that seems to have been replayed almost every year since then. Clapper proved prophetic this time as the Bruins prevailed, 6–5, handing Les Canadiens their first defeat of the season.

Less than a week later, the Canadiens returned the compliment with a 5–3 triumph at the Forum. One of the grating aspects of the feud, from the Montreal viewpoint, was the presence of Paul Bibeault, who had been loaned to Boston because of the wartime goalie problems. When Clapper revealed that Frankie Brimsek, Boston's pre-war goalie, was being mustered out of the U.S. Coast Guard, Irvin swiftly demanded that Bibeault be returned to Montreal. As expected, the Bruins balked at the demand, and the level of enmity between the two clubs reached a new high.

This hostility was translated to the ice when the teams collided at the Forum on

January 5, 1946. Goalie Bill Durnan, already acclaimed the greatest since Vézina, and possibly even better than Vézina, had to leave the game with a double fracture of the hand. Boston captain Milt Schmidt, who collided with Durnan, injured his hip, and soon the chaps had more or less decided to forget the puck and run at each other. Elmer Lach, who was regarded as the number-two center in the league after Bill Cowley, took care of the ratings by crashing the Bruin, Cowley, to the ice with a heavy body check. Cowley left the rink with a compound fracture of the wrist. Les Canadiens then took their toll on another third of the Kraut Line when Ken Reardon checked Bauer, injuring the Bruin's shoulder. By the time the final buzzer had sounded, Pat Egan, of Boston, had twisted his knee, and Murray Henderson had hurt his shoulder. Practically overlooked in the mayhem was the result of the game — 4–2, Montreal! The Canadiens also scored a victory over Ross and Clapper. Now that Durnan was injured and Brimsek was back in the Bruins' lineup, the Boston club was compelled to return Bibeault to Les Canadiens.

Durnan's temporary absence braked the Canadiens Express. With the less proficient Bibeault in goal, the Montrealers slipped to third place in mid-January. What's more, Irvin's gravest fears about opponents ganging up on Richard were born out. Maurice, who by this time had been nicknamed "the Rocket," staged a stirring bout with Murray "Muzz" Patrick of the Rangers, who was once heavyweight champion of Canada. A few weeks later, huge Reg Hamilton of the Black Hawks slugged toe-to-toe with Richard for three minutes before the linesmen could separate the pair.

When Durnan finally returned to the nets on February 9, Les Canadiens launched their successful offensive that would carry them to first place. The Punch Line led the attack, with Toe Blake motivated by his approach to the two-hundred-goal plateau. He achieved it on February 17 at Madison Square Garden, scoring a spectacular goal with less than a minute to play. The score was tied, 4–4, as Irvin dispatched the Punch Line to the ice with the overhead clock ticking away the final sixty seconds.

"In a violent rush," commented Kerr N. Petrie writing in the New York *Herald Tribune*, "Elmer Lach smashed through the Rangers' defense and forced the opening. Blake salvaged the puck and will remember the game it won for many years to come."

Kenny Reardon, who in subsequent years was to battle with numerous Rangers, reopened his war with the Garden spectators by scuffling first with a Ranger and then a railbird in the front row. "The crowd appeared to think Reardon should have been hung, drawn, and quartered," said Petrie, "but beyond the usual shower of paper and minor refuse there was no scene worthy of the name."

Having defeated the Rangers, Les Canadiens took a firm hold on first place and didn't relinquish it for the rest of the season. They clinched the league championship on March 14 and gamboled along the rest of the route, as individual players fattened their averages and collected the usual awards. Durnan won the Vézina Trophy for the third successive time and was now regarded as superior to Vézina. Blake, who received only one minor penalty all season, was awarded the Lady Byng Trophy, for combined ability and gentlemanly conduct, and Les Canadiens prepared for another march to the Stanley Cup, fully aware of the previous year's disappointment.

Paced by the Punch Line, they demolished Chicago, 6–2, in the opener of the best-of-seven semifinal. The Black Hawks sent several players on marauding missions against Richard, and Don Grosso of the Hawks emerged with a major penalty for fouling the Rocket. In the second game, Chicago's truculent defenseman, Johnny Mariucci, clashed with Richard, but the Rocket would not be daunted; nor would the Canadiens, who easily triumphed, 5–1.

"No player in hockey history has been so illegally shackled and interfered with by a host of personal checkers and shadows as has Rocket Richard," said Bill Roche. "Small wonder that he occasionally blows his top. Maurice should know a lot about the sour science of pro wrestling, for he has had nearly all the headlocks, arm scissors, and other grips and grabs applied on him in ice action. Further, if all the high sticks that have been thrust at his head were laid end to end he'd have quite a flourishing lumberyard."

The avalanche of wood notwithstanding, Richard & Co., eliminated the Black Hawks with 8–2 and 7–2 wins and prepared for their meeting in the Stanley Cup finals with the hated Bruins.

The Bruins tossed a scare that the Canadiens in the curtainraiser at the Forum on March 30 when they held a 3–2 lead, late in the third period. But Murph Chamberlain tied the score before the final buzzer, and the Rocket escaped from his check to blast home the winner in sudden-death overtime.

Boston obviously wasn't about to wilt. Goals by Pat "Boxcar" Egan and Bobby Bauer sprung them up to a 2–1 lead with less than ten minutes remaining in the second game, when Butch Bouchard released a long shot that escaped Frankie Brimsek. Once again the teams were thrust into the cauldron of overtime, and now it appeared the Bruins would prevail.

Speedy Don Gallinger found an opening in the Montreal defense early in the overtime period and dashed unmolested toward Durnan. "The Canadiens goaltender waited coolly for the Boston winger," said the *Associated Press* dispatch, "and just as Gallinger was preparing for his shot Durnan snatched the puck from him."

Minutes later, Jimmy Peters of Les Canadiens virtually duplicated Gallinger's effort, except that when Brimsek lunged for the puck, Peters slipped a low shot under him and the Montrealers won the game. The Canadiens then won the third match, 4–2, but Terry Reardon, now wearing a Boston uniform, snapped Montreal's winning streak with a sudden-death goal in the fourth game.

The Bruins fought gamely to avert elimination and managed to hold Montreal to a 3–3 tie after two and a half periods of the fifth game. It was then that Blake, despite an ailing back, drove in the winning goal. Chamberlain and Hiller added scores later in the period, and Les Canadiens had won the Stanley Cup for the sixth time in the team's history.

If championships had been won on paper, the Canadiens would have repeated again during the 1946–47 season when they finished in first place, six points ahead of the Toronto Maple Leafs. But the Habs encountered a hot, young Leaf club in the playoffs and to the amazement of the hockey world, were eliminated. The Punch Line would never be the same after that, and neither would the Canadiens — until the next dynasty arrived in the early 1950s.

The Detroit Red Wings, 1936–37

Detroit's First Dynasty — Red Wings, 1936–37

When most hockey fans recall superior Detroit hockey clubs, they invariably hark back to the Jack Adams' managed teams of the late 1940s and early 1950s, that headlined Gordie Howe, Ted Lindsay, and Terry Sawchuk.

Few are aware that an earlier Detroit club was just as competent in a number of ways and, in some cases, even better. Unfortunately, the Red Wings, circa 1936–37, played in the midst of The Great Depression, at a time when hockey did not obtain the brand of coverage it was to receive during the post-World War II era in the United States.

Thus, many of the feats of Goalie Norm Smith, as well as the top line comprising of Marty Barry, Herb Lewis, and Larry Aurie, went relatively unnoticed when compared with their standard of excellence. In 1935–36, for example, the Detroiters not only led the American Division (24–16–8), but also topped the entire league.

They remained on the fast track during the playoffs, first disposing of the Maroons in three straight games and then the Maple Leafs, three games to one. A season later the Motor City six was just as good. Again they recorded the best mark of all (25–14–9), confirming it in the playoffs with a three-games-to-two semifinal decision over the Canadiens and a similar job on the Rangers.

The Barry-Aurie-Lewis line was the toast of the league, but right behind them were some impressive attackers, not the least of whom was Syd Howe, a gifted scorer whose accomplishments were later overshadowed by Gordie Howe, who was in no way related other than the fact that both wore the red jerseys.

Ebenezer (Ebbie) Goodfellow was another excellent but underrated forward, as was Johnny Sorrell, Wally Kilrea, and Gord Pettinger. Coach, Jack (Jolly Jawn) Adams, could always count on a number of punishing bodychecks thrown by his big-chested defenseman, Wilfred (Bucko) McDonald, one of the hardest hitters the game has known.

The Red Wings reign was as abrupt as it was impressive. Following the two consecutive Stanley Cups, they plunged out of the playoffs and would not be a major threat until after the outbreak of World War II.

In their prime, the Wings did everything right. Adams was a splendid motivator, although he occasionally allowed emotion to dominate his thinking. Goaltending was excellent and, of course, there *was* that brilliant trio up front.

The Thirties Red Wings lacked the staying power of Adams' Lindsay-Howe-Sawchuk clubs, nor could it match depth or goaltending. (Terry Sawchuk was a better goaltender overall than Smith.) But for its time it was a vaunted power, and ranks with the all-time best.

Failures of the Detroit Red Wings in the post-Gordie Howe era and right up to the present, tend to erase the glitter of yesteryear when Jack Adams molded the Red Wings into one of hockey's mightiest organizations.

"We are not the Yankees of hockey," Adams would snap. "The Yankees are the Red Wings of baseball!"

National Hockey League history proves Adams's point. Since Detroit was admitted to the NHL in 1926, they have finished in first place 13 times and have won the Stanley Cup seven times, a record unsurpassed by any other American team in the league.

Detroit's dominance of puckdom was so awesome during the period from 1949 to 1955, that their opponents regarded it as a monumental feat even to tie the Red Wings in a game. In that era, the Detroiters finished first for seven consecutive years, an achievement the Ruthian Yankees never matched, even at their very best.

Reaching that pinnacle was not simple. There was a time when Detroit hockey fans were quite happy if the hometown skaters came off the ice with a tie. But that was in 1926, the team's rookie season in the NHL when the team was known as the Cougars.

Hockey had arrived in the Motor City via Victoria, British Columbia, when a syndicate composed of the Townsend-Seyburn interests of Detroit purchased the Cougars of the defunct Western League for $100,000. This brought players such as Jack Walker, Clem Loughlin, Art Duncan, Frank Foyston, and Frank Frederickson to Michigan. In time, Foyston, Walker, and Frederickson were inducted into the Hockey Hall of Fame, but their initial efforts were rather dismal during that opening 1926–27 season.

When the 44 game schedule ended, Detroit had won 12 games and lost 28 for the dubious distinction of finishing at the bottom of the American Division. That was, perhaps, the least of their problems. The club was forced to play in adjoining Windsor, Ontario, because the new Olympia Stadium on Grand River and McGraw in Detroit had not yet been completed.

As a result, fans of the new team did not exactly take the Cougars to their hearts. The militant disaffection was reflected in a vital area, the gate, where the Cougars dropped $84,000 in the first year and appeared hellbent for bankruptcy. Club president, Charles Hughes, of the Detroit Athletic Club, was not one to lose either on the ice, or at the box office. Since the hockey club's investors also included a member of the Ford family and a Fisher of Fisher Body fame, improvements in performance had to be made. One happy change made by Hughes eventually made Detroit a hockey powerhouse.

Hughes, with a little help from NHL president Frank Calder, signed Jack Adams — who had played NHL hockey with the Toronto Arenas, the Toronto St. Patricks, and the Ottawa Senators — as manager-coach. Hughes found he was dealing with an exceptionally galvanic personality who had been one of the best players in hockey history. Adams would do anything to win and rarely concerned himself with the consequences.

Once, during the 1918–19 season, Adams with the Arenas became engaged in a wild fight with Sprague Cleghorn, another robust skater. The Governor General of Canada was a front row spectator at the match and one whose criticism could have meant Adams's expulsion.

"It was a real slugfest," Adams later recalled. "Funny, I never did hear what the Governor General thought about it, but I thought I saw a distinguished-looking man clapping his white-gloved hands."

Adams brought to Detroit the successful style of play that had made him an outstanding hockey player through the years, a brand of hockey that frequently enraged his foes.

"Adams," said Alfie Skinner of the Toronto Arenas, against whom Adams played for many years, "was an awful slasher. Some fellows would slash and you'd hardly feel it through your pads. But when Adams swung his stick at a vulnerable part of your anatomy, he swung hard. He meant to hurt! On the other hand, he'd take punishment without a murmur. He'd never complain when anyone whacked him. A guy like that you had to admire."

President Calder must certainly have admired Adams when Jack walked into the NHL office prior to the 1927–28 season and asserted that he was man for the vacant Detroit job. Calder agreed and telephoned Charlie Hughes to set up an appointment.

Adams then met Hughes and revealed the same brashness, a characteristic for which he was renowned. "I'd been involved in winning the Stanley Cup for Ottawa," said Adams, "so I told Hughes that he needed me more than I needed him."

Hughes must have agreed, because he signed Adams to a contract and told him to get started building a winner. A year later, Hughes knew he had taken the right course. From a dismal 12–28–4 record, the Detroiters climbed to the .500 mark, winning 19, losing 19, and tying 6 games. It wasn't a good enough record for a Stanley Cup berth, but there was no question that the road to the cup had opened for Detroit. The following season Detroit, with a new nickname, the Falcons, finished third in the American Division.

Adams soon discovered that building a winner required more than native enthusiasm. Money was necessary to buy and sign players, but the Depression had hit the motor industry and loose cash was as distant as the Stanley Cup. One night Adams allowed a fan in to Olympia Stadium in exchange for five bags of potatoes.

"If the greatest star in the game was made available to us for $1.98," said Adams, "we couldn't have afforded him."

The turning point towards better times for the team was reached in 1933, when the franchise was bought by James Norris, Sr., a grain millionaire with a fervent love of hockey. Norris had played hockey for the Montreal Amateur Athletic Association's famous Winged Wheelers. He suggested a new team name, the Red Wings, and an insignia symbolic of the industry which dominates the city.

A no-nonsense type, Norris was even brasher than Adams. He laid it on the line with the manager. "I'll give you a year on probation," Norris warned, "with no contract."

Adams may not have had a written pact with Norris, but he quickly gained the millionaire's confidence as well as access to his bankroll to sign superior players.

He bought Syd Howe (no relation to Gordie) from the St. Louis Flyers for $35,000. Howe was soon playing the brand of hockey that eventually put him in the Hall of Fame. Hec Kilrea was purchased from Toronto for $17,000, and the Wings were off, flying toward the top.

By the 1935–36 season, the Adams-Norris combine was the best in hockey. The manager was not only off probation, but had become so friendly with his awesome boss that he referred to Norris as "Pops."

Adams put it this way: "Pops was the bankroll and the boss, and after he took over Detroit hockey never looked back."

By March 22, 1936, the final day of the 1935–36 season, Detroit was perched atop the American Division with a record of 24 wins, 16 losses, and 8 ties for 56 points, the best record in either division. In Marty Barry, Herb Lewis, and Larry Aurie, the Red Wings boasted the best offensive unit in the league. Their distinguished efforts were reinforced by the exploits of Syd Howe, Johnny Sorrell, Hec Kilrea, and a big broth of a shooter named Ebenezer Goodfellow.

"Goodfellow," a member of the Detroit family recently commented, "was Gordie Howe before Gordie Howe came along!"

In the prime of his career, Normie Smith provided Detroit with more than adequate goaltending, fronted by capable defensemen like Bucko McDonald and Doug Young. However, the Red Wings had yet to bring the Stanley Cup to Detroit, a fact that was fast becoming a negative obsession with its fans.

In 1935–36, the National Hockey League was still divided into two sections, a Canadian Division including the Montreal Maroons, the Toronto Maple Leafs, the New York Americans, and the Montreal Canadiens, and an American Division including the Red Wings, the Boston Bruins, the Chicago Black Hawks, and the New York Rangers. The Red Wings would face the first place team in the Canadian Division, the Montreal Maroons, in the opening round of the Stanley Cup playoffs.

Judging by their respective records, which were almost identical, the Maroons and Red Wings would be in for a difficult series, with bookmakers at a loss as to whom to list as the favorites. The opening game of the series at the Montreal Forum on March 24, 1936, proved how evenly matched they were.

Led by Hooley Smith, Baldy Northcott, and Jimmy Ward, the Maroons presented one of the most formidable attacks in the league. The Red Wings countered with their front line of Barry, Lewis, and Aurie.

Despite the notable scorers on both teams, three periods of play elapsed without either club scoring a goal. This meant sudden-death overtime; the first team to score would win the game. Although the Forum crowd was excited about the prospect of sudden death, there was some reason to suspect this might be an exceptionally long night. For one thing, the teams were getting excellent goaltending from Normie Smith in the Red Wing cage and Lorne Chabot of the Maroons. For another, there was precedent for a marathon match. On April 4, 1932, the Toronto Maple Leafs and Boston Bruins played past 1 A.M. in what had been the longest NHL game on record.

By the time the Maroons and Red Wings had played through the second overtime without a goal, the crowd began to get restless. The players, of course, were laboring on badly chopped ice that didn't have the benefit of modern resurfacing machines in vogue today. Nevertheless, they plodded on past midnight with no end in sight.

When the sixth period began, a cascade of cheers went up from the previously numbed crowd. Perhaps they hoped to inspire the Maroons to a spirited rush and a score, but this didn't happen. Neither team scored and the teams moved into the seventh period, as a handful of fans streamed to the exits.

Despite the hour, the majority of spectators remained in their seats. By now the monumental contest became an obsession with both players and fans, and everyone seemed determined to see it through to a conclusion, no matter what happened. Nothing very much happened in the seventh period, but the eighth — or fifth sudden death — period loomed as the decisive one.

Near the end of the period, Marty Barry, the Red Wings' accomplished center, was approaching collapse. With what energy he had at his command, Barry sent a pass to Herbie Lewis that catapulted his wing into the clear for a play on goal. He moved into striking distance and released a hard shot that obviously beat goalie Lorne Chabot. As Lewis prepared to raise his stick in the traditional victory salute, he heard the puck clang off the goal post. It rebounded harmlessly to the corner where Hooley Smith retrieved it and began a counterattack with as much danger as Lewis's play.

Smith was accompanied on his rush by Baldy Northcott. There was a choice, either Smith could make the play himself, using Northcott as a decoy, or he could try the pass. At first, Smith cut sharply toward the net, giving the impression he would go it alone. But, at the precise moment, he skimmed the puck to Northcott who shot hard at the Red Wing net. However, Normie Smith anticipated the play, caught the puck on his pad and steered it to teammate Doug Young who reversed the field.

Now, it appeared that each team was bent on a wild kamikaze attacks in the hopes of bringing the game to a sudden end. Young raced along the boards until he reached Maroon territory. Then, he fired wildly, but the puck suddenly hit Maroon defenseman Lionel Conacher's skate and changed direction, sliding straight for an empty side of the net. It appeared to be equadistant between Young and goalie Chabot. The Red Wing skater lunged for it, but before he could get his stick on the rubber, Chabot smothered it with his glove. Shortly thereafter the period ended and the teams had completed eight scoreless periods of play.

Four minutes and 46 seconds after the ninth period began, the teams had broken the longest-game record set by Toronto and Boston and, still, there was no end in sight. It was past 2 A.M. and many of the spectators were fighting to keep their eyes open, not wanting to miss the decisive goal if it ever was to be scored.

By this time, the veterans of both teams were fatigued beyond recovery. It was essential to employ the players with the most stamina and, naturally, those with even a smidgen of energy remaining were the inexperienced younger skaters. One of them was Modere (Mud) Bruneteau, a native of St. Boniface, Manitoba, who had just one season ago played for the Wings' minor league team, the Detroit Olympics. He was the youngest man in the longest game, equipped, Jack Adams believed, with the strongest legs. Adams was the Detroit coach and he remembered, before he died: "The game settled into an endurance test, hour after hour. One o'clock came, and then 2 A.M., and by now the ice was a chipped, brutal mess. At 2:25 I looked along our bench for the strongest legs and I scrambled the lines to send out Syd Howe, Hec Kilrea and Bruneteau."

As a rookie on a loaded first-place club, Bruneteau saw very little action during the season and scored only two goals while achieving no assists for a grand total of two points. But he was young and at the 12-minute mark of the ninth period, Mud Bruneteau was in a lot better shape than most of his teammates or opponents.

Adams' instructions were typically explicit. "Boys, let's get some sleep. It's now or never!"

Bruneteau surrounded the puck in the Detroit zone and passed it to Kilrea. They challenged the Montreal defense, Kilrea faking a return pass, then sliding it across the blueline. Bruneteau cut behind the defense and retrieved the puck. "Thank God," he says, "Chabot fell down as I drove it in the net. It was the funniest thing. The puck just stuck there in the twine and didn't fall on the ice."

There was a dispute when the goal judge neglected to flash his red light, but referee Nels Stewart arbitrated. "You're bloody right it's a goal!" Stewart announced, and put up his hand as a signal. After 116 minutes and 30 seconds of overtime, the Red Wings had defeated the Maroons, 1–0.

There was a wild, capering anticlimax. Bruneteau's sweater was removed, not delicately, by his relieved associates. One fan thrust a $20 bill on Bruneteau as he left the ice. Other exuberants reached for their wallets. "There I was, my stick under one arm and my gloves under another, and, laughing, I grabbed money in every direction!"

When he reached the Detroit dressing room, Bruneteau tossed a bundle of bills on a rubbing table. "Count it," he told Honey Walker, the trainer, "and split it for the gang." The windfall was gratifying for professionals in a depression year: $22 for each member of the Wings, including Adams, Walker, and the stickboy.

Mud Bruneteau's shot went into the net at 16:30 of the sixth overtime or 2:25 A.M. Eastern Standard Time. Normie Smith, who was playing in his first Stanley Cup game, was limp when it was over. He had stopped 90 shots in all. "We were all pretty much all in," Smith recalled years later, "but very happy."

Another hero of that marathon game was Red Wings' defenseman Wilfred (Bucko) McDonald. Although the record books don't show it, McDonald knocked a Maroon to the ice on the average of every five minutes. And many years later, offered proof of his devastating performance.

"The reason somebody kept track was because this oil dealer from Detroit had offered me $5 for every knockdown," said McDonald. "We agreed on a limit of $200 so I didn't quite make it. But he did pay me $185, which was a lot of money in the 1930s. Of course, he never dreamed I'd have so many chances to collect. Also, the ice got slushy as the evening wore on so the Maroons became easier to hit.

"This was the first game of the playoffs and we were in a tough situation; we hadn't beaten the Maroons all season," he recalled. "I was expecting a busy night because we figured a lot of hitting would intimidate the Maroons and put them off their game. So all I ate at noon was a boiled egg and a dish of ice cream. Fourteen hours later, we were still playing. I was bloody hungry.

"On in the overtime, Hooley Smith of Montreal told me he'd hit me over the head if I bodychecked him once more. 'Take your best shot,' I said. I was wearing a helmet, see. He did let me have it and got a penalty, of course. This could have been the break that decided the thing but we couldn't score on the power play."

Meanwhile, Bruneteau sat on his bed in Montreal's genteel Windsor Hotel near 5 A.M. on March 25, 1936, still unwinding from a Stanley Cup playoff that he had won for the Detroit Red Wings less than three hours before. He was about to undress after a beer celebration, when there was a knock on the door. He sat very still, not caring to be disturbed. The knocker persisted. Finally Bruneteau let his visitor in, somewhat startled to recognize the Montreal goalkeeper he had beaten to end the weary marathon. Lorne Chabot, dark eyes staring under a thicket of black brows, had come to call.

"Sorry to bother you kid," Chabot said, "but you forgot something when you left the rink." Then, handing Bruneteau a puck, "Maybe you'd like to have this souvenir of the goal you scored."

Bruneteau mused on the long-gone moment several years ago: "Can you imagine that such a great man as him would do such a thing for a rookie? I remember him standing there in the door, big, handsome guy with a kind of fat-looking face. I felt, I guess, funny. He came in and we sat on the bed, and talked for a long time."

Bruneteau was a journeyman, mutely remote from stardom until one goal left him with reverberating notoriety. Afterward, apart from 35 goals scored in the wartime season of 1943–44, he was undistinguished.

"The publicity never ended," he said. "It could've happened to a lot of guys who were better players. I was just another guy named Joe."

Adams's gratification paused short of hoping prolonged games would become habitual. "Rotten ice produced rotten hockey that was torture for the players and boring for the fans. I knew the NHL had to do something."

Adams discovered what to do in the spring of 1938, when the Red Wings and Montreal Canadiens toured Europe. "I noticed one night at an ice show that the attendants swept the surface with sheepskin brushes and then flooded it before the next show." He recommended ice-flooding between periods to the NHL governors, and in 1940–41 resurfacing became mandatory. "That legislation speeded up play, because it meant the players didn't have to skate through slush late in the game. It convinced me that there'll never be any approach to Bruneteau's overtime record. There are too many shots and too much wide-open play to permit long stretches with no goals."

The impetus gained from the Red Wings' marathon opening-game win was enough to lift the Red Wings to a three-straight playoff victory over the Maroons and a four-game win over the Toronto Maple Leafs for the Stanley Cup. Smith, the alter hero of the marathon match, lost both trophies he had hoped to obtain as souvenirs.

His goalie stick was autographed by every member of the Red Wings, but somehow wound up in the hands of a Judge John Scallen. "I also was supposed to get half the puck that was in play at the finish of the game," said Smith, "but I don't know what became of that."

Nor did he get his name inscribed in the record book that lists the longest game. That honor was bestowed on Modere (Mud) Bruteneau, the rookie who had scored only two goals all season.

Joy was rampant in the Motor City, although the championship was won at Maple Leaf Gardens in Toronto. After the game, Norris tossed a party for the Red Wings at a local hotel, where president Calder presented the Stanley Cup to the Detroit owner. The victory had special significance for Jack Adams and Hec Kilrea, who had been teammates nine years earlier on the Ottawa Senators when Ottawa won the Stanley Cup.

At first, defending the cup appeared to be an easy assignment for Adams and his men. His roster was mighty from the goal to the forward line, and even such promising rookies as defenseman Jimmy Orlando were unable to crack the varsity. Then the 1936–37 season got underway, and disaster followed disaster at Olympia. Captain Doug Young suffered a broken leg and was lost for the season, soon followed to the sidelines by Orville Roulston, another broken leg victim. When Detroit's leading scorer, Larry Aurie, broke his ankle early in March, 1937, Adams wondered if and when the bad luck would ever end.

In spite of the injuries, the Red Wings prevailed. They finished first in the American Division for the second consecutive year, winning 25 games, losing 14, and tying 9 for 59 points, once again tops in both divisions.

The first obstacle enroute to the Cup was a Montreal Canadiens team adorned with stars like Aurel Joliat, Johnny "Black Cat" Gagnon, and Toe Blake. Detroit swept the first two games of the best-of-five series at Olympia 4–0 and 5–1 without the injured Larry Aurie, but the Flying Frenchmen rebounded to win the next two, forcing a fifth game at the Forum in Montreal.

For the second time in two years the Red Wings were involved in a sudden-death playoff classic. Ebbie Goodfellow had lifted Detroit into a 1–0 lead, only to see it erased by a score by Bill McKenzie for the Canadiens. From that point until 12:45 A.M. (51 minutes and 49 seconds of overtime), the clubs traded shot for shot without result. It was then that Hec Kilrea lined a blast that eluded goalie Wilf Cude, giving Detroit a 2–1 victory in the game and a 3–2 edge in the series.

Catapulted into the Cup finals against the New York Rangers powerhouse, Adams was once again confronted with potential calamity. Goalie Norm Smith, who had injured his elbow in the opening round, was forced to retire during the first game of the finals on April 6, 1937, at Madison Square Garden. The Rangers bombed Detroit 5–1 and appeared to be heavy favorites to capture the Cup, since Smith was ruled too incapacitated to play for the rest of the series.

Smith was replaced by Earl Robertson, a second-string goaltender of hitherto questionable ability. However, the questions about Robertson's talent were answered during the next three games. He beat New York 4–2 in the second game. He lost 1–0 in the third, but then shut out the Rangers 1–0 to tie the series at two apiece, leaving one game to be played in the best of five.

The deciding bout was played at Olympia on April 15. Once again, Robertson was invincible. He blunted the best drives hurled at him by Frank Boucher, Lynn Patrick, Neil Colville, and Alex Shibicky, while Marty Barry scored twice for Detroit and Johnny Sorrell punched home a third goal. Detroit won both the game and the Stanley Cup, becoming the first team to finish first and win the Cup in consecutive seasons.

Adams now committed one of the few mistakes of his long coaching and managerial career. After much soul-searching, "Jovial Jawn," as he was affectionately known to chums, decided to permit the championship roster to remain intact, on the theory that what produced two Stanley Cups in a row was good enough to produce a third.

It didn't.

The plummet of the Red Wings in 1937–38 could conservatively be described as catastrophic. Not only did they fail to retain their hold on first place, but they didn't even gain a playoff berth. Without looking for scapegoats, Adams accepted all the blame.

"I stood pat," said Adams, "when I should have been dealing. After this flop, I'll never hesitate to bust up championship clubs."

The Boston Bruins, 1938–41

Boston's Kraut Line Era, 1938–41

It was entirely appropriate that "The Edmonton Express," Eddie Shore, should power the Boston Bruins to their first Stanley Cup in 1929 and still be with the Hub City six a decade later, when Beantown celebrated its second championship season in 1939.

Granted, Shore no longer was the overpowering force he had been in the late 1920s and early 1930s, but he still was a muscular marvel even in his declining years when the Bruins became the dominant team during the regular season, starting in 1937–38.

As with most power teams, the Bruins excelled in every area, beginning behind the bench. There was no smarter coach than Art (Lil Arthur) Ross; no better forward unit than The Kraut Line from Kitchener, Ontario, featuring Milt Schmidt centering Woody Dumart and Bobby Bauer; and an airtight defense including Dit Clapper, Flash Hollet, Jack Portland, and the ubiquitous Shore.

Goaltending was the envy of the league. The Bruins already had an ace in Tiny Thompson and then, somehow, found an even better netminder in the American-born (Eveleth, Minnesota) Frankie (Mister Zero) Brimsek. The latter was in goal for the Cup win.

The Bruins' excellence was reflected in the standings. They produced the best record in 1937–38 (30-7-11), 1938–39 (36-10-2), and 1939–40 (31-12-5), not to mention 1940–41 (27-8-13).

They were mean — how could they not be with Shore in the lineup? — when they had to be, and magnificent in every offensive department. Center Bill Cowley was, arguably, the most underrated playmaker of all time and

Mel (Sudden Death) Hill was the best clutch playoff scorer of the pre-World War II era. Second-liners such as Roy Conacher, Herb Cain, and Red Hamill would have been starters on any other team.

What is surprising about the Bruins who marauded through the NHL during the late 1930s is that they didn't win at least three Stanley Cups. They didn't even survive the first round in 1938, losing in three straight to the Toronto Maple Leafs and totalling only three goals in the process. While they did obtain revenge, winning The Cup, the following spring, the Bruins could not survive their opening playoff series in 1940. A New York Rangers team that was destined to win The Stanley Cup that year ousted Boston four games to two, although the Bruins held a two games to one advantage at one point.

But it was difficult, if not impossible, to contain the Boston machine for very long. The spring of 1941 was witness to a splendid seven-game semifinal series in which the Bruins defeated Toronto four games to three. They disposed of the Detroit Red Wings in four straight contests to wrap up The Cup.

That was it for The Krauts. The onset of World War II inspired Schmidt, Dumart, and Bauer to enlist in the Royal Canadian Air Force and other Boston stars joined the armed forces as well. The 1942 playoff edition of the Bruins was disposed of in two games by Detroit, signalling the end of The Kraut Era.

Placing the Kraut Bruins among the all-time teams was not an easy task, although it would have been a lot simpler had they won the "middle" Cup in 1940 thereby making it three in a row. Then, there is the War Factor, just as it was for the 1940 championship Rangers. The Kraut Line was in its absolute prime at the time Schmidt, Bauer, and Dumart departed for war duty. Ditto for goalie Frank Brimsek, who enlisted in the U.S. Coast Guard and never was the same after his return in the mid-1940s. Had the war not interfered, the Bruins would have been serious Cup contenders in 1942, 1943, and 1944, because the nucleus of stars would have been intact and ripe for winning.

A high rating still is in order for Boston, primarily because the Bruins presented one of the best lines of any era, a magnificent goalie, and a back-up corps that was deep in every department. They made only one mistake; they let the 1940 series against the Rangers escape their grasp.

It has been said that no act in the hockey world could follow Eddie Shore's extravaganza in Boston Garden. Shore was all things to all hockey people, but in Beantown he was God for too long to allow one mere mortal to replace him. Thus it was appropriate that when Shore's star began to descend, in the late thirties, it would require three forwards and a kid goaltender to allow Bostonians to ease Eddie out of their minds.

The three forwards — Milt Schmidt, Woody Dumart, and Bobby Bauer — and goaltender Frankie Brimsek gave Boston the nucleus of a marvelously strong and versatile hockey club, which frequently dominated the NHL in the years leading up to America's entry into World War II.

Shore was still king in Boston when Schmidt, Bauer, and Dumart were learning their hockey fundamentals in Kitchener, Ontario. They were the Three Musketeers of teenage hockey in Kitchener, playing as a unit for the city's Junior team. Inevitably, the scouts drifted their way, and the Bruins had the good fortune to lead them to the NHL.

Although Schmidt was regarded as the best of the three, Dumart and Bauer were the ones invited to try out with and eventually play for the Boston Cubs, a farm team of the Bruins. The younger Schmidt was advised to remain home in Kitchener. He was only 17 and considered too young even for the Boston Cubs.

Bauer and Dumart knew better. "You're making a big mistake," they told Bruins manager Art Ross when they arrived at Boston Garden. "Milt Schmidt is every bit as good as we are, if not better."

Ross was unmoved. When the 1935-36 season began, Schmidt remained at home while the other two learned what pro hockey was all about. Fortunately for Ross, they never stopped pestering him about their pal back home; they exerted as much energy badgering the Bruins manager about Schmidt as they did trying to score goals on the ice.

It wasn't until September, 1936, that Ross got the message. He invited Schmidt, Bauer, and Dumart to the training camp of the Providence Reds, a Boston farm club in the old International League. But Ross wasn't about to let well enough alone. "Look here, Schmidt," he told the flabbergasted rookie. "I don't believe that anyone can be as good as your two friends say you are. Now the three of you get out there on the ice, and we'll see what this is all about!"

At this juncture a lesser man than Schmidt might have fallen on his face — the victim of a buildup to a letdown — but with Bauer on his right side and Dumart on his left there was no way he could fail. The three dazzled their opponents with their footwork, passing, and shots. As expected, Schmidt was the best of all; even Ross was willing to concede that.

"I guess he's pretty good, all right," said Ross, who knew that he had three jewels in hockey crown. "But it seems to me that I remember there were some fellows around here telling me that."

At first they were dubbed the "Sauerkraut Line" in honor of Kitchener's favorite appetizer. Later it was shortened to the "Kraut Line." But no matter what they were called, the three were poison to the opposition. Before the 1936-37 season was half over, Ross realized that at least two of them — Schmidt and Dumart — were ready for the NHL. Bauer would have to wait.

The Bruins manager summoned them to Boston and told Milt and Woody that they would skate with veteran Dit Clapper. Schmidt was awed by the rapid rise; he dispatched a paycheck to his mother in Kitchener with a note saying: "Please bank this for me. I'll need it fairly soon because I won't last long in this league."

Schmidt never had to worry. He was in the NHL to stay, and so was Dumart. A season later Bauer was elevated to Boston and the Kraut Line soon established itself as one of the most formidable in the NHL. Dumart was rugged, Bauer was chunky, and Schmidt was all steel. Despite his youth, Milt made it clear that if there was to be any rough stuff on the ice, the enemy would have to contend with him, especially if the foe decided to pick on his less destructive mates.

"What Schmidt has done to some of his enemies," observed a Boston writer, "was nothing more than calculated vivisection."

"Black Jack" Stewart, the burly and surly Detroit Red Wings defenseman, once mauled Bauer so badly that Bobby was forced out of the Boston lineup for several weeks. "Before the game was over," said a reporter, "Milt banged into Stewart, who had to be carted off the ice." Black Jack remained out of the Detroit lineup for ten games.

Schmidt was not indestructable, but it required a terribly serious injury to keep him out of the Bruins lineup. For one full season he played with a shoulder separation. In one game, his ankle was cut, a knee wrenched, a shoulder bruised, and his groin strained. In another, his jaw was broken by an opponent's stick, and Schmidt was fed through a straw for several weeks. When he returned, he was wearing a mask that fitted over his head and under his chin, with a steel brace over the area where the bones had been broken.

The Bruins were playing the Red Wings that night, and almost immediately, Herbie Lewis of Detroit brought his stick up against Schmidt's chin. "I'm gonna carve you up for nine stitches," Schmidt vowed as the men lined up for the next face-off.

Seconds later, Lewis was down on the ice, his face a bloody pulp. He was carted to the dressing room, and, sure enough, nine stitches were taken in the Detroiter's hide.

Occasionally, a Schmidt vendetta had a humorous touch to it. During Milt's rookie season, the Bruins were playing the New York Americans when Eddie Wiseman of the New York sextet suffered severe cuts about the face. Normally the perpetrator would have been given a five-minute penalty for drawing blood, but referee Mickey Ion wasn't sure which Bruin was the culprit. The official finally demanded that coach Art Ross select one of his skaters to occupy the penalty box for the infraction against Wiseman. Ross pointed to Schmidt.

Two years later, Wiseman was traded to the Bruins. When the former Americans ace entered his new dressing room, Schmidt extended his hand and reminded Wiseman of the night his face had been bloodied. "Oh how I wanted to cut somebody up for stitches for that one," said Wiseman, "but I never found out who laid the lumber on me."

A big grin broke over Schmidt's face, and he said: "Never mind. Justice was done. It was me, but I want to apologize. You know I don't go around hurting people. Anyway, you're on my side now."

Wiseman mulled over the apology for a moment. Then he replied: "For a guy who doesn't like to go around hurting people, you certainly push a lot of them around on the ice. But, like you say, I'm on your side. You're somebody else's worry now."

The Kraut Line provided Ross with a remarkable team, but it wasn't until two years later, when Frankie Brimsek arrived on the scene, that Ross beamed over what many critics regard as the finest Bruins hockey club of all time.

Like the Krauts, Brimsek had a tough act to follow. Cecil "Tiny" Thompson, who had been the regular Boston goaltender, won the Vézina Trophy four times between 1930 and 1938. Naturally, Thompson was revered up and down the coast of New England. It was incredible for Bostonians to believe that a young *American-born* goaltender had been designated by Art Ross as heir-apparent to the beloved Tiny.

Brimsek learned his hockey, playing for Eveleth (Minnesota) High School and later for St. Cloud Teacher's College. The Bruins moved him on to their Providence farm club, and in November, 1938, Ross did the unthinkable: he sold Thompson to the Detroit Red Wings and promoted Brimsek to the varsity. Obviously, Brimsek and Schmidt were cut from the same cloth. Frankie was virtually immune to pressure, and he took up where Thompson had left off.

In his second game, Brimsek shut out Chicago 5–0 on the road and returned to Boston Garden for his first home game. Bruins fans, who had been loyal to Thompson for so many years, were wary of the kid from Eveleth. And the kid knew it.

"The crowd was so quiet that first night, that I could hear them breathe and feel their cold eyes on my back," said Brimsek.

The spectators did not seem to bother Brimsek. He played as if he didn't have a worry in his body. When the final buzzer sounded, the Bruins were on top, 2–0, for Brimsek's second straight shutout!

His next game, on December 11, 1938, was against the mighty New York Rangers. This time the Bruins scored three goals, and the kid goalie had done it again: another shutout.

In his next game, Brimsek was beaten. The Rangers scored twice (Boston had three), and his record ended, after 231 minutes and 54 seconds of shutout goaltending. Just to prove it was no fluke, he soon began another shutout string; this one of 220 minutes and 24 seconds duration, against the Canadiens, Red Wings, and New York Americans.

He obviously deserved the nickname coined for his achievements — Mister Zero.

Brimsek's remarkable goaltending occasionally stole the headlines away from Schmidt, Dumart, and Bauer. And when the Kraut Line was not in the news, a crafty center named Bill Cowley managed to get the ink.

In many ways Cowley was the most underrated cog in the mighty new Boston wheel. He had come to the Bruins via the defunct St. Louis Eagles, but he was placed at left wing rather than center, his natural position. Cowley's enormous playmaking abilities were stifled, until Babe Siebert convinced Bruins coach Frank Patrick that Cowley was better situated at the pivot position. "That kid can fly," said Siebert. "Put him at center, and he'll rattle in the goals."

Patrick took the advice. Cowley was slow to prove himself, and he didn't really show what he could do until the Bruins went up against the Canadiens at the Forum in Montreal. With the score tied in the final period, Cowley broke free with his pal Siebert right behind. Canadien goalie Wilf Cude braced himself for what appeared to be a natural play — a pass from Cowley to Siebert. "Beat him yourself," yelled Siebert. "It's your play kid!"

Cowley was almost atop the goalie. It seemed that the Boston center would have to circle the net in order to make a play on goal, but at the last split second Cowley released a backhand shot that whizzed past Cude. From that point on, Cowley could not be stopped.

He led the Bruins in scoring during the regular 1938–39 season — finishing third in the league only five points behind the leader, Toe Blake of Montreal — and was as responsible as Brimsek and the Krauts for the Bruins's awesome record of 36 wins, 10 defeats, and 2 ties. They finished in first place, a full 16 points ahead of the Rangers

"*Are the Bruins that good?*" The question was asked throughout the NHL, as Boston prepared to meet the Rangers in the opening round of the playoffs. Observers agreed that the winner of the Boston–New York series would march on to the Stanley Cup.

The Rangers trained their defenses on Cowley and the Krauts, and Boston's balance made itself felt. When the teams skated into overtime tied 1–1, a relative unknown named Mel Hill suddenly burst into prominence. It took three sudden-death periods to do it, but Hill finally took a pass from Cowley and beat Ranger goalie Davey Kerr for the winning goal — at 1:10 A.M.

By the time the second contest had ended, the Rangers were forgetting the Krauts and concentrating on Hill. Once again he took a Cowley pass during the first sudden-death period and fooled Kerr at 8:24. The Bruins led the series 2–0.

The Rangers took another battering, a 4–1 defeat, in the third game. Nobody gave New York a chance to counterattack, except the Rangers themselves. They salvaged the fourth game, 2–1, won the fifth by the same score in sudden death, and tied the series at three apiece with a 3–1 triumph in the sixth game.

The seventh and final game has been called one of hockey's most thrilling Stanley Cup battles. The score was tied 1–1 through regulation time. As heartbeats thumped faster and faster, the evenly matched clubs fought through two sudden-death overtimes without a score.

More than seven minutes had elapsed in the third overtime when the Bruins lifted a page right out of their old script. Cowley skated behind the Rangers net, detected Hill in front of goalie Bert Gardiner, and ladled a perfect pass to his buddy. Before Gardiner could move, the puck was in and a Bruin had a new nickname: Mel "Sudden Death" Hill.

As expected, the Bruins romped over Toronto in the Cup finals, winning the series 4–1. Cowley was the leading playoff scorer, with 3 goals and 11 assists, for 14 points in 12 games. Brimsek topped the goaltenders, allowing only 18 goals in 12 games for a 1.50 goals against average.

Meanwhile, the Krauts were improving with every season. At the end of the 1939–40 campaign, Schmidt led the NHL in scoring, and Dumart and Bauer were tied for second place. It was a toss-up as to which of the three was most important.

Dumart, the heavyweight, was invaluable as a checking forward; Schmidt was the master playmaker. As for Bauer, Schmidt once described him by saying: "Bobby was our team . . . my right arm."

The Bruins finished first again in 1939–40, but only by a skimpy three points over the Rangers. Lester Patrick, the New York manager, had assembled a team that was every bit as strong as the Bruins. So it was no great tragedy for the Bruins to bow out of the Stanley Cup playoffs in six games, at the hands of the Rangers.

At this point it appeared that the Bruins were growing stronger, while the Rangers were remaining static. Boston again led the league in 1940–41. Bill Cowley was on top of the scoring list again, and the Bruins romped to the Stanley Cup, first wiping out Toronto in a tough seven-game opening round, then shellacking the Red Wings in a four-straight sweep of the finals.

By this time, however, the winds of war had blown across Europe, and Canadians were enlisting in the armed forces by the thousands. Among them was the nucleus of Boston's hockey empire.

Among the first to go was the Kraut Line. In February, 1942, the dynasty came to an end, when Schmidt, Bauer, and Dumart enlisted together in the Royal Canadian Air Force. They played their farewell game at Boston Garden against the Canadiens, and, as expected, they pulled off the last act with a masterful flourish, beating Montreal 8–1.

"It was the biggest thrill of my career," said Schmidt. "Our line got eight or nine scoring points, and when the game was over, the players from both teams picked us up and skated off the ice while the organist played *Auld Lang Syne*."

The Bruins finished third in 1941–42 and were eliminated from the semifinal round of the playoffs by Detroit. From then until the war's end, they struggled along with a makeshift lineup. In 1945, the Krauts returned, but the three and a half years of lost hockey had taken their toll. The Krauts — and the Bruins — never were the same.

Bauer was the first to retire, in 1947, but he was persuaded to return for one game in the 1951–52 season, when the Bruins signed him to a *one-game contract*. The occasion was Schmidt-Dumart Night at Boston Garden, and the fans came out to see the great Krauts and to root Schmidt on to his two-hundredth goal.

Milt had 199 goals as the face-off opened the game. Bruins coach Lynn Patrick sent them out as a unit early in the game, and for a brief moment the clock was rolled back on the dynasty that once was.

Bauer ignited the spark with a crisp pass to Dumart at center ice. Woody took it in stride and fired a stunning blast at Chicago Black Hawks' goalie Harry Lumley, who managed to thrust his body in front of the shot. The rebound caromed directly to Schmidt, who shot the rebound past Lumley.

At first, Boston Garden resounded with thunderous cheers. Then a hush developed as the public address announcer delivered what was to be the last announcement of its kind — "Boston goal by Schmidt, with assists from Dumart and Bauer!"

The New York Rangers, 1928–33

Lester's Rangers 1928–33

For major-league hockey to be considered "big time," it would have to be accepted and take root in North America's media center, New York City. The team that could popularize the NHL in the Big Apple would not only make money for itself, but also help the NHL immeasurably in terms of its ranking with other major sports.

The New York Rangers did just that, but only after receiving considerable pioneering help from other sources. One of the major misconceptions is that the Rangers were the first significant team in the New York metropolitan area. Actually high-quality hockey had been featured in Manhattan as far back as the turn of the century. It was not uncommon for the St. Nicholas club to host top-notch visiting Canadian teams with stars such as the widely-acclaimed Fred (Cyclone) Taylor.

With construction of the "new" Madison Square Garden on Eighth Avenue and 50th Street near Times Square in 1924, the need for a New York NHL representative was recognized. With the help of Canadian friends such as Windsor sportswriter William McBeth, bootlegger William (Big Bill) Dwyer bought an NHL franchise and the New York Americans began play in the 1925–26 season. They did so well at the gate that Madison Square Garden Corporation thought it would be a good idea to install its own team. Thus, the Rangers were born the following year.

The Broadway Blueshirts, as they were nicknamed, were fathered by two of the smartest hockey men of all-time, Conn Smythe and Lester Patrick.

Smythe signed a number of key players prior to the opening of the season, but abruptly quit the team following a dispute with the Garden high command. The erudite Patrick completed Smythe's work and then some.

For starters, the Rangers boasted one of the finest forward lines ever to grace the ice in Frank Boucher and the Cook brothers, Bun and Bill (Boucher and Bill Cook are in the Hockey Hall of Fame). Their razzle dazzle stick-handling and passing captured the fancy of New York fans and the Rangers became instant sensations on Broadway. In addition, the club boasted such notables as the defense pair of Ivan (Ching) Johnson and Clarence (Taffy) Abel. Johnson proved to be one of the hardest checking blueliners of his time, while Abel was no slouch in that department either. Rounding out the squad was Iron Man Murray Murdoch and a sparkling French-Canadian defenseman, Leo Bourgault. Topping off the roster was an accomplished goaltender named Lorne Chabot. At first, there was concern about the Rangers' ability to draw in New York because of the uncertainty about two NHL teams surviving in the market.

The anxiety produced some weird happenings including the hiring of a pair of strange press agents named Bruno and Blythe. Bruno and Blythe believed that the Rangers would never draw fans unless they appealed to New York's ethnic population. "The Rangers," said Bruno, "need a Jewish player." To which Blythe added, "And an Italian player, too." But, alas, the Rangers had neither a Jew nor an Italian in their lineup in 1926. That being the case, Bruno and Blythe *put* a Jew and an Italian *in* the lineup. They decided that the Jew would be the Rangers' French-Canadian goalie, Lorne Chabot. Bruno changed his name to Chabotsky. Blythe then went to work on forward Oliver Reinikka and converted him to Ollie Rocco. Poof! You're Italian! Unfortunately, neither player enjoyed his nom de glace. What's more, the Canadian hockey writers knew Chabot and Reinikka for what they really were and lampooned Bruno and Blythe. As a result the two press agents became ex-press agents faster than Chabot could shoot the puck to Rocco — rather Reinikka.

Such shenanigans were unnecessary. Patrick swiftly whipped the Rangers into competitive shape, and in no time at all they not only outshone the Americans at Madison Square Garden, but became one of the most challenging clubs in the entire ten team league. Their Stanley Cup triumph in 1928 was as much a tribute to Patrick's personnel as it was to his teaching ability.

"There's more to coaching a hockey club than standing behind the bench," Patrick would say. "That's almost the least important phase of the job — watching your men when a game is in progress. It is incumbent upon you initially to build up their morale and then maintain it, and before you can do that you must have acquired the confidence in your judgment and you must know the man.

"When it comes to teaching hockey to my young men," Patrick continued, "I say as little as possible and avoid blackboards and diagrams. I've seen a lot of players in this league who've been blackboarded half to death so that when they go on the ice they're completely befuddled and the simplest plays hold terrors for them."

Lester proceeded to illustrate. "Once I had a fellow on this club who made a simple play wrong for three years," he recalled.

Hockey's Babe Ruth, the incomparable Maurice (Rocket) Richard, captain of *Les Canadiens* during their greatest years.

Jacques (Jake the Snake) Plante: adroit, innovative, eccentric, and arguably the greatest goalie of all time.

The majestic Jean Beliveau, captain of the Montreal Canadiens from 1960 through 1972.

Bernie (Boom Boom) Geoffrion, hard shooting right wing of Montreal's five-Stanley Cup dynasty, 1956–60.

The Canadiens at the very peak of their dynastic run. This 1957–58 edition could be THE finest aggregation the NHL has ever seen.

Only one American team has ever won four straight Stanley Cups. The New York Islanders won their fourth in 1983, beating Edmonton in four straight.

Photo: Bruce Bennett

The New York Islanders' answer to Rocket Richard, Montreal-born Mike Bossy, fastest gun of the early 1980s.

Photo: David Bier

After a relatively poor start, Guy Lafleur emerged as the most exciting Canadien of the 1970s.

Photo: Bruce Bennett

Prime Minister Pierre Elliott Trudeau helps Serge Savard lift yet another Stanley Cup.

Montreal's last dynasty spanned 1976–79. The 1976 edition (pictured here) was as strong as any of the four Cup-winners.

In the spring of 1948, the Maple Leafs finished first, and then won their second Stanley Cup in what would be a three-straight Cup reign. Syl Apps, the captain, retired after this picture was taken.

Wayne Gretzky played on four Stanley Cup winners in Edmonton before being traded to the Los Angeles Kings.

Combining remarkable strength, speed, toughness, and leadership quality, Mark Messier complemented Wayne Gretzky on Edmonton's remarkable clubs of the 1980s.

Paul Coffey, the Bobby Orr of the late 1980s, helped Edmonton to three Stanley Cups: 1984, 1985, and 1987.

In the clutch, goalie Grant Fuhr produced big saves for the Edmonton Oilers' first four Cup wins.

Photo: Courtesy Hockey Hall of Fame

When Punch Imlach orchestrated three consecutive Stanley Cup wins for Toronto, 1962–64, he adroitly blended veterans with youth.

Six-time Hart trophy winner Gordie Howe (*centre*) was the great offensive threat of the early 1950s Red Wing powerhouses, leading the NHL in scoring in 1951, 1952, 1953, and 1954.

Derek Sanderson could score as well as he could check on the 1970 and 1972 Boston Champions.

Bobby Orr (*right*) starred on two Bruins Stanley Cups — 1970 and 1972 — along with Derek Sanderson, seen here in a Rangers uniform.

Photo: Bruce Bennett

Boston Bruins goalie Gerry Cheevers liked to paint stitch marks on his mask to indicate where the puck would have cut him had he not been protected.

The Rangers won their first Stanley Cup in 1928, guided by hockey's Silver Fox, Lester Patrick.

Champagne was not available when the Rangers won their last Stanley Cup in 1940 at Maple Leaf Gardens. Manager Lester Patrick and goalie Frank Boucher flank goalie Davey Kerr.

After winning the 1940 Cup, the Rangers dispersed before a team photo could be taken. This montage has to suffice.

Conn Smythe was the manager and Maple Leaf Gardens was brand new when the Toronto club won its first Stanley Cup in 1932.

Toronto's Kid Line, circa 1932. (*Left to right*) Charlie Conacher, Gentleman Joe Primeau, and Harvey (Busher) Jackson.

Photo: Courtesy Hockey Hall of Fame

Charlie Conacher went to a photo studio for this formal photo. He was among the most popular Toronto athletes of all time.

Bobby Clarke was the star center and captain of the Philadelphia Flyers' Stanley Cup winners in 1974 and 1975.

Most critics agree that the essential ingredients in the Flyers' two Stanley Cup championships was the goaltending of Bernie Parent.

"One night in a tight game he made it right and it won the game for us. Afterwards, in the dressing room he said to me, 'Now I've got it. I wouldn't have believed that anybody could be as stupid as I've been.' "

" 'Never mind about that,' I said. 'Now that you know how to make the play, keep making it that way.' "

With the Cook brothers and Boucher providing the nucleus, the Rangers remained the dominant force through the early years of the Great Depression and succeeded in burying the Americans, as far as the intra-city rivalry was concerned. The Rangers won the Cup again in 1933 with the Cooks, Boucher, Johnson, and Murdoch providing the impetus. Ironically, the winning goal in 1933 was scored against ex-Ranger netminder Lorne Chabot who was then with the Maple Leafs. Here's how Boucher described it:

"About eight minutes along in the overtime period, Bun and Bill and I were completing a shift. In fact, Bunny had already gone to the bench for a breather, and Butch Keeling had hopped over the boards to replace him. Bill and I were heading for the bench, too, when suddenly Butch came up with the puck and fired a rink-wide pass to Bill who, seeing an opening and Butch with the puck, had quickly switched direction. He took the pass in full stride at the Toronto blueline along the right-wing boards and cut quickly toward the goal. He said afterwards that he could see a wide opening at Chabot's right as he zipped in.

" 'Lorne gave me the whole stick side,' Bill grinned. 'I just fired for that hole.'

"He hit it, and for the second time in our seven-year history, the Rangers were Stanley Cup champions."

To understand how the Rangers became one of the more extraordinary teams in the NHL's formative decade, one must first comprehend the background and leadership qualities of the original New York hockey patriarch Lester Patrick.

It is safe to say that Lester (alias the Silver Fox) was more responsible for the Ranger three (1928, 1933, 1940) Stanley Cup championships than anyone. A great hockey team requires superior leadership, and Patrick demonstrated that early in his hockey career when he and his brother Frank created an entire hockey league, the Pacific Coast League.

A defenseman, although he had forward's instincts, Lester could never understand why forwards, and only forwards, were the puck-carriers. In those days, just past the turn of the century, the defensemen had only one assignment — halt the attack.

"Of course, at Brandon, Lester was expected to behave like a defense player," wrote Elmer Ferguson, the dean of Canadian hockey writers, "but instinct and temperament proved to be too strong."

Rather than resort to the prosaic and boring technique of lifting the puck into the enemy's end of the rink when he captured it, Lester stunned the Brandon spectators by digging his skates into the ice and rushing headlong toward the goal. Although he missed his shot, Lester left both the opposition and his teammates awed by the unorthodox performance and, at the end of the period, he was summoned to the Board of Directors' room.

"What is the meaning of this?" they demanded of Lester.

He replied with the impeccable logic that was his hallmark in later years: "Why not let defensemen rush if it works — and if the fans like it?"

Unable to cope with Patrick's reply, the Directors acknowledged his point and decided to try it again in the next period.

Lester then proceeded to score a goal, and in 1903 this was as unheard of as flying to the moon. The crowd loved it, and from that point on, defensemen have become as much a part of an attack as the two wings and center. Conceivably, if Lester had not decided to make that rush in Brandon, Bobby Orr might never have been more than a defenseman who hurled the puck from one end of Boston Garden to the other.

But Patrick had just begun to innovate. When he arrived in Brandon it was traditional for defensemen to stand in front of each other, like the point and cover-point players in lacrosse. "That doesn't make sense," Lester observed. "It would be a lot more logical to have the defensemen to line up abreast." This time the Directors listened without rebuke, and once again Patrick proved his point. From then on the tandem defense became the vogue.

After revolutionizing defensive hockey in Brandon, Lester returned to his father's lumber business in Montreal where he was signed by the strong Montreal Wanderers hockey club. From 1903 throughout 1905 Canadian hockey was dominated by the Ottawa Silver Seven, a club which won the Stanley Cup three consecutive years. But in March 1906, Ottawa went up against the Montreal Wanderers, led by Lester Patrick, and were defeated in the two-game, total-goal series 12–10. It was Lester who scored the 11th and 12th goals for Montreal, thereby helping to win the Stanley Cup.

By now the Patrick name was so renowned in hockey circles that when a wealthy group of businessmen in Renfrew, Ontario, decided to organize a major league team, they went after Lester. He readily signed with the Renfrew Millionaires at a salary of $3000 for 12 games. The fee was regarded as astronomical, but it inspired other promoters to come up with equally large offers for other stars and set in motion the big-time professional hockey movement.

Meanwhile, Lester's father had decided that his lumbering fortune — and future — was in the Pacific Northwest rather than Montreal, so he moved his family to British Columbia where Lester once again helped the Patrick enterprise; this time it was by scaling, felling, hauling, and sluicing the giant trees of the Fraser Valley. Usually, brother Frank was at his side and whenever they'd take a break from lumbering, talk would switch to hockey and what they could do about cashing in on the certain eventual boom in the sport.

Their conclusion resulted in one of the biggest gambles in sports history. The Patricks decided to construct a chain of ice rinks throughout the Pacific Northwest and operate a professional hockey league, with teams in each city. With the aid of a $300,000 note from their father, Lester and Frank poured all their savings into what was to become the Pacific Coast Hockey league. They faced not only the uncertainty of public opinion, but also the dubiousness of hockey players as well as others who couldn't envision a league embracing Seattle, Victoria, Edmonton, Calgary, Regina, Vancouver, and Saskatoon.

But in 1911, the Pacific Coast Hockey League was born and, for the first time professional hockey thrived in the United States. A Patrick enclave was established in British Columbia, with Lester taking over the Victoria sextet while Frank ran the Vancouver club.

Any doubts about the wisdom of creating a major hockey league in the West were erased as soon as the schedule began. Starved for evening entertainment, the citizens of Seattle, Vancouver, Victoria, and the other cities in the league welcomed Patrick's organization and Lester and Frank responded with a determined effort to improve the brand of hockey being dispensed.

It was the Patricks who introduced the penalty shot to hockey, as well as numbers on players' jerseys and the new offside rule that enabled a player to pass the puck from behind the opponent's net to a teammate skating in front of it.

The idea for the penalty shot was inspired while the Patricks were visiting England. They had gone to a soccer match and were enthralled by the excitement produced by the penalty shot in the game; consequently, it became part of their ice hockey rules as soon as they returned. Likewise, the scheme for numbering players was the result of a day in a baseball park when the brothers realized that they couldn't identify many of the participants. "If we can't tell who these guys are," said Frank, "it must be the same for our fans watching hockey."

The next season, all Pacific Coast Hockey League players wore numbered jerseys. Fans not only relished the innovation, but bought so many souvenir programs that promoters up and down North America picked up on the idea and soon "You can't tell the players without a program" became a byword in American sport.

Speeding the flow of a hockey game became an obsession with the Patricks. They were particularly appalled by the way a referee could slow the game down to a virtual halt by an endless series of penalties. At times, each side could be reduced to two men including the goaltenders and the games then became a bore. As a result, the Patricks invented the "delayed-penalty" system that insures four skaters on the ice, no matter how many infractions are called.

They then legalized kicking the puck in certain areas of the rink and also introduced the assist to the scoring records. "Practically every forward step taken by professional hockey between 1911 and 1925 can be traced to the keen mind of Frank Patrick and the practical knowledge of Lester who tried out every rule first to prove its soundness," wrote Arthur Mann. "Between the two they just about made the game what it was before it hit the big cities below the border."

Thanks to Lester and Frank, the blue lines made their appearance in the Pacific Coast League in the 1914–15 season. To preview the fans, Lester informed the local newspapers and detailed explanations of the purpose of the blue lines were printed in each league city. Needless to say, a bit of confusion resulted, especially in Lester's "home" city of Victoria. He liked to joke about some of the bafflement, and he frequently told the story of the day his crack defenseman Ernie "Moose" Johnson was asked by a fan to explain the blue-line rules.

Johnson laughed. "What's the blue line all about?" he repeated.

"Don't ask me, bud. As far as I'm concerned there's only one rule in hockey — you take the puck on your stick and you shoot it in the net!"

Although Lester was basically a defenseman and also played rover in the seven-man game, it was his affection for goaltending that would occasion a handful of remarkable exploits between the pipes. The earliest of these occurred in Victoria when Patrick's goalie, Hec Howler, was ejected from a game. Lester decided to replace him but chose not to wear the traditional pads because he found them too cumbersome. He went into the nets with the simple defenseman's attire and foiled all shots hurled by the Vancouver team. When it was over, Patrick dismissed his feat with typical logic: "I worked on a simple principle — only one puck could come at a time. I stopped each shot and we won!"

After gaining some practical experience in the nets, Lester decided it was ill-advised to retain a rule that forced goaltenders to remain on their feet when making saves. The Patricks promptly changed the regulation, and from that point on goaltenders began flipping, flopping, splitting, and doing anything possible to keep the puck out of the net.

While all this was going on, the Patricks were simultaneously engaging in a blood war with the NHL for supremacy in professional hockey. With such cities as Toronto, Montreal, and Ottawa in its fold, the NHL presented an awesome challenge, but Lester and Frank were undaunted. "They fought the National League," wrote Elmer Ferguson, who was covering the game at the time, "raided it, took a whole champion team away on one of their forays, and forced the National League to terms."

The high point of Lester's managerial career at that time was reached in the spring of 1925 when his Victoria team took on the Montreal Canadiens in the Stanley Cup finals at Montreal. Victoria won the opener 5–2 and the second match 3–1 in the best-of-five playoff. Paced by Howie Morenz's three-goal "hat trick," the Canadiens topped Victoria 4–2 in the third game, but the visitors, guided by

Frank Frederickson's deft passes and his two goals, then routed Montreal 6–1 to take the series.

Flushed with success, Lester sought new worlds to conquer. He didn't have to look far; Boston and the New York Americans already had entered the NHL, and franchises were being sought for Detroit and Chicago as well as for a second team in Manhattan. The demand for players was never greater, and while a paucity of talent still existed in the East, nobody questioned the endless stream of stars in Patrick's Pacific Coast League.

Lester, always the shrewd businessman, fulfilled the demand by selling his Victoria team to a Detroit group, while negotiating the sales of other Pacific Coast League players to the NHL teams. When Conn Smythe walked out on his organizational job with the Rangers prior to the 1926–27 season, Colonel John Hammond, president of the infant New York team, promptly hired Lester as coach. Frank Patrick turned up as an NHL director, and eventually found his way to Boston where he coached the Bruins.

As Johnny-Come-Latelys in Manhattan, the Rangers were forced to play catch-up with the New York Americans who already had captured the imagination of the city's spectators. It would require some superior hockey dealing in order to ice a presentable team, and it was Lester who not only made the Rangers, but developed them into a club that almost immediately outclassed the rival Amerks. Patrick's background in the Pacific Coaast League was his forte; he knew ace players the Easterners had never heard of and made the most of his knowledge.

He remembered a brother act from Saskatoon, Bill and Bun Cook, who had been overlooked by the other franchises. He signed them to a Ranger contract. Then, there was a former member of the Canadian Royal Mounted Police named Frank Boucher. Together with the Cooks, Boucher was to provide some of the most stimulating offensive hockey ever seen.

Although they were born a year after the Americans, the Rangers immediately developed their own legion of fans, and an intense rivalry developed between the two New York teams. The Rangers had an advantage, having acquired the Cooks and Boucher. Bill Cook led the NHL in scoring, and the Rangers finished first in the American Division, while the Americans finished fourth in the Canadian section.

According to Canadian hockey biographer Ron McAllister, the Ranger dynasty actually was born on the first night Lester Patrick's team skated on the Garden ice for the 1926–27 season. Their opponents were the Stanley Cup champion Montreal Maroons, loaded with such stars as Reg Noble, Hap Emms, Dunc Munro, Babe Siebert, Nels Stewart, and Clint Benedict in goal.

To the astonishment of the veteran Maroons, neither team scored through the first two periods of play. As the third period rolled on, a stirring crescendo of cheers descended on the Rangers from the highest reaches of the Garden balcony, and the players responded.

Bill Cook stole the puck from the Maroons and sent a pass to Boucher, who relayed the puck to Bun Cook. The Montreal defense boxed Bun into a corner and seemed to have stalled the attack. According to McAllister, "Bun fought and dug like a terrier after a groundhog and sent a pass out to brother Bill. He grabbed it and raced straight in on Clint Benedict to beat the goalkeeper's dive with a low shot.

"After what seemed years, the bell rang, and the game was over. Bill Cook and his Rangers had defeated the defending NHL champions! That was the real beginning of the New York Rangers as a hockey team."

In their first playoff test, the Rangers ran head on into a hot Boston Bruins team for a two-game total-goals series. In the first game, at Boston, the teams skated off with a 0–0 tie, but Boston annexed the round with a 3–1 win at Madison Square Garden.

Patrick realized that there still was some building to be done if he was to win the Stanley Cup, and by the 1927–28 campaign he believed that all the necessary ingredients had been added. All that remained was for him to heat gently and stir.

The Cook-Boucher line was augmented by a rock-ribbed defense of Taffy Abel, Ching Johnson, and Leo Bourgault. Other stars included Murray Murdoch, Paul Thompson, Alex Gray, Billy Boyd, and Laurie Scott. They formed the nucleus of a team that would be at or near the top of the NHL for years to come.

Bill Cook was supplanted as the American Division's leading scorer by linemate Frank Boucher, and the Rangers, after finishing second behind Boston, routed Pittsburgh in the first playoff round. Then they gained revenge against the Bruins with a 5–2 victory in the two-game total-goals series, which catapulted them into the Stanley Cup finals — a best-of-five showdown against the mighty Maroons.

To some observers it was the hockey duel of the century. The powerful Montreal sextet represented the most hardened professionals on ice. The Rangers were kids by comparison, but they were enormously skilled and determined. And they had wise Lester Patrick to orchestrate their clever moves.

Playing all games at Montreal's Forum because a circus had occupied Madison Square Garden, the teams squared off on April 5, 1928, and the Maroons muzzled the Rangers 2–0. That set the stage for one of hockey's most memorable moments.

During a play in the second game, Rangers goalie Lorne Chabot was severely injured and unable to continue. Not having any substitute goaltender on his roster, manager Lester Patrick himself decided to skate between the pipes and replace Chabot.

This seemed preposterous. Patrick was all of 45 years old, and his experience as a player was basically in a defense position. Only once did he play goal, when Hec Fowler, his goalie on the Victoria Cougars, was thrown out of a game.

Bill Cook scored for the Rangers early in the third period, but the Maroons tied the score. The game went into overtime, and Patrick held fast until Frank Boucher sank the winner at 7:05 of the first sudden-death period.

The Maroons won the third game 2–0, and it appeared that they would dispose of the Rangers. However, the gallant New Yorkers would have no part of any defeatist talk. Chabot was replaced in goal by Joe Miller, who surprised the hockey world by shutting out the Maroons, 1–0, in the fourth match.

On April 14, 1928, the climactic fifth and final game was played at the Forum. Once again, the lithe Frank Boucher, considered the cleanest player ever to skate in the NHL, was the hero, scoring the winning goal in the Rangers 2–1 triumph. In some respects it was one of the most exciting scores ever made. The Rangers were playing shorthanded at the time, and Boucher had been dispatched to the ice by Patrick simply to rag the puck and kill time. Nobody anticipated a Rangers goal.

But Boucher controlled the puck at center ice and played it off the boards in the direction of Maroon defenseman Dunc Munro. The quick-witted Boucher realized that the puck didn't have much speed on it and that it was slowing down midway between himself and Munro. When Munro dashed for the rubber, Boucher realized he had his chance.

"As I raced Munro for the puck," Boucher recalled, "I could almost hear him think, 'By God, I can't get there in time.' He seemed to stop in one motion, and then he changed his mind and went for the puck again. By this time I was there and just swooped over to one side, fooled him, and had a clean breakaway to goalie Benedict. I just shot the puck the same place I had before, and it went in."

Thus, in only their second year of competition the Rangers were the world champions of hockey.

The Rangers didn't win back-to-back Stanley Cups, but they continued to be a threat, mostly because of Boucher and the Cook Brothers. "Bill Cook," said Patrick, "is the brainiest player I ever saw and the greatest right-winger of all time."

They were good enough to develop themselves as one of the foremost hockey clubs at a time when the NHL was still establishing itself in New York. The Broadway Blueshirts, as they were known in those days, rightfully earned the title of the "classiest team in hockey."

The Montreal Canadiens, 1930–31

The Howie Morenz Montreal Canadiens, 1930–31

Ever since the oldest of hockey fans can remember, the Montreal Canadiens have been nicknamed "The Flying Frenchmen," even in times when their lineup is predominantly English-speaking. There was, however, a time when the *Habitants'* lineup was truly representative of French-speaking Quebec.

In the 1920s and 1930s, when Montreal sported two NHL teams, the Canadiens and Maroons, there was a clear-cut line of demarcation between them. The Maroons represented Montreal's English-speaking minority while the Habs skated for the French majority. And, boy, did they ever skate!

Ironically, it was an English-speaking Canadian of Swiss parentage who, more than anyone, symbolized The Flying Frenchmen. His name was Howie Morenz and he was true to his assorted nicknames such as The Stratford Streak and Mitchell Meteor. Morenz's end-to-end rushes were so captivating that he inspired at least two American millionaires to decide to invest in NHL franchises and emerged as the first true superstar of the league's golden era of the late 1920s.

Teamed with petite Aurel Joliat — and later Johnny (Black Cat) Gagnon — Morenz cut a dazzling figure as the Canadiens became one of the continent's predominant teams. This was attributable to balance from the goal (George Hainsworth) to defense (Marty Burke, Sylvio Mantha, Albert Leduc) to the attack where Morenz and Joliat were complemented by adroit center Pit Lepine and right wing Wildor Larochelle.

They didn't peak until the 1929–30 season, when the Montreal teams finished in a 51-point dead heat for first place in the NHL's Canadian Division. But the Maroons were quickly eliminated in the first round by Boston, while the

Canadiens began their march to The Stanley Cup with preliminary playoff wins over Chicago and the Rangers. In a two-game final, the Habs defeated a mighty (38–5–1) Bruins team 3–0 and 4–3.

Both the Bruins and Canadiens remained the best teams through the 1930–31 season. Morenz was better than ever, and Joliat not far behind. Instead of meeting in the finals, Boston and Montreal collided in the semi-finals and it was, as expected, a gem. In a best-of-five series, the Canadiens prevailed 3–2 in the fifth game. Advancing to the finals, Montreal took on the Black Hawks, and again were taken the limit. Each of the first four games was decided by one goal.

Game Five, at The Forum, was scoreless until 9:59 of the second period when Black Cat Gagnon took a pass from Joliat and beat Charlie Gardiner in the Chicago net. Morenz clinched the shutout win at 15:27 of the third period and the Canadiens had their second Stanley Cup in a row.

The Habs had legitimate designs on a third straight championship, something that was unprecedented in big-league professional hockey at that time. Their credentials were formidable. During the 1931–32 campaign, they finished first again (25–16–7) but had the misfortune of meeting the Rangers, first in the American Division, in the semi-finals. Montreal took the opener of the best-of-five series, 4–3, but it was all Rangers after that. The New Yorkers swept three straight and the Habs were history.

Where do they stand in history? In a reasonably good position, thanks to Morenz and Joliat. The pair did as much for offensive hockey as any duet in the game before or since. Their selling power was as vital as their artistry. Fans streamed to the rink to see The Stratford Flash the way fans do today to view Mario Lemieux.

The balance between offense and defense was neat and the goaltending among the best of its time, if not all time. That the Canadiens failed to win three Cups in a row is more a tribute to the overall NHL balance than a knock against one of the more colorful and competent versions of The Flying Frenchmen.

One-two combinations in hockey are still prevalent in today's hockey, as evidenced by the Mike Bossy-Bryan Trottier duet of the early 1980s New York Islanders and Wayne Gretzky and Jari Kurri of the Edmonton Oilers a few years later.

Among the one-two units of the past, few were as memorable or as colorful as the pair who provided Montreal hockey fans with more than their share of excitement during a period of severe economic crisis across Canada.

It also was a time when competition in the NHL was extraordinarily keen. "Every kid in Canada wanted to be a hockey player," noted one observer of the scene, "not merely because it was glamorous but because it was a way to make a living at a time when it was pretty darned tough to get a job — any job. So, why not get paid playing hockey."

Between the Boston Bruins, the New York Rangers, and the Toronto Maple Leafs, the Canadiens had their hands full getting to the top, but the combination of Aurel Joliat and Howie Morenz would eventually give them the needed edge. Joliat was a little French-Canadian who wore a black baseball cap and defied opponents to knock it off his head. Morenz was a youngster from Ontario whose career would climb and dip like a roller coaster. Thanks to Canadiens boss Leo Dandurand, the climbs would considerably outdo the dips.

Hero-hungry French-Canadian fans lavished affection on their beloved hockey team from the very start. Fortunately, there were heroes aplenty on the club that proudly wore the *bleu, blanc, et rouge* uniform of Montreal. For typecasting purposes, the team's first captain and manager, Jean Baptiste "Jack" Laviolette, epitomized what was most appealing about the Montreal sextet. A speedy, lyrical skater, Laviolette had what one observer described as "a mane of theatrically long black hair, which streamed behind him when he came swooping down the ice to set up shots on goal for Edouard 'Newsy' Lalonde and Didier 'Pit' Pitre."

By the time World War I had ended, the Canadiens already had captured the first of what eventually would be a record-breaking number of Stanley Cups, emblematic of professional hockey's world championship. Their manager and coach, Dandurand, emerged as one of the most adroit talent-finders in hockey, and by the early twenties, he had molded a team whose competitive fire and aesthetic appeal were enormous. "*Les Canadiens sont synonyme de la vitesse,*" (the Canadiens are synonymous with speed) boasted Montrealers. Obviously, there were many great players on this dynasty in the making, yet they were a diverse group in the most interesting of ways. Two skaters, more than any others, symbolized this fascinating team.

One of them was Joliat. The other was Howie Morenz, a youngster from Ontario with not an ounce of French blood in him.

The son of a railroad man, Howie was born in 1903 in Mitchell, Ontario, a hamlet about 13 miles from Stratford. A little fellow, the young Morenz was often severely beaten by the older boys with whom he played hockey in the neighborhood games. From time to time he'd return home so badly cut and bruised that he often considered quitting the game; but his love for hockey was so passionate that he inevitably returned to the rink. Soon he was the star of the Stratford team, which journeyed to Montreal for a playoff game.

Dandurand happened to be in the stands on the night that Morenz dipsy-doodled around the hometown defensemen from the start to the finish of the game. Leo conferred with his aide, Cecil Hart, and both agreed that it would be prudent to sign Morenz before the Maroons, Hamilton, Ottawa, or Toronto beat them to it.

Leo was occupied with his horse-racing business in Montreal, and he delegated Hart to handle the negotiations. Cecil was given two blank checks and two contracts, one to be signed by Howie, and the other by his father. The offer was for three years starting at $3,500 for the first season with increases each season thereafter. Cecil took the first available train from Montreal to Stratford and expected little difficulty in signing the lad.

But when he arrived in Stratford, Hart was somewhat astonished to discover that Howie was working for the Canadian National Railroad with his father. What's more, his father had no intention of permitting his son to forsake the good life of railroading for such nonsense as hockey. But the money was awfully big, and the elder Morenz finally modified his position. "If my boy thinks he'd like to spend his life that way," he said, "then it's up to him to say."

Howie paused for a moment, looked uncertainly at his father, and said he would sign the contract. Both Hart and Dandurand believed that their troubles were over when Cecil returned to Montreal with the Morenz signatures, but a month later Leo received a letter post-marked Stratford. It was from Howie, and it read: "I am enclosing a cheque and contract to play hockey for your club. Owing to several reasons, of which family and work are the most to consider, I find it impossible to leave Stratford. I am sorry if I have caused you expense and inconvenience, and I trust you will accept the returned contract in a sportsmanlike way."

Leo wasn't about to give up that easily. He phoned Howie and invited him to Montreal to discuss the matter at greater length. Morenz accepted and the next day told Dandurand face to face that he rather preferred his situation at home. He had a nice job in the railroad car shops and was able to play in the Ontario Hockey Association's Intermediate Division. He was, after all, a hero in Stratford, and he didn't mind telling Leo some of the stories about hockey back home. One night, he recalled, his opponents actually tried to use police force to stop him from scoring.

This happened when Howie's Stratford team was playing a game in the town of Preston. Between the first and second periods, a constable appeared in the Stratford dressing room accompanied by what appeared to be a vigilante group of Preston rooters. The officer presented Morenz with a summons for malicious damage to property. The policeman charged that Howie, upon rounding the net at his usual breakneck speed, *had sliced the rubbers of the goal judge* who was stationed immediately behind the cage.

Strange as it may seem, the constable was serious about his mission, and he planned to haul Howie off to court. Stratford supporters offered five dollars for the rubbers provided they were delivered to the Stratford dressing room.

Milt Dunnell of the *Toronto Daily Star*, himself a native of the Stratford area, reported that the charge was dropped after the offer to repay the goal judge was made.

"The goal judge kept his damaged rubbers," said Dunnell. "After all, he had his pride."

Dandurand was suitably impressed with these tales and told Morenz so. But Leo was operating a hockey team for a profit as well as for fun, and he told Howie that his contract had to be honored. Morenz couldn't control himself. He burst into tears and revealed to Leo what was *really* bothering him: he didn't think he was good enough to play in the NHL. What's more, Dandurand was told that he would have to accept the consequences if he *forced* Howie to play and thereby to lose his job in the car shops.

"The kid touched a soft spot," Leo admitted later, "and I had all to do to keep from letting him off the hook. But something inside of me said, 'No, don't you do it.' And when we were through talking, I told him I was certain he could make our team and that I expected him to show up at training camp that November."

Morenz did show up at camp and, for a while, it seemed to everyone concerned that he had made the wrong move. As was the custom then, the veterans tried their best to intimidate the rookies, and each day his bruises multiplied. But it was also obvious that his skills were enormous, and soon the veterans were finding it more and more difficult to keep up with "Lightning Legs." Anyone who saw Morenz play in that rookie year was quick to admit that he was a star.

"He was the picture player," said Nels Stewart, a member of the Hall of Fame. "Howie had the grace and speed to finish off plays like no one else could."

Raw speed was Howie's forte, and he gained a varsity center ice berth on the Canadiens. Within weeks he was dubbed the "Stratford Streak," the "Mitchell Meteor," and assorted other appellations that almost, but never quite, described his presence on the ice. "The Kid's *too* fast," said one observer. "He'll burn himself out."

Morenz scored his first goal for Montreal against Ottawa on December 26, 1923, before 8,300 spectators at the spanking new Ottawa Auditorium, a curious-looking egg-shaped rink. Ottawa's Senators dominated the NHL that season, thanks in part to a minuscule defenseman named Francis "King" Clancy, who would go on to become one of hockey's most delightful personalities as a referee, coach, and vice-president of the Toronto Maple Leafs. Clancy vividly recalled his first clash with Morenz.

"Weeks before I ever played against him," said Clancy, "I had read story after story about this kid, and I couldn't believe any boy that age could be *that* good. The stories also said he was making a lot of the veteran defensemen look like fools. I made up my mind that Clancy wasn't going to be one of them."

Clancy gave Morenz a once-over in practice and concluded there was nothing very special to him. "He was only an inch taller than I was," said Clancy. "That gave me the confidence I needed for starters.

Morenz captured the puck and launched a rush in Clancy's direction. King's linemate covered the other Canadiens forward, enabling Clancy to get a clear shot at Howie, who by this time was under a full head of steam. King had sized up the situation as well as he could. Morenz was a left-handed shot; he figured to cut to his left when he reached pokechecking distance.

"I remember telling myself," Clancy recalled, "get nicely set on your feet, watch a quick reverse, and you got him."

Morenz barreled right in on King and neither zigged nor zagged. He released a snapshot, skated right into Clancy, and bowled him on his derriere. Howie didn't score on the play, but as he returned to center ice, Clancy pulled himself together and warned the rookie: "One more run like that, and I'll knock your block off."

The kid was unimpressed. After digesting Clancy's warning he replied that he planned to pull off the very same play as soon as he received the puck again. "Believe it or not," said the King, "he did *exactly* what he said he'd do."

Dandurand took a paternal interest in Morenz, even to the point of boarding him with an elderly Scottish lady who ran a rooming house in Montreal. Leo asked her to keep an eye out for Howie just in case he got homesick and decided to depart for Stratford. Sure enough, early one morning Dandurand was awakened with a phone call from the lady.

"Young Morenz is gone," she said, half weeping. "He left last night and hasn't returned since."

Thinking Morenz might have been sight-seeing on the town, Leo suggested that the landlady go back to sleep and phone him again later in the morning. But by 9:00 A.M. Howie had not returned, and Leo was genuinely worried.

There were several possibilities. One, naturally, was that Howie had decided to leave the big city and return to Stratford. Another was that he had gone on the town and was still collecting himself. Or possibly the kid was simply overwrought from the previous night's game and had to unwind somehow.

It was Dandurand's custom to hold a meeting the morning after the game, followed by a luncheon with his players. Thinking that Morenz might have gone there, Leo decided to go straight to the Mount Royal Arena. Sure enough, Howie was in the dressing room, looking none the worse for wear.

He had gone on a tour of Montreal — from Bonaventure Station to the Canadian National Railways yard in Point St. Charles and finally back to the city. His roaming was to be a standard operating procedure in years to come and one that would amaze teammates and sportswriters alike.

Morenz scored 13 goals in his rookie season, finishing in a tie with Jack Adams for seventh place in scoring. He was well on his way to becoming the glamour boy of hockey, a man admired as much by his opponents as by his teammates and fans. Howie played the game as cleanly as was possible in those rambunctious days of chronic stick fights and butt ends.

In a game at Madison Square Garden, he knocked out four of Bun Cook's front teeth with the end of his stick as the pair was battling for the puck. Howie immediately dropped his stick and helped Bun off the ice. Later Cook explained, "It was just an accident. Howie wouldn't pull anything like that intentionally."

Morenz was a superstar in his second year of big-league play. He finished second in scoring to Cecil "Babe" Dye of Toronto and was doing things with the puck that astonished even such skeptics as Conn Smythe, founder of the Maple Leaf empire.

"The trouble is," said Smythe, "that writers are always talking about what a great scorer Morenz is, which is true enough. But they overlook the fact that he's a great two-way player."

According to Smythe, Morenz executed "the most amazingly impossible play" he had ever seen in hockey up until that time. It was accomplished against the

Boston Bruins, who had a big, rugged team, and had managed to ram Morenz forcefully into the boards on more than one occasion. Somehow Morenz responded to the battering by skating even faster than he had before he was hit. Finally, Eddie Shore and Lionel Hitchman of the Boston defense prepared to sandwich Morenz between their powerful bodies as he tried to split the defense. Suddenly Howie leaped forward and crashed through like an auto speeding past two closing railroad gates at a crossing.

Just then a Bruin forward swerved in behind his defense to intercept Morenz. Seeing that he couldn't elude the checking wing, Howie released his shot from 25 feet in front of the net. The shot missed the goalpost by a few inches and caromed off the end boards right back to the blue line and onto Shore's waiting stick.

The Bruin defenseman, one of the speediest rushers hockey has ever known, orbited into a breakaway with all the Montreal players caught in Bruin territory along with Morenz. "I was watching Howie all the time," said Smythe, "and I saw him follow up his shot with a long leap in preparation to circling the net. To this day I can't figure out how he managed to stay on his skates as he rounded the cage."

Meanwhile, Shore was away at top speed for the Montreal goal. Nobody in the rink, let alone Smythe, doubted that the Bruin would have plenty of time for an easy play on goal and a likely score. Nobody except Morenz. Howie put his head down and dashed in pursuit of Shore. "He flashed from the net to the blue line," said Smythe, "faster than I can say 'blue line.'"

Shore was about to enter the final stages of his maneuvering, when Morenz suddenly cut directly *in front* of him, released the puck from the Boston player's blade, and immediately changed direction for another play on the Bruin goal. "Shore," said Smythe, "was absolutely dumbfounded. As for me, I actually was unable to move my mouth, I was so awed by the play. Morenz had done what he was to do for years to come — he took my breath away!"

Many respected hockey analysts claim that Morenz was singly responsible for the successful expansion of the NHL into the United States in the 1920s. It was no secret that New York promoter Tex Rickard became a hockey fan the moment he spied Morenz in action. Not long afterward, Rickard introduced the Rangers to New York.

One observer wrote: "There isn't a team in the league that has not in some way been affected by some aspect of Montreal hockey, even if the link is as tenuous as the Detroit Red Wings' crest, which is based on the old Montreal Athletic Association's winged wheel."

But the historian was quick to point out that Morenz was the leader of "the most exciting team in hockey from the mid-twenties to the mid-thirties." He adds, "While most fans remember Morenz mainly for his blistering speed and his headlong rushes on goal, he also provided one of the most remarkable examples of the passionate dedication to the game — to winning — that has been another characteristic of Canadien teams. Many people say, of course, that Morenz's fierce involvement in hockey, and in the Canadiens, led to his untimely death, although Morenz's dedication is not unique in the annals of the Montreal team."

Few opponents ever got the better of Morenz when Howie was in his prime, although Joe Primeau, the crack Toronto center, did just that one night when the

Canadiens and the Maple Leafs were locked in a Christmas Eve match. The teams were tied 1–1 after regulation time, and nobody scored in overtime. When the siren sounded to end the game, both clubs headed for the dressing room until they were halted by the referee. Apparently the timekeeper had erred by ten seconds, and the referee ordered the players back to the ice to play out the remaining unused time.

This act of recall nettled Morenz, who was anxious to get home to his family. Before the referee dropped the puck, Howie urged Primeau not to touch it after it hit the ice; that way the ten seconds would be squandered, and everybody could quit for the night. Primeau understood Howie's point, but he had no intention of complying. When the puck hit the ice, the Leaf center slapped it to the left side, where winger Busher Jackson gathered it in and roared toward the Montreal goal. His shot fooled goalie George Hainsworth, and Toronto won the game 2–1.

This goal necessitated another face-off, and Morenz was furious. He glared at Primeau as they went through the ritual of the last face-off and told him in no uncertain terms that he would get even. He did so less than a week later, when the teams clashed again. Nobody could touch Howie for the three periods of regulation time, but he couldn't get the puck past the Leaf goalie.

At last the teams went into overtime, and Morenz took possession of the puck immediately after the opening face-off. Bobbing and weaving through the Leaf defense, Howie worked his way right up to the goal mouth before depositing the puck where it belonged. Primeau, who was known as "Gentleman Joe," recalled that Morenz never said a word to him after scoring. "He had promised to get his revenge," said Primeau, "and he did. There was nothing more to say."

The episode reflects the competitive spirit of Morenz, and only those who were with him at the time can honestly portray the quality of his emotion. One of them was Elmer Ferguson, the veteran Montreal writer who had traveled to Boston one weekend with the Canadiens.

"It was a dark, muggy sort of morning, the way Boston gets when the fog rolls in from the sea on March days and nights," Ferguson recalled. "But it didn't seem possible it could be time to get up, and still be this dark, when the knock sounded on my hotel room."

Ferguson rubbed his eyes and wearily strode to the door. When he opened it, there was Morenz fully dressed as if ready to take an early morning stroll along the Charles River. "Howie," asked Ferguson, "don't you think it's a little early to be getting up? It's still dark. Where are you going?"

"I'm not getting up," said Morenz. "I haven't been to bed yet. I've been out walking around the streets, thinking about that play I missed. I lost the game for the team, and there's no use going to bed, because I won't sleep."

The play that so disturbed Howie was a face-off he had lost to Cooney Weiland of the Bruins. A split second after the referee had dropped the puck, it flew into the air. Weiland batted it down with his hand and promptly shot it into the net in the same motion. The goal won the game for the Bruins. Eight hours later, Howie was still blaming himself for the goal, as he slumped into the chair in Ferguson's hotel room. "He buried his face in his hands," said Ferguson. "His shoulders shook because he was crying like a little boy. He was heartbroken. He felt that he alone was responsible for the defeat. . . . In all the history of hockey there never was a more sincere competitor."

Morenz always arrived at the dressing room at least an hour before game time. "He'd restlessly pace around the long promenade," said Ferguson, "as highstrung as a thoroughbred that is being readied for a race."

It was easy enough for Montreal players and writers to wax ecstatic about Morenz, and it was not uncommon for opponents to do likewise. But when the opponent happened to be Eddie Shore, the fiercest defenseman in the game, Morenz knew he had arrived!

"He's the hardest player in the league to stop," Shore admitted. "Howie comes at you with such speed that it's almost impossible to block him with a bodycheck. When he hits you, he usually comes off a lot better than the defenseman. Another thing that bothers us is his shift. He has a knack of swerving at the last minute and that can completely fool you. Everybody likes Howie. He's one player who doesn't deserve any rough treatment."

Howie's ascendancy came at a fortuitous time for the Canadiens because they were about to be challenged by the newly formed Maroons. In 1924, Dandurand sold half of the Canadiens' territorial rights in Montreal to the owners of the Canadien Arena Company, who owned the new Montreal Forum. Dandurand's asking price was $15,000. When Chicago and Detroit applied for franchises, the NHL formally announced that the league was to receive $50,000 in return for entrance into the league. Dandurand later admitted that his generosity in permitting the Maroons to become NHL members wasn't as altruistic as it looked on paper. "I figured that having an English team to compete with the French Canadiens would make for a great rivalry," he said later, "and I was proven right."

Dandurand's shrewd wheeling and dealing brought the Stanley Cup to Montreal in 1924 following victories over Ottawa, Vancouver, and Calgary. The feat was hailed in Montreal with appropriate enthusiasm, but with a dignity and hilarity that has never been matched in the team's long history.

Instead of the traditional ticker-tape parade that greats the contemporary Stanley Cup champions, the august University of Montreal honored the 1924 Canadiens. A public reception was held at the city's national monument, during which each player received what amounted to an honorary degree from the university. The highlight of the civic affair, of course, was the presentation of the Stanley Cup.

That formality dispensed with, Dandurand herded his players to his home for a private party. Members of the team, including Vézina, Sprague Cleghorn, and Sylvio Mantha, made the trip in private cars. En route to Chez Dandurand, Leo's automobile broke down and required a rather hefty push. One by one, the Canadiens emerged from the car, including Cleghorn, who had been nursing the Cup on his lap. When Sprague got out of the car, he placed the Stanley Cup on the sidewalk and joined in the pushing brigade. It took several minutes to get the car up and over the hill, and when this was accomplished, the quartet jumped into the car and jubilantly drove off to Leo's house.

Madame Dandurand was delighted to see her husband and the players when they arrived, and she was anxious to pour some of the newly concocted punch into the Stanley Cup. She asked Leo where it was, and he asked Cleghorn where he had put it. Sprague nearly collapsed when he remembered that he had left it at curbside. An hour had passed, but Leo and Sprague returned to the site and found the Cup undisturbed.

The Canadiens had their share of French-Canadian stars to complement Howie, and the one who did it best was the smallest of all, Aurel Joliat. Morenz and Joliat worked together through the years, and when they retired, they had identical scoring totals — 270 goals.

Like Morenz, Joliat was a native of Ontario. He learned his hockey on the frozen Rideau River, along with Bill and Frank Boucher. In time Joliat graduated to a fast league in western Canada and arrived in a Canadiens uniform, when Dandurand decided to unload the aging Lalonde.

Aurel weighed 135 pounds at his heaviest, but his size never bothered him. It apparently motivated him to compensate with a vast repertoire of stickhandling maneuvers and pirouettes. "He transported the world of ballet to the hockey arena," said one admirer. To which Aurel replied, "A fellow *needs* finesse when he weighs only 135 pounds!"

Joliat teamed up with Morenz in the 1923–24 season. The pair jelled right from the start, although Aurel was to prove that season that he could excel with or without Morenz at his side. The Canadiens had gone up against Calgary in the playoffs, and Morenz's shoulder was broken after he was hit successively by Red Dutton and Herb Gardiner. That's when Aurel took over. In the third period he intercepted an enemy pass and circled his own net to gain momentum.

"I traveled through the entire Calgary team," said Joliat, "and faked a shot to the far corner of the net. But even as I let it go, I sensed I was covered on the play. So I kept going, rounded the net, and backhanded a shot into the open corner. I tumbled head over heels after that one. We went on to win the Cup, and I consider it the best goal I ever scored."

Joliat was a constant source of annoyance to his larger opponents. Once, after Aurel had thoroughly confounded Toronto's Babe Dye with a series of fakes, the distressed Dye skated over to Dandurand at the Montreal bench and said: "I'm tired of chasing that shadow of yours — that Frenchman, Joliat. Move him over to center, Leo, hold a mirror to each side of him — you'll have the fastest line in hockey."

Morenz and Joliat traveled together both on and off the ice. In the summer of 1926 the two went to work together at Washington Race Track in Chicago, which just happened to be run by Dandurand and Cattarinich. Joliat was the prudent type, and Morenz was a wild bettor with very little self-control.

One day that summer, Howie bought a pair of $50 straight tickets at odds of $7^{1}/_{2}$ to 1. When he got home in the evening, he suddenly decided to check his racing program with the mutual tickets he had in hand. He discovered those that had been bad bets, but realized that his winning tickets were gone. Then it all came back. He had inadvertently tossed them away with some losing tickets that afternoon.

He quickly dressed, hailed a cab, and told the driver to take him out to the track, although it was now the middle of the night. The somewhat perplexed driver drove right up to the racetrack gate, which, of course, was closed. Nonplussed, Morenz pleaded with the watchman to open the gate and promised that if he found the ticket, he'd give the watchman a reward.

The obliging watchman hauled out a kerosene lamp and watched Morenz crawl around on his hands and knees until he actually found both winning ducats. With a typical Morenz turn of generosity he gave $50 to the watchman and another $50 to the cab driver. The next day he cashed in his ticket and instructed the racetrack treasurer to turn $100 of it over to his favorite charity.

Dandurand was like a father to Morenz, and he had pleaded with Howie not to gamble. But like any good father, Dandurand understood the young man. He said: "He'd take all sorts of gambling chances in hockey games, and he was inclined to do the same in money matters."

Leo should have known. He had been wheeling and dealing all his life at both racetracks and the hockey rink. Dandurand was one of the most lovable characters in Montreal sports, always willing to lend a hand to anyone who'd come along and ask. When the Pacific Coast and Western Canada leagues collapsed in 1926, and the players were sold by Frank and Lester Patrick to the NHL clubs, it was Dandurand who helped to arrange some of the deals for the Patricks. Frank and Lester respected Leo and were particularly appreciative of his help in arranging the player transfer. Indeed, it was just this altruism that resulted in the Canadiens' acquiring *another* star.

The player was defenseman Herb Gardiner, of the Calgary sextet, who was somehow overlooked by the other NHL teams when they were stocking up on western players. One night, the Patricks and Dandurand were dining at Leo's home when Dandurand casually mentioned that Gardiner was certainly good enough for the NHL. "I agree," said Lester Patrick, "and you can have him for one dollar!"

That was Patrick's way of repaying Dandurand for all the help he had given him. The trio completed the deal on the spot, and Gardiner eventually developed into one of the most formidable defensemen in the history of the Canadiens "This had to be my best bargain," said Dandurand.

Well stocked on offense and defense, Dandurand realized that his major project would be finding a replacement for the legendary Vézina. Immediately after goalie Vézina collapsed at the start of the 1925–26 season, the Canadiens replaced him with Alphonse "Frenchy" Lacroix, who obviously couldn't handle the job. After five games, Lacroix was removed. Then Herb Rheaume played 29 games for Montreal, but he also left much to be desired.

Once again, luck played a hand in the Canadiens' favor. When Newsy Lalonde was traded to Saskatoon for Aurel Joliat, Lalonde went searching for a goaltender and found an exceptionally courageous young man playing in Kitchener. The son of a plumber, George Hainsworth soon persuaded Lalonde that he was major-league caliber, and Newsy signed George to play for the Saskatoon Sheiks of the Western Canada League.

But Newsy, like so many of the Canadiens before and since, had strong ties to his alma mater in Montreal. One day he wrote a letter to Dandurand, advising him that it would be worthwhile keeping Hainsworth in mind. "This kid," wrote Lalonde, "could be the one to take Vézina's place if Georges ever retires."

This was not exactly startling news to Dandurand because he and Vézina had watched Hainsworth play for Kitchener a few years earlier, when Georges had actually entertained thoughts of retiring. Vézina was greatly impressed with Hainsworth, and Dandurand knew it. "That night," Leo once told Bill Roche, "Vézina really chose his own successor in the Canadiens' net."

Dandurand launched his pursuit of Hainsworth in earnest as soon as Vézina entered the hospital. But since Hainsworth was under contract to Saskatoon through the 1925–26 season, Leo's hands were tied. As soon as the Western League dissolved, Dandurand was free to negotiate with the little goalie, and Leo was right there with a bid.

Dandurand didn't sign Hainsworth without some grave reservations. After all, there was the delicate matter of finding a *suitable* replacement for the venerated Vézina. Unlike his predecessor, Hainsworth measured only 5'6", compared to the tall, distinguished Vézina. And furthermore, at 33 years old, Hainsworth seemed to be approaching the end, rather than the beginning of his major-league career.

Hainsworth's debut was less than impressive. He was beaten, 4–1, in the season opener at Boston, and he returned to Montreal, where Ottawa outscored the Canadiens 2–1. This defeat was followed by a 2–1 loss to the Maroons, thus confirming the suspicions of Canadiens fans that Hainsworth was an unworthy successor to Vézina.

"From their point of view," observed Ron McAllister, "everything George did was wrong. Their loyalty to Vezina was a living thing."

The criticism notwithstanding (one sportswriter referred to him as "a lowly substitute"), Hainsworth played every one of the 44 games on the Canadiens' schedule and finished the season with a goals against average of 1.52, topped only by Clint Benedict of the Maroons, who registered a 1.51 mark. But George led the league in shutouts, with 14, and he outgoaled Benedict in the first round of the Stanley Cup playoffs.

Little by little, the Canadiens fans began warming to Hainsworth. He won the Vézina Trophy in the 1927–28 season with a remarkable 1.09 goals against average and managed to improve on that in 1928–29, allowing only 43 goals in 44 games, for a 0.98 mark. It would be presumptuous to suggest that Hainsworth ever commanded the same total adulation of Montreal fans that Vézina enjoyed, but by January, 1929, Hainsworth had certainly become a hero to many French-Canadians. It was a single performance, however, that captured their imagination.

On the night of January 24, 1929, the Toronto Maple Leafs were visiting the Forum. As the Canadiens were peppering Hainsworth in the pre-game warmup, a practice shot caught the goaltender unaware and smashed into his nose, knocking him unconscious. A bloody mess, Hainsworth was carried to the dressing room. A call went over the Forum loudspeaker for Montreal's spare goalie, but he couldn't be located.

Meanwhile, the team physician worked over Hainsworth's broken nose, attempting to reduce the swelling around his eyes and cheeks. The blow was so severe, however, that there was little the doctor could do, and within a matter of minutes the swelling had completely shut one eye. "Bandage me up," Hainsworth insisted, "I want to get out there."

Neither the doctor nor the Canadiens had much choice. Ten minutes later George skated out to his position for the opening faceoff. The Forum crowd reacted with a distillation of jubilation and fear. The goal-hungry Maple Leafs immediately swarmed to the attack and bombarded Hainsworth with every variety of shot at their command.

"George appeared to be enjoying himself," said one viewer. "He seemed to laugh with mad glee after stopping each shot."

Veteran reporters could hardly remember seeing the fans sit down throughout that game. Hainsworth portrayed a hockey version of Horatio at the bridge, and soon George himself was yelling and screaming along with his fans. "His face," wrote McAllister, "one-sided and bulging, feverish and red from excitement and injury, loomed livid and macabre above the forest of sticks and whirling forms crowding close about him. This was his night of nights!"

The Maple Leafs managed to jam one shot behind him, but the inspired Canadiens also scored a goal, and the game ended in a 1–1 tie. From that point on, Hainsworth was a Forum hero. He played 7 full seasons, until he was 40 years old.

Hainsworth seemed to improve with age. In 1928–29 he recorded 22 shutouts in 44 games and continued to excel for the Canadiens until the 1932–33 campaign. The entire Montreal team from Morenz to Hainsworth was in a slump that year. The disaster reached a climax on February 21, 1933, when the Canadiens visited Boston and were demolished 10–0 by the Bruins. Dandurand was furious with Hainsworth, who had given up several easy goals, and he made up his mind to trade George at the earliest opportunity. The result was one of the quickest deals in hockey history.

It happened after the season in which the Canadiens were dispatched from the playoffs by New York. Dandurand had been brooding over Hainsworth's play for a long time. One afternoon in a Toronto hotel room, he picked up the telephone and called Conn Smythe, manager of the Maple Leafs, whose goalie was Lorne Chabot.

"Would you be interested in trading Chabot for Hainsworth?" Dandurand asked.

"Certainly," replied Smythe, who promptly hung up.

Dandurand could be forgiven if he thought the whole brief sequence had been a bizarre dream. He phoned Smythe again to be sure the whole idea wasn't a gag in the mind of the Toronto boss. Thus assured, the two agreed to announce the trade the next day, and the deal was completed.

Chabot played only one season for the Canadiens, and he registered a 2.15 goals against average; Hainsworth's mark was a less impressive 2.48. But Hainsworth lasted three full seasons in Toronto, during which time the Leafs twice led the league. Then he returned briefly to Montreal in 1937 before retiring.

"George was one of the greatest goaltenders," said a Montreal observer, "but he had the misfortune of battling the ghost of Vézina as long as he played for the Canadiens."

The seeds of the world championship team that Dandurand had planted in the mid-1920s finally bore fruit in the playoffs of 1930. Les Canadiens went up against the Chicago Black Hawks in the first round of a two-game total goals series and emerged with a 1–0 win at Chicago before 17,476 spectators, the largest crowd to see a game in the Windy City until then. Next they returned to Montreal, where the teams played a 2–2 tie. Thus the Canadiens came off with a 3–2 edge in goals and moved on to the semifinals against the Rangers.

Paced by Gus Rivers, who scored at 68:52 of sudden-death overtime, a new record, the Canadiens won the opening game 2–1. Hainsworth shut out New York 2–0 in the second and final match, giving Montreal the right to meet the Boston Bruins in the Stanley Cup finals. Boston was heavily favored to rout Montreal, but Hainsworth was too much for the Bruins in the opener, and he stopped Boston 3–0. The Bruins hadn't lost two consecutive games that season and were expected to rebound in the second game of the best-of-three series, but the Canadiens prevailed, 4–3, and captured the Cup.

Dandurand wasn't one to stand pat. He embellished his lineup with a small slick forward named Johnny Gagnon. Swarthy and black-haired, with quick darting moves, Gagnon was placed on the line with Morenz and Joliat and immediately was dubbed the "Black Cat." He was to become one of the foremost Canadiens forwards in the years ahead.

With the Gagnon-Morenz-Joliat line leading the way, Les Canadiens finished first in the Canadian Division of the NHL and faced Boston, champions of the American division, in the first round of the best-of-five series. As expected, it was a superb series; they went down to the fifth game with the clubs tied at two apiece.

Montreal grabbed a 2–0 lead in the finale at the Forum, but the Bruins counterattacked and tied the score, forcing the game into sudden death. It was finally resolved when, after 19 minutes of furious skating, Marty Burke passed the puck to Wildor Larochelle, who beat Tiny Thompson in the Bruin goal.

In the meantime, the Chicago Black Hawks, coached by Dick Irvin, a man who was to play a major part in the Canadiens saga, reached the finals against Montreal. Cleverly directed by Irvin, the Black Hawks stunned the Canadiens by taking a 2–1 lead in games, and a 2–0 lead in what could have been the fourth and Cup-winning game for them. But "Black Cat" Gagnon rallied Montreal with two goals, and Pit Lépine followed with two more. The Canadiens triumphed, 4–2.

The finale was the type of match that has since been referred to as "typical playoff hockey." Both teams accented a close-checking defense game, also known as "kitty-bar-the-door," waiting for the break that would lead to a score. The Canadiens finally got it, and the Black Cat once again was the scoring hero. Morenz supplied the second goal, and the Canadiens won their second straight Stanley Cup.

A year later, the Canadiens led the Canadian Division again, but this time they were wiped out in the opening Stanley Cup round by the American Division champion Rangers, 3–1. Like the more contemporary Montreal teams, the Canadiens of that era accented style rather than strength. They were an artistic bunch with one collective flaw: size was always against them. The Morenz Line, for example, was nothing more than a collection of half-pints as compared to the behemoths on the other teams. Consequently, whenever an opposing coach planned strategy against Montreal, he would give serious consideration to mauling the smallest of the Flying Frenchmen.

Big, bruising Eddie Shore started one brawl by cross-checking minuscule Johnny Gagnon across the bridge of his nose with his stick. Minutes later, Sylvio Mantha of the Canadiens clashed with Shore. A bloody fight developed, with referee Cooper Smeaton in the middle trying to separate the pair. Peacemaker

Smeaton took three of Shore's hardest blows and fell to the ice with two broken ribs.

Faced with the possible extinction of his team unless the league intervened, Dandurand protested Boston's behavior to both NHL president Frank Calder and Charles Adams, president of the Boston sextet. Dandurand had the naiveté to expect Adams to punish Shore, a suggestion that received a huge laugh in Boston. Calder responded by fining Shore $100, and Adams protested that Shore was not permitted the right to defend himself.

Adams continued the feud with Calder until he resigned as an NHL governor, on February 11, 1933. The decision was regarded as a triumph for Calder and Dandurand and a curious event for hockey in general. The essence of Adams's resignation was his displeasure with the NHL "gag rule," which provided a $1,000 fine for criticizing another NHL official. By resigning, Adams cleverly placed himself beyond the ken of the rule, yet in a position to denounce Calder and Dandurand as much as he pleased.

The Bruins weren't the only players taking runs at the smaller Canadiens. Conn Smythe's big Maple Leafs also had their strategy settled when the teams clashed. Since Gagnon had developed into one of the most formidable scorers on Montreal, Smythe decided that the Black Cat should be softened up. He chose husky forward Busher Jackson to handle the job. From the opening face-off, Jackson crashed headlong into the surprised Gagnon. The Black Cat knew Jackson as a pleasant chap off the ice and asked him why he was battering him so violently.

"Sorry, Johnny," Busher replied. "That's orders."

Each time Jackson floored Gagnon, the Leaf would look down at the crumpled Canadien and repeat, "That's orders."

Finally, in utter desperation, Gagnon shot back: "Hey, Busher, how long these goddamned orders for?"

Gagnon, like most of his teammates, had a sparkling sense of humor, and it was briefly abetted by a huge French-Canadian named Jean Baptiste Pusie. Considered the funniest man to lace on a pair of skates, Pusie played for the Canadiens in 1931, 1932, and 1936. He was never at a loss for words, although his English was often fractured beyond repair. Once after Montreal lost a game, a teammate berated Jean Baptiste in the dressing room for his lack of teamwork. He wanted to know why Pusie hadn't passed the puck to him.

"I skate h'up de h'ice," said Jean Baptiste. "I no see you. I skate around de net; I no see you. Den I look h'up; an' I see you. But I cannot pass de puck, because you are park' in de penalty box!"

Dandurand wasn't doing much laughing in those days. His dynasty began crumbling in the 1932–33 season, and he wasn't sure why. The Morenz Line was intact, the goaltending and defense appeared to be sound, and the rest of the roster could hardly be considered inferior. Some of the players, including Gagnon, later charged that they couldn't get along with Newsy Lalonde, who was coaching the team at the time. The behavior of some stars confirmed this thinking. Overlooking Lalonde's part in the slump, Dandurand threatened to shake up the team and even went so far as to put Morenz on the trading block. At one point late in the season it was rumored that Leo had fined Gagnon $200 for indifferent play.

Leo established himself on the side of the coach and immediately began probing the minor leagues for potential replacements. Oddly enough, he took Morenz with him on a trip to Hamilton, Ontario, and it was Howie's advice that led to a vital acquisition for the Canadiens several years later.

Dandurand had heard some good things about a forward line with the Hamilton Tigers, of the Ontario Hockey Association's Senior League, and after watching the Tigers in action he asked Morenz whom he liked best. "Toe Blake and Herbie Cain," Morenz replied.

"I agree," said Dandurand.

A day later, Leo phoned the NHL office and requested that the pair be placed on the Canadiens' reserve list, thereby reserving them for his club. As a philanthropic gesture, Dandurand agreed to permit Cain to play for the enfeebled Maroons and later agreed to have his intracity rivals sign Blake. In each case, Leo reserved the right of recall, a stipulation that was to be very significant in the late thirties. Both Blake and Cain were eventually to become 200-goal scorers in the NHL.

Such Maroons-Canadiens amity was not reflected on the Forum ice. The English-French rivalry had been well established in the thirties, with the bigger Maroons having the edge in the fighting, if not in the scoring. On February 22, 1934, the Maroons edged the Canadiens 1–0 at the Forum. The game was enlivened by a bout between Morenz and Cy Wentworth and accentuated by a melee around the Canadiens bench when Lalonde attempted to behead Hooley Smith, the Maroon captain, with his stick. Dandurand couldn't restrain himself either, and he connected with a few well-placed jabs at Smith, while referee Mike Rodden tried to haul the Maroon out of danger.

In a startling turn of events, Frank Patrick, a managing director of the Canadiens, disclosed the following day that both Lalonde and Dandurand would be fined $100 apiece for their belligerence. More significant was the fact that fights such as the Morenz-Wentworth affair were beginning to take a toll on the Canadiens' star. Howie's physical condition continued to deteriorate in the playoffs, won by Chicago, when he crashed into the end boards and broke a thumb. Proof of Morenz's eroding scoring abilities was evident in the final statistics of the 1933–34 season: he finished 48th on the list, with only 8 goals in 39 games.

Dandurand was a sentimentalist, but he was also a businessman. He knew Morenz was slipping, and he also realized that the Morenz name could command some interesting players in a trade. Dealing the Stratford Streak was probably the most difficult decision of Leo's long career in sports. But Howie himself was despondent about the booing he was receiving from the Montreal fans, and he suggested to Dandurand that he be traded.

Morenz was 33 years old at the time, and he had obviously slowed down. Just before the 1934–35 season, Dandurand dropped his bombshell — Howie Morenz was traded to the Chicago Black Hawks!

After 11 years with the Canadiens, the most popular Montreal hockey player since Vézina was being cast adrift. In addition, Dandurand dispatched Lorne Chabot and Marty Burke to the Black Hawks in exchange for Lionel "Big Train" Conacher, Roger Jenkins, and Leroy Goldsworthy.

In honor of his friend, Dandurand tossed a farewell dinner for Morenz and solemnly told the audience, "As long as I'm associated with the Canadiens, no other player will wear Howie's number seven." Dandurand's promise was kept by his successors, and to this day the Montreal management has honored that vow.

The shake-up was beneficial to both the Canadiens and Morenz. Although he was admittedly unhappy in Chicago, Howie played a scintillating game for the Black Hawks. He scored against his old teammates in the final game of the season at the Forum, in which Chicago triumphed 4–2. Howie received a standing ovation from the Montreal crowd. A season later, Morenz was dealt to the Rangers, but he was a shadow of his former self. New York's Lester Patrick was happy to return him to the Les Canadiens for the 1936–37 season.

Wearing the *bleu, blanc, et rouge* once more proved to be a tonic for Morenz. True, he had lost his old get-away power, but he was reunited with his old buddies, Gagnon and Joliat, and every so often he'd bring the Forum crowd to its feet with one of the exquisite Morenz rushes.

He was doing just that on the night of January 28, 1937, when a Chicago defenseman caught him with a bodycheck, sending Morenz hurtling feet-first into the end boards at the Atwater Street side of the north-end net. It wasn't a normal spill, and Howie lost all control as he skidded toward the boards. When his skate rammed into the wood, a snap could be heard around the rink, and Morenz crumpled in excruciating pain.

Howie was rushed to the hospital with a badly broken leg, and there was some doubt that he would recover in time to return for another season of play. Once in the hospital, the 36-year-old Morenz began brooding. Instead of recuperating, he suffered a nervous breakdown. Then he developed heart trouble.

Nobody is quite sure what transpired in the hospital to bring about the utter deterioration of Howie's condition. One theory has it that he was overwhelmed by well-intentioned friends, who filled his room with flowers, books, and candy. "The hospital," said one visitor, "looked like Times Square on a Saturday night. The continual stream of visitors tired him."

Perhaps too late, hospital officials forbade all but Howie's immediate family to visit him. Then early on March 8, 1937, Morenz was given a complete checkup. He appeared to be rallying, but the analysis was deceptive. A few hours later Howie Morenz was dead.

In *Hockey Heroes*, Ron McAllister theorized: "Probably Morenz realized that even if he did recover, he would never be able to make a second comeback. And when he could no longer see visitors — his one link with the game that had become a whole life to him — the future must have looked terribly black. The terrific strain under which he played that last season, against younger and fresher men, had brought him to a complete breakdown; only genius and drive and know-how had kept him abreast of the game at all."

The funeral service for Morenz was held at center ice of the Forum, where thousands filed silently past his bier. Andy O'Brien, of *Weekend Magazine*, recalls the scene, as thousands of hockey fans lined up outside the rink that Morenz had made famous: "Outside the crowd was so great, we of the press had to enter through the boiler room on Closse Street. As I walked below the north end, profound silence left an impression of emptiness, but at the promenade I stopped in breathless awe. The rink was jammed to the rafters with fans standing motionless with heads bared."

The NHL paid an official league tribute to Morenz on November 7, 1937, by sanctioning an All-Star Game at the Forum. In it, the Canadiens and Maroons combined forces to challenge a select squad of NHL stars, including Frank Boucher, Charlie Conacher, and Eddie Shore. The All-Stars won, 6–5, and some 8,683 fans contributed $11,447 to a fund for the Morenz family. Howie's uniform was presented to his son, Howie Morenz, Jr.

The death of Morenz signaled the end of a significant era in Montreal hockey history, and it was also the prelude to the downfall of the Canadiens in the NHL. They reached their nadir in the 1939–40 season, finishing last in the seven-team league. Leo Dandurand had sold his interest in the club, and the new management realized that it was time for a major housecleaning.

The Boston Bruins, 1929

The Original Bruins, Starring Eddie Shore

Since the Bruins were the first team to represent the United States in the National Hockey League (first season 1924–25), one would think that the club, having been around the NHL for so long, might have more than a few Stanley Cups in its collection. But in its 65-year history, the team from Massachussets has had precious few truly great teams. The most recent was from the Orr-Esposito period; in the pre-World War II years, it was the Kraut Line club of the late 1930s; and before that, the original Bruins.

It took exactly three years for the original Boston club to climb from the NHL's cellar to the top of the American Division. In the 1927–28 season, Boston led its sector with a laudable 20-13-11 mark.

The playoffs were another story. Boston was eliminated in two games by the Rangers, but hardly felt a need to rebuild. In a period when NHL teams operated with small rosters and some players were capable of playing an entire 60 minutes of a game without substitution, the Bruins had a distinguished roster.

Appropriately, in an age that stressed defense, the Bruins two best players were defenders; goalie Tiny Thompson (his goals against average in 1928–29 was 1.18) and defenseman Eddie Shore.

Very few hockey players over the years have been able to almost singlehandedly carry a club by sheer force of ability and character, but Shore was one of them. His desire to play the game was unquenchable despite injury, and he powered the Bruins as a leader par excellence. Add to that an ability to deliver crunching bodychecks, as well as a knack for puck-carrying and goal-scoring that was unusual for defensemen in that day.

Shore's defense partners, Lionel Hitchman and George Owen, also were highly-skilled performers. Up front, the team featured Aubrey (Dit) Clapper, who later would star on defense for the Bruins, Harry Oliver, Cooney Weiland, and Perk Galbraith, all top-ranked forwards.

The Bruins finished first again in 1928–29 with a 26–13–5 mark, and they romped through the playoffs without a second wind. In the semifinals, Thompson hung a pair of 1–0 shutouts on the Montreal Canadiens before Boston closed the series with a 3–2 triumph.

In the finals, Shore & Co. faced the defending Stanley Cup champion Rangers. Thompson sparkled in Game One, producing a 2–0 shutout. He had the Rangers blanked for 46 minutes and 48 seconds of the second game before Butch Keeling of New York beat him. The final score was 2–1 and Boston had its first Stanley Cup. (Thompson's goals against average was 0.60.)

The Bruins were even better in the regular season following their championship. They won 38 games, lost but 5, and tied 1. The Montreal Maroons had the second best record, a full 26 points behind Boston. But the playoffs were another story. After ousting the Maroons three games to one in the semifinals, the Bruins collided with a red-hot Canadiens squad in the finals, losing in two straight, 3–0 and 4–3.

The regular season superiority was maintained in 1930–31, although the Bruins were not quite as strong (28–10–6) as they had been a year earlier. Not even Eddie Shore's heroics could overcome the Montreal jinx. In a best of five series, Montreal prevailed three games to two. The Bruins collapsed after that, finishing last in the American Division.

One Stanley Cup hardly qualifies the Shore Bruins for the top of the heap, but the combination of the Cup and four consecutive first place finishes during a highly competitive era ensure the Bruins of a place on the list of top teams.

Over the years, Boston's notorious "Big, Bad Bruins" have earned their reputation as the roughest, toughest band of swashbuckling skaters hockey has ever known. Such hard-nosed moderns as Wayne Cashman, Ken Hodge, and Bobby Orr have been carrying on a tradition that had its roots on a farm in Cupar, Saskatchewan.

It was there that Eddie Shore, who one day would mold the Bruins' image, learned to play hockey and, perhaps more important, learned to endure the most extreme forms of pain and hardship.

The family of Thomas Shore lived on a farm of 36 square miles. "We ran about a thousand head of stock, all told," said Shore. "We had about 400 head of horses and 600 head of cattle."

Eddie Shore worked long and hard on the farm. Later in his hockey career, Shore would drive through a blizzard from Boston to Montreal in a 1928 automobile without a windshield and play a game that same night, scoring the winning goal. Unbelievable as the feat might have been, it is understandable in the light of the toughening-up process he experienced on the Saskatchewan farm.

One of the most grueling of Shore's chores was his regular battle to break "outlaw" horses. With keen ferocity, the horses would rear, stamp, and lunge wildly, trying to heave young Eddie off their backs. "It was my delight and pleasure to break in a lot of those horses," said Shore, "and doing so helped me build the legs and body I needed to play professional hockey for 19 years."

By the time he was 12 years old, Eddie was supervising the hauling of harvested grain into town. "Sometimes I drove a 4-horse team pulling a wagon loaded with 150 bushels of grain for 20 miles or 40 miles round trip. That is a lot of mileage for a 4-horse team."

The game of hockey did not make an impression on young Eddie's life until he enrolled at Manitoba Agricultural College in Winnipeg. His brother Aubrey, who was a year-and-a-half older, was a superior hockey player, but Eddie had absolutely no interest in sports. Aubrey kindled his kid-brother's competitive fires by suggesting that Eddie just didn't have the makings of a good hockey player. The words were uttered with just the proper mixture of humor and contempt.

"I told Aubrey that anybody could be a hockey player," said Eddie. "Then I set out to prove it. The college had an outdoor rink, and all that winter when I got through with my classes, I'd get dressed and go out on that ice with a hockey stick and a puck."

The fact that the temperature had dropped to as low as 50 degrees below zero did not deter the sinewy kid, although in later years, Eddie would recall the abject intensity of the cold. "Lot of times I'd have one or two inches of hoarfrost on my shoulders and back. My ears, nose, cheeks, and feet froze. But I was determined to be a hockey player. The more Aubrey ridiculed me, the more determined I got."

Before the winter had ended, Eddie had gained a berth on the college hockey team. He was clumsy, a poor skater who had to compensate for his deficiencies by trying just that much harder. Still, the last thing on his mind was a career in professional hockey.

Then an event occurred that would have a lifetime bearing on Eddie, the Boston Bruins, and the history of hockey itself. His father decided to quit his successful farming business and try his hand at a western Canadian steel business. The steel business soon went bust, and Thomas Shore lost just about everything he owned, including Eddie's tuition. Not particularly distraught, Eddie left school and headed for Melville, Saskatchewan, a town renowned for its first-rate amateur hockey team. He managed to win a position on the Melville Millionaires, and off the ice he worked at odd jobs around town. "I was a bit of a carpenter, a bit of a barber, and a fireman on the Canadian National Railways," Shore recalled.

More important, he was learning fast how to be a superior hockey player. The rough edges were there, to be sure, but Shore's zest for battle was so overwhelming that he soon burst forth as the best player on the Millionaires. He was certainly the toughest. However, his coach believed that Shore was more valuable to the Millionaires on the ice than in the penalty box, and this feeling almost led to an early demise of Eddie's career.

The Millionaires were playing a rough Winnipeg Monarchs sextet in a championship match, and Shore was under the strictest orders not to draw a penalty, no matter how viciously he was attacked. Somehow sensing that Shore was being restrained, the enemy skaters took great liberties with the Melville ace. They bludgeoned him with their sticks and pounded him with their bodies. Shore was knocked out three times. After the third kayo, Eddie was carried to the dressing-room, and he remained unconscious until his teammates walked in to undress. He had lost six teeth, suffered a broken jaw, and had his nose broken.

More significant, though, was the fact that Shore had managed to play 50 minutes of the 60-minute game, and the Millionaires had won! It was the turning point in Eddie's career. Not only was he not intimidated by violence on the ice, he seemed to relish the assaults. He pressed on for bigger and better jobs in professional hockey.

At first he bounced around from Vancouver to Regina to Edmonton, with only modest success. By 1925, his abilities had been honed to sharpness, and he was recognized as a potential ace and unquestionably one of the roughest athletes in tough western Canada.

Once, in 1925, he demonstrated this toughness prior to a series with the Victoria club. Eddie had suffered a 14-stitch cut on his left leg just above the knee. The injury was a lot more severe than it appeared in the newspapers, and Eddie was in terrible pain as the Edmonton club departed by train for Victoria.

When the train arrived at Vancouver, the Edmonton players alighted and proceeded to the night boat for Victoria. Shore kept trying to put pressure on his bum leg, but the pain persisted. However, his teammates were feeling no pain, particularly Art Gagne and Johnny Sheppard, each of whom grabbed a crutch and tossed it overboard.

Shore couldn't have cared less. That night he took his position on the Edmonton blue line and played the entire 60 minutes of the match. Author Ed Fitzgerald wrote, "He played even though all the stitches popped out of that jagged cut early in the game. He played even though his thick woolen stockings and his canvas hockey pants were soaked in blood and the pain got so bad that he hardly felt it anymore, he was so numb. He refused to come off the ice.

"The people who were there swear that he was one of the most effective players in the game. Immediately afterward he went into a hospital, and they wouldn't let him out for a week!"

While Shore was rapidly earning a reputation as an exceptionally courageous and competent skater in the Western Canada League, eastern sporting moguls began reshaping the face of the National Hockey League. The 1924–25 season was a turning point; Boston's Bruins became members, thereby establishing themselves as the first American team in the NHL.

By any standards, the rookie Boston club was militantly inept. The Bruins finished in sixth place with an awful record of only 6 wins and 34 losses. A year later they climbed to fourth place, but once again they missed the playoffs.

Obviously the Bruins needed a superstar.

As luck would have it, such aces as Eddie Shore, Harry Oliver, and Perk Galbraith were being offered at bargain basement prices. Bruins owner Charles Adams promptly offered $50,000 — half of it in cash — for the trio of Shore, Duke Keats, and Frank Boucher in a seven-man package.

Boucher was sold to the newly organized Rangers, and others were dealt to the new Detroit team that had also joined the league.

During the summer of 1926, the NHL once and for all shed its Canadian provincialism and emerged as a truly inter-American organization. An American division, composed of New York, Boston, Chicago, Pittsburgh, and Detroit, was formed to compete with the Canadian Division, made up of Ottawa, the Canadiens, Maroons, New York Americans, and Toronto Maple Leafs.

Nobody knew it that summer, but the first Boston hockey dynasty had begun to form, and Eddie Shore was to be its general. Until Shore came along, the Bruins lacked a definitive image. They were both amusing and pathetic, effervescent and fumbling; but if you tried to find an adjective that would adequately describe them, you wound up with nothing.

Eddie Shore changed all that. From the moment he tugged on the gold, white, and black jersey, the operative word was tough. With very rare exceptions it was to remain the most singular characteristic of the team, even in the days when it appeared to be loaded with lightweights.

In some ways the unadulterated roughness of the Bruins is an anomaly. After all, Boston is America's seat of culture, the home of Harvard, the acme of gentility. One would expect the Boston hockey team to represent all that is pure and artistic in the sport. But it didn't quite attain that level, partly because of Shore and partly because of Boston. The best explanation of the phenomenon was supplied by the incisive Canadian author and television personality Peter Gzowski, who once diagnosed the Bruin psyche.

"There are really two cities in Boston," Gzowski explained. "On the one hand there is the old Puritanistic headquarters of the Cabots and the Lowells, the Boston of Beacon Hill and Back Bay and John Phillip Marquand, of Harvard Yard and bone china and the Isabella Stewart Gardner museum. On the other hand there is the lusty, saloon-tough seaport of the shanty Irish, of Mayor James Curley — and before him of 'Honey Fitz' Fitzgerald, whose descendants have crossed the tracks to the side of lace curtains and high success — of gay wakes and oyster bars and Rocky Marciano, the shoemaker's son from suburban Brockton, and of Boston

Garden, or, as Bostonians of both persuasions say, Gaaden.

"There is no confusion about which Boston is reflected by the Boston Bruins. Although every team in the NHL (East Division) eventually came to personify its home city, none has held more consistently to a single style, over the years, than the Bruins. They are as delicate as stevedores . . . at a poker table they are the burly, boisterous redhead in the corner, ready to give the first man who says he's misplayed a hand a good rap in the mouth. They seem to take as much pleasure out of knocking someone down as in scoring a goal. The Bruins have played the game with a joy-through-brawling that is as Boston Irish as a last hurrah."

None of this would have been possible without Shore. Consider what the Bruin character might have been like if Frank Boucher, the champion Lady Byng (good conduct) Trophy-winner, had come to Boston, and Shore had been dispatched to New York. The Bruins would have belonged to the Cabots and Lodges.

Ironically, manager Art Ross wasn't convinced that Shore belonged on the Bruins when Eddie reported to training camp in the autumn of 1926. Eddie had demonstrated his toughness in the minor leagues out West, but Ross wasn't so sure the big fellow with the slicked-back hair could make it with the big leaguers. The answer was supplied in a training camp scrimmage. Hard-hitting veteran Bruin Bill Coutu wasn't particularly enamored of Shore's behavior, and during practice one day Coutu punched Shore in the mouth. The rookie returned the blow, and it seemed a truce was declared. A few minutes later Coutu lumbered along the ice like a rhinoceros, picking up speed with every step. Everybody in the rink knew he was bearing down on Shore but not because he wanted to score a goal. He was after Eddie's head.

Shore instinctively realized that Coutu had him lined up for a pulverizing bodycheck, so he dug his skates into the ice and crouched for the blow. Coutu hit him amidships, but Shore was immovable. He held his ground as the veteran crashed to the ice, stunned and embarrassed. When Shore returned to the bench, he discovered that he hadn't escaped without injury. His ear was soaked with blood and it hung as if it had been sliced with a razor.

The trainer rushed Shore to a physician, who stopped the bleeding but announced that the ear would have to be amputated! Eddie, who had accumulated a wealth of questionable medical "knowledge," challenged the diagnosis. "I want to see another doctor," he demanded.

One after another, the physicians reiterated the original diagnosis: the ear would have to go. But Shore persisted until he found a doctor who would stitch the ear together. It was not a simple procedure. With the aid of a mirror, Eddie instructed the physician as to how he wanted the job done, almost like a customer telling a barber how to part his hair.

Rarely did a rookie skate in the NHL with the impudence of Shore. He was brash beyond belief. Al Silverman, former editor of *Sport* magazine, observed, "It has been written that man is the cruelest of the animals, and also the most maligned; that man is capable of dealing out merciless, inhuman punishment, and yet is just as capable of absorbing such punishment. Man endures all, say the philosophers. Well, in real life this is true only of certain extraordinary men. Men like Eddie Shore."

In his second NHL season, Shore set a league penalty record with 166 minutes' worth of fouls. The boisterousness that personified Shore was immediately translated to the Boston crowd. Soon it was impossible to determine which was the catalyst for mania, the frenetic Bruins audience, or Shore. To this day, visiting managers, coaches, and players denounce the ferocious behavior of Bruins fans as if it were a contemporary phenomenon (in 1969, Ranger forward Reg Fleming titled a magazine article "Boston Fans Are Animals"), but this behavior was manifested the night Shore made his debut. The hysteria was magnified a hundredfold when the new Boston Garden was opened, November 20, 1928.

Like most other aspects of Boston, the new home of the Bruins played second fiddle to its New York City counterpart. It was smaller and considerably uglier than Madison Square Garden in Manhattan. Because it was integrated with North Station and hidden behind elevated tracks, the new arena's architectural features were practically buried from view. Always ugly, it has somehow managed to deteriorate in appearance and hospitality. Some of those present suggested that the behavior of Bruins fans on opening night set humanity back several centuries, establishing the tone for Boston hockey forever. Others insist that Bruins fans are delightfully ebullient and the most faithful in captivity. In any event, columnist Stanley Woodward recreated the scene on the pages of the *Boston Herald* in horrified tones. "It was a riot, a mob scene, reenaction of the assault on the Bastille. It is estimated that 17,500 persons, 3,000 in excess of the supposed capacity of the Garden, saw the game."

One might have expected the crowd to behave once it obtained entrance to the rink, but good manners were forgotten in that frenetic atmosphere. When referee George Mallinson ruled a Bruin foray offside, the fans bombarded the ice with garbage.

The game itself carved the mold for the future developments. Boston played host to the Montreal Canadiens and, despite harassment from the crowd and some lusty bodychecks by Shore and company, the visitors won the game 1–0. Tall, dark, and handsome Sylvio Mantha sent the 17,500 rooters home depressed when he outwitted Bruin captain Lionel Hitchman and scored with only two seconds remaining in the second period. Reviews of the game sounded almost as if they had been written about the classic 1969 Montreal-Boston playoff round at the Garden.

"A constant stream of fresh Boston skaters, three and four to a position, emanated from the players' box and carried the game interminably to the Canadien end of the rink," said Woodward. "But the most virulent attacks were fruitless against the sturdy checking of the Canadiens defense and the matchless goaltending of George Hainsworth."

As if the general air of exuberance generated by Boston fans wasn't enough, Shore was also infuriated by Ross's machinations. "He played up the villain in Shore by various stunts," wrote Al Silverman.

One of the best stunts — or worst, depending on one's sense of the dramatic — was to keep Eddie off the ice when his teammates appeared for the opening face-off. When the play was first executed, fans thought that Shore had been injured and began to think that they wouldn't be getting their money's worth for the night. Precisely at that moment, the band would break into a chorus of "Hail to the Chief," and Shore would trot out in a matador's cloak.

Boston fans interpreted the episode as the height of drama and humor, but opponents took a dim view of the shenanigans. Some foes griped about it, and at least one decided on a countermeasure.

One night the obstreperous New York Americans were visiting Boston Garden. They silently observed the boring Shore ritual to its conclusion. Then, before the referee had an opportunity to drop the puck for the opening face-off, the Americans departed en masse to their dressing room. A minute later, they returned with a rolled up carpet, which they proceeded to unroll before the incredulous fans. When they reached the end of the rug, the noted American player Rabbit McVeigh crawled out. He got to his feet and blew kisses to the audience and the opponents, with special attention to Shore.

Shore was humiliated by the Americans' act and immediately decided he would no longer go through the cape routine, Ross or no Ross. But hockey promoters have been known to permit their intelligence to lag behind the masses, and Ross thought that the absurd behavior was essential to the game. Actually the Bruins could have done without cheap promotional tricks and succeeded admirably. They had a quality team, and they drew fans without gimmicks.

By the 1927–28 season, the Bruins had finished in first place. They repeated their performance in 1928–29 and won the Stanley Cup in 1929 with a three-straight sweep over the Canadiens in a best-of-five series. Shore had refined his playing style to a point at which his offensive ability matched his brutal defensive play, and he was regarded as one of the best all-around players in the NHL. Encounters with Rabbit McVeigh, the Montreal Maroons team, and a New York goalpost put him on a pedestal of durability that he shared with no one else.

The McVeigh incident was innocent enough. Shore had been checked to the ice by an Americans' defenseman, and he lifted himself to his skates just as McVeigh approached. It was too late for the Americans' forward to sidestep Shore, so he leaped over the kneeling Bruin. McVeigh's razor-sharp blade didn't quite clear Eddie; it sliced him between the eyes, knocking him back to the ice and out cold.

As the blood gushed from the wound, it appeared that Ross's prophecy about Shore's ultimate doom was to be fulfilled. The Boston trainer and a doctor skidded out to the fallen player in an attempt to pump some life into his inert, blood-smeared body. Eventually Shore regained his feet, skated to the bench, and had the trainer put a piece of tape on the gash. He resumed playing immediately and performed as if the accident had happened to some other player.

His clash with the Maroons was even more severe. Several of the Montreal players had decided that Shore was too liberal in his manhandling of them. During one game, one of them tore open Eddie's cheek with his stick blade, and another sliced his chin. With triphammer consistency, the Maroons clobbered Shore, and in the waning minutes of the game Shore was felled by a clout in the mouth that removed several teeth. He had to be carried from the rink after lying unconscious on the ice for 14 minutes. In that one game, Shore had accumulated more wounds than some players receive in a lifetime of pro hockey. He had a broken nose, three broken teeth, two black eyes, a gashed cheekbone, and a two-inch cut over his left eye.

He returned to action in the next Bruins game. When friends tried to commiserate with him, he dismissed their platitudes abruptly. "This is all part of hockey," he replied. "I'll pay off."

His high-speed collision with a goalpost at Madison Square Garden left the steel upright intact but cost Shore three broken ribs. The damage was so severe that the Bruins left Shore in the care of a physician and entrained for a game in Montreal. The doctor eventually escorted Eddie to a nearby hotel and left momentarily to register Shore at a hospital.

"Now Eddie," the doctor cautioned, "I want you to stay in your room until I can come back and take you over to the hospital."

The doctor should have known better. He left the hotel, signed up for a hospital room, and returned to Shore's room to escort the wounded player to the infirmary. The door was wide open, and there was no trace of the player or his baggage. Eddie had stumbled to the lobby and had hailed a cab for Grand Central Station, where he purchased a ticket for the late train to Montreal. He arrived in time for the game with the Canadiens. That night he scored two goals and an assist.

Shore's brave exploits did much to erase his image as a ruthless, insensitive player. Were it not for an incident in the 1933–34 season, Eddie might well have completed his long NHL career completely on the positive side, at least in the eyes of the fans.

If the Boston-Toronto bitterness had not exploded in such intensity, Shore might have averted the catastrophe; if he had realized who his tormentor was, the episode might have been minimized. But it didn't happen that way.

In the early thirties, Ross and Conn Smythe, the Toronto Maple Leafs manager, had ignited what was to be a long and bitter feud. The intercity hockey rivalry hit a new high in hostility early in December, 1933, and for good reason. The Leafs and the Bruins were the two best teams in hockey during the 1932–33 season, and they proved it by finishing first in their respective divisions.

They collided in the first round of a best-of-five Stanley Cup playoff. Four of the five games went into sudden-death overtime. Boston led the series 2–1 but lost the next game, and the teams battled in the deciding game. They played without a score through the regulation three periods in the deciding game. Then they played 100 minutes of overtime without a decision, at which point Smythe and Ross enjoyed one of their few moments of agreement. The two managers asked NHL President Frank Calder for permission to stop the game and resume it the following night. "Nothing doing," said Calder. The game was resumed.

Early in the sixth overtime, Shore attempted a clearing pass, but it was intercepted by Andy Blair of Toronto. Blair spotted Ken Doraty and slipped a pass to the little forward, who raced in and scored the winning goal at 4:46 of the sixth overtime, or 164:46 of the game.

Shore was the goat of the longest game played in the NHL up until that time, and he was reminded of this several times by the Toronto players. The animosity spilled over into the 1933–34 season and was quite evident on the night of December 12, 1933, when the Leafs and Bruins met at Boston Garden.

Exactly what inflamed Shore to detonate one of the most widely discussed episodes in hockey history remains debatable to this day. However, most observers agree that the incident started when the Leafs were killing a pair of overlapping penalties and simultaneously nursing a lead. Toronto coach Dick Irvin dispatched defenseman Red Horner and King Clancy and inserted Ace Bailey up front as his lone penalty-killing forward. George Hainsworth was in the nets.

Bailey was a splendid stickhandler, and he tantalized the Bruins with some uncanny bobs and weaves until the referee whistled a stoppage in play. At that point, Ross summoned Shore to the bench and whispered some advice to him. When Shore returned to the face-off circle, Bailey won the draw and continued to dazzle the Bruins with his footwork. Exhausted at last, Bailey skimmed the puck down the ice into the Bruin end of the rink. Shore retrieved it and began picking up speed in his inimitable locomotive fashion.

Confusion regarding subsequent events arises at this point in the play. Frank Selke, Sr., who was at the time of the incident assistant general manager of the Leafs, contends that Shore tried to round Clancy, was tripped by the minuscule Toronto defenseman, and lost the puck to the Leaf. Selke assumes that Shore was intent on retribution and charged at a player who he thought was Clancy. Actually it was Ace Bailey, who had dropped back to Clancy's vacated defensive position and whose back was turned to Shore.

In an extensive article about Shore, Al Silverman asserted that Shore was bodychecked by Horner and went after the Toronto ruffian after he recovered from the fall.

"Raging," said Silverman, "Shore went after Horner, mistaking Ace Bailey for Horner."

"Whether he mistook Bailey for Clancy," wrote Selke in *Behind the Cheering*, "or whether he was annoyed by his own futility and everything in general, nobody will ever know."

But this much is known. Shore gained momentum as he moved back toward the play in Boston territory, and soon he was skating at full speed as he approached Bailey from behind. According to Selke, he struck Bailey across the kidneys with his right shoulder. The impact of the blow was so severe that Bailey described a backward somersault, and he landed on his head with such force that onlookers could hear the crack all over the vast arena.

Selke, who was sitting in the front row of the press box, had one of the best vantage points in the building. He described the incident this way: "Shore kept right on going to his place at the Boston blue line. . . . Bailey was lying on the blue line, with his head turned sideways, as though his neck were broken. His knees were raised, legs twitching ominously. Suddenly an awesome hush fell over the arena. Everyone realized that Bailey was badly hurt. Horner tried to straighten Bailey's head, but his neck appeared to be locked. Red skated over to Shore, saying, 'Why the hell did you do that, Eddie?'

"Shore, little realizing how badly Bailey had been hurt, merely smiled. His seeming callousness infuriated Horner, who then hit Shore a punch in the jaw. It was a right uppercut, which stiffened the big defense star like an axed steer. As he fell, with his body rigid and straight as a board, Shore's head struck the ice, splitting open. In an instant, he was circled by a pool of blood about three feet in diameter."

At that moment the Bruins, as one, vaulted the boards and charged at Horner, but teammate Charlie Conacher rushed to Horner's side and the two held their sticks in bayonet position. "Which one of you guys is going to be first to get it?" Conacher demanded. The Bruins suddenly conducted an orderly retreat to assist Shore and to see if Bailey was still alive.

For 19 minutes Bailey lay unconscious while doctors worked frantically over him. An ambulance was summoned to rush him to the hospital, where he teetered percariously on the brink of death. He had suffered a cerebral concussion with convulsions, and it appeared that he would not recover. Before he was removed to the hospital, Bailey looked up at Selke from the dressing room table and he pleaded, "Put me back in the game. They need me."

As Selke and others suspected, Bailey was in danger of dying, and only immediate surgery would save him. A day after the injury, two brain surgeons familiar with that type of damage were found in Boston. They operated on Bailey, thinking he had suffered only one concussion. After the initial surgery, however, they discovered he had suffered two. A week later another operation was performed.

Few held out hope for the player, and the Toronto management made plans to have Bailey's body shipped back to Canada. Two weeks after the injury, Ace appeared to be slipping into an irretrievable condition, but he was attended by two unflaggingly spirited nurses, who kept urging him to "Keep fighting."

Suddenly Ace took a turn for the better, and he was released from the hospital two weeks later. Meanwhile, Shore had taken a turn for the worse in the eyes of hockey fans and officials. He was suspended by the NHL, and cries for his permanent suspension were heard from New York to Chicago.

When he was sufficiently recovered, Bailey graciously minimized Shore's dilemma by saying, "We didn't see each other coming.

When Eddie heard that, he replied, "I wish we had. I'd have slugged him — and nobody ever got hurt that way but Shore."

The Bruins sent Shore on a recuperative vacation, and a month later the NHL concluded that since Eddie had never before suffered a match penalty for injuring an opponent, he would be reinstated. He returned to the Bruins lineup in January, 1934, neither penitent nor restricted in his play.

Shore played 14 seasons in the NHL, 13½ of which were spent with the Bruins. Four times he was awarded the Hart Trophy as the league's most valuable player, and he was named to the All-Star Team seven times. The best estimates place Shore's total number of stitches in excess of 970. His nose was broken 14 times, his jaw shattered five times, and all his teeth had been knocked out before his career was over. He barely missed being blinded in both eyes and nearly lost an ear.

The Bruins finished in last place in the American Division during the season of the Shore-Bailey incident, but they recovered admirably to recapture first place the following year. Those opponents who suspected that Shore would become more temperate were unquestionably dismayed when he returned. Old feuds were reopened, and new ones, especially with younger players, started.

Because of Shore, the Bruins cultivated keen disputes with several teams, but the Leafs and Rangers remained at the top of the hate parade. Over the years, the New Yorkers were a more skilled but smaller club than the Bruins, and generally they absorbed more abuse than they distributed. But when former Canadian heavyweight champion, Murray Patrick joined the Rangers in 1937, the New Yorkers temporarily gained the balance of power. Patrick was the Rangers policeman, and he objected to Shore's abuse of Phil Watson, New York's young and rather small center. Shore once cracked Watson in the head and sent him to the hospital with a concussion.

"He was tough," Patrick recalled. "You had to be sure to get him first."

Frustrated to the point of paranoia by the Bruins' physical superiority over the Rangers, New York hockey fans waited impatiently for the day when Shore would get his comeuppance at the hands of Patrick. Oddly enough, it happened because of a confrontation involving Watson and Jack Portland, a Bruin defenseman. Muzz Patrick was observing the two-man battle without interfering when he noticed Shore stealthily move in on Watson from behind. "He started massaging the back of Phil's neck with his stick," wrote Al Silverman in his Shore chronicle. "Disturbed by the two-to-one odds against his teammate, Patrick rushed Shore and attempted to wrest him away from Watson. Shore wheeled around and swung at Patrick, hitting him on the shoulder. In a trice, Patrick let his two leather gauntlets slip off his hands. He retracted his fists and then — bomb-bomb-bomb — he smashed Shore three times in the face."

"I could feel his head squash when I hit him," Patrick admitted later.

After game officials intervened, Shore left the ice with a cut eye and lip and a nose broken in two places. He headed straight for the medical room, received stitches, and was back on the ice ten minutes after the fight had started.

Every so often, Eddie would have an off-year, and critics would charge that the law of diminishing returns was taking its toll on the aging star. But Shore had a knack, irritating to opponents, of bouncing back with even more élan the following year. He did it the season after his suspension and repeated the feat in 1937–38, after what most Shore fans regarded as his worst season. Eddie played only 18 games in 1936–37. The Bruins finished second in the American Division but were quickly dispatched from the playoffs by the Maroons. A broken vertebra had sidelined Eddie, but he was in perfect shape when he returned in the fall of 1937. He won the Hart Trophy and a spot on the First All-Star Team.

His hair was thinning, and his legs reacted just a trifle slower than before. Eddie Shore's star was in its descent, although he was to remain a player for a few more years, and then to become one of the most controversial team managers the game has known.

By the late 1930s, Shore was overshadowed by the glamorous young Bruins — the Bill Cowleys, Milt Schmidts, and Bobby Bauers. They were fast and smart, and they were awfully good hockey players.

But there never has been a player in Boston — or perhaps anywhere — as good and as smart and as tough as Eddie Shore. From 1926 through 1939 he made the Bruins a very special hockey club. There will never be another team like it because there will never be another Eddie Shore.

The New York Rangers, 1940

The Rangers' Last Glory Team, 1940

Every season, when the Rangers meet the New York Islanders at Nassau Coliseum, the Broadway Blueshirts can expect to hear a chant cascading down from the upper reaches of the arena. "NINETEEN FORTY! NINETEEN FORTY!!" is the Islanders fans way of reminding the frustrated Rangers that the wealthy club from Madison Square Garden has not won a Stanley Cup since Clark Gable starred in Hollywood and motorists drove an automobile called the Studebaker.

On April 13, 1940, Bryan Hextall of New York slipped the puck past Toronto Maple Leafs' goalie, Turk Broda, in the first period of sudden-death overtime to clinch the Rangers' third Stanley Cup. The New Yorkers haven't won one since.

By rights, the Rangers should have won several Stanley Cups during what was a brief, but glorious golden era on Broadway. After winning their second Stanley Cup in 1933, the Rangers grew old under coach Lester Patrick, and a massive rebuilding process resulted in a young and vibrant squad that began asserting itself in the late 1930s.

Patrick built the club around Davey Kerr, a sharp goaltender who benefitted from a rock-ribbed defense unit headed by captain Art Coulter and abetted by Ott Heller, Joe Cooper, and Walter (Babe) Pratt, each above average in his own right.

What distinguished the Rangers' overall balance was not one, but two, truly threatening forward lines. One featured Phil Watson at center, along with Bryan Hextall (Ron Hextall's grandfather), and Lynn Patrick (Lester's son), while a second included the Colville Brothers, Neil and Mac, along with Alex Shibicky.

In 1937–38, the Rangers finished second to Boston in the NHL's American Division with a 27–15–6 record, but they failed to clear the first playoff round against their bitter rivals, the New York Americans. The following season saw the NHL reduced to seven teams in one division. This time the Blueshirts put together a 26–16–6 mark, good enough for runner-up spot to the Bruins once more. The pattern repeated in 1939–40 when Patrick's sextet amassed a 27–11–10 record.

A year earlier, the Bruins had disposed of New York in a seven-game semifinal that wasn't decided until eight minutes of triple overtime. In 1940 the Bruins were just as good, but the Rangers were better. "There was never a team with so many strong players at every position that ever played better than the Rangers did that spring," says Herb Goren, who covered the NHL for the *New York Sun*. "It was a team without a weak link."

This was evident in the four games to two semifinal playoff win over Boston and a similar triumph over Toronto in the finals. Patrick had as many capable goal-scorers as he had playmakers. His defense was as airtight as any could be, and Kerr had reached his pinnacle. (During the regular season Davey compiled a 1.60 goals against average.) Toughness was abundant, particularly since the defense now was manned by Lester's younger son, Murray (Muzz) who had been heavyweight boxing champion of Canada.

With this core, the Rangers should have remained on the NHL's highest plateau for years, yet they slipped to fourth place (21–19–8) in 1940–41 and exited the playoffs in a six-game semifinal with the Maple Leafs.

One "problem" was goaltending. Davey Kerr went from superb (1.60 goals against average) to merely average (2.60) for him in the matter of a year and retired after the 1940–41 campaign. He was replaced by James (Sugar Jim) Henry, a capable youngster from Winnipeg.

While Henry wasn't in Kerr's class, average-wise — in his rookie year, Sugar Jim produced a 2.98 goals against mark — Henry was a winner and so were the Rangers; at least in the regular season. They finished with 60 points (29–17–2) in a highly competitive year, edging the Maple Leafs by three points and the Bruins by four. Bryan Hextall was the scoring champion, while linemate Lynn Patrick led in goals, and his other linemate Phil Watson topped the NHL in assists.

With the inventive and popular Frank Boucher behind the bench, the Rangers were favorites in the 1942 playoffs. And since they finished first, the Blueshirts should have opened the series with the opening two games at Madison Square Garden. But the fates intervened. The Ringling Brothers Circus caused a quirk in the scheduling and the series began at Toronto where the Leafs won 3–1. That was just the jump the underdogs needed, and they went on to beat New York four games to two.

Poof! Just like that, the Rangers bubble burst. World War II was raging in Europe and the Pacific and, one by one, the Ranger stars left for the armed forces. Jim Henry, Muzz Patrick, Art Coulter, Babe Pratt, the Colville Brothers, and Alex Shibicky all departed, and the Rangers fell to the bottom of the league in 1942–43 never to recover.

The Rangers would remain an NHL doormat through the end of World War II and into the post-war period. For years, New York hockey fans would wonder "what might have been," had the war not decimated such a high quality, inventive squad.

Curiously, the 1940 Rangers would take on a magical quality as the decades passed, mostly because the Blueshirts never won another Stanley Cup, and in the 1989–90 season "celebrated" the 50th anniversary since Broadway last hailed a Cup-winner.

Despite some impressive one year credentials, the 1940 Ranger squad cannot be included with the top or even middle echelon group of all-time teams, simply because the Rangers lacked staying power. Glittering as the lineup may have been, just one Stanley Cup and one first place finish is not good enough when so much more was possible.

Quite likely it would have been a more positive story had World War II not altered Lester Patrick's plans. But, as William Shakespeare once noted, "There is much virtue in if."

If Rangers' president, general manager, and coach, Lester Patrick, had succumbed to charges of nepotism, his club never would have blossomed into a dominant team of the late 1930s and early 1940s, and it certainly would never have won The Stanley Cup.

But in his sons Lynn and Murray (Muzz), Lester saw two gifted hockey players who belonged on the team, whether the fans or the newspaper critics liked it or not. Or whether Lester liked it or not because he, above all, was extremely wary of having even one — let alone two — of his boys skate for his Rangers.

Patrick had carefully watched his sons' development from their days as amateur athletes. "The most amazing thing of all," said Lester, "was that the situation was never planned — or even dreamed. I never steered or pushed the boys. It just happened."

When Lester opened the Rangers training camp that autumn of 1933, Lynn had earned a starting assignment with the strong Montreal Royals amateur team, a farm club of the Maroons. Muzz was not inclined towards hockey at that time.

An 18-year-old who weighed in at 215 pounds, Muzz preferred pro football and six-day bicycle racing. Watching Muzz in action, an insightful athletic critic could tell that he had the rare spirit of a winner. His father was just such a critic.

"Muzz," said Lester, "had started that six-day race with Gerard Debaets of Belgium. He was pushed around, bounced on and off the track like a handball. He was big and fast and game, but he wasn't a six-day bike rider. Well, he was for a while. He stuck it out gamely through the fourth day, but injuries made him quit. I hoped this had cured him of six-day riding, and it did.

"Now, he decided to become heavyweight champion of the boxing world. When? As soon as the track season was over. He had promised to run the half-mile. He did, too, in June, and he set a new record."

Meanwhile, Lynn had played so well for the Royals that Lester invited his son to the Rangers training camp in the fall of 1934. Lester was hypercritical of his son. The last thing he wanted to be accused of was nepotism. Above all, Lester wanted a winning team, and he certainly didn't think that Lynn had matured enough for the Rangers. He told some of his associates so, and some of them disagreed.

"Are your eyes going bad, Lester?" Frank Boucher asked. "Lynn is a pro. He's ready."

Boucher wasn't alone. Several of the Rangers pestered Lester, but the one who counted most was the captain, Bill Cook. His argument was persuasive. "You'd better sign the boy to a contract before somebody else does," he warned.

That did it. Lynn was signed to a Rangers contract and assigned to the third line. Knowing Patrick's high standards and his fear of charges of favoritism, his associates realized how difficult a decision it had been for the man who had grown to be known as the "Silver Fox of Hockey."

Lester's gravest fears were realized. A New York hockey writer suggested that Lester had bypassed better players to sign his son. There was the charge, loud and clear. Lester was furious, and he launched into a rare tirade against the newspaperman.

"You haven't hurt me," Lester thundered. "You're gnawing at the foundations of the game itself. To us, hockey means playing to win — brother against brother, father against son. It's a sacred precept that a foul mind like yours can't understand. My son made this team on skill alone, as any Ranger would tell you. In my opinion you're not fit to write about this sport."

Whether Lynn was fit to play for the Rangers was yet to be determined. He was to be tested by opponents and fans alike. They reddened Lynn's ears, calling him a prima donna and a daddy's boy, but Lynn was too strong a character and too good a hockey player to be thwarted.

Perhaps the best proof of Lynn's ability was provided by none other than Conn Smythe, who offered Lester $20,000 — at that time a lot of money — for Lynn less than two years after he made his New York debut. That left only Muzz on the sidelines, and Lester worried about him, concerned that the big fellow would get hurt as a boxer.

But Muzz could take care of himself. He knocked out 203 pound Phil Keating in two rounds and won the amateur heavyweight championship of Canada. All before he was 21 years old.

Muzz studied under veteran trainer Jimmy Bronson at Stillman's Gym in New York City. The plan was to move Muzz into the pro ranks on June 28, 1936, but first he was scheduled to meet Bill Gould for the Catholic Youth Organization's championship. The date was May 11, 1936, and Muzz ousted Gould. He was ready to go pro — or so Bronson thought.

What Muzz neglected to tell the trainer was that he had made a promise to his mother that he would quit fighting after the Gould fight, and he kept his promise. Bronson's heart was broken, but boxing's loss turned out to be hockey's gain.

Lester wanted to be as careful about easing Muzz into the NHL as he had been with Lynn, so the youngster was broken in with the Rovers, the Rangers top amateur team, then Philadelphia, a strong minor pro club. By the 1938–39 season, the two Patrick boys were Rangers teammates: Muzz on defense and Lynn on left wing.

The Patrick boys lifted the Rangers to heights experienced only by the Cook brothers and Boucher. The Cooks were gone, and Boucher had moved behind the bench to coach the Rangers, while Lester handled the managing.

They were a marvelous crew, finishing second behind Boston in the 1939–40 season, but knocking the Bruins out of the playoffs in a six-game opening round. Some observers believed that Muzz provided the inspirational lever over Boston. Until then, the Bruins had been a hardrock crew, dominated by the ever-rough Eddie Shore. But Shore overdid it on one occasion, and Muzz moved in on Shore and battered him to the ice. The Bruins were never the same.

The Patricks were not the only brothers making the Rangers a winner. Neil and MacColville worked the second forward line between Alex Shibicky. The trio would have been a first line on any other team but on the Rangers, the top unit comprised Lynn Patrick, Phil Watson, and Bryan Hextall. Boucher once described that line and some of his other aces thusly:

"Phil, the center, was a very unusual fellow with a most unusual temperament. Despite his Scottish name, he was a Frenchman, either laughing in a high-pitched squeal, or so low in spirits as to be in tears. His volatile nature surfaced particularly later on when he became the Ranger coach in the early 1950s. If the team was going well he'd beam and preen and shout, 'That's my boys.' When we lost, though, he'd grow bitter and shriek at the players, often in front of the writers. When he was excited, Phil's English grew confused and he was almost always excited in his early years with our club. Once, Johnny Gottslieg, the great old leftwinger of the Hawks, was needling Phil on the ice, and finally in exasperation Phil screamed at him, 'You . . . you . . . you been-has, you!' Gottslieg was leading the Hawks in scoring at the time.

"Hextall was Watson's rightwinger, though a left-hand shot, a hardrock of large bone structure and taciturn nature who could score off his forehand or backhand equally well. I always dreaded playing Detroit when the Wings had a body-thumper named Black Jack Stewart on the defense. Every time they met, Hex and Black Jack belted each other. Neither would give ground, so it was a succession of hammerings which could be heard all over the arena. Surprisingly enough, neither ever seemed to lose his temper; they simply revelled in the bumping.

"We used to alternate Clint Smith, Alf Pike, Dutch Hillier and Kilby Mac-Donald on our third line. Smith, called Snuffy, was a small fellow but exceedingly clever. He was hard to hit and was an expert on faceoffs and digging the puck from the corners. Pike, who like Lynn and Neil and Phil would coach after I was named general manager, joined us in my first season as the team's deep thinker. He'd been an outstanding junior player in Winnipeg. I remember that a few days after he reported to training camp in the fall of 1939 he and Lester got bogged down on contract negotiations. When Alf told me that the difference was $500 I told him that if Lester didn't give it to him, I would. As I've said, I was making $4500 then but I was determined to succeed and was convinced Pike would help us. And so Alf went to Lester and told him he'd decided to sign. Lester was puzzled, naturally enough, and probed Pike to find out why the boy who'd been so stubborn had suddenly relented, and finally Alf admitted I'd said I'd give him the $500. Lester bawled hell out of me for being soft, but my gamble — for it really had been that, I suppose — paid off; Lester came up with the five hundred.

"Dutch Hiller was the best skater on a club that could fly, a team whose skating and puck-handling abilities often have reminded me, in retrospect, of some of the best Montreal Canadiens free-wheelers. Dutch wasn't too big but he simply glided with an unusual gait in which he seemed to lift himself above the ice with each stride, and he became a consistent scorer, too. Kilby MacDonald was also a smooth and assured skater with a gliding stride. He could play on any line, filling in if players were injured, and was great to have around, pleasant, friendly, outgoing. All in all it was a wonderful team. In fact, I'll say it now: It was the best hockey team I ever saw."

The semifinal victory over the Bruins sent the Rangers into the cup finals against the Toronto Maple Leafs, a team that finished eight points behind New York during the regular schedule, but was capable of winning big games. Because of commitments at Madison Square Garden, the NHL decided that the first three games of the best-of-seven series would be played on New York ice, and the remainder would be fought in Toronto. But after the second game, the circus showed up — a day early — through some misunderstanding, and the Rangers and Leafs were to finish the series in Toronto. This change unnerved the New

Yorkers, who had won the first pair of matches at home by scores of 2–1 and 6–2. Playing before their home crowd, the Maple Leafs rose to the occasion, tying the series on 2–1 and 3–0 triumphs. The Rangers appeared to be in trouble — until the Patrick boys took over.

The fifth and pivotal game went into sudden-death overtime tied at 1–1. Back and forth, the players raced in the extra period, desperately trying for the score. More than ten minutes had passed without a red light when Lester Patrick watched his son Lynn clamber over the boards with linemates Phil Watson and Bryan Hextall.

A masterful playmaker, Watson dispatched a neat pass to Lynn Patrick, who hurled the puck past Toronto goalie Turk Broda at 11:43 of the overtime period. The Rangers were winners, 2–1.

New York needed only one more win to capture their first Stanley Cup since the halcyon days of the Cooks and Boucher, but Toronto wasn't about to play dead. The Leafs held the Rangers to a 2–2 tie, with only three minutes remaining in regulation time.

At that point, Watson appeared to have beaten Broda cleanly, but the referee disallowed the score on the ground that a Ranger player had one foot over the "crease" (a line that runs a yard in front of the goal.) Watson was so piqued by the decision that he spat in the referee's face.

Once again, sudden death was required. Both Lester Patrick and Boucher valiantly tried to keep the players "high" after the depressing setback on Watson's near-goal. Apparently they succeeded. Lynn Patrick's line took the ice, and at 2:07 of the period, Watson passed to Bryan Hextall. This time there was no denying the New Yorkers. They had won the Stanley Cup!

The next season, 1940–41, was virtually the last Lynn and Muzz played together. World War II had begun, and Muzz joined the army, the first NHL player to do so. Starting as a buck private and serving in Italy and France, he emerged five years later as a captain.

Lynn played on, recording his greatest years. In 1941 he scored 44 points and tied Hextall for the most points scored on the club. The next year he scored what then was a remarkable total of 32 goals, second only to Bill Cook in Ranger history at that time. In 1943 he led in assists with 39 and in points with 61. Then he entered the army as a private, and he came out two years later as a first lieutenant.

The 1940 Stanley Cup victory was the last for the Rangers. When Muzz left for the armed forces, a good chunk of the New York spirit departed, and Lynn's exit severely depleted the team's resources. When the war ended, the brothers tried to pick up where they had left off with the Rangers. But they just didn't have it anymore.

It was more than appropriate that when Lynn and Muzz retired as players, their dad, Lester, the illustrious Silver Fox, retired from the Garden after 20 memorable years.

And when the Patricks departed, the Rangers no longer were serious contenders in the NHL race.

The Toronto Maple Leafs, 1932

The Gashouse Gang — Toronto Maple Leafs, 1932

One can only guess at the number of Stanley Cups the early 1930s Maple Leafs would have won had they maintained a modicum of decorum between games. But this was hardly the style of a team that was justifiably nicknamed "The Gashouse Gang On Ice."

Like their baseball Gashouse counterparts, the St. Louis Cardinals of Dizzy Dean, Pepper Martin, and Frankie Frisch, the Maple Leafs were a wild bunch, given to pranks and more pranks, as well as some delightfully dependable hockey.

Managed by brash Conn Smythe, the Leafs started the season of 1931–32 ineffectively behind coach Art Duncan. They were 0–3–2 after five games, when former Black Hawks' ace Dick Irvin took over behind the bench and steered a 23–15–5 course the rest of the way.

Irvin had several things going for him, not the least of which was a forward line that ranks very close to being the best of all time, and was every bit as good as the Rangers' terrific trio, featuring the Cook Brothers, Bill and Bun, alongside Frank Boucher.

Toronto's counterpart was younger, faster, and infinitely more irreverent. On left wing, Harvey (Busher) Jackson had everything, including sex appeal. He could score, arrange goals with neat passes, and skate with the best of them. Right wing Charlie Conacher owned one of the hardest and most accurate shots of his time, and center Gentleman Joe Primeau, who knit the unit together, was a playmaker extraordinaire. "There were few better blends of talent," said Smythe.

The talent did not stop there. Behind Jackson-Primeau-Conacher (appropriately named The Kid Line), was a collection of solid forwards including Ace Bailey, Andy Blair, Harold (Baldy) Cotton, and Frank Finnigan.

Likewise, the defense, man for man, was as good as the league had seen. It featured a little man with immense talents named Frank (King) Clancy; a large studious poke-checking ace, Clarence (Hap) Day; a mean bodychecker who also could fight, Red Horner; and steady Alex (Kingfish) Levinsky. Together, they offered excellent protection for goalie Lorne Chabot who, previously, had starred for the Rangers.

"We can beat the opposition any way they want," said Smythe. "If they want to play rough, we'll oblige. And if they want to go with the finesse game, we can do that, too."

Smythe's words were underlined during the playoffs by a string of victories that took the Maple Leafs right to the Stanley Cup finals. After ousting Chicago in the opening round, the Leafs then edged the Montreal Maroons and advanced to the finals against the always powerful Rangers with the Cooks and Boucher.

The best-of-five playoff for the championship was no contest, reading more like a tennis match, 6–4, 6–2, 6–4. Just like that, the Rangers were out and the Maple Leafs owned their first Stanley Cup.

Unquestionably, they should have won more. The talent was there, especially The Kid Line, and so was the coaching of Irvin. But the Gashouse Leafs bore a striking resemblance to an equally powerful Black Hawks squad of the early 1960s led by Bobby Hull and Stan Mikita. Both clubs were too undisciplined to be successful over the long haul, and neither could win more than one Cup. Yet in a short period of time, The Gashouse Gang left an indelible imprint on the league, both on and off the ice.

■ If nothing else, the building of the first championship Maple Leafs team confirmed the fact that Conn Smythe was every bit as impressive a creator of franchises as he led people to believe. "Conn not only put his money where his mouth was," said one newsman, "but he also put a winning team where his mouth was."

While he was acknowledged for having been the force most responsible for finding the talent needed by the original New York Rangers before the Broadway Blueshirts took the ice, Smythe never got full credit for that because of the arrival on the scene of his successor, Lester Patrick. Nobody could be quite sure whether the Rangers success was due to Smythe's early work or the takeover by Patrick.

But once Smythe returned to Toronto, there was no mistaking his talents. No sooner had he received his walking papers, Conn returned to his hometown and began seeking out sporting business ventures, and he soon discovered that the city's professional hockey team, the St. Patrick's were up for sale.

What an opportunity! Smythe could return immediately to the NHL, prove the Rangers had been wrong in sacking him, and develop a winner that Toronto so sorely needed. He formed a syndicate and bought the St. Patrick's for $165,000, a fair sum in those days. Conn wasn't keen on the name, St. Patrick's, so it was changed to Maple Leafs and in 1927 Smythe became the general manager. The NHL would never be the same.

At the time, the general consensus around the league was that Smythe would be a colossal failure, but he proved the doomsayers wrong. Using revolutionary techniques, Smythe immediately gained an edge on his opponents. One such plan was the instigation of rigorous pre-season training programs for his players. Up to that time, the pro squads had customarily reported a day or two before the first game, in mid-November, and it was Christmastime before they had played themselves into top shape.

According to sports historian Herbert Warren Wind, "Smythe assembled the Leafs in Toronto two weeks before the start of the season, set up a training table for them at a local hotel, engaged a Canadian Army calisthenics instructor to put them through a rigorous drill each morning, and required them to play golf or volleyball or to go hiking in the afternoon."

The idea paid off handsomely. Soon the Maple Leafs had begun drawing large crowds to their rink, the Mutual Street Arena. Always thinking big, Smythe was concerned that the old building wasn't big enough for the brand of club he was building, and he decided that a new rink, bigger even than Montreal's Forum, would be built.

Friends and business associates cautioned him that the time was not ripe for such an imposing venture. The Depression had leveled too many businesses in the United States and Canada to encourage anyone to build as lavish a building as the 12,000-seat Maple Leaf Gardens proposed by Smythe. But he refused to listen to the warnings, and at length, he managed to obtain pledges for what he thought would be the necessary capital.

A few estimations fell short, however, and Smythe found himself with insufficient funds. Fortunately, Smythe's trusty aide, Frank Selke, had previously made his living as an electrician (on the maintenance staff at the University of Toronto) and also held the post of honorary business manager of his local union. When pledges were needed, Selke called together the business agents of the building-trades unions and persuaded them that the members who would work on Maple Leaf Gardens should accept 20 percent of their wages in Gardens stock. They agreed, and the directors of a large Toronto bank, impressed by Selke's ingenuity, voted to purchase $25,000 worth of stock. That move inspired other investors to join the bandwagon, and work on Smythe's Maple Leaf Gardens was begun in June, 1931.

Now all Smythe needed was a championship team to go with his championship rink. He had been working on this project for some time, and the dividends were beginning to accrue. Always thinking on the grand scale, Smythe pulled off the biggest deal in NHL history in 1930 when he persuaded the Ottawa Senators to part with Francis "King" Clancy, one of the greatest rushing defensemen in the game. A smallish player for a defenseman, Clancy nevertheless was enormously skilled and had one of those rare, galvanic personalities that inspired the rest of the team. Smythe paid $35,000, a fabulous figure at that time, for Clancy, and he sent two players, Art Smith and Eric Pettinger, to Ottawa.

Clancy complemented the Leafs as both an artist and an entertainer. Already there were so many jokers on the squad that the Leafs were known as "The Gashouse Gang of Hockey." Their offensive nucleus was provided by Joe Primeau, Charlie Conacher, and Harvey "Busher" Jackson, a young trio appropriately dubbed the "Kid Line." Conacher weighed in at 198, Jackson at 183, and the lithe Primeau at 147. By the 1930–31 season they had captured the imagination of fans around the league with their inventive plays and razzle-dazzle speed.

"They clicked," wrote Ed Fitkin, who later was Leaf publicist, "because all three were passionately determined to make good. In practices they would work out trick plays and then put them into operation during a game."

No play was unorthodox for the Kid Line. Typical was the development of a maneuver later to be known as the "Baseball Play." One day Conacher and Primeau were discussing offensive strategy when Charlie said: "How about that baseball play — you know, the one where a guy fields the ball and instead of throwing it straight at the baseman, he tosses it to the bag, and the other guy races over and takes it in mid-air right on the base. The old double-play move."

"Yeah," said Primeau, "but what's that got to do with us?"

"Well," said Conacher, "we could work the same thing. Instead of you taking the puck and laying a pass on my stick or Jackson's stick, you change your tactics. You carry the puck, and we'll lay back. You draw the other guys over and toss the puck to the open wing. Either Busher or I will take it, and we'll have a clear road to the goal."

The idea was broached to Jackson, who approved immediately. Taken off the drawing board and tried on the ice, the play was an instant success. Primeau decoyed the enemy by luring them to him; then he'd shovel a pass to the open wing, and either Jackson or Conacher would whiz by, untouched by the foe.

That season, Conacher finished second in scoring, Primeau finished fourth, and Jackson came in seventh.

The Gashouse Gang was embellished by two other noteworthy characters, Reginald "Red" Horner and Harold "Baldy" Cotton. Crude and exuberant, Horner was a defenseman totally without fear. If Smythe had suggested that Red should skate through the end boards for him, Horner would have bashed his head against the wood and, no doubt, would have gotten through to the other side.

Naturally, much of Horner's bashing was directed against the opposition, and he rapidly became one of the most hated men in the league. At times, Horner would so enrage the enemy that the feeling would infect the minor officials at foreign rinks. Once Horner stickhandled his way through the Bruins at Boston and sent a pass to a teammate that resulted in a goal. Ordinarily that kind of play would result in an assist for the playmaker, but the Boston goal judge ignored Horner. "I wouldn't give that big so-and-so the time of day," was his explanation.

By contrast, Baldy Cotton was a workmanlike scorer, and he worked well with Andy Blair and Ace Bailey. Cotton's chief function with the raucous Leafs was to play fall-guy for the pranks instigated by Conacher and Clancy. Since Cotton was known to be suffering from a fear of heights, many a gag was planned around that weakness.

Cotton was not much of a diplomat, and he constantly antagonized Conacher. Once he did so in a New York hotel room, and Conacher responded by hanging Cotton, feet first out of the window until Harold apologized.

"You can imagine what a shock we got seeing Baldy hanging out the window," Primeau recalled. "He looked like a ghost, and he was yelling like a madman."

A few weeks later the scrappy pair had another argument. This time Conacher turned a bed upside down on Cotton, pinning him to the floor. Then he stuffed pillows around him, hemmed him in with heavy chairs, added desks to the barricade, and walked out of the room.

As a benevolent gesture, Conacher did take the telephone receiver off the hook, enabling Cotton to yell loud and clear for the hotel desk clerk to send help. A detective was summoned and, thinking that someone was being murdered, dashed up to the room to relieve Baldy before Conacher could get more than two blocks away.

Another player fond of a jape was defenseman, Clarence "Hap" Day. He appeared to be a quiet, distinguished gentleman, but often he was as wild as his colleagues. Day and Conacher once spent an evening with Clancy on an occasion when King was feeling particularly proud of himself. For some reason Clancy kept referring to his "wonderful" physique until Day and Conacher decided that some reprisal was in order. Since Clancy was half naked, the plot was readymade.

They sourrounded Clancy, who was considerably smaller than either of the pair, and carried him out onto the balcony. Then they locked the door and forced the semi-nude Clancy to exhibit his physique to any passerby who happened along.

King pleaded with his oppressors to open the door, suggesting that the cold weather was not the best tonic for him. "Well," snapped Day, "if you have such a wonderful physique, you should be able to stay out there all night."

Fortunately the humor was confined to off-rink activities. There was no joking about construction of Maple Leaf Gardens. Work began in June, 1931, with

November, 1931 as the target date for completion. Smythe wanted to have Maple Leaf Gardens ready for the opening game of the 1931–32 season.

Few people believed that it was possible to erect a building of such magnitude in so short a time. But on November 12, 1931, a crowd of 13,542 squeezed into the new building, and the Maple Leafs played host to Chicago's Black Hawks. The visitors took the win 2–1, but Maple Leaf Gardens stole the show. It was the perfect showplace for hockey, with not a bad seat in the house. Smythe had done the impossible for his hockey team, and now it was time for his team to reward him and the fans with a Stanley Cup.

At first the Leafs seemed spellbound by their new surroundings, and they couldn't get themselves untracked. When they lost their first five games, Smythe decided that coaching was the problem. He fired Art Duncan and replaced him with the mercurial, but wise, Dick Irvin, who formerly had coached the Chicago Black Hawks. The change was another of Smythe's genius strokes.

Under the supervision of Irvin, the Leafs won and won and won. The Kid Line moved up to the top of the scoring list, and Toronto went to the top of the league. Legends began to develop around the Maple Leaf aces, and soon the Leafs themselves began to invent stories. When Busher Jackson's speed was said to be better than that of Montreal's great Howie Morenz, Hap Day offered an amusing answer:

"Busher is so fast that one night in Montreal he circled his net, started down ice, and shot the puck when he was nearing center. And do you know what? He was traveling so fast that he caught up with the puck and passed it before it got to the blue line!"

A serious hand injury to Conacher on February 7, 1932, crippled the Maple Leafs drive for first place. They ultimately finished second, four points behind the Canadiens, and girded for the opening playoff round against Chicago. Smythe's dream was to bring the Stanley Cup home to his spanking new building, but the Black Hawks were having no part of it. They edged Toronto, 1–0, in the two-game total-goals series and had the Leafs on the ropes. But Day proved the hero in the second game, tying the score and setting the Kid Line in motion. When it was all over, Toronto had won the round, 6–2.

Next on the agenda were the Montreal Maroons, a rugged club led by Charlie Conacher's older brother, Lionel. The two-game total goals series stood at a tie, 1-1, after the first game. The decisive second match was a gem that took the breath of every fan in Maple Leaf Gardens.

Early in the third period, a shot by Maroon Hooley Smith dropped Toronto down by a goal and appeared to seal the fate of the Leafs. But the Maple Leafs were not daunted; they charged over and over again at the intrepid Montreal defense.

As the overhead clock ticked toward the halfway point in the third period, Hap Day captured the puck behind his net, picked up speed at the Toronto blue line, and zoomed in on the Montreal back-line. Bobbing and weaving, Day eluded the Maroons defenders and went head on with the goalie Flat Walsh. Day threw a feint, and Walsh went for it. Hap flicked the puck over the fallen goaltender, and the game was tied.

"Never before," wrote Fitkin, "had the Leafs been given such a tremendous ovation. Even staid businessmen in the boxes leaped to their feet, grabbed their neighbors, male or female, and hugged them with sheer delight."

Neither team scored again in regulation time, but Smythe's men had the momentum. They pressed the attack in sudden-death overtime. The coup de grace was delivered late in the first overtime period.

Time and again the Kid Line tried and failed to finish off the Maroons. Meanwhile, rookie Bob Gracie sat on the bench fidgeting for action. As the period rolled on without result, Gracie pushed himself close enough to coach Irvin to deliver a message.

"I've got a feeling I'm going to get that winning goal tonight for you," said Gracie. "Let me out there on the ice."

Irvin waited for a whistle and a face-off. He motioned to Primeau, Jackson, and Conacher to return to the bench. In their places he dispatched Gracie, Andy Blair, and Frank Finnegan. "Go get your goal kid," yelled Irvin.

Before a minute had elapsed, Gracie released a shot from just inside the Maroons blue line that beat goalie Walsh. Pandemonium reigned in Maple Leaf Gardens. The din was so loud that few people — including Gracie — heard referee Mike Rodden blow his whistle for an offside. The goal did not count. Irvin soon yanked Gracie and his linemates, and the Kid Line returned, only to be foiled again.

There were fewer than three minutes remaining in the period when Gracie took the ice again. Brimming with confidence, he turned to official scorer Bill Graham and chuckled: "You can chalk me down for the winning goal right now, Bill."

Graham laughed and replied: "First you'll have to show me."

The puck was dropped. Blair got control of the rubber and spotted Gracie racing toward the Maroons zone. The pass was ideal, and the skinny kid let fly.

It was a dynamite drive. Walsh partially blocked it with his leather leg pads, but the puck hit the pads and kept going, right into the net. This time there was no mistake and no offside. And Gracie, the slick-haired rookie with the wan look, was given a hero's escort off the ice on the shoulders of his teammates.

Impossible as it may have seemed to the skeptics, Smythe's Leafs had reached the Stanley Cup finals. Their rivals were the New York Rangers, a team hated by each and every Toronto player, for good reason. Before the season had ended, Rangers' manager Lester Patrick had scoffed at Conn's club. "The Maple Leafs aren't much of a team," said Patrick. And when the playoffs began, Patrick put it another way, saying that the Maroons were the only team he feared — in short, that the Leafs would be pushovers if New York and Toronto ever did meet.

Well, now they were meeting, and Patrick began eating his words as early as the opening game on Madison Square Garden ice. The upstart Maple Leafs forged to a 5–1 lead. Then they nearly blew it. The Rangers came on strong to reduce the margin to 5–4 only to see Toronto counterattack and leave the ice 6–4 victors.

The arrival of a circus forced the Rangers out of Madison Square Garden, so they switched their next home game to Boston Garden. This time New York came on like gangbusters, grabbing a 2–0 lead and justifying their role as the series favorites. Then the Kid Line took over.

First Jackson broke the ice, and then Conacher tied the score. When Jackson was given a two-minute penalty early in the third period, the Leafs stunned New York by charging to the attack. Clancy and Primeau batted passes back and forth like table tennis balls until Clancy reached the goal mouth. His shot went wide, but the perky defenseman retrieved the rubber and somehow managed to persist until he brought the puck around the net and stuffed it past Rangers goalie John Ross Roach. Conacher and Primeau added goals, and the Leafs won the game, 6–2, leading the best-of-five series, 2–0.

Now the Maple Leafs fans waited to see if their team was for real. It didn't take long. Blair scored twice in the opening period, and Jackson scored in the second. There was no stopping Smythe's big, blue machine.

Perhaps the most symbolic event of the game occurred late in the second period, when Charlie Conacher sent one of his hot-potato shots from just inside the blue line. The blast was so penetrating that it caught goalie Roach under the heart and sent him reeling back into the net.

Somehow Roach managed to straighten up and clear the puck before dropping his stick and falling to the ice, his hands painfully holding his throat. To the onlookers it appeared that Conacher had actually killed the goalie with his shot. But Roach soon responded, and after a five-minute respite, he resumed the game.

Like Roach, the Rangers were far from dead. After Finnegan and Bailey made it 5–1 for Toronto, the New Yorkers staged a game comeback in the third period.

Bun Cook scored for the Rangers, and Gracie got one back for the Leafs. It was 6–2 Toronto when slick Frank Boucher scored two quick ones for New York. All of a sudden, Toronto's lead was reduced to two, and the Rangers were coming on strong.

But the capacity crowd roared encouragement, and the Kid Line regrouped. Clancy and Day stiffened the defense, and the Toronto boys checked the Rangers at every turn. At last, the seconds ticked away, and the Toronto Maple Leafs became the first team ever to make a clean sweep of the Stanley Cup finals and the first Maple Leaf team ever to win the cup.

They were a marvelous crew, this Gashouse Gang, and they proved their mettle the following season by finishing first in the Canadian Division, fulfilling Conn Smythe's pre-season wish. They repeated the first-place effort for three straight seasons, confirming their excellence, but they did not win the Stanley Cup in any of those years.

The Gashouse era in Toronto ended in the 1935–36 season when Toronto finished second to the Maroons in the Canadian Division and were beaten by Detroit in the Stanley Cup finals. It was then that Joe Primeau retired, and the Kid Line broke up. When that happened, Smythe knew that the handwriting was on the wall, and it was time to rebuild.

The Montreal Canadiens, 1916

The Original Flying Frenchmen

Only one National Hockey League team has roots that are traceable to a period that precedes the birth of the NHL in 1917. The Montreal Canadiens were organized shortly after the turn of the century, and almost immediately captured the imagination of sports fans in the Quebec metropolis.

Wearing their *bleu, blanc, et rouge* uniforms, the Canadiens (also known as the Habitants, Habs, or Flying Frenchmen) became favorites for a number of reasons, the most significant of which was that they were very good.

Their first captain and manager, Jean Baptiste (Jack) Laviolette, dazzled spectators with his skillful skating and good looks. Under the direction of George Kennedy, who helped found the "Club Athletique Canadien" in 1910, the Habs improved enough in the ensuing years to challenge for The Stanley Cup.

By the 1915–16 season, "Club Athletique Canadien" (later to be known as Club de Hockey Canadien), sported some of the best talent ever to hit the ice. Edouard (Newsy) Lalonde, Didier Pitre, Goldie Prodgers, and Bert Corbeau were the Mario Lemieux, Wayne Gretzky, Steve Yzerman, and Grant Fuhr of the day. The Canadiens were universally hailed as one of the premier professional hockey clubs and confirmed that compliment by winning the first of a seemingly endless string of Stanley Cups.

No hockey team in the world can match the tradition of the Canadiens, and this quality has been of great value to the team right up to the present. But it all began more than seven decades ago with the first Cup-winning Canadien team.

To understand the manner in which the Montreal Canadiens developed into one of the most imposing dynasties in sport, it is necessary to go back to the origins of the team and trace its growth to the present.

Surely, no club had had greater impact on The Game, its fans, or distinguished citizens such as New York Islanders' president and general manager Bill Torrey, himself a native of Montreal.

After his club had become the first American team ever to win four Stanley Cups in succession, Torrey was asked if the Islanders had become a dynasty. Torrey chuckled at the suggestion.

"To me," said Torrey, "the Montreal Canadiens are the real dynasty. After all, they've won 23 Stanley Cups, which means we've got to win 19 more just to tie them, not something I expect to see in my lifetime."

Few would argue with him, nor would anyone challenge the assertion that the *Habitants* have meant more to the French-speaking citizens of the province of Quebec than any other institution short of the Roman Catholic Church.

"We don't own the Canadiens, really," said Senator Hartland Molson when he assumed the presidency of the club in 1957. "The public of Montreal, in fact the entire province of Quebec, owns the Canadiens. This club is more than a professional sports organization. It is an institution, a way of life."

Few would argue with the Senator's observation today, but back in 1909, Le Club de Hockey Canadien was nothing more than the germ of an idea nurtured by a few men involved in one of hockey's first inter-league wars.

It was appropriate, to say the least, that hockey's most controversial team over the years should be born in the midst of a fierce battle between arena entrepreneurs in Montreal. It all started when officials of the Eastern Canada Hockey Association, the major league of its time, selected the Westmount Arena in Montreal as the site of its games. The decision was tantamount to the mayor of New York, choosing Shea Stadium over Yankee Stadium for all New York home baseball games.

The decision infuriated the owners of the Montreal Wanderers Hockey Club, and with good reason. The Wanderers were the property of the Jubilee Rink — which had the misfortune of utilizing only natural ice — and the Wanderers' backers immediately perceived they were being victimized by a hockey squeeze play.

Their suspicions were confirmed when the E.C.H.A. held its annual meeting on November 13, 1909. Representatives from Ottawa, Quebec, and Montreal complained about the sale of the Wanderers to P.J. Doran, who owned the Jubilee Rink, and who naturally wanted the Wanderers' games played there. Opponents pointed out that the Jubilee was too small and generally too inconvenient, let alone unprofitable.

Hockey finances in the early years of the twentieth century varied from rink to rink. Club owners in the E.C.H.A. favored Montreal's Westmount Wood Avenue rink because the operators received 60 percent of the gate receipts, while the clubs received 40 percent. In turn, the teams handled such items as players' salaries and travelling expenses, while the arena was responsible for practice ice, heating dressing rooms and showers, advertising, and other miscellanea.

The question perplexing the E.C.H.A. high command was how to outfeint the Wanderers. The ultimate strategy was an example of front-office chicanery that hasn't yet been matched by today's high pressure moguls. On November 25, 1909, the E.C.H.A. simply dissolved itself and then reincarnated the league with the sobriquet "Canadian Hockey Association."

To create an aura of legality, it went through the motions of "granting" franchises to Ottawa, the Montreal Shamrocks, Quebec, the Nationals, and All-Montreal. Each team paid an initiation fee of thirty dollars (today it would cost a minimum of twenty million dollars to get into the National Hockey League) with an annual upkeep fee of twenty-five dollars.

Naturally, the Wanderers applied for membership. There was nothing particularly unusual about it other than the fact that P.J. Doran was advised that his application had been rejected! P.J. wasn't the only club owner who was upset about the reversal. George and Jim Barnett, owners of the Renfrew (Ontario) Millionaires, had also made a pitch for entrance into the C.H.A. Their representation was made by J. Ambrose O'Brien, a big man in Ontario mining circles and an "angel" behind a couple of teams in northern Ontario.

The events that day in the corridors of Montreal's Windsor Hotel would have made an excellent scenario for a Marx Brothers movie. O'Brien, who happened to be in town on other business, dropped over to the hotel, walked up to Room 135, and put in a bid for a Renfrew franchise. The C.H.A. governors treated his request with the same amusement they would reserve for a suggestion that hockey be played in mud.

Laughed out of Room 135, O'Brien was heading for St. Catherine Street when, by pure chance, he encountered Jimmy Gardner, an official of the Wanderers. The two losers-of-the-moment were exchanging condolences when they suddenly realized their respective team obituaries were a trifle premature. They quickly rented Room 129 in the Windsor Hotel, within shouting distance of the C.H.A. meeting, and began plotting the destruction of their oppressors.

The scheme was so rudimentary, that they both wondered why it had taken more than a minute to dream up. If the C.H.A. wouldn't have them, they would do the next best — if not the better-thing. They would form their own league. For starters, they had the Wanderers, a respected and established outfit. O'Brien, himself, owned teams in Cobalt and Haileybury, Ontario, and his pals, the Barnett brothers, had title to the Renfrew club. That made four teams, which was a good start, but not good enough for the ingenious O'Brien and Gardner. They agreed that a metropolis such as Montreal could support still another team, but not another team dominated by English players, as the Wanderers were.

"It was Gardner who suggested that a French team should go well in Montreal," O'Brien explained at the time of his induction into hockey's Hall of Fame. "Gardner also advised me to get Jack Laviolette as manager. Newsy Lalonde's name was mentioned as a likely player. There were several others who eventually joined the club."

If anybody could come up with French-Canadian hockey players, it was the French-Canadian Laviolette. Given such assurance from Laviolette, representatives from Renfrew, Cobalt, Haileybury, and the Wanderers convened in

Montreal on December 2, 1909. In a "secret" conclave, they formally organized the National Hockey Association of Canada which ultimately became the National Hockey League, now embracing three Canadian cities and eleven in the United States.

Fred Strachan of the Wanderers, the association's first president, immediately sanctioned franchises in the original four cities. Right from the start, the N.H.A. betrayed a vigorous survival instinct. Its life appeared very short-lived when the Barnett brothers developed second thoughts about the project and decided against participation, thus detonating the league's first crisis. This, however, was resolved with dispatch, not to mention a few thousand dollars, when J. Ambrose O'Brien and his father, M.J. O'Brien, took title to the Renfrew organization and reentered the league. And just to prove his good faith, M.J. presented a brand-new trophy to the league which would be presented to the champions each year.

Unlike the relatively inexpensive Stanley Cup, the O'Brien Trophy was created by Hemsley's, the distinguished Montreal firm, and was composed of solid silver extracted from the rich veins of Cobalt, Ontario. The trophy was all well and good, but there was still the matter of a fifth hockey team, a project now in the hands of the flamboyant Laviolette.

Jack's assurance that he could produce the French-Canadian skaters was not a fragile promise. Thanks to his downtown Montreal restaurant, Laviolette was meeting athletes on a daily basis. What's more, a group of his cronies would convene regularly for exhibition games in and around Montreal.

The N.H.A. held another meeting on December 4, at the Windsor. Once again, a bizarre tableau unfolded. The N.H.A. moguls gathered in Room 129. At that very moment, officials at the established C.H.A. opened their meeting a few doors away in Room 135. Neither meeting was secret, and reporters from Montreal's English- and French-language newspapers patrolled the hotel for reports about the impending confrontation.

One possibility was that the C.H.A.'s antagonism toward the Wanderers would be reversed and the Wanderers would be welcomed back to the fold. Another was that the two leagues would merge into one big prosperous, if not happy, family. Still a third report had it that three clubs were prepared to bolt the C.H.A. and march down the hall to apply for membership in the baby league. However, none of these developments materialized.

The N.H.A. opened the meeting with the announcement that the fifth team, to be known as Les Canadiens, had applied for membership, and that T.C. Hare of Cobalt, Ontario, would put up security for the franchise, with a special proviso that the club be transferred to French-Canadian owners at the earliest possible date.

A dozen yards away, owners of the C.H.A. teams rebuffed suggestions that the Wanderers be readmitted and became more and more intransigent in their discussions about the new league. While reporters suggested that the Wanderers had been pushed right out of the C.H.A., the league governors piously denied that any such thing had happened, although it obviously had. Little did they realize that their power play was inadvertently a death blow, although the coup de grace didn't immediately occur.

Whatever the case, the C.H.A. had its original wish. It had divested itself of the need to play in the Jubilee Rink and was prepared for another profitable season. Meanwhile, the N.H.A. agreed that both the infant Canadiens and the Wanderers would share the Jubilee ice and all that remained was the matter of signing up hockey players — which was when the fun really started.

The secret word was "money," and if the C.H.A. had it, then the spanking new N.H.A. had it with double digits. What made the intruders so strong was the bankroll of O'Brien who was coining money with his silver mines in northern Ontario, not to mention assorted other enterprises in a growing Canada. Antitrust laws were unheard of in Canadian sport at the time, so nobody was particularly disturbed by the fact that the O'Brien family controlled four out of five teams in the new league, the exception being Montreal's Wanderers. Besides, it was difficult to dislike Ambrose O'Brien. He had played hockey at the University of Toronto and betrayed a hyperchauvinistic loyalty to Renfrew and its neighbors, particularly when the self-appointed sophisticates of Montreal would try to put him down.

"The ridicule of the cities," said Toronto *Daily Star* sports editor Milt Dunnell, "merely stiffened O'Brien's determination. It was his fierce pride in his hometown of Renfrew that led to the founding of the Canadiens and what now is the N.H.L."

O'Brien's intense motivation to make a success of his team was reflected in the bidding for hockey players. At the time, Lester Patrick, who later organized and ran the New York Rangers, was one of the most distinguished players in Canada. Patrick was playing in western Canada, and liking it, at the time O'Brien began developing his team. Naturally, Ambrose telegraphed an offer to Patrick who was highly amused by the temerity of a small-town team like Renfrew thinking it could afford his salary. But just to pursue the gag, Lester wired a demand for $3,000, which by today's standards would be tantamount to $500,000. At the time, the highest-paid player in all hockey was Tom Phillips and he was receiving only $1,800 a year.

Lester went a step further and insisted that his brother, Frank, also be imported by the Renfrew club at a salary of no less than $2,000!

To the complete bafflement of the Patricks, O'Brien swiftly approved the terms, and both Lester and Frank were soon on a train heading east. But Ambrose didn't stop there. He lured Hay Miller and Fred Whitcroft from Edmonton for $2,000 apiece. That was just for starters.

"By the time O'Brien was finished," said Baz O'Meara, former sports editor of the Montreal *Star*, "he had assembled the greatest galaxy of stars ever seen on one hockey team."

Odie and Sprague Cleghorn, Cyclone Taylor, Herb Jordon, and Steve Vair were a few of the members. Curiously enough, Renfrew never did win the Stanley Cup, a disappointment that O'Brien never overcame. "I guess," he once explained, "the trouble was that we had too many stars."

Nevertheless, O'Brien's freedom with the dollar inspired Laviolette, who was zeroing in on the best French-Canadian talent available. His first coup was the signing of Edouard "Newsy" Lalonde, one of the toughest and most adept players available. Then he trained his sights on Didier Pitre, who was playing for the

Nationals of the C.H.A. Pitre was a speedy right wing who seemed to be a natural for Les Canadiens.

Laviolette was well aware that Pitre had signed an $1,100 contract to play for the Nationals, so he responded by putting $1,700 on the table. When Harry Trihey, the Nationals' attorney, learned of the counter-offer, he announced that Pitre was risking a $2,000 fine, not to mention a jail sentence, if he dared play for the Canadiens.

Now the Canadiens were on the spot, but they had no thoughts of backtracking. Laviolette huddled with Pitre and assured him that the $1,700 was his to keep no matter what happened.

On January 5, 1910, the Canadiens were scheduled to meet the Cobalt team on the natural ice of Montreal's Jubilee Rink. By this time, Pitre's case had splashed across the papers, and the N.H.A. had captured just the publicity it required to launch its first season. Montrealers filled the venerable building, partly out of curiosity for the new Canadiens, and partly for the excitement over whether or not Pitre would defy the Nationals and skate for Les Canadiens.

When Didier finally did step on the ice, a swelling roar developed among the crowd of 5,000 and it was to continue virtually unabated, as the Canadiens rebounded from 3–0 and 6–4 deficits to tie the game in regulation time, and win the contest in a sudden-death overtime. But it wasn't only the pulsating triumph nor Pitre's appearance that captured the imagination of the crowd; there was also the essential element of quality hockey that the N.H.A. was offering, and needed to survive. Seasoned critics raved about the "speed, even balance, furious rushes, tension, skill, and combination play" that the match featured. If the opening game was any barometer, both the N.H.A. and Les Canadiens were there to stay.

Despite the legal threats generated by the Nationals, Didier Pitre remained with the Canadiens. Nothing came of the court action, and Didier developed into one of the first French-Canadian heroes of Les Canadiens. This right-winger had extraordinary get-away speed and quickly became the target of his slower rivals. Once, in a game against Ottawa's Senators, Eddie Gerard, the enemy captain, assigned his ace, Cy Denneny, to guard Pitre.

"No matter what I did," Denneny recalled, "Didier would get away for a shot on goal."

During the intermission, Gerard suggested it might be more practical, if not prudent, to clout Pitre on the lower part of his legs, the theory being that this would enrage Didier and distract him from his pursuit of goals. When this stratagem failed, Gerard suggested that Denneny try haranguing him with insults.

"There wasn't a name in the book that I didn't call him," said Denneny, "but that didn't seem to rile him either."

When the game finally ended, Gerard and Denneny consoled themselves with the knowledge that they had done everything in their power to needle Pitre. "A little later," Denneny revealed, "we discovered our mistake. Didier didn't fathom a word of English!"

Meanwhile, the interleague rivalry was turning into a war of attrition. Montreal was now loaded with five top-rated teams, and crowds soon began tailing off at some rinks. A C.H.A. match between the Shamrocks and the Nationals drew only 800 spectators, and there were murmurings of merger once again.

The once-powerful C.H.A. betrayed signs of panic, and on January 15, 1910, both Ottawa and the Montreal Shamrocks "jumped" the venerable league for the new N.H.A. This signaled the beginning of the end for the C.H.A.

Despite such notables as Pitre, Joe Cattarinich, Ed Decarie, Art Bernier, and Richard Duckett, Les Canadiens finished in last place in their first season, with a poor record of two wins and ten losses. Their English-speaking rivals, the Wanderers, finished first with an 11–1 record and went on to win the Stanley Cup of 1910.

Controversy continued to follow Les Canadiens as the club prepared for its second season. A onetime wrestler and sports promoter by the name of George Kendall (who operated under the name Kennedy) took an ad in the Montreal *Herald*, asserting that the name "Canadiens" actually was the property of the Club Athlétique-Canadien, which was a registered and incorporated outfit. Since Kennedy owned the club, he made it abundantly clear that he would demand the N.H.A. eliminate the name Les Canadiens.

But Kennedy was not a hard man to deal with if the deal was right. His plan was to obtain an N.H.A. team, which he did when O'Brien presented him with a franchise for $7,500. An entanglement of legal red tape over the rights to Newsy Lalonde developed into a head-on collision between Kennedy and O'Brien. The mining tycoon argued that Lalonde had become the property of Renfrew, but Kennedy countered that Newsy belonged to Les Canadiens. The league eventually resolved the dispute by ordering Lalonde to Montreal. It was a decision that would have a long-standing beneficial effect on the Canadiens' franchise.

A native of Cornwall, Ontario, Lalonde was nicknamed "Newsy" during a brief stint working in a newsprint plant. Canadian author Bill Roche once described him as "the greatest French-Canadian athlete of all time and one of the best who ever laced on a skate or fondled a lacrosse stick."

Lalonde broke into pro hockey with Sault Ste. Marie when he was only 18. In his first game against Pittsburgh he discovered that the defensemen had a habit of backhanding the puck into the air when they wanted to clear the puck from their zone. "Once I figured that out," Newsy revealed, "I made a point of getting in front of them and then, suddenly, swerving around so that I actually had my back to the defensemen."

Lalonde soon proved there was method to his madness. The next time a Pittsburgh player attempted to clear the puck, Lalonde executed his pirouette. The puck struck him in the back and slipped through his baggy hockey pants to the ice directly behind him. He then deftly spun around, captured the puck, and skimmed it into the net. Newsy executed the same maneuver twice in the same game, and Sault Ste. Marie came out on top, 3–1. "After that," he said, "I was in pro hockey for good."

With Newsy leading the team in scoring with 16 goals in 16 games, Les Canadiens finished second in their second season. But Lalonde wasn't the only ace on the team. By a strange coincidence, the club had acquired a 22-year-old goaltender from Chicoutimi, Quebec. His name was Georges Vézina, and he was to become so good, the N.H.L. was ultimately to strike a trophy in his name to be awarded to the best netminder in hockey.

Like so many other Montreal stars who were to follow him, Vézina was a product of a small French-speaking city in the province of Quebec. Chicoutimi sits on the edge of the dark Saguenay River, which flows into the blue St. Lawrence at historic Tadoussac. It was in this setting that young Georges learned his hockey, although, admittedly, he learned it in a curious way.

Georges was an excellent goaltender — the best in Chicoutimi at the time — but he had developed a habit of playing without skates. For some peculiar reason he found the idea of wearing skates a bother, and it wasn't until two years before he graduated to Les Canadiens that he actually learned to wear skates while tending goal.

Conceivably, the Montrealers would never have discovered Vézina were it not for a chance exhibition game between Les Canadiens and the local Chicoutimi club on February 23, 1910. The match between the awesome professionals from Montreal and the patchwork amateur outfit figured to be so one-sided that only a handful of fans turned out for it.

Chicoutimi hardly looked like a formidable foe, except for the six-foot goalie, wearing a red-and-white Habitant *toque* on his head. Leaning against the goalpost, the tall, lanky Vézina appeared almost too bored for words. But once the overpowering Canadiens sliced through the fragile Chicoutimi defense, Vézina suddenly responded with a peripatetic style that thoroughly dumbfounded the likes of Pitre, Lalonde, and Laviolette. Joe Cattarinich, who both goaled for and managed the Canadiens, began imploring his men for a goal as if his club were playing in a Stanley Cup battle, but Vézina would not be beaten. Vézina's overmatched teammates began rallying behind their goaltender and scored two goals against the Canadiens.

By the time the third period had begun, the Chicoutimi skaters had skated themselves to exhaustion. They had scored their goals and proved a point, and now it would only be a matter of minutes before the stars from Montreal swept them off the ice. Wave after wave of Canadiens shooters swept in on Vézina, testing him with backhanders, forehanders, and short-pass plays around the net.

By the middle of the third period it was no longer a question of whether the Canadiens would win the game, but rather would they ever put the puck behind Vézina? The young goalie seemed nonplussed by the whole affair — he was the only person in the building who showed no emotion — as he acrobatically fended off the enemy shots. When the game ended, the kid who was soon to be nicknamed "the Chicoutimi Cucumber" had prevented Les Canadiens from scoring a single goal.

Cattarinich was as impressed as he was flabbergasted and immediately urged George Kennedy to sign the youngster, although it almost surely meant the end of Cattarinich's own career in the Montreal nets. Kennedy obliged by inviting both Georges and his brother, Pierre, who had scored the winning goal, to Montreal. Georges made his debut in the *bleu, blanc, et rouge* Canadiens' uniform on December 31, 1910, and played for Montreal for 15 years.

As personalities go, Vézina was as strange as any who have ever graced the NHL. He never signed a contract with the Canadiens, preferring a gentleman's handshake with his manager, first Cattarinich and later Leo Dandurand. Georges abstained from smoking and drinking, and was liberal to a fault when it came to "loaning" cash to friends. More often than not, it was never returned, but Vézina never seemed to mind. Certainly, as the father of 20 children, he could have used the money. One of his sons was named Stanley, having been born on the night the Canadiens won the 1916 Stanley Cup.

Vézina was beaten, 5–3, by Ottawa in his debut, but went on to post a league leading 3.9 goals against average in his rookie year as the Canadiens finished second to Ottawa. He didn't miss a game all season and played in every Canadiens game until November 29, 1925.

Thanks to Vézina, Lalonde, Laviolette, and Pitre, Les Canadiens rapidly obtained a distinctive image, which they have retained to the present day. "The Canadiens' charm is Gallic," observed Peter Gzowski, broadcaster-editor and one of the most perceptive writers on the North American continent. "And the headlong, passionate way they have always played hockey has helped to make them the national team of French Canada in a way no team representing *all* of Canada, with its diverse, unmelted ethnic strains, could hope to parallel, and I have sometimes wondered if their rallying cry, '*Les Canadiens sont la*,' is not a better motto for the national spirit of French Canada than '*Je me souviens*.' "

This sensitivity to the French spirit of Les Canadiens was evident as far back as October 11, 1911, when the N.H.A. governors ruled that the Canadiens were to sign only French-speaking players. Conversely, all other teams, by rule, were forbidden to sign French-speaking skaters. Incidentally, at that same meeting, the league responded to a request of W.E. Northey of the Montreal Arena and eliminated the position of rover, thereby reducing the number of players on each team from 11 to 6.

A cloud of anxiety hovered over the meeting when it was learned that Lester and Frank Patrick were organizing a Pacific Coast League that would directly compete with the N.H.A. for players. Having departed Renfrew, the Patricks began raiding the eastern teams for team members and it was the Canadiens who suffered some of the most severe losses, including Newsy Lalonde who signed with Vancouver. Without Lalonde, the Canadiens finished in last place, although Vézina once again produced the best goaltending average. A year later, however, the Canadiens entered negotiations with the Vancouver sextet and regained Newsy's contract.

By this time, Newsy had earned a reputation as one of the roughest players in the game. His clashes with "Bad" Joe Hall, who later became a teammate on Les Canadiens, were studies in jungle brutality, but Newsy didn't reserve his venom for Hall. On December 22, 1912, the Canadiens played their hometown rivals, the Wanderers, in an exhibition game to unveil the new Toronto hockey rink. Midway in the game, Lalonde dispatched Odie Cleghorn of the Wanderers into the boards with such force that Odie's brother, Sprague, charged across the rink and smashed Newsy across the forehead with his stick. The blow just barely missed Lalonde's eye and he required 12 stitches to close the gaping wound.

The episode didn't go unnoticed officially and a constable served a summons on Cleghorn. Sprague turned up in a Toronto court and was fined $50 for his efforts, not to mention an additional $50 fine slapped on him by N.H.A. president Emmett Quinn. Cleghorn was also suspended for four weeks, but such was the *laissez-faire* atmosphere of pro hockey at the time, that Sprague absented himself from only one game and then promptly returned to the Wanderers' lineup with inpunity.

A year later Newsy was at it again. On December 30, 1913, the Canadiens were in Quebec City to help unveil the new hockey rink with a match against the hometown Bulldogs. Lalonde bashed Joe Hall across the head with his stick, opening an eight-stitch wound. Hall, who had a craggy face and a neatly parted haircut, was not one to forget such a misdemeanor. When the same two clubs clashed again on January 14, 1914, in Montreal, there was no mistaking Hall's program for the evening. He had his eyes on Newsy from the start and finally connected with a lusty body check that crashed Lalonde into the boards so vigorously that Newsy required ten stitches to close *his* wound.

Lalonde's distillation of fury and finesse had a very beneficial effect on the Canadiens, who became first-place threats by mid-season. It was then that they became involved in big-league hockey's first classic overtime game.

It happened on February 18, 1914, in Montreal against Ottawa at a time when it was still commonplace for players to skate an entire game without substitution. On this night, the two evenly matched clubs exchanged end-to-end rushes for the full three periods without a goal being scored, sending the match into sudden-death overtime. By the early minutes of the extra period, skaters began collapsing on the ice even without being hit by an opponent; they were that tired. The agony was ended finally after 6 minutes and 40 seconds of sudden death on a goal by Ernie Dubeau of Les Canadiens. Exactly a week later, the Canadiens visited Ottawa and this time lost a sudden-death game to the home team after *30 minutes* of overtime.

In later years, Les Canadiens would be coached by men whose decibel count was as high as their boiling point was low. Both Dick Irvin and Toe Blake, Irvin's successor, often seemed to be on a treadmill to the N.H.L. office for one disciplinary reason or another. What has generally been overlooked in the cases of Blake and Irvin is that precedent was set for vitriolic Montreal coaches as far back as 1914, when George Kennedy displayed a temper that would have made both Blake and Irvin appear decorous by comparison.

One of Kennedy's more flamboyant displays occurred at the conclusion of an especially bitter contest with the Wanderers in which, oddly enough, Les Canadiens won, 6–5. In a scene that was later reenacted by Blake with referee Dalton McArthur, manager Kennedy assaulted referee Leo Dandurand as soon as the game ended. Interestingly, it was the same Dandurand who later helped purchase Les Canadiens from Kennedy's widow in 1921.

At the time, though, Dandurand was infuriated with Kennedy's behavior, particularly because N.H.A. president Quinn's failure to suspend the Canadiens' manager appeared to suggest tacit approval of the assault. In those early days of pro hockey, it was not unusual for either players or executives to fight their cases on the editorial pages of the local newspapers, and Dandurand did just that. He wrote a letter to Quinn in the Montreal *Herald & Daily Telegraph*, which printed it as follows:

"The Wanderers vs. Canadiens match, decided Saturday night at the Arena, was full of incident. The worst part of it, no doubt, was the injurious manner in which I was treated by Mr. George Kennedy and the assault that he committed upon me as he left the ice when the game was finished. Obeying I know not what motive, Mr. Kennedy seized me and threatened me with blows, and at the same time speaking to me in terms unworthy of a dignified man. Mr. Kennedy failed in his duty as a sportsman, and accused me of not having fulfilled my functions as a paid umpire. He caught me by his fists before the spectators, players, and officers of the Canadien club.

"I was afraid of receiving some severe blows and I believe that only my coolness under the circumstances saved me from an unpleasant assault.

"Not content with having abused me in this manner upon my leaving the ice, the general manager of the Canadiens came back and insulted me in the worst manner in the umpires' room, calling me a _____ before Messrs. Waud of the *Daily Mail*, W.J. Morrison of the *Gazette*, E.C. St. Pierre of *Le Canada*, Mr. Robertson, proprietor of the Toronto Hockey Club, C. Hoerner, John Dunlop, Tom Melville, Dave Power, Cecil Short and yourself. These are the facts and I hope you will take them into your serious consideration.

"Mr. Kennedy may think himself authorized to consider me incapable, but I refuse him the right to insult me and my honor as a gentleman in the way he has done.

"I have written enough to convince you that this time an end should be put to a deplorable situation among professional hockey players."

Quinn had more urgent matters to consider than Dandurand's letter. The season ended the day after the referee dispatched his missive to the newspaper, and both Les Canadiens and Toronto had finished in a tie for first place. Quinn ordered a two-game total goals play-off, opening in Montreal and closing in Toronto. The Canadiens sloshed their way to a 2–0 win in the first game on a soggy natural-ice surface made virtually unskateable by mild weather. In the second game, played on excellent artificial ice in Toronto, Les Canadiens were defeated, 6–0, and thus were prevented from playing in the first East-West competition for the Stanley Cup.

The truculent Kennedy was no more affectionate with his own players than he was with referees such as Dandurand, especially when it came to financial matters. By the beginning of the 1914–15 season, it was becoming fashionable for a few star players to think in terms of organizing hockey's first players' union.

Ironically, Art Ross, who later became manager of the Boston Bruins and was one of the most frugal moguls in hockey, started the stick-handlers' union movement in 1911 by launching a brief players' revolt. He feuded with owners again late in 1914 and this time was supported by Lalonde of the Canadiens. Newsy became one of Montreal's first hockey holdouts when he refused to accept a $1,000 contract from Kennedy. Kennedy replied by fining him $100. The manager further announced that he would subtract $100 from Lalonde's salary for every week he refused to play. Les Canadiens launched the season without Newsy and promptly lost four consecutive games.

The impasse was broken when Lalonde signed a "secret" contract on January 9, 1915, but he played only six games before injuries compelled him to retire for the remainder of the season. Newsy's feud with management torpedoed the

Canadiens as contenders, and they finished the season in last place with an appalling 6-14 record.

In a sense, the last-place trauma had a cathartic effect on the team. Newcomers such as Howard McNamara and Goldie Prodgers replaced Jimmy Gardner, Ernie Dubeau, and Harry Scott. Lalonde returned, apparently rejuvenated from the previous season's woes, and Les Canadiens appeared ready to spring themselves right back to the top of the N.H.A. With Prodgers leading the attack with two goals, the Canadiens launched the 1915–16 season with a 2–1 victory on the road against the Toronto Blueshirts. They were on their way.

A week before the season had ended, the Canadiens clinched first place and completed matters on March 18, 1916, defeating Toronto, 6–4. Newsy scored two goals in that game and won the scoring championship, finishing five points ahead of Joe Malone and Cy Denneny. The stage was now set for Les Canadiens to meet the Pacific Coast Hockey Association's champion Portland Rosebuds in a best-of-five series for the Stanley Cup in Montreal.

As playoffs go, the 1916 Stanley Cup final was one of the best of the early editions. The teams were tied two games apiece when they faced-off on March 30 in the rubber match. They matched goals early in the game and appeared destined for sudden-death overtime, when Goldie Prodgers scored for the Canadiens. Georges Vézina was impregnable in the nets from that point on, and Les Canadiens won the game, 2–1, and captured the Stanley Cup. Each member of the winning team collected $238, while the losers rode home with $207 in their pockets.

To bolster his defense for the 1916–17 campaign, George Kennedy obtained Harry Mummery from Quebec. If nothing else, Mummery was distinguished for his size and girth, tipping the scales at 258 pounds. It was axiomatic that Harry had the appetite to go with it, a discovery made by Kennedy when Mummery checked in to his office after arriving in Montreal.

Harry shook hands with his new boss and in the next motion presented him a bill for $107, which covered his dining expenses from Brandon, Manitoba, to Montreal. (Remember that $107 in those days would be close to $800 in purchasing power today.) Kennedy was in no humor to tacitly accept such a toll, and inquired just what Mummery had to eat on his jaunt across two provinces.

In a trice, Harry itemized his six meals a day as well as a few side dishes, not to mention one quart of cream with every meal. Kennedy was prepared to concede the six meals a day but the cream was a bit much!

The two argued back and forth for several minutes until Mummery rose from his seat. Was he going to strike Kennedy? Nothing of the kind. "George," he said rather matter-of-factly, "I'm getting hungry. And I'm going to charge it to the club if you don't pay up pretty soon."

With visions of three-figure food bills in his head, Kennedy calmed his defenseman and promptly doled out $107 in crisp new bills. It was a wise decision because Mummery was soon to play an excellent defense for Les Canadiens, teamed with Bert Corbeau. However, Kennedy, perhaps because of the staggering food bills, traded Harry to Toronto the following season. He returned to Les Canadiens in the 1920–21 season and scored a very impressive 15 goals. The next year he was dealt to Hamilton, and Mummery finally retired after playing in Saskatoon for the

1922–23 season. According to hockey people, his food bills have never been matched before or since.

But of the early Canadiens, Newsy Lalonde clearly established himself as the most distinguished of all. "He not only had class," said Elmer Ferguson, dean of Canadian sportswriters, "but Newsy oozed color. Once he scored nine goals in a game his team won with an eleven-goal performance. He was born about fifty years too soon."

With Newsy playing the best hockey of his life, Les Canadiens managed to beat Ottawa for the right to compete again for the Stanley Cup in 1917, only this time they traveled to Seattle for their defense of the world championship. After winning the opening game, 8–4, the host club took over and proceeded to smother Montreal by scores of 6–1, 4–1, and 9–1 to capture the Cup and end an era for Les Canadiens.

The Chicago Black Hawks, 1961

Chicago Black Hawks, 1961

There never has been a more promising, yet disappointing, championship team than Rudy Pilous's representatives from the Windy City. The promise was in such names as Bobby Hull, hockey's Golden Jet; Stan Mikita, one of the most creative small centers of all time; magnificent Glenn Hall, appropriately dubbed Mister Goalie; and Pierre Pilote, one of the more accomplished offensive defensemen in the pre-expansion era.

"We had some wonderful hockey players," said Pilous, "and a lot was expected of us. In that one year (1960–61) we certainly caused quite a commotion."

Actually, the commotion had started a few years earlier, but for a more negative reason. During the early 1950s, when the NHL was in extraordinarily deep financial straits, the Chicago franchise came perilously close to passing right out of the big-league mainstream. Saved by the Wirtz family, the Black Hawks began a massive rebuilding program.

The league was so concerned about the franchise that stronger teams like the Toronto Maple Leafs and Montreal Canadiens were urged to siphon off a couple of their lesser players and ship them to Chicago. From the Montrealers, the Black Hawks obtained Ed Litzenberger, a forward with more than a little promise. Defensemen Jim Thomson and Gus Mortson, well past their prime and in trouble with Toronto owner Conn Smythe over union activities, came from the Maple Leafs.

More important was the decision to turn the entire Chicago hockey operation over to Tommy Ivan, who previously had helped develop a hockey dynasty in Detroit. As Black Hawks' general manager, Ivan promptly set to work creating a widespread farm system with scouts sprinkled across Canada from coast to coast. One of the most important outposts was the St. Catharines, Ontario farm club in the Ontario Hockey Association's Junior A division.

One by one, the St. Catharines' products made their way to the NHL. First it was Pilote, followed by Elmer (Moose) Vasko, Ken Wharram, and Mikita. Their contributions were evident in the standings. From a non-playoff team in 1957–58, the Black Hawks jumped to third place the following year, with 15 more points than they previously had.

Ivan didn't rely on his farm system alone. Goalie Hall arrived from Detroit by way of a trade with the Red Wings, while Ab McDonald was a contribution from the Canadiens, along with Dollard St. Laurent. Rangers' reject Jack Evans would prove to be the Gibraltar of the Chicago defense.

"We hit our stride in the 1960–61 season," says Hall who had become the best goalie in hockey, "but we knew that the Canadiens had won five straight Stanley Cups and whatever we had accomplished in the regular season would mean nothing if we didn't beat them in the playoffs."

If there is one reason above all others for the Black Hawks to make the all-time list, it's the fact that Rudy Pilous's team was the only one powerful enough to stop the Canadiens' Stanley Cup streak. It is worth remembering that Montreal's five-straight-Stanley-Cup-winners to this day is the all-time hockey dynasty. Beating them required, not only a monumental effort, but a stupendous team as well. That is precisely what the Black Hawks were at that time and place.

After disposing of the Canadiens, Bobby Hull and Company took on Gordie Howe and the Detroit Red Wings in the finals. It was no contest. Chicago topped Detroit in six games with Glenn Hall excelling in goal, while Hull and Mikita dominated the assault forces.

"We looked good enough to win a couple more Cups," said Hall. "The guys were young and the talent, obviously, was there. We were looking forward to some big days ahead."

A year later, the Black Hawks wiped out the Canadiens in a six-game semifinal and seemed good enough to win another Cup. They took on Punch Imlach's Toronto Maple Leafs in the finals but couldn't cope with the formidable Leaf defense. The decisive sixth game — Toronto led three games to two — was played at Chicago Stadium. If any match was symbolic of the Black Hawks of that era — great promise, a big buildup, and a major letdown — this was it. Game Six was a vintage thriller; a zero-zero tie well into the third period. At 8:58, Chicago Stadium turned into a cacophonous cavern, as Bobby Hull beat Leafs' goalie Dan Simmons for the opening goal. Every conceivable piece of debris, including two ink bottles, was thrown on the ice as the fans celebrated what they thought was the winning goal. Little did they realize they had halted their team's momentum. A delay of more than ten minutes was required as workmen cleared the ice. The delay enabled Imlach to regroup his forces and plan a new strategy. When the game resumed, Toronto scored almost immediately on a goal by Bob Nevin and won the game and the Cup on Dick Duff's score at 14:14.

Chicago's defeat told reams about the team. Superb as they were as scorers, they were deficient on defense. Their individual stars often seemed greedy and at odds with each other. The Black Hawks seemed to emphasize style over substance, and when they were wiped out of the 1963 semifinal playoff by Detroit, four games to two, Pilous was fired and replaced by Billy Reay. To many, this was an egregious sin against Pilous. His 1962–63 record was 32-21-17. Chicago finished with 81 points, only one behind first-place Toronto. But Rudy was accused of being too lax with his players and made a scapegoat for a dozen skaters who didn't pull their weight in the playoffs.

Reay hardly was an improvement. In 1963–64 the Black Hawks slipped to third place and went out in the first round, four games to three. They were third again the following season and this time made a determined run at the Cup. They defeated Detroit in a seven-game semifinal and then met the Canadiens for the Cup. The series went the full seven games but the Black Hawks came up empty in a decisive Game Seven. Jean Beliveau scored within 14 seconds, and by the end of the period the Canadiens led, 4–0, which was the final score.

For all intents and purposes, this was the end of the major Black Hawk Cup challenge. Hull and Mikita remained the offensive nucleus until 1972 when the Golden Jet defected to the World Hockey Association. Hall remained a first-rate goalie, but got little help on defense, and in 1967 was claimed by the St. Louis Blues in the NHL's first expansion draft.

It can be said, then, that the Black Hawks' position on the all-time team list is solely due to their performance in 1960–61. Certainly, they were not in a class with such long-term titans as the Canadiens of the 1950s or the Islanders of the 1980s. But one look at their roster is convincing enough that they were a uniquely powerful offensive unit with an impressive defense — at least for one year — and a truly superior goaltender.

In addition to Hull and Mikita, the offense was balanced by tough Murray Balfour, slick Tod Sloan, and speedy Ken Wharam. The defense was big, mean, and smart. Jack Evans had the best year of his lengthy career and Elmer (Moose) Vasko was not far behind. Pierre Pilote, Dollard St. Laurent, and Al Arbour were also exceptional.

Insiders argue that the Black Hawks *could* have taken the Cup in 1962 and 1963 had Pilous been more of a taskmaster and had the stars showed the same dedication and mental toughness as the Maple Leafs. This was not to be and, to the great consternation of Windy City fans, the Black Hawks never won another Stanley Cup.

As the Fabulous Fifties came to a close and the Swinging Sixties got under way, the National Hockey League began to undergo many changes. During the sixties, the NHL would experience unprecedented expansion, the advent of the curved hockey stick, and an increase in popularity throughout North America. But perhaps the most unusual event of all occurred in the 1960–61 season when, for the first time in 23 years, the Chicago Black Hawks won the Stanley Cup.

The Chicago team of 1960–61 featured several of the game's brightest stars, including four who would eventually be named to the Hockey Hall of Fame. During the many years between Cups, the Hawks were one of the worst teams in the league, but they somehow survived, and when they finally did win it all, it appeared as though they would dominate the league for years to come. Although they were near the top of the standings for many more years, the Hawks never recaptured the Stanley Cup, and now another three decades have come and gone and the Windy City stills yearns for another championship. The city and the franchise have hoped in vain for a taste of the bubbly again, and though they have a storied history behind them that has been highlighted by some great individual efforts, the fact remains that the Hawks have only won the Cup once in the past 2 decades.

At the height of their losing years, the Hawks became a frustrated team and often resorted to beating the opposition with their fists if they couldn't beat them on the scoreboard. During the forties, the Hawks' number one policeman was a burly blueliner named John Mariucci. Mariucci was a former football player from the University of Minnesota and he was totally fearless. In the early 1940s he was involved in one of the most brutal fights in the history of the game when he locked horns with Detroit's Black Jack Stewart in a bout that lasted an incredible 15 minutes and left both combatants bloodied and dazed. After being escorted to the penalty boxes, the two continued to battle until they were exhausted to the point of collapsing. Mariucci was a battered hockey player that symbolized the Chicago franchise. The Black Hawks had hit rock bottom.

Enter Mr. James Norris. Norris was a millionaire who was the majority owner of Madison Square Garden and also a big shot in the boxing world. Norris hung around with many celebrities from the Broadway crowd and he had also been known to associate with a few underworld characters who were members of his International Boxing Club. He was a big sports fan and when he had the opportunity to purchase the Black Hawks he didn't hesitate to take advantage of the situation. Along with Mr. Arthur M. Wirtz, the two gentlemen invested hundreds of thousands of dollars in an attempt to save the flagging franchise and keep hockey alive and well in Chicago.

As a result of more than a decade of failure, the Black Hawks were in deep trouble in the mid-1950s. Attendance was way down, and the franchise was not making any money. Players did not want to play for what was being called "The Siberia of Hockey" and the fans did not want to come out to see a loser. In an attempt to save hockey in the Windy City, the National Hockey League came up with a sort of Marshall Plan to help salvage the team. The "Help Save the Hawks Plan" was instituted, and each of the other clubs in the league was asked to donate several players to the Chicago club. Many of the players who were sent to the Hawks were those who had been trying to form a players association, an effort that met a great deal of resistance from the owners. In those days the players did not have the leverage that most professional athletes enjoy today, and it was the owners who decided which players were to be "donated" to the Hawks.

Despite the controversy that surrounded the plan to save the Hawks, the combination of the league's efforts and the duo of Wirtz and Norris helped revitalize the Hawks and, by the late fifties, they once again became competitive. During the 1957–58 season, the Black Hawks still missed the playoffs, but they made great strides towards post season play, and Norris was confident that success was in the not-to-distant future for the team. The optimism was even more justified when a muscular, blond haired 18-year-old forward joined the club that season. His name was Robert Marvin Hull and he could skate like the wind!

Though he tallied only 18 goals during his rookie season in 1957–58, one look at Hull on the ice and you could tell he had superstar written all over him. He could out skate any player in the league, he was as strong as a bull, and he possessed the most powerful slapshots that anybody had ever seen. The only reason he did not capture the Calder Trophy that year was because another first year man by the name of Frank Mahovlich scored seven more goals than Hull. But Hull's not winning the Rookie of the Year award was not important to the people of Chicago. What mattered was that, after years of misery, the club finally had a foundation on which they could build upon. And build they did!

In Hull's second season, the Black Hawks accomplished something they had not been able to do since World War II — they made the playoffs. Hull improved over his previous year's statistics by picking up 18 goals, and his reputation quickly spread throughout the hockey world. In the 1959–60 season, the Hawks made the playoffs again, and Hull took another step towards becoming one of the league's premier players by winning the Art Ross trophy for the first time. "The Golden Jet" totaled 81 points by notching 39 goals and adding 42 assists. He was named a first team All-Star and in only his third season, his 118 mile per hour slap shot had become legendary. He was the heart and soul of the Black Hawks and the action seemed to center around him. The Chicago faithful roared every time he stepped out on the ice, and they sat on the edge of their seats each time the "Jet" streaked down his wing looking to terrorize the opposing goalie.

At the start of the 1960–61 season, the Hawks and their fans could sense the club was really coming together. Revolving around Hull and being supported by a host of other stars, the Black Hawks stormed into the playoffs and took aim at the Stanley Cup. Hull, once again, was one of the top scorers and an All-Star. The team was led by the "Million Dollar Line" that comprised Bobby, along with Red Hay and Murray Balfour. The trio was put together by Rudy "The Mouth" Pilous who was now the head coach of the Black Hawks, and he was well aware of the prize he had in Hull. After years of frustration, the Cup was within reach, and when the team made it to the finals in April of 1961, there was no stopping it. Led by "The Golden Jet", the Chicago Black Hawks defeated the Detroit Red Wings and were crowned champions!

Bobby Hull went on to have a marvelous career after the championship season in spite of not winning another Cup. In 1962, he became only the third player to score 50 goals and won his second Ross trophy. He won the scoring title once again in 1965–66 when he put together a slate of 54 goals and 43 assists for 97 points. He also won the Lady Byng trophy in 1965 and he was twice named the league's M.V.P. in both 1965 and in 1966. The Point Anne, Ontario native finished his N.H.L. career with 610 goals and 560 assists for a total of 1,170 points, which obviously were enough to get him into the Hockey Hall of Fame. Hull also gained a great deal of attention when he jumped to the upstart W.H.A. for a large sum of money near the end of his career.

Although he ultimately regretted leaving the National Hockey League for the new league, Hull's biggest disappointment is having not won another Stanley Cup with the Hawks. Despite the stock of talent and several trips to the finals, Chicago was never able to pull off the championship after the 1961 season. Some people blame this on the lack of depth on the squad, while others claim it was the life in the fast lane the team led off the ice. Whatever the case, Bobby Hull did all he could during his fabulous career that eventually saw his number retired and hanging from the rafters of two separate arenas.

But Hull was not the only superstar that helped guide the Black Hawks to their Stanley Cup victory in 1961. Glenn Hall was an outstanding goalie who broke into the league in 1952 with the Detroit Red Wings, but was unable to displace the great Terry Sawchak until 1955–56. He won the Calder trophy that first year by posting 12 shutouts, and he complimented that with another stellar performance, winning 38 games the following season. However, Jack Adams shipped him to Chicago in 1957, and from then on he became a fixture in goal for the Black Hawks for the next ten years. He earned the nickname "Mr. Goalie" although he was known as "Gool" to his teammates. He led the N.H.L. in shutouts four times in his career and he was an All-Star eight times. "Gool" is credited with developing the "butterfly" style of goaltending and he captured the Vézina Trophy in 1963.

Hall had a strange habit of throwing up before each game as part of his mental preparation — he claimed he didn't feel right if he didn't empty his gut just before he hit the ice. His teammates found this ritual a bit weird but they didn't care what "Mr. Goalie" did as long as he won. His performance in the Cup finals in 1961 ranks right up there as one of the great goaltending achievements in playoff history. It was Hall's back-to-back shutouts in the two key games against Montreal that helped bring the Stanley Cup to Chicago. Hall finished his career having appeared in 906 games and posting a GAA of 2.51, all of which led to his induction into the Hall of Fame in 1975.

The captain of that championship team, Pierre Pilote, was a fellow from Kenogami, Quebec. The rangy defenseman who won the Norris Trophy for three straight years beginning in 1963, was just coming into his own when the Hawks went on their stretch run in 1961. Rugged and fearless, Pilote led the way that year with 6'3" Elmer Vasko, and together these two formed the backbone of the Chicago defense that also featured a young Al Arbour on the blueline. Much of the team's success is credited to Hall's goaltending and the consistent play of the defense.

Other members of the championship squad included Eric Nesterenko, Tod Sloan, and Ron Murphy. This trio formed the checking line and they were tough in the corners. Nesterenko was a bear of a man who finished his career with more penalty minutes than games played, and he later starred in the hockey movie "Youngblood" after his career was over.

Another valuable member of the championship squad was Earl Balfour (no relation to teammate Murray), a player of marginal talent who specialized in killing penalties. Eddie Litzenberger was also a forward who contributed more than his fair share to the championship team.

Complimenting Hull on the "Million Dollar Line" were center Red Hay and Murray Balfour. Hay was a unique specimen in those days, as he was one of the first hockey players to make it to the N.H.L. after receiving a college degree. Hay broke into the Chicago line up in 1959 after earning a Bachelor of Science in Geology from Colorado College. His father had convinced him to go to college and it turned out to be a move he didn't regret. After playing 506 games in the league and scoring 386 points, Hay retired at the age of 32 and became a very successful businessman. The other member of the "Million Dollar Line", which got its name from coach Pilous, was Murray Balfour. Murray was the checker of the unit, the guy who would go into the corners and come out with the puck. He then usually dished it off to Hull, who more than once buried the disk behind the goalie. Balfour was a strong man who enjoyed a rough, but clean style of play and this earned him the respect of his teammates as well as the opposition. During the 1961 playoffs, he was rewarded for his efforts as he tallied five goals and ten points in the eleven games. He scored a pivotal playoff goal against Montreal in the third overtime. Unfortunately, tragedy struck four short years later when Murray Balfour died of lung cancer.

As explosive as the top line was for the Hawks in 1961, the biggest reason for their Stanley Cup win probably was the play of the team's second line, aptly called the "Scooter Line." This trio consisted of Ab McDonald, Ken Wharram, and a little bundle of energy from Czechoslovakia named Stan Mikita. Wharram was a speedy skater who joined the Black Hawks in 1958 and he played an integral part in the Cup drive. Ab McDonald joined the club in 1960 after being a part of two consecutive Stanley Cup winners in Montreal and he helped round out "The Scooter Line." It was Mikita, however, who really made the line go.

Stan Mikita was born with the name Stanislas Gvoth in the town of Sokolce, Czechoslovakia in 1940. He came to Canada as an eight-year-old boy when his parents felt he would be able to lead a better life in North America since the Communists had taken over his home land. It also didn't hurt that his aunt and uncle could not have children and had asked Stan's parents if he could come to Canada with them. So in the winter of 1948, young Stan, who cried the entire trip, left his home and began a new life with his aunt, Anne, and uncle, Joe, in St. Catharines, Ontario.

It didn't take long for Stan to take a liking to all of the sports that the Canadian boys played, especially ice hockey. Of course there were the expected problems that come with being a foreigner, and Stan was involved in more than his fair share of fistfights along the way. He couldn't speak the language at first but he learned quickly, and it wasn't long before he understood such words as puck, shoot, and score. He was taunted and called a D.P. (displaced person) but as he got older, he let his natural athletic ability do the talking for him, and he soon gained the respect of friends and foes alike.

While just a teenager, Stan became the star of the local junior team called the St. Catharines Teepees. He led the team in scoring every season and while still at the tender age of 13, he had already caught the eye of Rudy Pilous, who would eventually be Stan's coach on the 1961 team that won the Cup. Aside from hockey, he also excelled in soccer, basketball, football, lacrosse, and baseball. He did so well at baseball that several major league baseball teams wanted him to tryout as a catcher. But hockey was Stan's true love and he never doubted that he would play in the National Hockey League.

Late in the 1958 season, Mikita made his debut in the NHL after a very successful junior career. The next season was Stan's first full one in the league and he appeared in 67 games, managing to score eight goals and total 26 points. But Stan was not very pleased with his output. It wasn't enough for him to make it to the big time — he wanted to excel. Because he wasn't very big, (a wiry 165 pounds) Stan felt he had to prove himself to the rest of the players in the NHL. He concentrated on his defensive play in his rookie season, while playing with "Terrible" Ted Lindsay, who was in the twilight of his career with Chicago. Stan might not have lit up the scoreboard too often that first season, but he sure did find out where the penalty box was as he amassed 119 penalty minutes, earning himself the nickname "La Petite Diable."

The "Little Devil" got under the skin of the opposition, and he also didn't exactly love the members of the press, but he made an impact his first year in the league and he seemed to be the missing ingredient for a Black Hawk Cup bid.

Bobby Hull was the number one star on the team and Mikita had to play in Hull's shadow, but Stan was the one who provided the spark to get the guys going. He was an intense competitor who burned with the desire to win and he accepted nothing less than 110% from himself as well as his teammates. In November, 1960, coach Pilous put Mikita together with Wharram and McDonald. The "Scooter Line" was born and the Hawks were on their way to the Cup!

Although he earned the reputation as a dirty player early in his career, Stan Mikita eventually changed his style of play and cut down his penalty minutes so drastically that he won the Lady Byng Trophy several times in the late sixties. In fact, Stan captured all three of the NHL's top awards (Hart, Ross, and Lady Byng) in both 1967 and 1968. He led the league in scoring four times and was an All-Star eight times. His career spanned 22 seasons, and he is immortalized in the Hall of Fame. However, despite his personal achievements, Stan Mikita would have traded them all in if his team, the Chicago Black Hawks, could have matched their accomplishments of 1961 — that is, win the Stanley Cup more than once.

The 1961 Chicago Black Hawks finished the regular season with a 29-24-17 mark, which was good enough for a third place finish. The team had been put together by Mr. Norris who claimed he spent more than a million dollars obtaining players from other teams. Of the 18 men on the club, 13 of them had been purchased from other teams, many from the Detroit Red Wings who were owned by Norris's brother and sister. Naturally, much controversy surrounded such a relationship, but the Hawks made the playoffs and were going up against the five-time defending Stanley Cup Champions, the Montreal Canadiens.

The great Rocket Richard had retired from the Canadiens the year before, but the scoring slack left by Richard had been picked up by Bernie "Boom Boom" Geoffrion who had scored 50 goals during the regular season. The Habs were still at the top of their game and they appeared to be on their way to cup number six, after taking the first game of the series by a score of 6–3. During that contest however, several Canadians were injured by the Black Hawks who had led the league in penalties during the season. Billy Hicke, Don Marshall, and superstar, Jean Beliveau all went down in Game One, and the Canadiens were screaming that the bigger Chicago squad was guilty of dirty hockey.

The second game was a much cleaner contest, and the Hawks prevailed 4–3 as Ed Litzenberger supported a strong game by Mikita when he scored the game winner with little time left on the clock. The third game was the most pressure filled of the series as the two teams battled into a third overtime stanza before Murray Balfour won it for the Hawks. The game proved to be more than just a loss for Montreal, as Geoffrion went down with a leg injury and it looked as though he would be done for the rest of the series. With both Beliveau and Geoffrion out of the line up, the Black Hawks liked their chances as they headed into Game Four, leading two games to one. But Montreal fired 60 shots at Glen Hall and tied the series at two games a-piece by winning 5–2.

In the fifth game however, Hall was as solid as a rock, and he shut out the champions, putting Chicago on the brink of a trip to the Stanley Cup finals. With his team on the verge of elimination, Geoffrion had the cast removed from his leg, took a shot of Novocaine and tried to play in an attempt to help his club. The effort proved futile however, and after just one shift "Boom Boom" was finished, and so were the Canadiens, as Hall blanked them for the second straight game. The five year run as Stanley Cup champions had finally come to an end for the battered and beaten Canadiens, and for the first time since the 1955 season, the Cup was going to find a home in the United States. Chicago was going to face Detroit for the Championship.

The Red Wings had won two Cups of their own in the early part of the decade and they had the great Gordie Howe on their side, so even though they had dethroned the champs, the Hawks still had a hard road ahead of them if they were to lay claims to Lord Stanley's trophy. Detroit had defeated Toronto in their opening round, and they were confident as they faced off against Chicago. But the Windy City hadn't tasted victory in 23 years, and even Gordie Howe wasn't going to stop them this time.

The final series began on the night of April 6, 1961 at a packed-to-the-rafters Chicago Stadium. The Golden Jet brought the full house to their feet as he tallied in the first period, and the home team was ahead by a 3–0 count barely four minutes later, when Hull slammed home his second of the game. Hall was spectacular the rest of the way, and Chicago hung on the take the first game, 3–2.

The series shifted to Detroit for the second game, two nights later, and this time it was the Red Wings who delighted their home town fans as they skated to a 3–1 victory. Alex Delvecchio scored two goals and Howe assisted on both of them, while goalie Hank Bassen held Chicago to a solitary score by Pierre Pilote. The best-of-seven series was now reduced to a best-of-five series as the scene moved back to Chicago for Game Three.

After a scoreless first period, the "Scooter Line" came to life and notched two of the three goals as the Hawks won, 3–1. Mikita broke the ice and Murray Balfour finished the Wings off with the third goal. Hull and Pilote each had two assists and Hall was once again outstanding between the pipes, allowing only a third period score by Howe.

An interesting trend was developing as the series went back to Detroit's Olympic Stadium for the fourth game. Up to this point, the home team had come away with the win and the Wings kept pace as they pulled out a squeaker and nailed down their second win by a score of 2–1.

With the series once again tied, it was back to Chicago as a rowdy, beer-drinking crowd of 20,000 jammed into Chicago Stadium. The Black Hawks did not disappoint the faithful as they broke a 3–3 tie and exploded for three goals in the third period. Mikita had two goals in the game and the fans showered their team with cheers as they skated off the ice. The Chicago Black Hawks were only one win away from that elusive prize!

The sixth game was played on April 16, 1961 and the Detroit fans cheered for the Wings just as heartily as their Chicago counterparts had done two nights before. They really got excited when the home team jumped out to a 1–0 lead after the first period. However, the Black Hawks were undaunted and they kept coming at the Wings until they got a break. Mid-way through the second period, the Red Wings went on a power play and were looking to increase their lead, when suddenly, Reg Fleming stole the puck and raced down the ice towards Bassen on a breakaway. Fleming lit the red light by tucking a low shot past the goalie for a shorthanded goal, giving Chicago a shot in the arm with the big play. The goal seemed to deflate the Wings, who gave up another goal to McDonald late in the period.

Detroit came out for the third period with their backs against the wall, but the Hawks were flying and they quickly dispelled any notions the Wings had of climbing back into the game as they scored three times to wrap things up. After 23 years of waiting, the Chicago Black Hawks and their fans were finally rewarded. The Stanley Cup belonged to the Windy City!

The Black Hawks continued to be a contender throughout the remainder of the decade, and they even made it back to the finals in 1962. However, they were never able to win it all again and, to this day, the franchise and the fans wait for another chance to drink from the Cup. Many of the players on that team had sensational seasons during the sixties. They won scoring titles, most valuable player awards, and featured many All-Stars. But the Cup has managed to elude them time and time again.

Many people feel that the Black Hawks had many individual stars but the team always lacked enough depth to go all the way. Others blame it on the fact that many of the Chicago players lived it up too much off the ice and that affected their performance on it. Regardless of the reason, the Black Hawks and their fans will have to be satisfied with the memories of that great 1961 team until the Stanley Cup finds its way back to Chicago.

The Philadelphia Flyers, 1974–75

The Broad Street Bullies — Flyers, 1974–75

It has been said, with some justification, that the Philadelphia Flyers did more to damage professional hockey's image than any NHL championship team. After all, they weren't called The Broad Street Bullies for nothing.

Coached by the unorthodox Fred (The Fog) Shero, the Flyers employed intimidation as a tool but, contrary to popular belief, the Philadelphians were not the first team to "win by the sword." They merely adapted the tactics previously used by the two-time (1970 and 1972) Stanley Cup-winning Boston Bruins and refined them for their roster.

Television helped magnify (and further damage) the Flyers' image. When Shero's club began winning big, TV sports had become a major force, and Flyers' fights were constantly played on news shows as well as the regular sports and hockey programming. The sum total was to blow the image of the Flyers far out of proportion to reality.

"We were a good, solid team, from Bernie Parent's goaltending to Bob Clarke's work at center," said Bill Barber, one of the outstanding Philadelphia forwards. "No team in the league ever worked harder for what we accomplished than us."

That, in a nutshell, explains why the Flyers made the all-time list. They *were* the hardest-working team ever! "When we beat the Bruins for the 1974 Stanley Cup," recalled Bill Clement, a member of the Cup-winners who now is a broadcaster, "they had Bobby Orr and Phil Esposito, but we just outworked them over the 60 minute game."

Shero's unorthodox (for the time) coaching also was a major asset. While many journalists tended to mock him for his ethereal aura, Shero, in fact, was a strategic marvel who was one of the first to import Soviet technique for application to the NHL.

Shero was one of the first to use an assistant coach and modify the five-man attack — as opposed to the standard three-forward system — to include the defensemen into the scoring unit.

But most of all, he stressed the value of the infantry. Shero noted that the team that regularly won the battles in the trenches — the corners of the rink and behind the net — was the team that won the most hockey games.

With footsoldiers such as Gary Dornhoefer, Ross Lonsberry, Bob (Hound) Kelly, and Orest Kindrachuk, the Flyers conquered "The Wall" and became the first expansion team to seriously challenge for The Stanley Cup.

They were able to do so because of a pair of the most inspirational leaders a coach could hope for; captain and center Bobby Clarke and goalie Bernie Parent. Clarke was the quintessential rah-rah type, but in the most practical kind of way. More often than not, his passes wound up on the stick of sharpshooter Reggie Leach and the Flyers found themselves leading yet another game. And when a slim advantage had to be preserved, Parent produced the saves.

Unlike other great teams, the Flyers lacked a dominant defenseman but, here again, the Shero unit system worked to perfection. Ed Van Impe, Joe and Jim Watson, and Andre (Moose) Dupont played within their limits and the system.

There was nothing flukey about either of the Flyers two Stanley Cup victories, the first in 1974, and the second in 1975. They were won by outgrinding the enemy. The Cup-winning game in 1974, a 1–0 win over the Bruins, was vintage Flyers. A year later they won The Cup by beating Buffalo 2–0. Same script.

The Flyers reached the finals again in 1976 but a vital element was missing, Parent. Responding to the lure of the World Hockey Association, he had departed Philadelphia and was replaced by the less efficient Wayne Stephenson. Philadelphia lost the 1976 finals in four straight games to Montreal and have never won another championship.

During the opening seconds of the third game of the Flyers-Penguins playoff in the spring of 1989, Philadelphia forward, Craig Berube, started a fight with Phil Bourque of Pittsburgh. The Spectrum crowd went wild, and once again the Flyers maintained their 15-year-old reputation as the Broad Street Bullies.

In the eyes of Philadelphians, the nickname has a positive connotation. After all, the original Bullies brought the Stanley Cup back to Philadelphia in 1974 and 1975. Fans in the City of Brotherly Love will never forget it. Yet to this day, many fans cannot fathom why and how the Flyers decided to adapt to the hit first ask questions last philosophy. It might be helpful if one recalled an ancient body-building advertisement which appeared in several magazines. It featured muscleman Charles Atlas with a drawing of a seaside brute kicking sand in the face of a beanpole wimp. The caption read "Do you want to be a 98 pound weakling?"

For several years of the Flyers early NHL life — they were born in 1967 as part of the major NHL expansion — they were the lambs of the league. For reasons that cannot be definitively assertained, the Flyer clubs, managed by Bud Poile and coached by Keith Allen, featured miniscule players like Simon Nolet in starring roles. The precious few "big guys," such as defenseman Larry Zeidel were hard-pressed to provide effective police action for the Broad Street Shrimps.

"We had some pretty good players," said Zeidel, "and we finished first in our opening year. But it was pretty clear that we didn't have enough muscle; at least not as much as some of the other teams."

The Flyers were pushed around for several seasons through the start of the 1970s until owner Ed Snider could take no more. Realizing that "might makes right" in the NHL (or at least the NHL of the 1970s), Snider had his scouts keep a lookout for beefy young skaters who could play hockey. And if they could fight, all the better. The transformation from the NHL's 98-pound weaklings into the Broad Street Bullies was a slow process, but the Spectrum high command was determined to push it through.

To do so, a capable leader was imperative. Vic Stasiuk was tried as coach and, despite a valiant effort, didn't quite succeed. For the 1971-72 season, Snider opted for the eccentric Fred Shero. Nicknamed "the Fog," because he frequently seemed to be transported into deep trances, Shero nevertheless was a consummately insightful hockey student. Furthermore, he implicitly believed in the notion that hockey games are won in the trenches; that is in the infighting along the boards and behind the net. He also subscribed to the Snider philosophy.

Although the Flyers failed to make the playoffs in 1971-72, they gradually acquired the type of player who would inflict more black and blue marks on the foe than the opposition would on Philadelphia. One by one the new Flyers made impact, and soon a solid nucleus of ruffians was in place.

Can the Flyers' Mean Machine Crunch This Bunch? The question sat atop an NHL schedule distributed throughout Philadelphia to hockey fans interested in purchasing season tickets. "This Bunch" happened to be then 15 other NHL teams who, during the next seven months, had the misfortune of getting in the Flyers' way.

Some victims did better than others. The big bad Boston Bruins, for example, were hardly bruised, but when they left the Spectrum they knew they had been in a hockey game. By contrast, the Vancouver Canucks were crushed like a saltine under a mallet. The others were blacked and blued and — in the case of Detroit — screamed bloody murder, demanding that the Broad Street Bullies be punished by NHL President, Clarence Campbell.

For sure, nobody scared the Flyers anymore; not even Boston. "In other years," said Bobby Clarke, "we'd play the Bruins in Boston and figure they had a two-goal lead to start with. Now it's even."

Only one figure frightened the Flyers and that was the black-and-white striped referee who, as the 1972–73 season progressed, began to take greater and greater note of the ferocious Flyers.

So did the strong teams of the NHL, although several required a rude awakening during the early months of the 1972–73 season. The regal Montreal Canadiens were just such a one. On the night of December 3, 1972, the Canadiens invaded the Spectrum and, instead of starting their first-string goalie, Ken Dryden, Montreal coach Scotty Bowman called on the inexperienced and little-used Michel Plasse.

Suitably provoked, the angry Flyers nearly ran the Montrealers out of the rink and stung the visitors with a 5–2 defeat. Still fuming even after the victory, Bobby Clarke betrayed the team's new pride by singling out coach Bowman for unusual criticism.

"Hasn't he (Bowman) got any respect for the Flyers?" snapped Clarke. "What's he doin' with the best goalie in the league sitting in the press box? When we saw Dryden wasn't dressed for the game a lot of us were teed off."

The more teed off the Flyers became the better, it seems, they played. By the end of 1972, they not only had established themselves as first-rate contenders in the West Division but also as the holy terrors of the league. The reputation resulted from a series of Pier Six brawls, smaller skirmishes, and a not-very-subtle assertion by the front office that Fred Shero's sextet would be delighted to beat up on anybody in sight.

One game more than any other underlined the ferociousness of the new Flyers, and from that point (December 29, 1972) on the Magnificent Mean Machine became the most fearsome thing on the ice since the Big Bad Bruins of 1969.

The incendiary event took place at Vancouver's Pacific Coliseum during the third period of a 4–4 tie. According to Vancouverites, the first and most disturbing act of provocation was supplied by Flyers' rookie Don Saleski who was beating up Barry Wilcox of the Canucks.

Saleski was doing such a destructive job on Wilcox that a Vancouver fan felt obliged to intervene on behalf of the local skater. The spectator reached over the boards and grabbed a handful of Saleski's abundant hairs.

"I thought he was going to pull me right off the ice," said Saleski, amazed.

The spectator made the mistake of perpetrating this act near the Flyers' bench. Immediately, the Philadelphians charged over the boards and engaged a flock of the loyal in combat. Sticks flew, heads ducked, and the police charged onto the scene. One gendarme, Corporal Donald Brown, attempted to pull the Flyers' spare goalie, Bob Taylor, away from the melee, but the officer himself wound up on the ground. The Vancouver spectators charged that the Flyers acted like animals, while Philadelphia coach Shero claimed there would have been no trouble if the authorities had heeded his warning.

"There were no cops in the runway at all," Shero protested, "and I had requested some. The people were hollering and throwing things in the first period and I expected trouble. I told an usher but he did nothing. Our law and order on the ice is maintained by a referee. If the fans reach out there and get involved they deserve what they get. This is as old as hockey itself."

The episode took place while NHL President Clarence Campbell was hospitalized for gall bladder tests in Montreal. His deputy, vice president Don Ruck, studied the game reports and issued what amounted to a mild slap-on-the-wrist to the belligerents.

"Under heavy provocation from fans," said Ruck, "a hockey player will react like any other human being. Analyzing something like this is like trying to crawl into somebody's mind. Some people have shorter fuses than others. What do you do when a lady spills coffee in your lap? Say thank you or punch her in the nose?

"It's unfortunate that fans can't remain in the area they purchased — and that's the same as the width of their butt."

Whatever the rationale, Philadelphia jumped to the top of the visiting team hate parade in Vancouver. Soon they'd be on top in Detroit, Buffalo, and Montreal as well. "The Flyers," said Chuck Newman of *The Inquirer*, "have earned the dislike of fans and officials throughout the league."

"Maybe we ought to lay low for a while," suggested Bill Flett.

To which rookie Bill Barber replied: "The referees will have to change. They can't make us change our style."

There certainly was no change in the Flyers' style on February 9, 1973, when they returned to Vancouver to defeat the Canucks 10–5 and tighten their grip on second place. They clobbered the club at every opportunity.

PHILLY BULLIES PACK MEAN PUNCH, declared a headline in *The Vancouver Sun*. And "villainous" was the adjective used by *Sun* reporter Arv Olson to describe the Philadelphia team.

Andre Dupont of the Flyers clipped Bobby Schmautz of Vancouver on the forehead with his stick. Dave Schultz belted Schmautz in a fight. And later, Schultz took on Dale Tallon of the Canucks. Tallon retired from the game with a seven-stitch cut over his eye and a pulled stomach muscle. These were just a few of the bouts.

Guerrilla warfare such as this caught the fancy of hockey fans across the continent. They regarded the Flyers as a throw-back to the pioneering days of the game when brawls were a dime-a-dozen and nobody thought twice about it. National magazines began zeroing in on Shero's warriors and, of course, the more puritanical element grabbed their typewriters and condemned the Broad Street Bullies for defacing hockey's good name.

When the 1973–74 season opened, the Flyers no longer could be taken lightly. Led by captain Bobby Clarke at center, the Bullies were strong at every position, especially goal where Bernie Parent would win 47 games, lose only 13, and tie 12, for a 1.89 goals against average. (His partner, Bob Taylor, was 3–3–0 and 4.26.)

Bill Barber was a whiz on left wing, while Rick MacLeish enjoyed one of his best years at center. Even the tough guys proved to be productive. When critics bemoaned the incessant fighting involving Dave (Hammer) Schultz, Flyers publicists would be quick to point out that in 73 games he collected 20 goals and 16 assists, for 36 points.

The Philadelphia defense was unspectacular, but solid. Veteran Ed Van Impe, a Chicago Black Hawks castoff, had become notorious for his vicious stickwork in front of the net but it served to keep the crease clear for Parent. His partners, Andre Dupont and the Watson Brothers, Jim and Joe, were no less indiscreet.

In addition to Schultz's intimidating tactics, Shero always could call upon Don (Big Bird) Saleski, Bob (Hound) Kelly, and Gary Dornhoefer, with a lot of extra help, when necessary, from Orest Kindrachuk, Terry Crisp, and Ross Lonsberry.

With the exception of Schultz, none of the Flyers was especially frightening, but the team operated as a voracious unit and, as such, did scare some opponents before the opening puck was ever dropped.

Because of all the furor about goonism caused by the media — and in many cases it *was* justified — there was a tendency to overlook the fact that the Flyers won most of their games because of skill, hustle, and puckstopping; all of which was reflected in the final standing.

"If the NHL wants to condone goon squads like the Flyers," said one reporter, "if the Canucks are silly enough to play along and the customers are suckers enough to buy it, who am I to say no? There's just one thing that bothers me. The Flyers play butcher shop hockey and succeed by the only measuring stick that counts. They win.

"Success breeds imitators. If they make it to the Stanley Cup final, how many more goon squads can we expect next season?"

The Flyers closed the 1973–74 regular season with their 50th win, a 6–2 triumph over Minnesota. They entered the playoffs on a roll and hoped to continue it against the upstart Atlanta Flames, coached by former NHLer Bernie Geoffrion.

It certainly looked like the Flames would need some football players to outmuscle the Flyers; the Broad Street Bullies were notorious for their vicious ways. The series opened at the Spectrum on April 9, 1974 and the Flyers smothered Atlanta, 4–1. Third-line center Orest Kindrachuk netted two third-period goals, and the team had a mere 13 penalty minutes in the game. Game Two was even more lopsided, with Philly winning 5–1. The star this time was winger Rick MacLeish, who popped in three straight goals in the second period to blow open the game.

The series switched to the Omni in Atlanta for Games Three and Four, but the change of arenas had no effect on the Flyers. Philly took the third game, 4–1, in one of the wilder playoff games in recent memory.

The game was 2–1 in the second when, just 16 seconds after a major brawl — the first of the series for Philly — MacLeish bore down on Atlanta goalie Dan Bouchard and apparently clanged one off the crossbar. But referee Dave Newell saw differently and signaled goal. That made Bouchard see red and the feisty goalie charged out after Newell and actually hit the referee! The goal counted, however, and it took the wind out of the Flames' sails.

Game Four saw Atlanta jump out to a 3–0 lead mid-way through the second. The Flyers got untracked thanks to inspirational Dave Schultz, who had just beaten Bryan Hextall silly. Andre Dupont scored 12 seconds after the fight and the Flyers won in overtime, 4–3, on Schultz's goal.

Noticeably absent from the Bullies bench was coach Fred Shero, who had been attacked late the previous evening. Shero had no recollection of the attack but, after waking up with a broken thumb and numerous cuts and bruises, he knew he could not coach. That meant assistant coach Mike Nykoluk would take over for Philly.

"We didn't find out until just before we went on the ice," said captain Bobby Clarke of Shero's accident. "I don't know how anybody felt about it. Mike said we owed the man something and it's obvious we do."

The response was slow, but the Flyers did win one for their coach. And themselves.

"This is the greatest team I've ever coached," said Shero. "I've had some pretty good teams, but this team is something special. They work like hell."

The Flyers had overcome one obstacle with relative ease on their road to the Stanley Cup. Now, a much tougher task lay ahead against a much tougher, more experienced team — the New York Rangers.

Led by the likes of Brad Park, Jean Ratelle, and Steve Vickers, and the superb goaltending of Eddie Giacomin, the Rangers would push the Flyers to the limit.

Game One opened at the Spectrum on April 20, 1974. The Flyers showed they had the upper hand from the very beginning. Just three minutes into the game, Bobby Clarke leveled Ranger Walt Tkaczuk with a big check that knocked the Ranger forward out of the game. Philly jumped all over the Rangers and won handily, 4–0.

Flyer goalie Bernie Parent hardly broke a sweat in facing 19 shots for the shutout. At the other end, Giacomin was harassed, held, and harried by the Flyer forwards, especially Gary Dornhoefer, who "shadowed" the Ranger goalie and prevented him from going anywhere.

"I've got to do something," laughed Dornhoefer. "I can't skate. I can't shoot. I can't pass. Everybody's got to do his thing."

The extra effort put out by "muckers" like Dornhoefer, Kindrachuk, and Dupont made the Flyers a complete team. Everybody *does* have to do his thing; that's what wins championships.

Game Two saw more of the determination and hard work by the boys from Broad Street. Ross Lonsberry, who quietly scored 32 goals during the regular season, netted two third-period tallies as the Flyers again shut down New York 5–2.

"I've said it before and I'll say it again," said coach Shero, "Ross Lonsberry could be our most valuable player this season."

This game also, included yet another disputed goal. Flyer defenseman Ed Van Impe flipped the puck towards the net, it deflected off a Ranger stick and trickled over the goal line before being snatched out by Giacomin. The red light went on and Giacomin went berserk, swinging his stick at the glass guarding the goal judge. He nearly hit ref Dave Newell — the same official that called the controversial goal in the Atlanta series.

"I took my glove off to make sure it wouldn't go over," said Giacomin. "I'd swear on a stack of Bibles it wasn't in."

The goal stood, making it 2–0 Flyers. They never looked back, heading to Madison Square Garden with a 2–0 series lead.

The Flyers again took a two-goal lead in Game Three, thanks to scores by MacLeish (his eighth playoff goal) and Dupont.

But Philly fell apart, thanks to penalty after penalty. Referee Bryan Lewis doled out 108 penalty minutes — 81 to the Flyers. The Rangers had 11 power plays to Philadelphia's three, and New York capitalized on two of them, one being Brad Park's game-winner at 8:53 of the third. New York won the game, 5–3.

"It was like he (Lewis) had a vendetta against us," said Flyer G.M. Keith Allen. "It was the worst-refereed game I've seen all year. The Stanley Cup semifinals and they send a clown like that."

The Flyers may have been griping, but NHL president Clarence Campbell held a closed-door meeting with the Philly brass to discuss the numerous fights and penalties.

"I was angry, very angry," said Campbell. "I was angry at the entire presentation. It injured the league's image in my opinion."

Game Four had less of the fighting, but no less of the chippiness. Neither team had a man in the box nearly all of the first two periods. The game was tight and the teams headed to overtime tied at one.

The overtime was full of excitement and Rod Gilbert's deflection at 4:20 of the extra session gave the Rangers a 2–2 series tie.

But more important to Philly was the loss of stalwart defenseman Barry Ashbee, who was hit in the eye by a Dale Rolfe shot two minutes into overtime. There was a lot of blood and Ashbee, a superb backliner who always played hurt, would not return in the playoffs — or ever.

"He's a clean hockey player," said Ranger wing Steve Vickers. "You don't care who he is. You don't like to see it happen. Just because there are hard feelings in a series like this, that doesn't matter. Hard feelings can't maim you."

Saddened by the loss of their fine defenseman and the loss of their two-game lead, the Flyers returned to the Spectrum for Game Five.

The Flyers took the game, 4–1, on the strength of clutch saves by goalie Bernie Parent and persistent checking — and cheerleading — by forward Terry Crisp.

"We could have been off and running in the first period," said Ranger coach Emile Francis, whose club led only 1–0 after one, thanks to Parent. "We had better chances in that time than we've had all series."

Crisp showed signs of the determination and decibel level he employs now as coach of the Calgary Flames.

"He was cheerleading all night," Shero said of Crisp. "He kept saying, 'Let's go get 'em. We can't fool around anymore. The whole season is riding on this game.'

"Other guys just yell and scream on the bench, but Crispie knows what he's saying. He sees the mistakes out there."

Game Six was back at Madison Square Garden and the result was the same as the previous five contests — the home team won. The Rangers scored three third-period goals to break a 1–1 tie and coasted to a 4–1 win. Flyer captain Bobby Clarke had several good scoring chances, but could not convert.

"I walked in alone twice," said Clarke. "If I score on either one, maybe the game goes a different way."

Game Seven started, as usual, with Kate Smith's inspirational singing of "God Bless America." The fans were cheering and the players were pumped, though it was the Rangers who opened the scoring as Billy Fairbairn notched one at 13:43 of the first.

Other than that goal, however, the first 40 minutes was all Flyers. They pummeled Giacomin with 37 shots and held a 3–1 lead after two.

"They outskated us and they forechecked," said Francis. "Hockey games are won in the other team's end and that's where Philly spent the first two periods. They were right on top of us and gave us no room at all."

But the Rangers would not fold. They pressured the Flyers and, despite numerous stops by Parent, cut the lead to 3–2.

The Flyers wanted no part of a close game and made sure of it right from the ensuing faceoff. MacLeish and Lonsberry worked behind the Ranger net and got the puck out front to Dornhoefer, who made no mistake. The man who had spent most of his time during the series screening the Ranger goalie now put one past Giacomin. Dorny's second goal of the game put the contest out of reach.

The Blueshirts got one back, but it wasn't enough. The final was 4–3 and the team that had been born merely six years earlier was now going to play for the Stanley Cup.

"If Dorny doesn't score, I think we're in trouble," said Clarke. "But somebody has picked somebody else up all year. It all goes back to the end of last season when we realized we had come together."

One of the happiest Flyers was veteran defenseman Ed Van Impe, whose steady defensive play and nurturing of younger players like Jim Watson helped bring Philly its first-ever shot at a title.

"I've waited for this for 14 years," said Van Impe. "Some people say that we have done so well already that this series is anticlimactic. I don't feel that way."

The series Van Impe was referring to was the Cup final showdown with the big, bad Boston Bruins. With talents such as Bobby Orr, Phil Esposito, and Johnny Bucyk leading the way, the Bruins had stormed through the opening rounds with ease and were well-rested when the two teams took the ice at Boston Garden on May 7, 1974.

Game One of the final was just as one might expect — close-checking and tight defense. The Bruins jumped out to a two-goal lead on scores by Wayne Cashman and Bobby Sheppard. But the Bullies never-say-die attitude brought them back, thanks to a second-period tally by Orest Kindrachuk and a third-period marker by Clarke.

The game stayed tied until the final minute of the third, when Flyer Cowboy Bill Flett stormed down the wing and cut past Bruin netminder Gilles Gilbert. He flipped the puck towards the unguarded goal, but it clanged off the post and the Bruins started down the other way.

The puck went into the corner in the Flyers' zone and Cashman literally ripped

Moose Dupont off the puck. Ken Hodge picked it up and feathered a pass to Bobby Orr. The superhuman defenseman blasted one by Parent, who himself had put in another superhuman effort. The red light flashed on at 19:38 of the third. Bruins three, Flyers two.

Philly felt they were jobbed by referee Dave Newell — yes, the same Dave Newell who had been involved in controversial calls in each of the first two Flyer series — on the missed call on Cashman. And they were disappointed about the crushing defeat.

"Having Orr score doesn't lessen the pain," said Crisp. "It could have been Sidney Glick from Oshkosh and it would hurt. What really hurts is that the play should have been dead long before."

With the Flyers still smarting from the previous game's loss, the Bruins could have made Game Two a blowout and they took another two-goal lead. But Philly closed the gap to 2–1, and with just 52 ticks left in the third, Rick MacLeish found defenseman Dupont cruising in the slot. Moose tipped the puck past Gilbert and the game headed to overtime.

Both teams had several chances in the fourth period, but Parent, stopping John Bucyk on a breakaway, and Gilbert, halting MacLeish and Crisp from in close, kept the game going.

Finally, 12 minutes into overtime, Flett found Clarke all alone at the side of the net. His first shot was stopped by Gilbert, but the rebound came right back to the Philadelphia captain, who made no mistake this time. The series was now tied.

"I didn't even know what happened on my first shot," said Clarke. "I was just waiting and hoping for a rebound. I got it.

"If we'd lost this one, we would have been tired going home. Now we're fresh as daisies."

The freshness showed as Philly took Game Three back in the friendly confines of the Spectrum, 4–1. They also took a 2–1 lead in the series, thanks to some superb efforts from role players.

With the score tied at one, Crisp made a beautiful one-man effort and muscled a shot past Gilbert at 15:43 of the first. Kindrachuk, already with four key playoff goals, notched yet another in the third to put Boston out of business.

Along with another important win came the loss of another important player, however. Gary Dornhoefer went down with a separated shoulder late in the third; he would not return for the remainder of the series.

"A guy like Gary is hard to replace," said Van Impe. "But we're gonna hang tough. We're too close now."

Van Impe played a big part in Game Four, blocking shots and rattling Bruin bodies to preserve a 2–2 tie into the third.

With just under six minutes left in regulation, coach Shero sent Lonsberry and MacLeish over the boards. He needed a right winger because of Dornhoefer's injury; he chose 21-year-old left wing Bill Barber, who was riding a nine-game playoff scoreless streak.

"I just put him out there and hoped I'd get lucky," explained Shero.

He did. Barber fired a wrist shot from the left boards past Gilbert at 14:25 of the third. The Spectrum crowd exploded. The Bruins hadn't even had time to catch their breath when, just over two minutes later, Dupont blasted one in. Philly had taken a 3–1 series lead, thanks to Barber and Shero's decision.

"The magical Shero could walk through a hail of bullets this season and shrug them off like a shower of Rice Krispies," wrote Jack Chevalier of *The Evening Bulletin*.

The Bruins had their backs to the wall as they headed home for Game Five, but coach Bep Guidolin felt confident.

"We'll come back and win this thing yet," said Guidolin.

His confidence spilled over into his players as the Bruins blew out Philly, 5–1, with Bobby Orr notching two goals and an assist. The champagne would have to wait.

"We just couldn't get anything going," said Lonsberry. "We were awful."

The Bruins were gaining confidence, but the Flyers had two powerful weapons on their side for Game Six: the Spectrum, where they sported an 8–0 playoff record; and Kate Smith, who sported a 36–3–1 record of her own when singing "God Bless America."

Ms. Smith's song whipped the Spectrum crowd into a frenzy. The first period of the sixth game was tight. The Bruins pelted Parent with 16 shots, but as he had done throughout the series and the entire season, the Flyer goalie stonewalled the opposition. The Broad Streeters skated off with a 1–0 lead thanks to a Rick MacLeish deflection of an Andre Dupont shot, MacLeish's 13th playoff goal.

The rest of the game belonged to Parent. He made the slim lead stand up with 30 saves, many of them brilliant. The Bruins continued to press into the final minutes, led by Orr, who had been on the ice for nearly half the game. But Clarke broke free for a clean breakaway with under three minutes to play. Orr not only caught the Flyer captain but seemingly stripped him of the puck. Ref Art Skov saw differently, however, and sent Orr off for holding with 2:22 to play. The Bruins protested vehemently to no avail. The remaining time ticked off and the game, and the series, ended. The brawling Broad Street Bullies were now Stanley Cup champions.

"The only word I can think to describe this feeling is fulfillment," said Crisp, one of the integral parts of the Flyer machine. "Right now, I'm numb."

Not only was it the Clarkes, Parents, and MacLeishes; it was the Van Impes, Crisps, Kindrachuks, and Duponts. Not to mention Dornhoefer, and Barry Ashbee, who still had not fully regained his eyesight.

"I'm only sorry the old man (34-year-old Ashbee) wasn't there with me on this day," said Dupont, fighting back tears. "I owe Barry so much."

Boston coach Guidolin felt Clarke should have taken the Conn Smythe Trophy as playoff MVP, but the prize went to the backbone of the team throughout the year — Bernie Parent.

"We are not the most talented team to ever win the Cup by a longshot," said Parent, "but it is the result of hard work. You don't realize how much damn hard work we put in for this thing and that is what makes it such a great experience. Even if you have a hundred million dollars, you couldn't buy the feeling we have right now."

The champs even drew praise from NHL president Campbell, who had criticized them earlier in the playoffs for their tactics.

"It's an occasion of rejoicing for everyone, not least of all the league," Campbell said. "It's the first breakthrough for the expansion clubs and probably the biggest event that ever happened to hockey."

The Cup was the culmination of six years' work, six years that turned a bunch of weak-kneed wimps into back-alley brawlers. Captain Clarke summed up his team best: "We're not just a bunch of Broad Street Bullies. We play good hockey."

The Flyers' 1974 Stanley Cup victory was viewed with skepticism in some quarters. While Philadelphia skaters certainly worked hard and received magnificent goaltending, they lacked a superstar of the Bobby Orr genre. Additionally, they still had to bear the cross of their bully image and never obtained the kind of respect that the Canadiens, Maple Leafs, or other championship teams received.

To do so, they would have to repeat their Stanley Cup win in 1975 as well as finish the regular season on a high level. To the Flyers' high command, this was not an unattainable objective. Snipers like Reg Leach, Bill Barber, Rich MacLeish, and Bobby Clarke were playing the best hockey of their careers. The defense was intact and Bernie Parent finished the season with a 2.03 goals against average.

If there was any doubt that the Flyers could conquer the NHL and the regular season, it was erased at the conclusion of the 80-game schedule. Philadelphia won the most games (51), lost only 18, and tied 11, for a total of 113 points.

"I had watched the team from its birth back in 1967," said ex-Flyers' defenseman Larry Zeidel, "and I have to say that the 1975 team was as strong as any team that played in the NHL for a long time."

Shero didn't have to be told that the first-place finish would be virtually meaningless if his club failed in the playoffs. The true test of the Flyers' greatness would come when they met the challengers in their defense of the Stanley Cup.

The Flyers opened the 1974–75 post-season against the Toronto Maple Leafs. Game One was at the Spectrum on April 13, 1975, and the game was not without controversy — the norm in Flyer playoff games. The Leafs, heavy underdogs in the series, took a 3–2 lead into the third period thanks to two power play goals on a five-minute advantage given Toronto when Andre Dupont was ejected from the game for head-butting Dave Dunn in a fight.

But Philly, always cool under fire, stormed past the Leafs with three scores in 2:37 in the third. Bill Barber tied the game at 9:25, hard-shooting Reg Leach banged home the go-ahead goal at 11:46, and just 16 seconds later, Jimmy Watson blasted one by Toronto goalie Gord McRae to put the game out of reach. The Flyers coasted to a 6–3 victory, with Rick MacLeish completing a hat trick with seven seconds to play.

Game Two saw more of the underrated Flyers coming to the fore. "Battleship" Bob Kelly notched two assists, and mucker Terry Crisp scored twice as Bernie Parent kept the Leafs off the board. The Flyers won, 3–0, and despite Toronto coach Red Kelly's statement that, "Our chances of winning the series are as good as when we started," all signs pointed to another Philly sweep.

Game Three was a strong reminder of Parent's Conn Smythe Trophy effort of 1974. The Flyer goalie dazzled the Maple Leaf Gardens crowd with impossible save after impossible save, even one off Ian Turnbull that Leaf goalie Doug Favell couldn't believe.

"Our whole bench jumped up, anticipating the goal," said Favell of Turnbull's shot. "Then, out of nowhere comes this skate and this stick. And the puck's in the corner. We must have looked crazy, all of us standing there."

Parent finished the night with 31 stops and his second consecutive shutout, 2–0. Things looked mighty bleak for the Leafs.

The Leafs looked sharp as Game Four started. Blaine Stoughton connected off a Dave Keon pass at 2:47 of the first and Toronto seemed ready to take command. But Reg Leach blew one by McRae under a minute later and Philly was back in it.

The teams traded scores and Barber's goal at 8:25 of the second put the Flyers ahead going into the third. The Leafs pressed and finally came up with the tying goal as Ron Ellis knocked in his second of the game at 13:23. The teams headed for sudden death.

The extra session was just over a minute and a half old when Dave Schultz, the Flyers' answer to Mel Hill, hopped over the boards. The Hammer had set up one OT score and scored one in Philly's drive to the Cup the previous year; he was true to form at 1:45 of this overtime, when he fed Moose Dupont for a 20-foot wrist shot that beat McRae and the Leafs, 4–3.

The Flyers had swept away another opponent and now headed into the semis on a roll. They would have to wait nearly two weeks before playing again, however, and it remained to be seen if the rest would come back to haunt them.

While the Flyers were taking care of the Leafs, another series was history in the making. The Pittsburgh Penguins had opened a 3–0 series lead on the young New York Islanders. It looked like a battle for Pennsylvania lay ahead.

But the upstart Isles blew past the Pens, winning the last four games of the series and shocking the hockey world. Now, however, they had to face the Stanley Cup champions, and things looked bleak for the upset-minded club.

Fortune seemed to be smiling on those Islanders, though, when Bernie Parent went down with a pinched nerve in his neck. The Flyers' superstar goalie would have to miss the crucial opening game. The start went to backup Wayne Stephenson.

The champs never batted an eyelash, squashing the Isles, 4–0; it was as if Parent had never left.

"We just played basic hockey, clearing the front of the net and blocking shots," said veteran defenseman Ted Harris, a new addition to the Flyers. "It was beautiful. It just shows how easy it can be done."

"The first save was the biggest one," said a relieved Stephenson. "I knew if I didn't make that one, I'd be in trouble. But the guys played great in front of me. They protected me all night."

Stephenson was in net again for Game Two, but his team faltered late in the game. What was once a 4–1 lead with more than half the game over, was a 4–4 deadlock thanks to a Denis Potvin slapper and two rebound goals by J.P. Parise. The Flyers looked nervous and worried.

New York's Bob Nystrom, a 27-goal scorer in the regular season but with nary a one in the playoffs, broke in alone on Stepehnson just 1:22 into OT. He tried to flip one over the Flyer netminder, but Stephenson stayed with him and turned the shot aside.

The Flyers then took control of the extra session and it finished at 2:56 with an apparent kick-in by Bobby Clarke. Ref Wally Harris signaled goal and the Isles were livid. They were also 2–0 down in the series, but the Flyers were wary of their striking ability.

"That's the kind of team we expected to see," said Flyer Orest Kindrachuk. "They just took over."

The teams traveled to the Nassau Coliseum for Games Three and Four. The question was, could the Isles recall some of the magic that boosted them past both the New York Rangers and the Penguins?

Game Three saw the return of Bernie Parent, and the Flyers responded by playing one of their strongest defensive games in history. Both Parent and Islander goalie, Chico Resch were at the top of their game, and the match was scoreless after two periods.

Just half a minute into the third, Reg Leach took a pass from Clarke as he steamed down the right side. He blew past Dave Lewis and threw a backhander behind Resch. That was all the scoring for the game, as the Flyers won their seventh consecutive playoff game, 1–0. The Islanders now found themselves in the same hole they had dug one round earlier. But this was the Champs they were facing, and the prospect of a comeback was faint at best.

The Isles were taking things one game at a time, and they stormed out to a 3–0 lead in Game Four. The Flyers wanted another sweep, though, and they came back with three goals of their own to tie the game. Philly was swarming the Islander net with seconds to play.

The puck popped free to Leach, who shot one past Resch. The red light went on. The Flyers celebrated. The officials conferred. It was ruled no goal because time had expired. The teams headed into the locker rooms to prepare for overtime. The Flyers were mad, but the green light had blinked on before the red one.

"There's absolutely no doubt in my mind that time had run out," said Coliseum clock operator Bob Ahrens.

The Islanders had been given a reprieve and they took full advantage of it. Jude Drouin flipped a backhand shot past Parent at 1:53 of overtime and the Long Island kids had come back from the brink once more.

Game Five was back at the Spectrum, where the Flyers hadn't lost a playoff game in two seasons. The fans smelled blood, but the Islanders weren't folding. They blew the Broad Streeters out of their own arena, 5–1. The momentum had shifted; the Flyers were the ones on the run and the young Islander team was now coming together.

"I don't know why we were so damn tight," said Flyer coach Fred Shero. "No reason for that. We were two games up, not them. But give them some credit; it's a real series now."

Not only were the Isles outplaying the Champions, they were outpunching them as well. As time wore down, Dave Schultz was sent over the boards to send a message to his opponents. But New Yorker Clark Gillies won a clear-cut decision over the Hammer; the Flyers were getting beaten at their own game.

Game Six, at Nassau, showed more determination from the Islanders and more tired play from the Flyers. A quick lead on a Ross Lonsberry goal was erased at 16:15 of the second on Denis Potvin's short side blast. The game stayed tied into the third.

The final period saw none of the usual Flyer tenacity. None of the extra effort. The Isles pressed in the opening minutes and backliner Gerry Hart fired in his own rebound at 3:42. Chico Resch and his teammates kept Philly in check for the rest of the game and the Islanders pushed the Flyers to a seventh game.

"We know this shouldn't be happening, but it is," remarked Terry Crisp. "It's like a bad nightmare where you run and run but get nowhere. About the only thing said in the dressing room after was Clarkie saying, 'We're lucky we have one game to redeem ourselves.'"

The Spectrum was rocking as Kate Smith made her first post-season appearance for "God Bless America." The Flyers looked ferocious and just 19 seconds into the game, Gary Dornhoefer shot a pill behind Resch. The boys from Philly looked like the champs from the word go.

The Islanders closed to 2–1 at the 5:02 mark, but Rick MacLeish pulled some more playoff magic and netted his second of the game just two minutes later. The Flyers had already pummeled Resch for three goals and they kept the shots coming.

The visitors managed only 15 shots on Parent and MacLeish completed his second playoff hat trick of the year with an empty-netter in the third. The Flyers, who had looked lackadaisical in losing three straight after winning three in a row, took the series with a 4–1 win and won a return trip to the finals.

"It was a combination of a lot of things," said vet Jim Watson. "Our team just played tremendous. It was great hockey, but what a tough series."

Things wouldn't get any easier for the Flyers as they had just two days to rest before taking on the Buffalo Sabres for the Stanley Cup. The Sabres had a mix of veterans such as Rick Martin and King Kong Jerry Korab to go with young stars like Jim Schoenfeld and Gilbert Perreault. The Flyers would need more efforts like the seventh game of the Islander series to take care of the Sabres.

Game One was a beautifully played game, scoreless after two. Parent shone in net again, robbing Perreault on four separate occasions. Buffalo goalie Garry Desjardins was strong in the Sabre nets, but Philly struck first as Bill Barber banged home an Ed Van Impe shot at 3:42 of the third. Ross Lonsberry converted a power play chance four minutes later and the Flyers were off and running to a convincing 4–1 victory. As usual, Philadelphia's savior was the man behind the mask.

"If Bernie doesn't come up with those first two periods, we lose the first game," said Joe Watson. "If it wasn't for him, we'd be behind. It's as simple as that. It was the sharpest I've seen him all year. He was the Parent of old."

Game Two belonged to another "old" superstar. Bobby Clarke set up Leach's opening goal and then scored the game-winner at 6:43 of the final period as the Flyers took a 2–0 lead in games.

The defense also shone, as the Sabres couldn't muster a single shot after Korab's tying goal at 2:18 of the third. Buffalo felt a trip back to the Aud would do them some good, but they knew they were not playing up to par.

"We're trying to make everything perfect," said Sabre coach Floyd Smith. "I think our inexperience in the finals is showing. We have to shoot more."

"We're used to having 20 feet to wind up for shots," said wing Brian Spencer, "but they're right on top of us. So now we have to forecheck and make their defensemen make the mistakes."

But, after only three minutes of Game Three, the Sabres looked just as sluggish as before. Barber and Don "Big Bird" Saleski each tallied to make it 2–0 early on. Saleski's goal was a 70-footer that Desjardins let into the top corner. The Flyers led 3–2 after one and vet Roger Crozier came in to replace Desjardins.

The game was 4–3 in the third. The temperature in the Aud reached 90 degrees and fog swirled around the ice. A bat even found its way into the arena. Things began to get slow, but young Buffalo defenseman Bill Hajt shot one by Parent at 9:56 of the third. The teams slowly skated into an extra period.

The overtime was filled with clouds and few shots. Both teams were exhausted from the heat in the building, and the game didn't look like it would come to an end. But Rene Robert slipped a short-angle shot by Parent at 18:29 to give the Sabres their first win of the series.

The fog lifted a bit for Game Four, but the Flyers couldn't get their heads out of the clouds. Jim Lorentz, who killed the aforementioned bat in Game Three, killed the Flyers' chances with a five-foot dunk goal in the second. Buffalo won, 4–2, and the Flyers seemed relieved to exit the Aud.

"I don't think we put out our best effort here," said Lonsberry. "We've got to play better to beat them. They're too good to just roll over and die."

The Flyers got things in gear in Game Five back at the Spectrum. Minus the fog and the various flying creatures, Philly bombed the Sabres, 5–1. The grinders did most of the scoring for the Flyers, as Schultz, Dornhoefer, and Bob Kelly all put shots past Desjardins in the first. Schultz added another and the Flyers were one win away from their second Cup in as many tries. One young Flyer who was enjoying their success was defenseman Larry Goodenough.

"I'm thankful whenever I'm not scratched," said the rookie. "I took enough cheap shots about it during the regular season. I feel like I'm a part of the team now."

The Sabres wanted to spoil the Flyer party, however, and they peppered Parent with 26 shots in the first two periods to just 18 for Philly. But Bernie stood tall — yet again — and the teams went to the third tied, 0–0.

Philly went to yet another unsung hero early in the third. Bob Kelly sneaked out from behind the net and stuffed one past Crozier just 11 seconds into the final period. And Parent, as he did in Game Six one year ago, made it stand up. Bill Clement sealed it with his first of the playoffs with three minutes to play. The final was 2–0 and Philadelphia silenced the Sabres and their critics, who said their win in 1974 was a fluke.

"This proves something to me and should prove a lot to the world," said Ed Van Impe. "You don't win this thing twice in a row without a pretty damn good hockey team."

The Conn Smythe Trophy winner was also a repeat. Parent, whose goals-against average for the 15-game playoff was a paltry 1.88, took the MVP for the second time.

"The guy deserves it," said Shero. "And more. Sometimes, I think we should give him part of our paychecks. He carried our whole team when we needed him. He'd come up with one of those clutch saves that seemed to give everybody a little lift and keep them going."

"Well, this is what it's all about," said Parent. "Last year, I said you couldn't buy this feeling for a hundred million dollars. They say there's nothing like winning it the first time.

"Well, I want to tell you, they're wrong. It's sweeter the second time around."

Even the opponents couldn't help but sing the praises of the superstar goalie.

"What's that they say in Philadelphia — 'Only God Saves More Than Bernie Parent?' " said Korab, forcing a smile. "Ha, God should have a season so good."

The Flyers had one more superior season left; 1975–76. Galvanized by the positive energy from the 1975 Stanley Cup triumph, they took over the Patrick Division once more and finished the season with 51 wins, only 13 losses, and 16 ties for 118 points, 17 more than the runner-up Islanders.

Toronto nearly derailed Shero's stickhandlers in the first round, but Philly came through four games to three and then beat the Bruins in five games. That carried them into the finals against the Montreal Canadiens who finished the regular season atop the Norris Division with 127 points, nine more than the Flyers!

In Game One at The Forum, Leach and Lonsberry banged home goals against Dryden, and the Flyers looked like they were off and running to another Cup. The Canadiens rallied to tie the count at two apiece in the second period. Larry Goodenough scored for Philly early in the third, but the Habs retaliated again when Jacques Lemaire tallied at 10:02 followed by Guy Lapointe at 18:38. The Flyers lost 4–3 and never got back into the series.

Each game was close but every time the final buzzer sounded, the Flyers were on the short end of the score; 2–1 in Game Two; 3–2 in Game Three; and, finally, 5–3 in Game Four. Bernie Parent's defection from the team prior to the season had, in the end, hurt more than anyone could have imagined but, more than anything, it was a matter of the Flyers meeting a dynasty-in-the-making. Montreal would win four straight Stanley Cups beginning in 1976, and it is to the Flyers credit that they did so well in the two previous years. They were a great team in their own rambunctious way, but surely not one of those belonging in the upper echelon.

The Chicago Black Hawks, 1934

Chicago Black Hawks' First Cup Winners — 1934

Over the years the Black Hawks and New York Rangers have been among the least distinguished "established" teams in terms of regular season and Stanley Cup accomplishment. Each team has won only three Stanley Cups since their formation in the 1920s. But each also has boasted distinguished clubs that have often been overlooked. The first Windy City cup-winner in 1934 is a case in point. Coached by the impressive Tommy Gorman, the Black Hawks featured a number of fascinating skaters, not the least of whom was Lionel (Big Train) Conacher who later was voted Canada's Athlete of the Half-Century. Other notables were defenseman Art Coulter, who later captained the 1940 Ranger Cup-winners, and left wing Paul Thompson.

Easily the top player on Gorman's club was its goaltender Charlie Gardiner, who could dramatically lead his team to a championship as few ever have before or since.

The Black Hawks earned their place on the list by fusing ability with color and an unusual flair for the dramatic. And nobody did it better than Gardiner.

Unfortunately, their ability to put two solid playoff years back-to-back was strangely reminiscent of Chicago's other two Cup-winners. A year after their championship, they were wiped out by the Montreal Maroons. The reason was tragically simple — Gardiner died after the compelling Cup win and the Chicagoans never recovered from the loss. Forever after, the Black Hawks brass lamented what might have been. They could only exult over the brief year of glory that was in 1933–34.

In the 1920s, the Chicago Black Hawks were a team that many spectators had difficulty taking seriously. The reason wasn't that the Windy City representatives lacked ability; it was more a matter of the club's origin and the unique problems of survival in the hockey thicket of that time.

Chicago's application to join the NHL was accepted in 1926, the same season the New York Rangers and Detroit Cougars (later to be known as the Red Wings) entered the league. The Black Hawk entry came by way of the Pacific Northwest. Multimillionaire Major Frederic McLaughlin of Chicago purchased a minor league team known as the Portland Rosebuds.

Even his most generous followers felt that the major was a man given to grave eccentricities. The purchase of the Rosebuds was considered one of his lesser aberrations. Hockey was not regarded with enormous affection in the Chicago of the mid-twenties, and there was considerable speculation that the major had been taken for a financial ride. But the Black Hawks' performance in the rookie season indicated that the major wasn't so foolish after all.

Coached by Pete Muldoon, the Hawks finished third in the five-team American Division, ahead of Pittsburgh and Detroit and only four points behind second-place Boston. They had obtained hard-shooting "Babe" Dye from Toronto, and Dye wound up fourth in scoring in the American Division, hard on the heels of league-leading Bill Cook of the Rangers. All in all, it was a more impressive debut than Major McLaughlin's Detroit rivals could boast.

Unfortunately for Coach Muldoon, his first-round opponents in the Stanley Cup play-offs were the Boston Bruins, who had the benefit of two years of big-league play behind them. Even worse, arena-leasing problems made it impossible for the Black Hawks to play their first game in Chicago, so the series opened in New York, and the Bruins romped to a 6–1 victory. In those days, the semifinals were decided on the basis of total goals scored in two games. To win, the Black Hawks would have to make up the five-goal deficit on unfriendly Boston Garden ice. The challenge was too much for the men from Muldoon. They fought Boston to a 4–4 tie and lost the series, ten goals to five.

Although impartial observers regarded this as a not too disgraceful turn of events for the Black Hawks, the perfectionist Major McLaughlin was not at all pleased. According to hockey legend, developed by Toronto columnist, Jim Coleman, he reportedly summoned Coach Muldoon to his office and reprimanded him for allowing the Black Hawks to go to pot. "Why," said the major, "this club was good enough to finish in first place."

"You're crazy," the infuriated Muldoon reportedly shot back.

"You're fired!" shouted the offended major.

As Muldoon was walking out of McLaughlin's office, he wheeled and looked his opponent in the eye. "I'm not through with you. I'll hoodoo you. This club will NEVER finish in first place." And, so, a hockey fable was born.

Major McLaughlin laughed contemptuously as his former coach stalked out. But as the years passed, the laugh turned to a frown and the Muldoon declaration became known as "the Muldoon jinx." For, try as they might, the Black Hawks could not get past second place.

Apparently, the "hoodoo," as Coleman had put it, began taking effect as soon as Muldoon was fired. When the Black Hawks reported to training camp for the

1927–28 season, their hopes of an improved record rested on the heavy shooting of "Babe Dye," who had scored 25 goals the previous year. "From what I saw of him in Winnipeg," recalled Marvin "Cyclone" Wentworth, a Black Hawk defenseman, "he appeared to be headed for another good winter."

By this time, the Chicago players had established a reputation for horsing around, and Dye was no exception. One of his favorite foes was teammate "Cyc" Townsend, also a forward. The two would elbow and butt each other on the ice like a pair of friendly goats, and they weren't at all reluctant to throw in an occasional trip or high stick.

One afternoon, the Dye-Townsend rivalry escalated to a point where they were fouling each other on almost every rush down the ice. As Wentworth recalled, "It developed into quite a contest."

On one rush late in the workout, Dye collected the puck and began accelerating in the direction of Townsend. For some unaccountable reason, Dye kept his eyes riveted on the puck and overlooked the fact that Townsend had extended his foot as a barrier.

"Dye was caught off guard and off balance," said Wentworth. "Townsend's boot plunked into him just above the ankle, and 'Babe' went down in a heap. He couldn't get up. His leg was broken."

Nobody blamed Townsend. The trip was all part of the horseplay. Nobody really thought that the accident was particularly tragic, either. But as the weeks passed, and Dye's condition failed to improve noticeably, it became obvious that the playful trip was ruining Chicago's bid for first place. One could almost hear Pete Muldoon cackling in the distance.

"The accident closed Dye's career," said Wentworth. "He was out of hockey that winter. And though he tried two or three comebacks later, he couldn't regain his old stride."

Without Dye to bolster their attack, the Hawks finished a dead fifth in the American Division and out of the playoffs. If they had anything worth cheering about, it was a young goaltender imported from the Winnipeg Maroons. His name was Charlie Gardiner, and he was slowly developing into one of the finds of the decade. Whenever he stepped between the goal pipes, he usually wore a broad smile. At first this seemed the height of presumptuousness, since his goalkeeping was scarcely flawless. But he worked diligently at his trade. "He would come far out of the nets and sprawl on the ice in an effort to stop a score," reported Canadian writer Ron McAllister. "And even when his own team had folded up, he fought on and tried to defend his goal."

During the 1928–29 season, the Black Hawks began to take on a happier face. They were about to move their home base from the old Chicago Coliseum to a mammoth new structure that was being built on West Madison Street. The Chicago Stadium would hold more than sixteen thousand people, making it the largest rink in the NHL. However, before the stadium opened, the Hawks were pushed out of the Coliseum and were without a home rink. Circumstances finally forced them to choose a bandbox arena in Fort Erie, Ontario, for their home games. One night, while playing the Boston Bruins in this unlikely rink, the Hawks' young goalie put on a spectacular show.

Eddie Shore, the premier defenseman of the Bruins, was zooming in on

Gardiner for a shot, when the Black Hawk goalie edged out of his crease to meet him. In this way, Gardiner trimmed down the shooter's angle and forced Shore to shoot wide of the target. Undaunted, Shore pursued the puck behind the net, but Gardiner wheeled around and tripped the big Bruin.

In those days the NHL awarded one-minute penalties to goalies, and Gardiner was ordered off the ice. While he sat out his foul, teammate Wentworth moved into the nets without the benefit of a goaltender's equipment and managed to blunt the Bruins' attack. Meanwhile, the impatient Gardiner was leaning on the boards, awaiting the moment when he would be sprung from the penalty box. Finally his sentence was over, and he leaped over the wooden boards and dashed headlong for the goal.

At the moment Gardiner was released, Boston defenseman George Owen captured the puck. He carefully aimed for the four-by-six-foot opening and drilled the rubber for what appeared to be a certain goal. But it never went in.

"Gardiner," wrote Jack Laing, a reporter for the *Buffalo Courier Express*, "racing over the ice in his heavy, cumbersome pads, leaped into the air like an agile shortstop and caught the puck halfway to the net!"

By 1929, Gardiner had improved so much that he finished second to the immortal George Hainsworth of the Montreal Canadiens in the race for the Vézina Trophy (awarded annually to the goalie whose team has the fewest goals scored against it). In 1932, he would finally win the coveted prize and be named to the All-Star Team.

In the 1929–30 season, the Black Hawks finished second to Boston, albeit a distant second. But they were eliminated by the Canadiens in the Stanley Cup semifinal. A year later they were runners-up to the Bruins again. However, this time they eliminated Toronto in the first round, New York in the second round, and advanced to the cup finals against the Canadiens.

The teams split the first two games at Chicago by 2–1 scores, and then Chicago took the lead with a 3–2 victory in triple overtime at Montreal. The Hawks needed only one victory in the best-of-five series to capture their first Stanley Cup. But Montreal took the next two games, 4–2 and 2–0, and won the series, three games to two.

Still the Hawks appeared to be in grand shape. They had acquired a respected coach in Dick Irvin, and his orchestration of the Chicago players gave every indication that better things were to come. But this was too much to expect from the Black Hawk franchise. Irvin left the team during the summer to accept a similar job with the Maple Leafs. It was also too much to expect Major McLaughlin to follow Irvin with an equally competent coach. Instead, the major chose a chap named Godfrey Matheson who had absolutely no big-league hockey coaching experience.

The major was captivated by Matheson's unique game strategy. But the more experienced players immediately sensed that they had acquired a loser. Defenseman Teddy Graham once cited some of Matheson's foibles:

"Matheson had coached only kid teams that had just one shift of players — one front line, one set of defensemen, and a goalie. He simply had no experience in changing lines."

When the players reported to their new mentor for game plans, Matheson informed them that only six of them would participate in the regular season's action and the rest would be able-bodied reserves. That left about twenty players with nothing to do but watch. The nucleus of the team consisted of Gardiner in goal, Taffy Abel and Helge Bostrum on defense, and Tommy Cook at center, flanked by Paul Thompson and "Mush" March.

The extras were informed that they were to pay close attention to the big team just in case they had to substitute for any of the regulars. "It was," said Graham, "enough to make a nut house out of any hockey camp."

Matheson added to the improbable situation by referring to each of his hard-bitten pros as "mister." The nonplaying players had to be content with an occasional spin on the ice before and after the special six conducted their practices. The major had left the preseason training in Matheson's hands, and the weird arrangement would very likely had remained the same had it not been for Bill Tobin, the business manager of the Hawks. Word had filtered back to Tobin's Chicago office about Matheson's unprecedented plans, and at first Tobin considered the reports as amusing balderdash. It wasn't until he arrived at the training base that he learned the truth.

"We got in touch with Tobin as soon as he arrived," said defenseman Graham, "and let him know what was going on. It was for our good and welfare as much as his."

What followed is something that would have been more appropriate in the screenplay of a W.C. Fields movie of that era. Confronted by Tobin, Matheson promptly turned in his resignation.

The major now had an opportunity to select any one of several qualified professional coaches to handle the promising team. Instead, he succumbed to one of his quirks, a desire to have Americans rather than Canadians associated with his team. For when he bought the Hawks, McLaughlin had made up his mind that someday he would staff his team with American skaters, although it was well known that the best players were Canadians. The major wasn't ready to put an all-American team on the ice for the 1931–32 season, but he decided to solve his coaching problem by selecting a United States-born individual.

His choice as Matheson's successor was Emil Iverson, who qualified for the job on the basis of one factor — he was an American. As for his other credentials, they included a stint as a figure skater and experience as a physical culturist. There was no indication that Iverson had ever coached a hockey club.

"The fact is," said Graham, "he was the Black Hawk trainer and never coached a day in his life."

With Matheson gone and Iverson at the helm, the Black Hawks headed for Toronto to open the brand-new Maple Leaf Gardens. If they weren't the worst-prepared team ever to open an NHL season, they were very close. Their foes, finely honed to lift the curtain on their handsome new arena, were eagerly awaiting the arrival of the Chicago sextet. The date was November 12, 1931.

The largest crowd to witness an indoor event of any kind in Toronto turned out to see the Chicago massacre. All the trimmings were there, right down to the bands of the Forty-eighth Highlanders and the Royal Grenadiers playing "Happy

Days Are Here Again." The opening ceremonies included the presentation of two floral horseshoes to the Maple Leafs. Eventually, the game started.

When it was over, Iverson's ill-trained, perplexed men were the most surprised people in the building. They had beaten the Maple Leafs, 2–1.

However, nothing the Black Hawks could do seemed to alter the Muldoon curse. They finished seven points behind the American Division leaders, the New York Rangers, and were rapidly eliminated by the New Yorkers in the opening playoff round. By this time, Major McLaughlin must have been wishing that Pete Muldoon had never entered his life. However, there was little he could do now but continue to experiment with new personnel and hope for the best.

In January, 1933, the major imported Tommy Gordon to manage the team. When Gorman arrived at Chicago Stadium he immediately realized that all was not quite normal with the Black Hawks. During a workout, Gorman watched Charlie Gardiner guard the pipes at one end of the rink. But when he glanced at the other end, a strange sight met his eyes. Instead of a substitute, practice goalie, Gorman saw a full-sized scare-crow manning the nets as if it were a paid goaltender. "The major's idea," Gorman later related, "was that players would learn to shoot so they could score without hitting the dummy. It was supposed to make them increase their accuracy."

While some observers no doubt could have made a good case for using the dummy, the idea didn't appeal to Gardiner. In fact, he considered it an insult to his profession. But the dummy was there to stay. As Gorman became acclimated to the new job, he realized that it was but one of an endless list of eccentricities that cloaked the franchise.

But Gardiner, who was bombarded with shots season after season, seethed with resentment during each practice. Finally, in January, 1933, he completely lost his cool. After a workout he skated to the other end of the rink and grabbed the dummy around the waist. Holding the straw man tightly in his grip, Gardiner lifted the pseudo goaltender over the boards and hauled him right into the Black Hawks' dressing room while onlookers watched in amazement. Then he beckoned to trainer Eddie Froelich and called over Bill Tobin.

"Listen, you guys," demanded Gardiner, "give that poor fellow a good massage. He's worked his feet off. Why, I haven't done a thing today!"

The troops knew better than to rile Gardiner. He was the one piece of pure gold on the roster and the lever that could catapult them to the heights of greatness.

In 1932–33, the Hawks finished fourth and out of the playoffs. The following year they rallied and launched their most serious assault on first place. That they failed by seven points and finished second to Detroit was no fault of Gardiner's. His goaltending had reached new degrees of perfection. He allowed only 83 goals in 48 games and scored 10 shutouts. In 14 other games, he permitted just one goal.

But astute Gardiner watchers perceived that there was something unusual about the goalie's deportment, and they couldn't quite figure out what it was. Gardiner had lost his jovial manner and appeared melancholy. "He suddenly grew more serious," noted one observer. "Instead of relaxing, he kept on shouting to his teammates, more than ever before. He became intolerant of mistakes."

There were many explanations for the goalie's behavior: it was Gardiner's seventh full year as the bulwark of the Black Hawks; perhaps he was tired of his

Atlas-style chore of holding up the team. "Or perhaps," wrote Ron McAllister, "he had a premonition about the future."

Unknown to everyone, Gardiner was suffering from a chronic tonsil infection. The disease had spread and begun to cause uremic convulsions. However, the goaltender pressed on. Winning the Stanley Cup became an obsession with him, and the Black Hawks responded by defeating first the Canadiens and then the Montreal Maroons. This put them in the cup finals against the awesome Detroit Red Wings, whose firepower included Ebbie Goodfellow, Larry Aurie, and Cooney Weiland.

The best-of-five series opened in Detroit and the Black Hawks won the first game, 2–1, in double overtime. In the second, also at Detroit's Olympia Stadium, the Hawks ran away with the game, 4–1. When the teams returned to Chicago for the third, and what appeared to be the final, game, all hands were prepared to concede the Stanley Cup to the Black Hawks. NHL president Frank Calder arrived from his Montreal office to present the prize to the Hawks, and Chicago Stadium was jammed for the event.

But it was not to be Charlie Gardiner's night. His body was wracked with pain and he prayed that he might recapture his physical condition of seasons past. By this time, coach Lionel Conacher and manager Gorman realized they had a weary and tormented player. "He's bad," said Gorman, turning to Conacher in the dressing room before the teams took the ice. "What do you think we should do?"

Gardiner knew the bosses were discussing him. With great effort, he lifted himself off the bench and walked over to them. "Listen," he insisted in tremulous tones, "I want to play. Let me play — for the Cup."

Gardiner took command at the Chicago fortress for two periods. But weariness and pain overcame him in the third, and he wilted before the Detroit attack. When the final buzzer had sounded Detroit had won the game, 5–2.

When the team returned to the dressing room, Gardiner collapsed on a bench. But he wasn't totally done in. "Look," he said to his depressed teammates, "all I want is one goal next game. Just one goal and I'll take care of the other guys."

As he took his place in the goal crease on April 10, 1934, Gardiner's body was already numb with fatigue. He had expected this and vowed to himself that only self-hypnosis would enable him to overcome the challenge of his ailment. For two periods, the game remained scoreless. Early in the third period he began shouting encouragement to his players, even though it cost him valuable energy. Then Detroit captured the momentum and the Red Wings seemed to be headed for victory. But Gardiner's flailing arms and jabbing legs held them at bay.

When the regulation time ended, the score remained tied, 0–0. Now the game would go into sudden-death overtime. But every minute more meant less chance for the disabled Gardiner to prevail against his well-conditioned foe, Wilf Cude, in the Detroit nets.

The referee finally whistled the teams back on the ice for the over time. Gardiner's teammates feared that he might collapse at any moment under the strain, as he had in the preceding four periods. But when he tapped his pads in front of the net for the face-off, he was wearing a broad smile, as if he knew something. And as the players began swirling at center ice, he waved his stick to the crowd.

Red Wings and Black Hawks crunched against each other for another period, and there was still no result. Another intermission was called, and then they returned to the ice for the second sudden-death overtime period. By now Gardiner was beside himself with pain, but he would fight it as long as he could stand on his skates.

At the ten-minute mark, tiny "Mush" March of the Black Hawks moved the puck into Detroit territory and unleashed a shot at Cude. Before the goalkeeper could move, the puck sailed past him, the red light flashed, and the Black Hawks had won their first Stanley Cup. Gardiner hurled his stick in the air and then just barely made it back to the dressing room under the thick backslaps of his mates.

Less than two months later he died in a Winnipeg hospital.

The death of Gardiner was terribly symbolic for the Black Hawks. In the seasons immediately following his passing, Chicago ceased to be an effective force in the NHL. Ironically, the next time they won the Stanley Cup in 1938, they did so with an under .500 record and a coach named Bill Stewart, who was also a major league umpire.

The Ottawa Silver Seven, 1905

The First Great Ones — Ottawa Silver Seven

The hockey played at the turn of the century was a far cry from the streamlined game featured by such modern clubs as the Edmonton Oilers, New York Islanders, and Montreal Canadiens. The slapshot, for one thing, was non-existent, sticks were primitive in construction compared to the modern high-tech devices, and players wore little in the way of equipment.

While it was a different game, it still was similar in many ways to the current pastime. The idea was to put the puck behind the goaltender and into the net. Leagues had formed, and the sport already had attracted hordes of fans in major cities on both sides of the border.

By the start of the 1900s, therefore, it was possible to isolate great players and great teams, although with less precision than we do today because of the appalling lack of statistics then.

The first of the truly high-calibre teams in the pre-NHL era was based in Ottawa and bore the name, The Silver Seven. (Bear in mind that each team iced seven skaters instead of six; the seventh being a rover.) They demonstrated with Stanley Cup wins just after the turn of the century that they had the best individual players and top teamwork in Canada; and they had the silverware to prove it. From 1902–03 through 1904–05, the Silver Seven won three Stanley Cups, becoming the first team in the 20th century to do so. In short, Ottawa, the nation's capital, boasted hockey's original dynasty.

For many years prior to the formation of the NHL, teams from across Canada battled for the right to call the Stanley Cup their own. During the early 1900s, just a few years after Lord Stanley of Preston paid a little less than fifty dollars for the small silver bowl that would bear his name, The Cup became hockey's most sought after prize. Almost a century later, the Stanley Cup is still hockey's most treasured possession.

Back in the Dark Ages of ice hockey, the game was played by amateurs and the teams consisted of seven players per side. The equipment was primitive, the rinks were outdoors, and the rules were vastly different than they are today. Still, the game required a great deal of skill and the players had to have stamina and strength, much as they do today. Despite all the changes through the years, the early pioneers of hockey developed the basic concepts that have evolved into today's sophisticated game of violent speed and grace.

One of the top teams from those early days was based in the capital of Canada, the Ottawa Silver Seven. Overlooked by most hockey writers and historians, the Silver Seven was undoubtedly hockey's first dynasty. They won the Stanley Cup in 1903 and did not relinquish it until the spring of 1905, after defending their title eight times. They were the first hockey club to win the Cup three years in succession, and they featured some of the best players ever to lace up the skates. In fact, five members of the Silver Seven are now fixtures in the Hockey Hall of Fame. In spite of the fact that the Silver Seven did not win their first Cup until 1903, some people claim Lord Stanley had earmarked the trophy for the club from Ottawa when he donated it in 1893.

The captain of the Silver Seven was a forward named Alfred Smith. Alf, a native of Ottawa, joined the Silver Seven after starting his career in Pittsburgh. He led the squad to the three titles before breaking up the team and forming the Ottawa Senators, who he also guided to a Stanley Cup three years later. Smith then retired and began a coaching career that included a stint with the New York Americans. The success that Smith enjoyed as both a player and a coach led to his place in the Hall of Fame.

Another Hall of Famer who was a member of the Silver Seven was a pint-sized chap by the name of Harry Westwick. The immortal Westwick was nicknamed "The Rat" for his small stature and pesky style of play. Harry joined the Ottawa club in 1895 and had his best season ten years later, when the Silver Seven captured their third consecutive cup. In 13 games during the 1904–05 season, "The Rat" notched 24 goals playing the "rover" position. In the days of seven players to a team, the rover played both offense and defense. Westwick retired as a player in 1907 and became a National Hockey Association (which became the National Hockey League in 1917) referee. He died in 1957.

Defenseman Harvey Pulford was another member of the Silver Seven who eventually was named to the Hall of Fame. Pulford was known as one of the best body checkers of his era but he also had the reputation of being a clean and gentlemanly player. He used his body to strip opponents of the puck much the same way Leo Boivin and Denis Potvin did in later generations. A well rounded athlete, Pulford also excelled in football, lacrosse, boxing, rowing, and squash. In fact, Harvey won a championship in each one of those sports during the course of his athletic career, which lasted until he reached his fifties.

Several other members of the Silver Seven included H.L. (Hamilton Livingstone) "Billy" Gilmour, goalie Dave Finnie, and defenseman Art A. Moore. Gilmour, who attended McGill University before joining the team in 1902, was another member of the team who made the Hall of Fame. During their three-year dynasty, the Silver Seven shuffled a few other players in and out of the line up, including two of Gilmour's brothers, Siddy and Dave, backup goalie Bouse Hutton, and defensemen Jim McGee and Charles Spittal.

Of all the players who contributed to the Stanley Cup victories, perhaps the most skilled and famous player of them all was a burly, blond haired centerman by the name of Frank McGee. To this day, the exploits of McGee are still regarded as some of the most remarkable feats in Stanley Cup history. Blind in one eye, the dynamic McGee scored an amazing 14 goals in the final game of the championship series versus Dawson City in January, 1905. Eight of those goals were scored in succession in less than nine minutes, and four of them were notched in 140 seconds. His sixth, seventh, and eighth goals were netted in a span of 90 seconds, a record that still stands as the fastest hat trick in Stanley Cup play. The final score of the game was 23–2, but the contest will always be remembered as the game in which Frank McGee set several records that will never be matched. Born in the 1880s, McGee retired from hockey with a total of 71 goals in 23 regular season games and 63 goals in 22 playoff games. The legendary McGee was killed in action while serving as a lieutenant in the Canadian Army in World War I. He is now immortalized forever as one of five members of the Ottawa Silver Seven in the Hockey Hall of Fame.

The Silver Seven captured their first Stanley Cup in the winter of 1903. In a two-game series, with the total goals determining the winner, Ottawa defeated the Montreal Victorias, 9–1. The first game ended in a 1–1 tie but the Silver Seven, led by all three Gilmour brothers along with McGee and Pulford, whipped Montreal 8–0 in the second game. The win gave Ottawa the Canadian Amateur Hockey League (CAHL) championship and the rights to the Stanley Cup. It is not known if captain Smith took a lap around the pond with the Cup hoisted above his head.

Later that same year, in mid-March of 1903, the Silver Seven had to defend the cup for the first time. The first challenge for Lord Stanley's hardware came from the Rat Portage Thistles (Rat Portage later became known as Kenora, Ont.), a band of young hockey players who traveled to the nation's capital with visions of winning the Stanley Cup. Rat Portage was a proud town (Pop. 2,312) located in northwestern Ontario and the people felt their team had what it took to claim the Cup. However, once the Thistles arrived in Ottawa, they realized that the Silver Seven were every bit as good as they claimed to be, as the home team won both games of the series, thus defending their championship for the first time. The second game of that series featured one of the most unusual events in Stanley Cup history when, during the height of the action, the puck disappeared through a hole in the ice. It is unlikely that this will ever happen again with the Stanley Cup on the line.

When the 1903–04 season began, the Silver Seven had withdrawn from the CAHL. After some controversy and much discussion, the trustees of the Cup allowed Ottawa the right to defend the trophy. And defend is just what they did.

The first challenge of the new season came from the Winnipeg Rowing Club but the result was the same as the year before. The Silver Seven defeated their challengers two games to none, with the first victory coming in December of 1903 and the clincher coming in early January of 1904. The following month, the Silver Seven beat the OHA champions from Toronto, the Marlboroughs. The Toronto team had one of the true stars of the time on their side, a fellow by the name of Tom Phillips who was, coincidentally, originally from Rat Portage. Unfortunately for Toronto, Phillips suffered an injury in the first game and he was unable to return for the second game. The Marlies may have been the champs of their league, but without Phillips they proved to be no match as the Silver Seven swept the two games, defending their title for the third time in less than a year.

The champions from Ottawa were set to take on the Wanderers from Montreal after disposing of the Toronto team, but a question of home ice led to such a debate that the series was called off. This was the second time in the history of Stanley Cup action that a series was called off. When the 1919 series was cancelled it was due to a flu bug that infected many of the players.

In March of 1904, the champs from Ottawa faced their most formidable challenge since winning the Cup a year earlier. The Manitoba and Northwestern League champion Brandon Wheat Kings, featuring a young defenseman named Lester Patrick, came calling for their crack at the Cup. Although the Silver Seven defended the Cup again by winning both games (by scores of 6–3 and 9–3), Patrick began making his mark on the game of ice hockey during this series. During one of the games, Lester, who is credited with being the original "rushing defenseman," became the first blueliner to score a goal in Stanley Cup play. Oddly enough, it was also during this series that Patrick stood in as the Wheat King's goalie when the regular net minder, Doug Morrison, took a penalty. During those days, goalies had to serve their own penalties and be replaced by another member of the team. In this instance, Patrick, who nearly a quarter of a century later would come off the bench to play goal for the New York Rangers and inspire them to a Stanley Cup, stepped in and guarded the cage. For the record, he stopped the only shot he faced, while Morrison paid his dues in the sin bin.

Despite the ground breaking performance of Lester Patrick, the Ottawa Silver Seven had once again defended their Stanley Cup, and were now the champs for the second straight year. Going into the 1904–05 season, the Silver Seven knew there would again be several more teams who would attempt to wrest the prized possession from the capital city. Little did they know, however, that one of the challenges would come from a band of hockey players who would travel more than 4,000 miles by land, sea, and dog sled to vie for the Cup.

The adventures of the Dawson City Klondikes and their quest for hockey's treasured silver cup is among the most incredible tales in the history of the game. Dawson City was the hub of the Klondike mining region and nearly 4,000 miles away from Ottawa, but the hockey fans in the hills of the Yukon had heard of the Stanley Cup and they thirsted for a chance to make it their own. A wealthy prospector named Colonel Joe Boyle formed the Klondikers by gathering up a collection of men who had come to the region in search of gold but were now looking for a way out. Mr. Boyle financed nearly $3,000 for the team's journey, and on December 19, 1904, with the town's entire population cheering them on, the Dawson City Klondikers began the longest and most bizarre trip any team would ever make trying to win the Stanley Cup.

The first 125 miles of the trek had to be covered by dog sled. Fortified by whiskey to brave the 20-degree-below-zero temperatures, the happy band of hockey players and their dogs traveled more than 90 miles in the first two days. But the third day saw the men and the dogs suffering from exhaustion, and they were so severely frostbitten that many of the players actually removed their boots so that their blistered feet would get some relief. As a result of the pain caused by the frostbite, newspapers and socks were all they could bear to keep on their feet.

The first stop for our friends from the Yukon was a port city on the southern coast of Alaska, called Skagway, which was the only exit to the rest of the world. Due to the frigid weather conditions, the dog sled caravan had not been able to travel as fast as they had planned, and by the time they arrived in Skagway, they had missed their boat to Seattle — by a mere two hours. Undaunted, the troops set up camp and waited five days before they were finally able to board the next vessel to Seattle. On New Year's Eve, a coal scow called the S.S. Dolphin took the team to Seattle where they boarded a train for the 200 mile trip to Vancouver. From there, they caught a Canadian Pacific mainliner eastbound to Ottawa. While on board the train, many of the players exercised by skipping rope in the trains smoking parlor.

The 24-day marathon finally ended when the Klondikers arrived in the capital city on January 12, 1905, one day before the best-of-three series with the Silver Seven was to begin. All the time the challengers were traveling by dog sled, boat, and train to make it to Ottawa, the home team champs were working out on their own ice, eating home cooked meals at night, and sleeping in their own beds. Nobody but Colonel Boyle gave his boys much of a chance. They were a group of unknown hockey players from all over Canada and the Silver Seven were, after all, the defending world champions.

Though the Klondikers put up more of a challenge than most people had expected, the Silver Seven won the first game by a convincing score of 9–2. Several of the players on the Dawson City squad were probably decent hockey players. Among them was a fuzzy-faced seventeen year old goalie by the name of Albert Forest. To this day, Forest is still listed as the youngest player in Stanley Cup history and the Three-Rivers, Quebec native earned the respect of the Silver Seven despite allowing nine goals.

Some of the other members of the Klondike squad included defensemen Jim Johnson, Dr. Randy McLennan, and the talented Lorne Hanney. Among the forwards were guys like George Kennedy, Hector Smith, and rover, Dave Fairburn. Norm Watts was another winger on the squad and it was his remarks regarding Ottawa's Frank McGee that have gone down in infamy as the words that stirred the sleeping bear.

Following the first game, Watts, who had opened a four-stitch gash on the head of Art Moore with his stick during the contest, publicly questioned the ability of McGee. Since McGee had only scored once, Watts seemed to imply that Frank McGee was a bit overrated. Though he was blind in one eye, the husky McGee could hear perfectly with both ears. In the second game, after hearing Watts' comments, he proved why he was considered one of the game's first superstars. He was unstoppable in the second game. He scored four goals in the first half and started the second half with his fifth, sixth, seventh, and eighth. By the time the game was over, McGee had scored 14 goals including the fastest hat trick ever recorded in the Stanley Cup play. The Silver Seven went on to a 23–3 thrashing of Dawson City and McGee set several scoring records that will never be threatened. The Champions from Ottawa had defended the Stanley Cup for the fifth consecutive time and the Klondikers were faced with the prospect of the trip back to the Yukon. Although they never even mounted a serious threat for possession of the Cup, the Dawson City Klondikers will always be remembered for their fantastic voyage just for a shot at the trophy.

The next challenge for the Ottawa Silver Seven came in March of that same year in the form of their old nemesis, the Thistles of Rat Portage. This time around, the Thistles felt they were more prepared as they had picked up ex-Wanderer Tom Phillips. Phillips, who was considered the most accurate shooter of his time, scored five goals as Rat Portage took the first game of the best-of-three series. With their backs against the wall, the Silver Seven held Phillips scoreless in the second game, and prevailed by a score of 4–2. The defending champs played more physical in the second game and used the slow ice surface to their advantage. Some stories claim that a few Ottawa partisans poured salt on the ice the night before in order to slow down the challengers, who won the first game by outskating Ottawa.

In the deciding contest, the Silver Seven won 5–4 on the strength of McGee's third goal, shortly after Phillips had scored to even things up. For the third year in a row, the Ottawa Silver Seven had the Stanley Cup all to themselves and there was no telling who was going to take it from them. They had beaten some of the best teams from all corners of Canada for three years running and their line up still featured several of the game's best players.

The following season saw the champs defend the title two more times before they finally relinquished it early in 1906. The seventh title defense came when the Silver Seven beat Queens University in two straight games. Queens University was the champion of the OHA but they put up little resistance as Alf and Harry Smith scored 15 goals between them in leading Ottawa. The eighth team that the Silver Seven defeated during their reign as champions came from the nearby railway town of Smith Falls. As was the case against Dawson City, Frank McGee was a one man team versus Smith Falls and their goalie Percy LeSeuer and the Silver Seven breezed to a two game sweep.

The final chance Ottawa had to defend the Stanley Cup was against the Montreal Wanderers, who Lester Patrick now played for. The series was going to consist of two games with the winner having scored the most goals and, after Montreal won the first game by a score of 9–1, things did not appear too good for the Silver Seven. In Game Two however, with Percy LeSeuer now in goal after being acquired at the conclusion of the previous series, the champs jumped out to a 9–1 lead just as Montreal had in the first game, and suddenly things were all tied up! But leave it to the amazing Lester Patrick to bring Ottawa back to reality. With less than two minutes remaining in the game, Patrick snapped home two goals past LeSeuer and clinched the Stanley Cup for Montreal. After almost four years and eight successful defenses, the Cup had been snatched away from the Ottawa Silver Seven.

Although they were only amateurs playing during the adolescence of ice hockey, the Ottawa Silver Seven were a great team. In a game that eventually would feature the dynasties of the Montreal Canadiens, the New York Islanders, and the Edmonton Oilers, the Silver Seven were hockey's first dynasty. They took on all comers and played a brand of hockey that set trends and helped mold the game. The great players like Frank McGee and Harvey Pulford will always be remembered for their scoring and checking abilities. The City of Ottawa may never get another chance to capture the Stanley Cup, but the Silver Seven carved a notch in hockey history that will always be considered among the greatest achievements in Stanley Cup history.

The United States Olympic Team, 1980

The Miraclemen of Lake Placid — 1980 U.S. Olympians

All the world loves an underdog — except, of course, the favorite who winds up being defeated by same — and that explains why the 1980 Olympic hockey team from the United States took on saintly appearances following the unforgettable gold medal victory at Lake Placid.

Uncle Sam's skaters proved not only to be memorable but also very significant. They opened the games for Americans into the NHL, and forever changed the league's attitude toward the professional qualities of skaters from below the 49th parallel. From 1980 on, Americans became more and more prominent in the NHL and by 1989, U.S. citizens such as Chris Chelios (Canadiens), Ed Olczyk (Maple Leafs), Joe Mullen (Flames), and Jimmy Carson (Oilers) were among the best players on Canadian teams.

In addition, the 1980 U.S. team introduced the advanced coaching techniques of Herb Brooks to the hockey world. Brooks broke from the traditional up-and-down NHL methods and developed a weaving style of play that matched the best the Soviets had to offer. He later brought his hockey philosophy to the NHL where he further changed the mode of play.

More than anything, the American win underlined the possibilities of an underdog team that plays like a *team*, in contrast to a considerably more powerful foe loaded with individual stars. Emotion can do wonders to a hockey club if properly channeled, and nobody refined the rah-rah spirit to proper advantage more than Brooks and his boys. They weren't the best team to play in the Olympics, but they certainly could go down as the most spirited of the underdog gold medalists.

The Dallas Cowboys have long been considered "America's Team," but for two weeks in February 1980, 20 college kids not only became America's Team, they became American heroes.

During the XIIIth Winter Olympic Games in Lake Placid, New York, the United States hockey team not only pulled off the greatest upset in Olympic history, they put USA hockey on a higher plateau, and forever opened the door to the NHL for American-born players.

When the United States team arrived in Lake Placid for the games, not many international hockey experts thought much of their chances. Since the inception of the Winter Games, the USA had one gold medal (in 1960), four silver medals (1924, '52, '56, '72), and one bronze (1936). During the previous Olympics, the U.S. finished fourth at Innsbruck, Austria. But there was one who believed he could make a respectable showing. He had an innovative system and was the nation's most successful College hockey coach at the time. He was Herb Brooks, head coach of the University of Minnesota Golden Gophers.

Brooks was no stranger to the USA Olympic hockey program. He was the last man cut from the gold medal team of 1960. He played on the team in 1964, and again in 1968, including five appearances with the National Team. A native of St. Paul, Minnesota, Brooks played his high school hockey at St. Paul - Johnson under Minnesota hockey legend John Mariucci, and was part of the state championship team his senior year. He moved on to the University of Minnesota where he played three years. Brooks began his coaching career at the University of Minnesota as a part-time assistant coach to Glen Sonmor in 1971–72. He then became head coach during his seven years there. He guided the Gophers to National Championships in 1974, '76, and '79, as well as the NCAA runner-up in '75.

Brooks was interviewed in Chicago by the Amateur Hockey Association of the United States (AHAUS) in 1978, and was named head coach of the 1980 Olympic team in February of that year. Shortly thereafter he formed an advisory staff to scout America's top amateur players from the college ranks. The staff included college coaches from around the country, as well as two pro scouts. One was Jack Button of the NHL Central Scouting Board, and the other was Rudy Migay, a scout with the Buffalo Sabres.

Throughout the remainder of 1978 and the first half of 1979, there was constant communication by Brooks and the advisory board. "That advisory board was the first of its kind, and it proved invaluable," said Brooks. "It was our feeling that there was a tremendous resource in American hockey, and to get them all on board pulling and pushing in one direction was very important. Sometimes regional favoritism comes to the forefront because of lack of communication, and that's not what we wanted."

One of the early problems in unifying the team was the problem of East vs West, the east coast players and the mid-west players. "I had grown up in Boston watching eastern college hockey," said defenseman Jack O'Callahan. "My impression at that time was that any player or coach from out west was a jerk, no matter who he was. It took us a while to settle the problem, especially since out of that original 30, 23 or 24 were from the west." Brooks solved that problem very quickly.

From a coaching standpoint, narrowing this team down from 30 players to the final 20 was, at times, gutwrenching. "When you get down to the final 4 or 5 cuts, it's really tough. You have your top 12 or 14 players, but after that it gets difficult," said Brooks. "We were looking for the right mold, the style of player that fits our system." One of those players who almost missed the final 20, and the initial 72, was Mike Eruzione.

"Rizzy" played his college hockey at Boston University, and was on the team that won the 1978 National Championship. He went on to join the Toledo Golddiggers of the IHL for the 1978–79 season. When the candidates for invitations to the '79 sports festival were being reviewed, Eruzione was virtually ignored. "Mike had a couple of black marks against him on our list, but Jack Parker (of BU), and Bill Cleary (Harvard), who were part of the advisory staff from the east, spoke very highly of Mike," said Brooks. "He wasn't a great skater, but he was older, had experience, and was a natural catalyst and leader."

Eruzione was in Toledo while this was brewing and he decided it would be in his best interests to see Brooks personally. He drove to St. Paul to see Brooks at the NCAA final four. "Mr. Brooks, I'm Mike Eruzione" he said to Brooks, while extending his hand.

"Mr. Brooks is my dad, I'm Herb" was Brooks' reply.

Rizzy thought to himself, "Oh god, this guy is crazy; this will be a long year!"

Another problem was defection from the Olympic team to the NHL by the festivals' top players such as Mark Johnson, Neal Broten, and Rob McClanahan. Agent Art Kaminsky represented a majority of the top players, and it took some strong persuasion to show Kaminsky that the pre-Olympic schedule would best benefit his clients, and prepare them for pro careers. From that moment on, Kaminsky became part of the fold. If Kaminsky hadn't endorsed the program, Brooks would not have had the players. After showing his plan to NHL GMs, those who had prospects on the team agreed that the Olympic team was a good idea.

Until that time, the zenith of an American players' career was playing on the Olympic team. While American players like Joey Mullen and Rod Langway had turned pro, the door was not entirely open to the Canadian dominated NHL. "I felt that the one accomplishment that I could make in hockey was to play on the Olympic team, to represent my country in Lake Placid," said O'Callahan. "At the time the pros were still a dream, not a reality."

Ken Morrow was another who felt the Olympic experience was important. "For me, it wasn't all patriotic, though that was a part of it. But playing for the Olympic team was a bridge to the NHL, and it was much better than playing in the minors."

The pre-olympic schedule consisted of games with the CHL, NHL, college teams, games in Europe, and a pre-Olympic tourney at Lake Placid just before Christmas. All in all, they would play 60 games in over four months, culminating with a game at Madison Square Garden against the Soviet Olympic Team.

It was during those 60 games that the players were introduced to Brooks's new system of hockey. At the time it was called "The Weave," for lack of a better name. Brooks felt that if the U.S. was going to compete against Europeans, they had to play like Europeans. "I wanted to develop the most effective system of hockey, mixing the Canadian school of thought with the European school of thought," said Brooks. "From the Canadian system we took our defensive strategies, and from the Europeans, we used the offense. In essence, we didn't have left wings, centers, and right wings, we had interchangeable forwards."

The tour of Europe was gruelling, with Brooks enforcing his theories of conditioning, skating, and fast-paced practices. If there was a time when the patience of the team was tested, it was during the time overseas. But the team stayed together, and the family unity was formed.

Just before the Lake Placid Invitational tournament in December of 1979, Eruzione was voted captain. For a player who was almost excluded from the tryouts, that was quite an accomplishment. At the tournament, the United States rolled over the Canadians, Swedes, Czechoslovakia, and the Soviet Union. But there was a catch here. The other teams, with the exception of Canada, had sent their second teams, not their Olympic teams.

Finally, after what seemed like an eternity, the pre-season concluded. All that remained was the game with the Soviets at Madison Square Garden on February 9, 1980.

The U.S. team brought a 42–14–3 pre-Olympic record into that game. The players were feeling pretty good about themselves. Two days earlier Brooks worried that his team was too confident. "We might need a good kicking to bring us down to earth," he said. On that night, 11,241 fans witnessed that kicking.

When the dust had cleared, the Soviets had emerged with a 10–3 win, powered by three goals from Vladimir Krutov. As well as losing to the Russians, the Americans also lost a player, defenseman Jack O'Callahan. Soviet defenseman Vyacheslav Fetisov checked "O'C" as he tried to complete an end to end rush. O'Callahan went up, and came down on the knee he had hurt four months earlier. As the team headed for Lake Placid the next day, Brooks had an important decison to make. Does he take Jack off the roster and fill his spot with a player on the taxi squad, or does he take Jack to Lake Placid as the sixth defenseman, and hope his knee recuperates fast? O'Callahan had earned his place on the team. Brooks kept him aboard.

The 10–3 drubbing hardly upset the Americans. Instead, it helped them. Brooks told his players that after the initial blitz, they had played the Soviets even.

"If anything, we just laughed about it," said O'Callahan. "We just got blown out of the rink."

The U.S.A. opened up the tournament against the Swedes on February 12, the day before the official opening of the games. Only 4,000 people showed up at the brand new Olympic Ice Center. The Americans were seeded seventh out of the 12 teams in the tournament. They were one of six teams in the Blue division, along with (in order of seed) Czechoslovakia, Sweden, West Germany, Norway, and Rumania. Most figured the US to finish third in their division. Going into the games, the Americans had a very loose feeling among them. After all, no one thought they would win anything. The players felt that they were prepared to do their best. They might lose 10–3 to everyone, but they were going to try their best.

Starting in goal for the U.S.A. was a 22-year-old native of Boston named Jim Craig. While at Boston University, he backstopped the 1978 Terriers to the

National Championship, beating Brooks's sextet on the way. He was a standup goaltender who had played the majority of the pre-tournament games. He had played in the 1979 World Cup, the last team Brooks coached before the 1979 sports festival.

Sweden opened the scoring at 13:34 of the first period when Sutre Andersson tipped Lars Molin's backhand past Craig for a 1–0 lead. After being outshot in the first period, 16–7, the Americans settled down in the second period and the opportunities came. With 45 seconds left in the period, defenseman Mike Ramsey started out of the American zone. He threw a pass that hit the skate of a Swedish defenseman and caromed to Dave Silk behind the Swedish defense. Silk found himself two on the goalie with Mark Johnson. "Silky" came in on the net and snapped a ten-footer past Swedish goalie, Pelle Lindbergh to tie the game.

The Swedes regained the lead when Tomas Erickson scored from out in front at 4:45 of the third period. Still, the Americans pressed on. A Mark Johnson slapshot narrowly missed as it hit the far post early in the period. With 41 seconds to go in the game and a faceoff in the Swedish zone, Brooks pulled Craig in favor of an extra attacker. Mark Pavelich won the faceoff and drew it back to the point for Ramsey. His shot was blocked at the point, and it caromed cross ice to Bill Baker, who dumped it around the boards. Buzz Schneider picked it up behind the net and skated towards the far side. He gave a soft pass to Pavelich at the side of the faceoff circle. "Pav" sent a cross ice pass where Baker was, but Baker was in the process of starting out of the zone. Seeing the pass, he changed directions, and let go a 45-foot blast that beat Lindbergh to the glove side at 19:33, and the same ended a 2–2 tie.

"In that game, we got great goaltending from Jimmy," said the injured O'Callahan. "We were not disappointed to tie, just happy not to lose. I figured Sweden was the second best team in the tournament, and we didn't lose."

The hero for the U.S.A., Billy Baker, had played for Brooks at the University of Minnesota, and captained the team that won the National Championship in 1979. In the typical fashion of a Brooks-trained player, he was modest about the big goal. "I hoped the goal against Sweden would enable us to go into the Czechoslovakian game with a little more confidence, and a little more momentum. If that's what it does, then I'm happy I could've contributed."

The U.S. approached the game with the Czechs the same way as they approached the Swedes, relaxed. This time, they were on an emotional high. Most hockey experts figured the Czechs for the Silver Medal, and predicted that no one would beat the Russians. The Czechs had one of the top lines in the world, with the Stastny brothers, Anton, Peter, and Marian. Other than momentum, the U.S. carried a slight psychological edge.

Looking back to the early 1970s, the United States had played remarkably well against the Czechs. No one could explain it, but it was there on paper. Before the game, Brooks told his team that they were going up against a tiger. "Go up to the tiger, spit in his eye, and shoot the bastard!" Brooks told his team. And they listened attentively as they did throughout the tournament.

The Czechs slightly outplayed the U.S. in the first period, though it was 2–2 at the end of one. In the second period, the U.S. mustered only five shots on goal, but connected twice to take a 4–2 lead into the third. The Americans came out flying and broke the game wide open when Phil Verchota scored at 2:59, and Buzz Schneider got his second of the game at 3:59 to make it 6-2. Schneider, and his linemates John Harrington and Mark Pavelich were predominantly a checking line, but that night they took it to the Czechs offensively, accumulating two goals and five assists. Craig stopped 28 shots as the U.S. won 7-3.

Coach Brooks's pre-tournament goal was to make the medal round. For that, they needed at least three, if not four, points from the games with Sweden and Czechoslovakia to put them in a position to do so. The tie and the win gave Brooks his three points, and the U.S. was rolling. The next opponent was Norway, which had tied the U.S. 3-3 on the European tour.

The Americans came out flat in the first period, showing an obvious emotional letdown. Geir Myhre scored at 4:19 to give the Norwegians the early lead. It stood as the only goal of the period.

"Herb came into the locker room and flipped out, telling us that we weren't that good, and we shouldn't rely on our talent," said Eruzione. The approach worked, as Mark Johnson scored less than three minutes into the second period.

"After the first period, we sat down in the locker room and said if we're going to win this game, we have to rely on hard work," said Johnson. "If we played our system, we'd win the contest." Schneider and Eruzione added goals that period, and the U.S. added two third period goals to skate off with a hard fought 5-1 decision.

The next challenge would be from Rumania, a team that was vastly outmatched by the Americans. Buzz Schneider, the 25-year-old native of Babbit, Minnesota, continued his outstanding play by notching a goal and an assist in the first period, as the United States built a 2-0 lead. Schneider, like Eruzione and Morrow, was one of the "old men" of the team, and someone Brooks looked to for leadership. Like his coach, Schneider was no stranger to the Olympic team, having played for the 1976 club under Coach "Badger" Bob Johnson, Mark's father.

The U.S.A. had the lead 4-1 after two periods. At 8:14 of the third period, Steve Christoff scored to make it 5-1, with an assist going to Jack O'Callahan. O'C was playing in his first game of the tournament. Some doubted he'd play in the games at all, but the dream of playing in the Olympics was not about to vanish because of a hurt knee.

When O'Callahan got to Lake Placid, he went right to the American medical staff, and started a power rehab, working on the knee up to five times a day. After receiving clearance to skate, O'C worked hard to get into playing shape, and Brooks rewarded his efforts by giving him his place on the American defense.

The Americans defeated the Rumanians 7-2, outshooting them 51-21. This was now a different team than the raw recruits who lost 10-3 to the Soviets just a week-and-a-half earlier. Brooks was now faced with a problem that he never expected. Overconfidence!

"Here we are, 3-0-1, and people are talking medal round and gold medal and we're getting a little cocky, a little overconfident," O'Callahan recalled.

Awaiting the Amricans were the West Germans. They were 1-3, but a better team than their record indicated.

Brooks was wary of the West Germans, because they enjoyed the same advantage over the United States that the Americans had held over the Czechs.

And look what happened there. A second problem arose during the pre-game warmups. A shot by captain Eruzione hit Craig in the neck. If there's one thing a goalie fears in a game, it's being struck in the head. But if it happens in practice or warmups, it not only infuriates him, but can throw him off his game.

Sure enough, the West Germans scored on their first shot on goal, *from the red line!* On the bench, Eruzione bowed his head and thought to himself, "Oh god, what have I done?!"

That goal at 1:50, as well as another through a screen at 19:45 staked the West Germans to a 2–0 lead at the end of the first period. After the poor first period against Sweden, Brooks used Rob McClanahan as a guinea pig to get at the team. The much publicized blowout obviously worked because the team came back strong. In this instance, the coach stayed quiet. He calmly told the squad to stay within its system, and the chances would come.

Through the first four games, the United States had yet to be held scoreless in the second or third period. This night would prove no exception. McClanahan got the United States on the board at 7:40, scoring off a semi-breakaway to pull the Americans to within one. With 1:30 remaining in the period, Neal Broten tied the game, and the U.S. never looked back. McClanahan scored again in the third period, again on a breakaway, and Phil Verchota put the U.S. up 4–2. That's the way it ended, and the Americans finished the Blue division round robin 4–0–1.

The Americans and the Swedes were tied for first place, but the Swedes were awarded the top spot thanks to better goal differential. Both the U.S. and Sweden went into the medal round with a point, by virtue of their 2–2 tie opening night. From the Red division, the Soviet Union (5–0) and Finland (3–2) advanced to medal round, with the Soviets having two points and the Finns none, because of the Soviets' triumph over the Finns during the round robin. The run for the gold began on Friday, February 22 as the United States faced the Soviet Union, who had outscored their opponents 51–11 through the first five games.

To hockey fans worldwide, the Russians had taken on all aspects of gods on ice. Since their masterful eight-game series with Team Canada in the 1972 Super Series, the Soviets had dominated the international hockey scene. In 1979, they came to Madison Square Garden for a best-of-three series against a team of NHL All-Stars and won the series 2–1, taking the deciding game 6–0.

The Soviets were captained by 35 year old Boris Mikailov, competing in his fourth Olympics. To the Soviet hockey fans back home he was known as "the Gordie Howe of Gorky Park." They had a 22-year-old left winger named Helmut Balderis, nicknamed Elektrichka, the Electric Train. With his blazing speed, he could have made speedster Mark Messier look slow. On defense was 30 year old Valery Vasilev, who owned a slap shot as loud as gunfire. But their strongest position was goal. At that time, Vladislav Tretiak was the world's premier goaltender. As a rookie, he almost stole the Super Series back in 1972, and had proven he was the international elite puck-stopper ever since. Surrounding that nucleus were such Soviet stars as Vladimir Krutov, Sergei Makarov, Alexsi Kasatonov, and Vyaceslav Fetisov.

If Brooks's goal was making the medal round, he certainly knew he would end up facing the Russians there. With this in mind, Brooks studied the Russians, and for the sake of his players, he humanized them. The Soviets were merciless in crushing Japan 16–0, beating the Netherlands 17–4, and routing Poland 8–1. But they had struggled against Canada, and had to come from behind in the third period. Even the world's best team can have an off day, but they even won on those days too.

Brooks picked up on their unenthusiastic attitude on the ice. The Russians had a machine, not a team. He poked fun at the Soviets when discussing them with his players. "Look at that Mikhailov, he thinks he's a god out there," Brooks told his boys. "He looks like Stan Laurel." Going into the game, the Americans felt that the Russians were there to win the gold medal, but not to earn it. Be that as it may, it was the same team that routed the U.S. 10–3 two weeks before.

With 10,000 people watching, the Americans set out to do the impossible. The game was scoreless until the 9:12 mark, when Krutov deflected Kasatonov's shot from the point behind Craig for a 1–0 lead. The Americans were well aware that they couldn't afford to fall behind by two goals, or more. They clawed at the Russian Bear, and with 14 minutes gone in the period, they inflicted their first wound.

Mark Pavelich, who already had a game-tying assist (Sweden), and a game-winning assist (Czechoslovakia) in the tournament, intercepted a pass at the American blue line. He headed along the wall with Schneider on the opposite boards, moving up with him. After crossing center ice, he threaded the needle to Schneider who crossed the Soviet line full speed. Schneider fired a routine slap shot, and surprisingly, the puck hit the net, and the score was tied. In describing the goal, ABC hockey commentator Al Michaels exclaimed at the time, "that's not the type of goal you expect Tretiak to give up!"

The tie didn't last long. Three-and-a-half minutes later, Makarov picked up a deflected pass from Golikov and snapped a ten-footer pass a startled Craig to give the Soviets a 2–1 lead. It stayed that way through the next few minutes, and it seemed the Americans would be content to take a one goal deficit into the locker room. With eight seconds to go, Ken Morrow fed Davey Christian heading out of the U.S. zone. Tretiak, in his book "The Legend" describes the play.

"Christian fired the puck at me from center ice. I made a sloppy save and the rebound went out in front of me, but there were no opponents near me anyway. But out of nowhere, came Mark Johnson."

Mark busted in from the neutral zone and got between two Soviet defensemen, gathered the puck and skated in on Tretiak. He made a small fake and slid the disk past Tretiak with one second to play in the period. Time expired as the puck lay behind the bewildered Tretiak, and the U.S. took a 2–2 tie, plus a lot of excitement to the dressing room for the intermission.

When they reached the ice for the second period, the Americans noticed #20 was missing from the Soviet crease. Instead, they saw a #1. Could it be true, yes it was. The Soviet coach, Victor Tikhanov replaced Tretiak in goal with backup Vladimir Myshkin.

The bear was wounded, and now it was time to go for the kill. But the only killing the American team and crowd witnessed was the death of their momentum. The Soviets played a masterful period, forcing the Americans to take foolish penalties. John Harrington was called for holding by referee Karl-Gustav Kaisla at

0:55. West German coach, Hans Rampf, had said at the conclusion of their game with the U.S. that the referee had been very lackadaisical in calling the Americans for penalties. Rampf went further saying the Americans will not win if they take penalties.

Out came the vaunted Soviet power play.

It took a little over a minute and a half for the Russians to score. Alexander Maltsev took a pass from Krutov at center ice and zipped behind the American defense. Maltsev showed that goalies are virtually defenseless when facing him on a breakaway. He glided around Craig and scored to give the Soviets the lead. After that, the Soviets threw a curtain around the American team, allowing it only two feeble shots on goal. Through two periods, the U.S.S.R. had outshot the U.S. 30–10.

Brooks knew the Americans couldn't afford to give up another goal. Craig had been outstanding and the Americans' conditioning was superb. They had skated stride for stride with the Russians. What the Americans needed was a spark to get them going. The longer they trailed, the stronger the Soviet armor would get.

With time running out on a power play, the Americans' Dave Silk crossed the Soviet line, and tried to hit Johnson with a pass as he headed for the net. The pass struck the stick of defenseman Sergei Pervuhkin, and caromed to Johnson. He snapped it quickly past an astonished Myshkin to tie the game at 8:39. "I felt that if we were winning, or at least tied, with nine minutes to go, we could beat them," said Eruzione.

With the score tied, "Rizzy" was sitting on the bench when Brooks called for his line to replace Schneider's. Buzz came to center ice and shot on goal, then headed to the bench. Eruzione jumped off the bench and joined the play. Fortunately for the Americans, Schneider's linemates didn't see him go off and chased the puck in the Soviet end. Myshkin had deflected the shot to the corner, and Harrington arrived first. He pushed the rubber along the boards to Pavelich. Surrounded by two Soviet players, "Pav" delivered a soft pass to the top of the circle — and Eruzione. The captain curled, used a Russian defenseman as a screen, and drove home the goal since labeled "the shot heard 'round the world."

The scoreboard read U.S.A. 4, U.S.S.R. 3. Time left, 10:00: 'I picked up the puck and thought two things," said Eruzione in describing the play. "The first was if the defenseman charges me, I'll pass it, and if he stays put, I'll shoot it. The goalie gave me the whole far side. As crazy as it sounds, I knew from the instant I let it go, it was going in. I just felt it.'

The toughest part was yet to come; holding the lead. Ken Dryden, the ex-Montreal Canadiens goaltender, was "color" commentator for ABC during the games. A veteran of many encounters with the Soviets, he told the viewers during those last ten minutes that the one thing about the Russians is they never allow you the chance to feel good. "Whether you're ahead by one goal or two, they can strike so quickly."

Craig agreed. "I knew that these guys could score seven goals in three minutes, but my guys were throwing their bodies all over the place, blocking shots with legs, heads, anything." Time seemed to move on the clock like a turtle in the home stretch. The Soviets were repulsed at every turn and at the five minute mark they launched a succession of successful counterattacks that worked until the final minute. Finally, with thirty seconds to go, the U.S. struggled to get the puck out of its zone.

As the crowd counted down the final seconds, Al Michaels shouted "Do you believe in miracles, YES!!" And with that, it was over.

The American players charged at Jim Craig, who had stopped 36 Soviet shots. Jack O'Callahan and Mike Ramsey fell to the ice in joy. Outside the Oympic Ice Arena, cheers and chants of U.S.A., U.S.A., U.S.A. could be heard on many streets. Fireworks lit up the sky like the fourth of July.

Inside, the Soviets stood motionless at center ice awaiting the traditional post-game handshake. Their faces were blank as they stared into the American celebration. The Soviets had never witnessed such an uproar, and on the handshake line, the first player Eruzione shook hands with even had a smile on his face.

In the Americans' locker room, tears of joy blended with screams of "We beat the Russians, I can't believe we beat the Russians!" President Jimmy Carter phoned Coach Brooks to congratulate the team. Brooks tried to quell the celebration, warning there was one more game to win, but his cries fell upon deaf ears.

"This is like a bunch of Canadian college football players beating the Pittsburgh Steelers," said Craig.

Meanwhile, Ken Morrow had walked out a side door to the Olympic Village to ice a sore shoulder. As he lay in bed listening to the radio, he bagan to comprehend the magnitude of the victory. Every station had listeners calling in to talk about the game. The Americans still had one more game to play. It would be on Sunday morning at 11 A.M. against Finland. Morrow remembers that one fan called in to say that "It didn't matter if they were playing the Montreal Canadiens on Sunday, they'd beat'em!"

On the other side, the Russians tried to analyze their defeat. TASS, the official Soviet news agency, released a statement concerning the issue: "Mistakes by the defense and goalies, as well as elements of confusion and a lack of concentration caused the defeat. To lose 4–3 to a team that we beat recently in New York is not easy to explain."

Sure it was, "we wanted it more," said Eruzione.

The next day at practice, Brooks skated the team through gruelling workouts. He held team meetings, before practice and after practice. There was no way he was going to let them get cocky, not with the gold medal on the line. "He skated our asses off," said O'Callahan. "For all those people who thought we went into that game cocky, overconfident, or on a downward side, forget it!."

Brooks let it be known that they were still grunts, and that they hadn't won anything yet. If any of the players thought Brooks was their friend now, they were sadly mistaken. He was still the coach, no matter who they had beaten the night before. It was still Herb's team.

Brooks remembers that practice. It was late morning and reporters were all over the Olympic Ice Center. The coach then employed on his players the last psychological tool to shake the team. "I needed to get them out of that euphoric feeling, I called the team meetings for that reason. Basically, I told them they weren't that good, that they were lucky. I said the win was a fluke. By design, I got them good and mad at me but I had to knock them down a notch."

Before taking the ice against Finland, Brooks spoke with the team briefly. At that point, there was really nothing more he could say to them. He pointed out that they couldn't overlook the Finns, and needed to display the same effort they showed against the Russians. Before walking out of the locker room, he turned and said calmly, "If you lose this game, you'll take it to your fuckin' graves." He paused, repeated it, and walked out. The players looked at each other and collectively said "No way these guys are stopping us. We didn't come this far to lose to the Finns!"

Before the game, Pittsburgh Steelers quarterback Terry Bradshaw came in to wish the team luck. That gesture pumped the team even higher.

The game followed the same basic script as the others. The Americans fell behind in the first period. The goal, scored by Jukka Povari, gave the Finns a 1–0 lead at 9:20. At the other end, Finnish goalie Jorma Valtonen was playing brilliantly. He stopped Johnson from point blank range with a skate save. Later, while on his back, he turned and picked off Steve Christoff's deflection in mid-air as it was heading for the net.

In the second period, the U.S. got on the board when Steve Christoff hit the mark, unassisted, at 4:39. Two minutes later, with Schneider in the penalty box, Mikko Leinonen tipped in Hannu Haapalainen's slap shot and the Finns regained the lead, 2–1. At this point, the Finns had been out-shot by the Americans 22–13.

"Valtonen was incredible, making some outstanding saves in the first two periods," said Eruzione. "I remember thinking to myself during the second period that this guy's gonna have the game of his life, and we're going to be shut down." At the end of two periods, it was Finland 2, the United States 1.

Throughout every game, the U.S. seemed to get a big goal to get itself in gear. Against Sweden, Silk's goal at the end of the second period to tie the count was that kind of goal. Eruzione's goal against Norway, and Schneider's goal against the Soviets were examples. The Americans needed an "ice-breaker" quickly to maintain the excitement they felt between the second and third periods.

This time the hero was Phil Verchota, who took Dave Christian's pass in the left circle and beat Valtonen to the far side at 2:25. It was Verchota's third goal of the tournament and it tied the game 2–2.

When the Finns lost the lead, they seemed to falter and the Americans went for the jugular. Just three-and-a-half minutes later, they took the lead when Robbie McClanahan stuffed home a pass from Mark Johnson at 6:05. But then the Americans began taking penalties. Broten was sent off at 6:48, then Christian got the gate at 8:45. They were fortunate to kill off each Finnish power play, but with only 4:15 left, Verchota was sent to the box, two minutes for roughing. Brooks dispatched Johnson and Christian to kill the penalty.

They forechecked tenaciously, creating a scoring opportunity for Christian, but he hit the post. The puck came to center ice where Morrow sent it into the Finnish zone. As Risto Litma chased it, Christian intercepted and found Johnson at the blue line. Mark's shot was stopped by the right pad of Valtonen, but before he set for a rebound, Johnson popped it home for a shorthanded goal and, more importantly, a 4–2 lead. America held its breath as time became the enemy of the Finns. And the final seconds ticked off the clock, Al Michaels, so excited he almost jumped out of the TV booth, screamed: "This impossible dream, *comes true!*"

The blue-shirted players mobbed Craig. A fan climbed onto the ice carrying an American flag and draped it around Craig's shoulders, just as Jim began to search for his father in the stands. Craig remembers the final minutes: "During the last few minutes of that game, I was thinking how great it would have been if Mom could've been here to see this," said the goalie, who's mother had passed away in 1977.

Telegrams poured in from all over the United States congratulating Brooks and the team, while the country went wild. At Radio City Music Hall in New York City, 6,000 people were settling in to watch the stage performance of the fairy tale "Snow White and the Seven Dwarfs." Instead, it was the fairy tale at Lake Placid that drew the loudest ovations, as the score was announced before the show. American Vice-President Walter Mondale, a native of Minnesota, was at the game and exclaimed after the victory, "this is one of the greatest moments I've ever been through, ever!"

In Winthrop, MA, a large crowd gathered outside Mike Eruzione's home, singing the "Star Spangled Banner" and "God Bless America." In Kansas City, a nationally televised NBA game between the Kings and Milwaukee Bucks was interrupted for a second singing of the "Star Spangled Banner" in honor of winning the gold medal. Three players on the court, Ernie Grunfeld, Phil Ford, and Quinn Buckner were part of the USA basketball team that won the gold medal during the Summer Olympics in 1976, and knew the special feeling within the 20 hearts of the American hockey team.

By this point, Brooks ban of the media was lifted, and the players reactions to the victories over the Soviets and Finns were being heard. "We're all a bunch of big doolies now," said Eruzione.

"No way we weren't gonna wrap up the gold," said Ramsey.

"We deserved it. We deserved every bleepin', bleepin', bit of it," said Craig.

Ken Morrow put it this way. "I was really proud, kind of like a writer when he won the Pulitzer Prize."

Mark Johnson: "We knew we were younger, and we knew we could outskate them, and we knew we were going to break our butts to beat them."

"I believe someone was in our corner somewhere, it was fate," said O'Callahan. "We were going to win those games, and it just didn't matter how because it was meant to happen. It was a once-in-a-lifetime thing, and I don't think it will ever happen again like that."

"There are still no words to describe the feeling I had," said Eruzione. "It wasn't sensational, it was better than that."

Among the unanswered questions was why Brooks didn't join the team celebrations on the ice after the wins over the Soviet Union or Finland. The coach had claimed he had needed to use the men's room, but there were other reasons. Brooks was not close to his players and he never let them see the real side of him, the human side.

"By design, I stayed aloof from the players," he explained, "I wanted to show that there was going to be no favoritism, no regionalism, and that's why I stayed away. I always thought that it was the players who are the workers, and if they do something good, they deserve the credit, not the coach. If I had gone out there on the ice to celebrate, the guys probably would have looked at me and said 'buzz off Herb.' "

"I think Herbie wanted to be close with us, and I think he loved every one of us," said Eruzione. "When we have our team reunion, Herb will have that chance. Finally, he'll sit and have a beer with us."

The team headed for Washington D.C. for a farewell lunch with President Carter. "I couldn't believe it when the White House called me to ask what I wanted to eat," said Craig. "I told them I wanted two lobsters. After all we did beat the red tide."

Captain Eruzione capsulized the miracle on ice: "We all came together six months ago from different backgrounds and ethnic beliefs . . . and we made ourselves a team. The saddest thing is that we will all go our separate ways."

How come this unknown team won a gold medal against all odds, while the 1984 and 1988 U.S. teams failed miserably? The answers are: a) they were taken too lightly; b) they were virtually unknown by their opposition; c) they were a better team than people thought; d) they had home-ice advantage; and e) there was no pressure on them to win a gold medal.

"The U.S.A. won't sneak up on anybody anymore," said Craig. "Not like we did anyway."

The 1984 team produced players like Pat LaFontaine, Chris Chelios, Al Iafrate, Ed Olczyk, Bob Brooke, and Scot Bjugstad. The 1988 alumni were equally impressive, boasting Tony Granato, Brian Leetch, Craig Janney, Chris Tererri, Kevin Stevens, and Kevin Miller. While these teams had quality players, they were missing the ingredients of the 1980 team, especially an insightful coach, who wasn't afraid to be tough, or innovative. Clutch goaltending was another factor.

The no-name 1980 team went from a seventh seeded squad to immortality in two incredible weeks. How good were they?

"Real good," said Eruzione. "Some guys are still in the NHL, and two are playing professionally in Europe. If Craig had waited until the start of the new NHL season to join the Flames, I think he would've been a real good NHL goalie. It wasn't that simple a decision for Craig though."

Kenny Morrow, who played on champions throughout his career, added, "Because of what we did, people tend to put us on a higher level, but talent-wise, we were a real good hockey club. Skating-wise, it was the best team I ever saw, including the Islanders of the early '80s and the Edmonton Oilers."

Jack O'Callahan said it best. "At the time, we were the best in the world."

The New York Americans, 1925–42

Hockey's Zaniest Team — The New York Americans

Why, you may ask, would anyone include a team that never won a single Stanley Cup, in a book that includes such distinguished teams as the Montreal Canadiens, New York Islanders, and Edmonton Oilers?

The answer is quite simple; the New York Americans, in their own quaint way, made an indelible imprint on the National Hockey League because they were different in every imaginable way. And while they never won a championship, the Amerks — as New York headline-writers loved to dub them — were one of the most entertaining teams ever to come down the pike.

They also had a philosophical link to the present era when "strike" seems to be a byword in baseball and football, and has been bruited about quite a bit in hockey recently as well. The Americans, strange as it may seem, were born as a result of professional hockey's first organized strike; the walkout of the Hamilton Tigers.

Their lack of championships notwithstanding, the Americans were well-sprinkled with stars, from their inception on Broadway during The Roaring Twenties through their collapse and forced departure from the NHL in 1942. In fact, their last goaltender, Chuck (Bonnie Prince Charlie) Rayner, eventually made it to The Hockey Hall of Fame.

No team in hockey history ever suffered from tragedy more than the Americans, right down to the very end when the team — sidelined during World War II because of personnel shortages — tried to return to NHL play in 1946.

Former star defenseman Mervyn (Red) Dutton, who later became owner of the team, had a plan to build a brand, new arena for the team in Brooklyn, across the river from Madison Square Garden. "We'd have a terrific rivalry with the Rangers," Dutton proclaimed. And he was right.

But Madison Square Garden, which owned the Rangers and had considerable clout on the Board of Governors, had monopoly on its mind. The Garden directors lobbied with the NHL and, in time, Dutton's bid to revive the Americans was thwarted.

It has been said that Red put a curse on the Rangers, saying they never would win another Stanley Cup because of their dastardly blockade of his bid. Interestingly enough, the Rangers have *not* won a Stanley Cup since then!

Children of the Roaring Twenties, fathered by a bootlegger and nurtured by a zany collection of fans, they were the New York Americans. They wore flamboyant, star-spangled jerseys matching in color their behavior both on and off the ice. They never won the Stanley Cup and never finished first, yet from their birth in 1925 to their unfortunate death in 1942 they captured the imagination of all who adored the underdog.

Curiously, it was a Canadian-born newspaperman covering sports in New York City who inspired bootlegger "Big Bill" Dwyer to launch the Americans. William McBeth, a sportswriter from Windsor, Ontario, believed that if hockey could be properly staged in Manhattan, it would be an instant hit. McBeth had his listeners and his backers, but he lacked one item: a major league arena. That, however, was supplied when Tex Rickard and his "Six Hundred Millionaires" built the "new" Madison Square Garden on Eighth Avenue and 49th Street in the early twenties.

McBeth realized that even though the new Garden had flaws (built primarily for prize-fighting, it lacked adequate sight-lines for hockey) there were 15,000 seats and enough good ones to satisfy even the most discriminating fan. But the Garden backers were ignorant and, consequently, dubious about hockey's potential, so McBeth had to go elsewhere for money.

His choice was "Big Bill" Dwyer, a character among characters in that era of wonderful nonsense. A native New Yorker, the pot-bellied Dwyer grew up in the area around the new Garden, living the life of a quasi-Dead-End Kid. He did a short stretch at Sing Sing Penitentiary and bounced around the West Side of Manhattan until Prohibition arrived. Dwyer's big moment came precisely then.

While others warily wondered whether to plunge into the gold-mine of rum-running and other "industries" created by the new law, Big Bill made his move fast — and the money rolled in even faster. By the mid-twenties Dwyer's empire comprised a couple of night clubs, race tracks, a fleet of ships and trucks, as well as warehouses and a full-fledged gang, appropriately stocked with the Jimmy Cagneys and Edward G. Robinsons of the day.

As far as McBeth was concerned, Dwyer was the perfect choice to back his team because Big Bill liked sports and wanted very much to improve his image by owning a hockey club. A little prestige never hurt any bootlegger, and owning the Americans promised a lot of it, possibly even the Stanley Cup as well.

The next step was finding a team. This, too, was accomplished in a typically bizarre manner. During the 1924–25 NHL season, the Hamilton Tigers went out on strike, marking one of the few times in sports history that a team ever marched on a picket line.

Led by Red Green, Hamilton players objected that the season was lengthened from 24 to 30 games, yet they had received no increase in salary. They demanded a $200 boost per man and instead got nothing but a stiff rebuke and $200 individual fines from President Frank Calder. The Hamilton players remained firm in their strike, and early in April, 1925, league governors got wind of Dwyer's desire to own a hockey team. They reasoned that the Hamilton problem could be simply resolved by selling the franchise to the Manhattan bootlegger and on April 17, 1925, it was agreed at an NHL meeting that the Hamilton club would be transplanted to New York at the start of the 1925–26 season.

The deal was officially confirmed on September 22, 1925, at a league conference in New York. Dwyer obtained both the franchise and the suspended players — quite appropriately he bought them even though their suspension had never been lifted — for $75,000. Thomas Patrick "Tommy" Gorman, one of Canada's more ebullient personalities, was chosen as manager, and the new team promptly was named the Americans — and just as quickly nicknamed the Amerks by space-conscious headline writers.

If Big Bill Dwyer was pleased, Bill McBeth was in his glory. The dream of bringing major league hockey to New York City was realized on December 15, 1925, when the Montreal Canadiens faced the Americans in the opening NHL game at Madison Square Garden.

Although the new Garden had already been open for business, the hockey premiere was greeted with the same respect and heraldry as the opening of the Metropolitan Opera House. Dignitaries from both the U.S.A. and Canada jammed the arena, most wearing white tie and tails. Marching bands paraded impeccably across the ice and then the Canadiens defeated the Americans 3–1, a fact immediately forgotten in the waves of champagne poured by Big Bill Dwyer during his post-game party.

When the Amerks finally drifted off cloud nine and back to the reality of a 36-game schedule, they played competitive if not championship hockey. Billy Burch scored 19 goals and finished seventh in the league; such redoubtables as the Green brothers, Shorty and Red, defensemen Leo Reise, Sr., and Alec McKinnon; and the peripatetic "Bullet" Joe Simpson gave New Yorkers plenty to cheer about.

Rather appropriately, McBeth was named publicity director of the team, and while successfully trumpeting their virtues throughout the Metropolitan Area, he also helped to produce the Americans' artistic downfall that first year. It happened because McBeth chose to single out Burch and Simpson for the loudest drum-beating. He christened Simpson "The Blue Streak from Saskatoon" and Burch "The Babe Ruth of Hockey." New Yorkers, unschooled in hockey fundamentals, seized upon the nicknames and immediately made these two their favorites, demanding a goal each time Billy or Joe would touch the puck.

Conscious of their newly created audience, Burch and Simpson responded by stressing their individual exploits. "Every time one of them passed to another player," wrote Frank Graham, Sr., who covered sports for the *New York Sun*, "the spectators howled in rage and disappointment. Seeking to please the customers, Billy and Joe did as little passing as possible. This resulted in spectacular but futile one-man raids on the enemies' nets and a rapid disintegration of the team play necessary to insure victories as the other players then all tried to get into the act as individuals."

A mild case of dissension followed, principally because Shorty Green was so ardent a team player that he couldn't accept the "playing-to-the-crowd" style of his colleagues. "There were frequently tears in his eyes following a losing game," noted Graham. "But nobody else seemed to care."

Nobody had time to care; the abundant distractions for the now adored Canadian boys kept them equally busy off-ice. Just a block away from the Garden sat the glittering White Way of Times Square with its wine, women, and song — mostly the first two temptations. Occasionally, Dwyer's bootleg hooch would find its way into the Amerks' dressing room with amusing results. One such incident occurred at the conclusion of the 1925–26 season. New York had finished in fifth place, respectably ahead of Toronto and the Canadiens, and had scheduled a post-season exhibition game at Madison Square Garden just prior to the arrival of Ringling Bros. Barnum and Bailey Circus.

As was normally the case, circus officials moved their animals into the Garden menagerie several days before the show opened, and in this instance the floating zoo was located about a hundred feet from the teams' dressing room toward the rear of the arena.

Following the exhibition match with Portland, the Americans were greeted with a case of bootleg booze which Simpson eagerly poured. After a few hearty rounds, "Bullet Joe" left the dressing room and headed for Broadway; somehow he made a wrong turn and walked straight into the menagerie, where he was greeted by a trumpeting elephant and several boisterous lions. Stunned to the core, Simpson wheeled in his tracks and fled back to the dressing room where he grabbed Percy Ryan, the Americans' trainer.

"Where in hell did that bad hooch come from?" Joe demanded. "Christ! I could swear I saw a herd of wild elephants out there."

Though there were plenty of laughs, the Americans had also managed to become a serious business proposition. In their first year they had proved hockey could be a money-maker in Manhattan, and had underscored this with enough big crowds to inspire Madison Square Garden Corporation to get into the act with a team of its own. This was easy to do because the Garden already was collecting a healthy rental from the Amerks — it also shared in their gate receipts — and the emergence of another New York team would create a stimulating rivalry, matching the Giants and the Dodgers in baseball.

Dwyer was making too much money on bootlegging at the time to care, but the Garden already was beginning to force his hand — when he first decided to bring the team to New York he had been assured that the Garden would never install a club of its own — and the high rent and other expenses eventually would hasten his downfall. But with the demand for illegal booze at an all-time high and an income too big to even count, Big Bill couldn't care less about what the Garden was doing to him.

The same carefree attitude characterized his players' deportment. Gorman had signed former great Newsy Lalonde as coach for the 1926–27 season, but even so awesome a personality as Lalonde couldn't control the laugh-happy Amerks. Their behavior was so notorious that even the official NHL history took note in its 1926–27 edition with the following observation: "Newsy Lalonde had his hands full with his rollicking crew of Americans who were living it up on Broadway. (Lionel) Conacher and Burch were suspended for breaking training after their loss to Detroit on March 15th."

Suspensions hardly proved a deterrent, especially when Conacher was involved. Once, he was playing cards in a hotel room with Billy Burch when Red Green tossed an apple core and hit Conacher on the head. Lionel jumped out of his chair and pursued Red down the hall until the elusive Green dashed into an empty room, locking the door behind him.

Conacher, who later was to be voted Canada's Athlete of the Half Century, reared back and charged at the door. In the process his shoulder rammed the door frame plus the wall and buckled the floor supports so badly that the hockey club had to pay $500 in repairs.

When the Americans weren't fighting among themselves they managed pretty well against the opposition, especially the Rangers. What made this rivalry so keen was the fact that the Madison Square Garden club, under the direction of Lester Patrick, had proved artistically superior to the Americans from the very start. In 1928, while the Amerks were floundering near the bottom of the league, Patrick's Rangers won the Stanley Cup. This infuriated Gorman, who was determined to produce a winner.

Prior to the 1928–29 season he began negotiating for Roy "Shrimp" Worters, a superb little goalie, and finally obtained him early in the season, thus giving the Americans the goalkeeping they needed. From opening night until mid-January, Tommy Gorman's crew held first place in the Canadian Division of the league, eventually finishing the season in second place — precisely where the Rangers finished in the American Division. That meant the intra-Garden enemies would meet in the first round of the playoffs which was to be a two-game, total goals series. The opener ended in a 0–0 tie and the second match was 0–0 at the end of regulation time. True to form, the Rangers finally won when Butch Keeling beat Worters at 29:50 of overtime.

The Americans-Rangers rivalry took on some peculiar turns. Once, Col. John Hammond, the Rangers' president, summoned Gorman to his office to complain about the Amerks' after-hours roistering. The Colonel went a step further and said at that very moment the Americans were cavorting around the corner at a big party.

Gorman wouldn't put anything past his skaters but something told him that the Colonel was, at the very least, in error. The Americans' manager got hold of two Garden detectives and headed straight for the notorious address. "When we got there," Gorman said, "we found a terrific party-drinking, singing, the works — and a helluva lot of hockey players. But they were all Rangers. Just happened to be Ching Johnson's birthday party."

Because of Dwyer's association with the underworld, it was not uncommon for the Americans' rooting section to be graced with submachine guns, blackjacks, and cowbells. "There were dark accusations," noted Frank Graham, "by rival coaches that referees and goaltenders and goal judges were intimidated by gangsters who had bet on the Americans and wished to insure their bets."

One night, the Americans lost because of an especially poor call by the referee, who was then chased down 50th Street by a horde of Amerk fans threatening his life. Fortunately, he had better stamina than the irate rooters and sprinted away unharmed.

The fans had plenty to beef about in 1929–30. After the glorious playoff year, the Amerks sank back to the cellar and Gorman went to work, again hoping to mold a winner. He traded Lionel Conacher to the Montreal Maroons for Hap Emms and Mervyn "Red" Dutton in a deal that was to have enormous import for the New Yorkers in years to come.

Dutton, the tough son of a wealthy Canadian, had a red mane and the temper to go with it. That he was playing big league hockey was tribute enough to his courage because during World War I, he had served overseas with the Princess Pats and nearly lost both legs when an artillery shell exploded a few feet away from him. At first doctors were prepared to amputate, but decided against such a measure and Dutton returned to Canada to recover and go on to star as a defenseman for Calgary and then Montreal before coming to New York. Right from the start, a camaraderie developed between Dwyer and Dutton; at least partly inspired by Red's love of a good time.

"We knew what Bill was," said Dutton who eventually became NHL president and later a millionaire building contractor, "but we loved him. Dwyer's policy was that nothing was too good for his players. Every time we won a game he'd throw us a big party. Worters used to say, 'Join the Americans and laugh yourself to death.' "

Worters no doubt remembered the time he and his teammates had played a game in Ottawa, then had to return to New York by train with only a three hour layover in Montreal. Before leaving Ottawa, Gorman phoned Dwyer in Manhattan with a report on the game. After listening to the account, Big Bill replied: "When you get to Montreal take the boys to dinner. Tell them to have all they want to eat and all they want to drink. If they've got any friends who can make the party, tell them they're welcome."

Big Bill didn't know it at the time — or maybe he did and wasn't letting on — but the party was over for him. The end of Prohibition loomed and friends began deserting him. He was convicted as a bootlegger and sentenced to two years in Atlanta, leaving the Amerks with many bills to pay. The problems weren't solved on Dwyer's return, but help was in sight when Dutton agreed to divert some of his family fortune to the Amerks. He, in turn, became playing coach of the club and continued helping Dwyer with grants in aid.

"Once I had to lend Bill $20,000 when he was down in Miami Beach," Dutton recalled. "He blew it all in one night in a crap game."

By the 1935–36 season, prohibition was just a memory and Big Bill Dwyer was a poor man, unable to support a hockey team. The NHL took over the club a year later, naming Dutton overseer while the endless debts were paid.

"We had a lot of headaches then," Dutton remembers, "because we always were short of money and had that tough contract with the Garden. Many's the day I'd look up at the sky and pray it wouldn't rain so we'd have a good crowd and could pay the salaries. Of course, the league would stand behind us, but I wanted the club to be able to pay the bills on its own."

Even with Dwyer out of the picture and the depression as a cloud over the sporting scene, the Americans managed to produce laughs. One reason was simply Dutton's own sense of humor; it surfaced at odd times. Joe Jerwa, a young defenseman, once made this discovery after Dutton had fined him $100 for a team infraction.

"Why not make it $200?" Jerwa suggested.

At this point Dutton got in on the spirit of things, replying, "Two hundred dollars it is! Now, Joe, do you want to go for $400?"

Jerwa laughed. "Heck, you can't fine me $400. I don't have that much coming to me."

Despite his problems, Dutton still managed to ice a competitive team. During the 1937–38 season, his Americans finished second in the Canadian Division and Red's protégé, Dave "Sweeney" Schriner, placed seventh in scoring. "What made me so proud," said Red, "was that I signed Schriner to his first pro contract. I brought him in, along with Art Chapman and Lorne Carr and together they made one of the greatest lines in hockey."

Once again the second place Americans faced the second place Rangers in the best-of-three playoff round. This time Dutton's sextet won the opener 2–1 on Johnny Sorrell's overtime goal. The Rangers rebounded, winning the second match 4–3 and setting the stage for the climactic finale on March 27, 1938, at the Garden.

The largest crowd of the season, 16,340 fans, jammed the arena and saw a pulsating contest. Paced by Alex Shibicky and Bryan Hextall, the Rangers jumped into a 2–0 lead, but Lorne Carr and Nels Stewart tied the game for the Amerks, sending it into overtime. Neither team could break the tie for three sudden-death periods before Carr finally scored the winner for Dutton and Company.

"That," Dutton states, "was the greatest thrill I ever got in hockey. The Rangers had a high-priced team then and beating them was like winning the Stanley Cup to us."

Unfortunately, the Americans were knocked out of the playoffs by Chicago, two games to one, in the next round and were never to achieve such lofty heights again, although their fans continued to root them on, just as Brooklyn's "Faithful" supported the Dodgers. "We had fans mostly from Brooklyn," said Dutton, "while the Rangers had the hotsy-totsy ones from New York."

A year later, the Americans made the playoffs only to be eliminated in the first round, two games to none, by Toronto. They slipped out of playoff contention in 1939–40 and finished dead last in 1940–41. World War II had broken out and many Canadian-born players quit hockey to join the Armed Forces. By 1940–41, Dutton had lost 14 of 16 players to the Canadian Army and other branches of the services.

Dutton's last ploy to save the franchise — the infusion of new blood — was blunted by the war. When the 1941–42 season started, he changed the club's name to the Brooklyn Americans; this was a token gesture to stimulate a Brooklyn-New York rivalry, although all American home games were still played at the Garden. The Amerks finished last again but, surprisingly, had come up with several young players such as goalie Chuck Rayner and defenseman Pat Egan, who showed considerable promise.

However, the war effort soon took Rayner and several other Americans, and at the start of the 1942–43 season, Dutton was forced to fold the club just when he was starting to pull out from under the debris of the Dwyer days. "We had begun to pay off a lot of Bill's debts," said Dutton, "and it looked as though we were going to come out all right. A couple more years and we would have run the Rangers right out of the rink."

And so, the Americans vanished, and a glorious hockey era came to a sad close.

The Soviet National Team, 1972

Russia's Best, 1972

Canadian hockey snobbism, pure and simple, is what prevented North American critics from appreciating the significant growth of hockey in the Soviet Union following World War II. From 1960 to 1970, so many developments had consumed the interest of North American fans it is no wonder that scant attention was paid to the burgeoning European hockey scene.

The NHL, for example, enjoyed a golden era in the 1960s, during which attendance climbed so dramatically that even the conservative club owners reluctantly approved expansion from the established 6 to 12 teams. And despite innumerable growing pains, the league continued to add new teams while big-league hockey prospered.

Prosperity was so rampant that even a new "major" league was formed and the World Hockey Association made its debut in 1972 after gathering considerable attention in its pre-natal months, before the first puck was officially dropped. With all this going on, it was not surprising that attention was deflected from Europen hockey, and since precious little news about the Soviet teams was available in the Canadian media, the Russian teams remained somewhat of a mystery to NHL experts.

Not that Iron Curtain bloc teams were completely ignored. Soviet teams began having an impact soon after World War II and in 1956, the Russians arrested attention, winning the Olympic gold medal. By 1960, teams from Moscow were touring North America but they were regarded more as curios than serious threats to the well-advertised supremacy of NHL teams.

"The Russians were doing some very special things in terms of practice technique as well as offensive strategy," said former U.S. Olympic coach Lou

Vairo. "But we were so consumed with ourselves at the time we hardly paid them any mind. That would come later."

Success followed success in the Olympics and international competition for the Soviets until it was no longer possible to ignore them. By the start of the 1970s, a few enlightened North American hockey leaders began to grasp the potential of European hockey as a source of talent. More and more NHL scouts visited the continent and returned with increasingly glowing reports about the rising quality of play. One such individual was Toronto attorney, R. Alan Eagleson, who doubled as a player agent as well as executive director of the NHL Players' Association.

Aggressive and enthusiastic to a fault, Eagleson helped arrange an unprecedented eight game tournament between a team of NHL stars and a similar team of Soviet stickhandlers. The first four games would be played in Canada and the remaining in Moscow. Although the tourney was billed as an exhibition series, it was clear to both sides that this would be hockey's first World Series.

Although the NHL dispatched scouts to analyze the Russians, little was known about their ability to compete against hard-nosed professionals, many of whom held the Europeans in contempt. Such disparaging behavior would eventually cost the NHL players dearly until they finally came to appreciate the skills and courage displayed by the Soviets.

Although Team Canada ultimately won the series, it was the Soviets who emerged with the most acclaim; and for good reason. Their teamsmanship — especially the five-man forward-defense combination — dazzled onlookers as much as individual efforts.

At first, North American viewers had a difficult time appreciating the Soviet stars because so little had been known about them. (Russians were not well-versed in the North American art of sports hype.) But as the games unfolded, it soon became readily apparent that the Europeans had as many virtuosos as the Canadian squad.

By far, the most apparent was goalie Vladislav Tretiak. A 20-year-old at the time of the 1972 tournament, Tretiak emerged from the series as the most talked-about — if not the best — goalie in the world. Within a decade he had become a legend.

Not as spectacular, but no less competent was the Russian defense. Aleksander (Rags) Ragulin, Viktor Kuzkin, Yuri Liapkin, Aleksander Gusev, and Valery Vasiliev matched NHL aces like Brad Park, Bobby Orr, Guy Lapointe, and Serve Savard every step of the way.

Up front, the Soviets were sensational, to say the least. Attacking formations combined speed, passing agility, and stickhandling finesse in a manner that had rarely been seen in NHL rinks. Within two games, forwards such as Aleksander Maltsev, Valery Kharlamov, Aleksander Yakushev, and Vladimir Shadrin became distinguished for their offensive skills.

While the Russian team did not win the series, it came away from the tourney glowing with all-time greatness as much for its collective effort on the ice, as for the impact it had on major league hockey for the next decade-and-a-half.

"We learned an incalculable amount from them," said Herb Brooks, coach of the 1980 U.S. Olympic team, who later coached in the NHL both in New York and Minnesota. "Certain plays we adapted from the Russians have become routine in the NHL today."

Unfortunately, none of the Soviets then were allowed to play in the NHL, so it is impossible to determine how they would have fared over an 80-game schedule and the playoffs.

What we do know is that they were able to play the NHL All-Stars even (or just about even) over a tension-filled eight-game set, and that alone was no mean feat.

Furthermore, Tretiak, was to prove one of the finest goaltenders of all time, while teammates such as Liapkin, Vasiliev, and Kharlamov were ranked among the best forwards of the 1980s. As for the Soviet team, the *New York Times* observed: "The Russian players were clean-cut, disciplined, phlegmatic and, above all, a team or, as they prefer to call it, a *kollektiv* with swift-passing, smoothly rehearsed pattern plays. Tall, baldish Russian head coach Vsevolod Bobrov endured the ulcerous tension of the games, expressionless and motionless at his bench, giving minimal instructions, and taking a laconic tone in his post-game comments about the refereeing and the results."

When it was over, the NHL knew that the Soviet Union now had become a true world hockey power. "Even before the series ended," said *The Times*, "the Canadians held some of the Russian players in awe."

They had every reason to do so, because in that autumn of 1972, the Soviets iced one of the most remarkable hockey units in the annals of sport.

The game of hockey was born, nurtured, and developed to its highest level in Canada. Although Canada's national game was officially lacrosse, everyone north of the 48th parallel recognized hockey as the *real* Canadian game. Nearly every player who skated in the National Hockey League was Canadian-born, as was every manager, coach, and trainer.

It was generally believed, not only in Canada but in Europe and Asia, that hockey belonged to the Canadians and that any Canadian team was better than a similar team from anywhere else.

All of this was emphatically true until the years following World War II. Then something unusual happened. The Russians, who previously had considered soccer their number one sport, became attracted to ice hockey. The Soviet Union was as far north and as cold as Canada. For millions there it was as natural to ice skate as to walk. Since the long, cold winters provided thousands of natural ice skating rinks from Leningrad to Vladivostok, the shift to hockey was natural and easy.

In the early 1950s, the Russian team was first recognized as a threat on the international hockey scene. It should be noted here that the top Russian players in all sports are considered "amateurs" and compete against other world-class amateurs. It is generally known that they train all year round and have few, if any, duties except excelling in sport. so in many respects they are the same as professionals in North American sport. By contrast, the top amateurs in Canada often had other full-time jobs and, anyway, they were usually either too young or not good enough to play professionally in the National Hockey League.

The Soviets made the first splash in 1954. The top Soviet team entered the world (amateur) hockey championships in Stockholm, Sweden, and played so well they reached the finals against a Canadian team comprising of the best non-professionals in North America. Although the Canadian amateurs were hardly of NHL quality, they *were* Canadians and therefore considered capable of beating anybody.

The Russians won 7-2, and the first chip had been delivered against Canada's image of world-wide hockey superiority. But this was only the beginning. Using unique training techniques and developing their own style, the Russians got better and better, while the Canadian amateurs remained static. And this was reflected in the results.

By 1962, the Russians, coached by Anatoli Tarasov and Arkadi Cherneshev, began a rampage of championship victories that was unparalleled in amateur hockey competition. From 1962 through 1972 the Soviets won 12 out of a possible 13 championships in Olympic and World hockey play.

As Canadian hockey critic Jock Carroll pointed out, Canada was left clinging to the idea that its *professional* players were still the best in the world. And even as the 1970s dawned, most hockey experts agreed that NHL players would make short work of the Soviet National team — if they should ever get the chance. The Russians, encouraged by international amateur hockey officials, still refused to meet professional opponents.

But then Soviet coach Tarasov startled the hockey world by revealing that the Russians would, in fact, be willing to play an NHL team. "I wouldn't care if we got beaten 15-0," said Tarasov. "The score won't matter. What will matter is to determine how our hockey players stand up to the best professionals in North America."

The machinery was set in motion to arrange the game, and after considerable haggling, officials of the NHL and the Soviet Ice Hockey Federation arranged for an eight-game series in September, 1972. The first four games would be played in Canada and the final set would be played on Russian ice.

"We used to listen to stories about Canadian hockey as if they were fairy tales," said Tarasov. "That the Canadians were invincible, that the skill of the founders of this game was truly fantastic."

Now thought the Canadians, the Russians would have a chance to see for themselves.

The Canadian team was to be composed of National Hockey League stars and coached by Harry Sinden, who led the Boston Bruins to the 1970 Stanley Cup victory. Sinden faced two obstacles. A new league, the World Hockey Association had been established and had attracted such superstars as Bobby Hull and goalie Gerry Cheevers. The NHL would not allow such renegades to play for Team Canada. Then too, the games would be held before the regular NHL season, and the coaches would have a minimum of training time to get the pro stars into condition and used to one style of play.

Nevertheless, Team Canada displayed an awesome collection of stars: defenseman Brad Park (New York), Bill White (Chicago), and Don Awrey (Boston); hard-shooting forwards Frank Mahovlich and Yvan Cournoyer (Montreal), Bobby Clarke (Philadelphia), and Phil Esposito (Boston); and goalies Ken Dryden (Montreal), Tony Esposito (Chicago), and Eddie Johnston (Boston).

North American hockey experts generally agreed that the Russians would be lucky if they weren't blown out of the rink by the third period of the first game. Some said Team Canada would win all eight games and by substantial margins. Coach Sinden reflected the optimism. "We're gearing to win the first game," he said. "We'll think about the second game after we've won the first. But I have complete confidence in the ability of our team to beat *any* combination of hockey players, any time, any place in the world."

The Russians went about their business with extreme thoroughness. They had spent years scouting the NHL teams, filming big-league games, and learning the best of the professional game while discarding the worst. They prepared carefully and thoroughly for their four games in Canada.

Team Canada, on the other hand, treated the Russians with a casualness bordering on contempt. Scouts were sent to analyze the Russian brand of hockey but they took the most cursory glance at the Soviet sextet. They returned fully confident that Canada would win, reporting that the Russians' most glaring weakness was in the net. Soviet goaltender Vladislav Tretiak was inferior, they said.

The boasts and predictions finally would be put to the test on September 2, 1972, when the opening face-off would take place in Montreal. By that day, all of Canada was in a frenzy, thirsting for the kill, awaiting the big victory of Team Canada, "the best hockey team in the game's history," according to Frank Orr of the *Toronto Star*.

There were 18,818 spectators in the Forum. The national anthems of Canada and Russia blared over the loudspeaker, then the game began. Almost immediately, Phil Esposito drilled a shot past goalie Tretiak and soon after, Team Canada scored a second goal.

It appeared that the dam had burst on the Soviets and that all the predictions of a grand — and total — Canadian victory would come true. And much quicker than anybody had suspected. Then, Esposito breached the Russian defenses once more and seemed to have a third Canadian goal on his stick. But this time Tretiak was equal to the occasion and blunted the drive.

The myth of Canadian supremacy was about to fall. Instead of retreating in disarray, the Russians regrouped and poured into Canadian territory, testing goalie Ken Dryden again and again. The NHL stars were flabbergasted. Gradually they just fell apart as a team before the astonished eyes of their fans. In no time at all, Russia had tied, then soared ahead, and finally put the game completely out of reach of the home team. When the final buzzer sounded, Team Canada had been humiliated by a score of 7–3!

"Seldom since Goliath contemptuously looked at David can an opponent have been so grossly underrated as we underrated the Russian Nationals," said an editorial in The *Toronto Star*. "All Canadians concerned shared in this error."

All of a sudden, Canadians realized that they no longer reigned supreme in the hockey world. NHL owners paid their compliments to the Russians in the only way they knew — by offering them professional contracts.

"How much do you want for Valery Kharlamov?" Toronto Maple Leafs President Harold Ballard asked Soviet hockey officials. "I'll give you one million dollars and a future draft choice."

The Russians said "Thanks, but no thanks" and began preparing for the second game of the series; this one at Maple Leaf Gardens in Toronto. A funereal air covered Canada as a result of the opening game defeat. Some NHL skaters admitted that it was foolish for players and correspondents to have been so overwhelmingly sure of a Team Canada sweep. "I never like going into a series being a favorite," said Boston's Phil Esposito, "no matter where I play."

Team Canada no longer was a favorite, but it was not an underdog either. Most experts believed that the second game would be critical in determining the remainder of the series.

The Canadians came through, and fans salvaged a little of their national pride. At Maple Leaf Gardens, Team Canada skated like a team possessed, and rumbled to a 4–1 victory over the Soviet National Team.

Chicago Black Hawk goaltender Tony Esposito was splendid in repulsing the skittering Russians, especially in the first period when the visitors threatened to bust the game wide open. And this time the NHL players used their bodies to greater advantage, checking more tenaciously than in a Stanley Cup final game. For a change, coach Sinden was pleased. "We didn't run around like we did in the first game," said Sinden. "We had control in position play."

The impressive performance filled Canadians with new confidence. The loss in the first game now was treated as a freak caused by over-confidence. On to Winnipeg the teams moved for game three.

More than anything, the third game seemed to symbolize the relative merits of both teams. By the end of the second period the score was tied 4–4. The clubs played through the final 20 minutes without another score and the game ended in a 4-4 draw. The result summed up in a dispatch by Tass, the official Soviet news agency: "The match proved that two really equal, splendid teams were meeting."

This was small consolation to 20 million Canadians who hoped for an overwhelming victory. There would be one more chance on home ice — in Vancouver. But all was not well with Team Canada. There had been some grumbling even before the series began. The NHL stars had interrupted their vacations to play. They were being paid very little. And there was always the chance they might be injured. After the series started, some top stars didn't get much playing time, and their complaints only made things worse.

More than 18,000 jammed the Pacific Coliseum in Vancouver for game four, expecting the best from Team Canada. Instead they were rewarded with an almost perfect game by the Russians and what frequently appeared to be a disorderly retreat by Team Canada.

Wave after wave of Soviet forwards penetrated the Canadian defenses, pouring five goals past goalie Dryden. Team Canada managed three scores against the acrobatic Tretiak, who was proving to be not inferior at all. The NHL players were subjected to a cascade of boos from their own fans, and after the game, several players openly criticized their countrymen for lack of support.

In any event, the Russians now led the series two games to one with one tie as the teams jetted to Moscow for the next four contests. It had become apparent, even to the most partisan NHL fan, that the Soviet hockey club was as good as, if not better than, the best professionals in North America.

"They play this game," said coach Sinden, "as though there were no scoreboard, no ups and downs. We don't."

Team Canada had several days to reorganize its forces before the series resumed on September 22, 1972, in Moscow. A short exhibition series had been planned for the NHL stickhandlers against Swedish teams as a leisurely tune-up for Moscow, but instead it was another small disaster which further upset members of the Canadian entourage.

Curiously, the most favorable forecast for Team Canada came from Soviet coach Vsevolod Bobrov. He predicted that the best Canadian play was yet to come. "Team Canada has not yet been on form," he said. "They had not trained much and were overconfident. Now they will be stronger. They will take these games more seriously. And they will be in better condition."

They were kind words, but the NHL embarrassment had not yet ended. In the pre-game ceremonies before the fifth contest, Phil Esposito skated toward center ice to accept a bouquet of flowers. Suddenly the magnificent Bruin skater wound up on his backside. "One of the flower stems had fallen off," Esposito later explained. "I stepped on it and was on my behind in a flash!"

That proved to be only the start of Team Canada's troubles. Twice the NHL aces built a three-goal lead, but the Russians struck back to tie the score. Ultimately the home team went ahead to capture the match, 5-4. "The Russians never let up," said coach Sinden. "They just keep coming at you."

The Soviets had now won three games, tied one, and lost one. Another victory would clinch the series. With three more games left on friendly Moscow ice, they seemed sure of triumph.

Nothing suggested that Team Canada was capable of a comeback. Apart from the three losses, the Canadian spirit had been further weakened by the walkout of several players. New York Ranger captain Vic Hadfield returned home to Canada because he disagreed with Sinden's coaching policies.

"Take a look at the captain of the Rangers going home because he can't win a place on the team," said John Forristall, one of Team Canada's trainers. His biting tone illustrated the ill-will on the Canada squad.

Team Canada may have been down, but something clicked in the sixth game. Neither team scored in the first period, and before the second period was two minutes old, the Russians had gone ahead on Yuri Liapkin's goal against goalie Ken Dryden. It was the eighth time the Russians had beaten the Montreal goalie by shooting low to his left, an obvious aspect of their strategy.

But then Team Canada returned to the offense. Rod Gilbert intercepted a Russian pass and skimmed the puck to teammate Dennis Hull. Hull fired at Tretiak and the Soviet goalie made the first save but allowed the rubber to rebound back to Hull. Dennis's second shot was true, and although nobody realized it at the time, that was the turning point in the entire series!

Less than a minute and a half later, Yvan Cournoyer converted Red Berenson's pass into another Team Canada goal. Then came a third score, this one from the stick of Toronto's Paul Henderson. The Russians struck back once to pull within one goal, but Dryden repulsed them throughout the third period, and Team Canada emerged with a heartening 3–2 triumph.

Two games remained for Team Canada and two wins were needed. It seemed impossible as the seventh game unfolded. The Russians mounted a 2–1 lead in the first period. But late in the period, Phil Esposito displayed his unique leadership qualities and tied the game with a goal.

Neither team scored in a tense middle frame, and then the clubs traded goals early in the third period. Now it was 3–3 and the stage was set for high drama. If the Russians could hold off the visitors and come up with a tie, they would come out winners of the series. If Team Canada could go ahead to stay, they would have a chance to win the eighth game and the series.

As the clock approached the 18th minute of the last period, Serge Savard of Team Canada passed the puck to Paul Henderson, who confronted a pair of Russian defensemen, a seemingly impregnable barrier. What followed was one of the most dramatic scores in the entire series.

"I tried to push the puck through the legs of one of them," said Henderson, "and I got a bit of a break on it. The puck hit his skate, deflecting it to his right, and that gave me the chance I needed. While he was looking for it, I moved around him. I had pretty good balance when I let the shot go. What I mean is, I put the puck exactly where I wanted it to go. Upstairs."

Henderson was knocked down on the play, but he kept his eyes riveted on the net. His frown turned to a gigantic smile as he watched the net bulge. At 17:54 of the final period Team Canada had gone ahead to stay. Final score: 4–3. Henderson had managed to tie the series, each team having won three and tied one. Everything now hinged on the outcome of the eighth and final match.

According to some observers, the normally methodical Russians were now in a panic. One loss at home would have been bad enough, but two straight defeats was humiliating. Now they faced the prospects of three losses in a row and defeat in the series. Despite their great performance so far, it was clear the final game meant as much to the Soviets as it did to Team Canada.

After two periods of hectic play it looked as if the Russians would prevail. Their splendid pattern passing plays and vigorous skating enabled them to mount a 5–3 lead in front of Tretiak's heroic goaltending. Team Canada gave no promise of reviving in the third period, and Ken Dryden seemed shaky in the nets.

But the prideful members of Team Canada believed otherwise. "We're better hockey players," insisted Peter Mahovlich. Then the NHL skaters went out in the third period to prove just how right he was. Phil Esposito scored at 2:27 to pull Team Canada within one goal. Nearly 11 minutes later, Yvan Cournoyer tied the score.

Now the Soviets are hanging on for dear life, hoping to escape with a tie. But Team Canada lunges for the Russian jugular, shooting for a sixth goal.

With less than a minute to go, the Canadians have made several great attempts, but the game still is tied, 5–5. Coach Sinden calls Peter Mahovlich to the bench and orders Paul Henderson onto the ice in his place. Phil Esposito gets the puck in front of the Russian goal and shoots. Tretiak makes the save but allows the puck to trickle away.

Henderson is there and shoots again. Tretiak stops it again but cannot control the puck. Henderson fires again and this time the puck slides under Tretiak's pads into the goal!

That's all there was to it. Seconds later Team Canada skated off the ice with a 6–5 triumph and a series victory — four games won, three games lost, and one tied.

Coach Sinden called it the greatest hockey game ever played and others seconded his motion. Certainly it was one of the most exciting.

But when the excitement died down, observers agreed that the Soviets had proven themselves equal to the best professionals in North America. "I don't think any of those Russians would have trouble finding jobs in the NHL," said Peter Mahovlich. "But only three or four of them would be invited to the All-Star Game."

The Team Canada-Russian series had reverberations which will be heard for years to come. It set big-league and amateur coaches to examining the Soviet style of play and conditioning techniques. The excitement created by the series brought new popularity for hockey, particularly in Europe, and now Russians are playing for NHL teams.

Some experts argued that the Canadians were the real losers because they had been favored to win eight straight games and were fortunate to squeeze out a last-minute triumph in the final game.

Perhaps the most accurate appraisal of all was made by Canadian author Henk W. Hoppener, who wrote when it was over: "We won the games. We lost a legend."